The Priesthood
of Christ

Introduction © Sinclair B. Ferguson 2010
Copyright © Christian Focus Publications 2010

ISBN 978-1-84550-599-8

This edition first published in 2010
in the
Christian Heritage Imprint
by
Christian Focus Publications,
Geanies House, Fearn,
Ross-shire, IV20 1TW, Scotland

www.christianfocus.com

Cover design by Alister MacInnes

Printed and bound by
Bell & Bain, Glasgow

Mixed Sources
Product group from well-managed
forests and other controlled sources
www.fsc.org Cert no. TT-COC-002769
© 1996 Forest Stewardship Council

FSC

The Priesthood
of Christ

John Owen

CHRISTIAN
HERITAGE

CONTENTS

CONTENTS

THIS EDITION

The contents of this book first appeared as an excursus in John Owen's exposition of Hebrews. The text here is unchanged apart from the following features, designed to make the book more user-friendly:

1. Approximately seven percent of the original text was in Latin. This has been translated so the whole book is now accessible to non-Latin speakers.
2. Subheadings, sometimes extending to four levels and largely based on the original numeric structure, have been inserted. The contents pages include primary and secondary subheadings to aid navigation.
3. Sentences enumerating more than five or six items, lists of more than one sentence, selected notes, and some 'short digressions' are broken off from the main text and displayed.
4. The style and placement of biblical references has been made consistent with modern practice and Roman numerals have been changed to Arabic.
5. Words such as 'unto' become 'to' and 'doth consist' becomes 'consists'.

INTRODUCTION

The Priesthood of Christ is now the fourth work of John Owen, the great Puritan theologian-pastor, which Dr Philip Ross has redressed in modern publishing clothes for a twenty-first century readership.

Some readers may find this particular work a greater reading challenge than either of the earlier volumes: *The Glory of Christ*, *The Holy Spirit*, and *Communion with God*. But the effort will prove to be immensely worthwhile. For this is a significant work on a major biblical doctrine. Owen himself believed it was probably the most substantial work to date on the theme. While it is now three hundred and fifty years old its burden addresses issues that remain vitally important today. Yet for Owen these 350 pages amounted to what nowadays would be referred to as an 'excursus' in a much larger work!

Who was this John Owen who was capable not only of writing these pages but another twelve thousand besides? — *The Priesthood of Christ* accounts for only part of one volume in an immense corpus of works.

In brief, John Owen was born in a vicarage in Stadhampton, near Oxford, in 1616. His early education was followed by studies at Oxford University (graduating B.A. in 1632), time spent as a private tutor, pastoral service in two congregations, first in Fordham in

Essex and then at Coggeshall (a congregation of over 2,000), service as a chaplain to Oliver Cromwell, a period as Vice Chancellor of Oxford University (in American terms, the President), ejection from the Church of England in 1662 as a 'Nonconformist,' and finally a period towards the end of his life when he served in pastoral ministry in a gathered congregation in Leadenhall Street, London. He died in Ealing (then a pleasant village, now a London suburb) in 1683.

A man of immense learning, Owen's collected Works extend to twenty-four substantial volumes. They fall, essentially, into four categories:

    (i) expositions of specific doctrines;
    (ii) pastoral and practical teaching;
    (iii) writings dealing with controversies;
    (iv) biblical exposition.

Dominating this last category is a massive exposition of the Letter to the Hebrews, well over 3,000 pages in length. 'It is' wrote Thomas Chalmers, 'a work of gigantic strength as well as gigantic size; and he who has mastered it is very little short, both in respect to the doctrinal and the practical of Christianity of being an erudite and accomplished theologian.'

The Priesthood of Christ (originally entitled *Concerning the Sacerdotal Office of Christ*) forms one of a series of introductory essays ('Exercitations' in Owen's now disused language). They contain material which nowadays might appear in a series of excursuses or appendices in which the author might review or further develop material which would be inappropriate in the body of the text, or be too extensive for a footnote.

In Owen's hands these exercitations are advance expositions in which he discusses important theological issues and points up their relevance. In relation to his commentary on Hebrews they serve a similar role to the one Calvin's *Institutes* play in relation to his commentaries, enabling him essentially to say to the reader 'For further discussion see the exercitations.'

Owen wrote for serious readers. ('If you have come like Cato into the theatre,' he greets his readers on one occasion, 'Farewell, you have had your entertainment'!). Thus this 'precursus' on Christ's priestly ministry is a work of such substance that it stretches the

powers of a culture more accustomed to the three or four sentence,
multi-paragraph pages of contemporary books. But the dividends
of thoughtful reading are immense.

It may help us as readers if two things are available to us before
we set out on the journey on which Owen will lead us: (i) A road
map to provide some sense of direction to the journey, and (ii)
some basic knowledge of the major individuals and theological
controversies singled out by Owen in his discussion.

A MAP FOR THE ROAD

Owen develops his theme in a logical and theological order. The
exposition begins with a discussion of the origin of priestly ministry.
Its necessity arises from the presence of sin:

> A supposition of the entrance of sin, and what ensued thereon
> in the curse of the law, lie at the foundation of the designation
> of the priesthood and sacrifice of Christ (see p. 68).

Owen does not mean that the plan of redemption is a divine
afterthought, a poor Plan B cobbled together because of the failure
of Plan A. Rather it is rooted in eternity in the inter-personal
purposes of the Father and the Son together with the Spirit. Readers
of *Communion with God* will recognise here Owen's profound
interest in the inner relations in the Trinity and their far reaching
implications.

There were, Owen argues, 'eternal transactions' between the
Father and the Son with respect to the work of redemption. These
were of a covenantal or federal nature.[1]

Owen shared with the earlier Scottish theologian, Robert
Rollock, the view that all of God's relations with respect to creation
and redemption are covenantal in nature. In particular he viewed
God's work in history unfolding in terms of four covenants:

---

1 'Federal' from the Latin *foedus-er* is a covenant or treaty. Owen's exposition here,
as in a number of places, provides the reader with a series of mini-seminars on
important theological themes. Pausing on them, without being frustrated that
the argument does not move with contemporary rapidity, will add to the riches
of the study.

    (i) a covenant of works made with Adam in creation;
   (ii) a covenant of grace, made with Adam following the Fall and fulfilled in the work of Christ;
  (iii) a covenant made through Moses, which he believed had aspects of both the covenant of works and the covenant of grace, and
  (iv) an inner-Trinitarian covenant between the Father and the Son, the covenant of redemption.

While it often comes as a surprise to readers of Owen to discover that his federal theology was not simply a reiteration of, for example, *The Confession of Faith*, he was by no means unique in holding the four covenant view, nor in particular the 'mixed covenant' view of Sinai.[2]

In view in these covenant purposes is the salvation of sinners for the glory of God—demonstrated in the manner in which he displays his wisdom, justice and grace in the gospel of Christ.

This plan then raises the question: What did this involve for the Son? Two things:

  (i) obedience (he becomes the Servant of the Lord), and
 (ii) sacrifice (he becomes the Suffering Servant who bears God's judgment on man's sin).

The covenant of grace, the covenant of redemption, the coming of Christ—these are all necessary for our salvation. Yet they remain the free act of God. The justice of God and the mercy of God are not opposed to one another (as though the former were an involuntary necessity while the latter is an act of voluntary condescension). God freely performs that which is necessary for man's salvation; he freely exercises the judgment against man's sin that his nature necessarily requires.

In the light of the fact that God has committed himself to our salvation in all persons of the Trinity, Owen continues, Christ had

---

2 This is all the more striking in the light of the fact that Owen was involved in the composition of *The Savoy Declaration* which simply echoed the Westminster document at this point. Clearly it was not a matter for which he would have gone to the stake.

to suffer what we deserve (it was an action of consequent absolute necessity given the prior commitment to save):

> The Lord underwent the punishment due to our sins in the judgment of God, and according to the sentence of the law; for how did God make our sins to meet on him, how did he bear them, if he did not suffer the penalty due to them, or if he underwent some other inconvenience, but not the exact demerit of sin? (p. 181)

The Father lovingly sent the Son in our place. Christ then became our substitute; the Father punishes our sin even when it is borne before him by his own beloved Son. For God hates sin, and not to judge it would impeach his own glory. Herein lies the heart and wonder of the cross—heaven's love and heaven's justice meet.

This is what makes the priesthood of Christ a necessity. He must become both sacrificing priest and sacrificial lamb. Owen argues — surely rightly—that without this perspective the cross cannot be the foundation for a coherent theology. Priestly, substitutionary, penal substitution is of the essence of the atonement. Any perspective on the atonement that denies or lacks the notion of penal substitution must fail to provide a rational for redemption from the guilt and power of sin.

Thus, for Owen, any theology of the atonement that reduces the work of Christ to either the kingly role (Christ conquers our enemies) or the prophetic role (Christ reveals the Father's love to overwhelm us and turn us from sin, or as an example to us of how to live in sacrificial love) disembowels the gospel. It cannot provide an adequate grounding for the cry of dereliction. The cross becomes either inessential, or too high a price for the blessing purchased by it. The cross cannot be fully explained as Jesus identifying himself with us in our need to show us the love of God. For, as James Denney pointed out long ago, if I see a man drowning in a river I do not demonstrate my love for him, nor do I rescue him by jumping in and drowning with him. No, the wonder of the love of God at the cross is that while we were sinners Christ died for us in order to justify us and save us from the wrath of God (Rom. 5:8–10). The cross is a revelation of love only because there God made Christ to be sin for us (2 Cor. 5:21), and a curse (Gal. 3:13).

Substitutionary self-sacrifice (eye for eye, tooth for tooth, man for man) is therefore essential to Christ's priesthood. He comes to act for the church before the face of God. His life, with its slow but divinely ordained journey to Calvary constitute his preparation for this ministry; his maculation, or sacrificial slaying and his oblation in his shedding of his precious blood are forerunners of his representation as he stands on our behalf before the throne of God.

Charitie Lee Bancroft was therefore right, after all:

> Before the throne of God above
> I have a strong, a perfect plea . . .

> When Satan tempts me to despair,
> And tells me of the guilt within,
> Upward I look and see him there
> Who made an end to all my sin.
> Because the sinless Saviour died
> My sinful soul is counted free;
> For God, the just, is satisfied
> To look on him and pardon me.

There Christ serves us as intercessor—not, in Owen's view, so much by formal representation of our needs in words audibly spoken to his Father and ours, but in a virtual manner (i.e. real and powerful way).[3]

But, Owen notes, Christ came 'in the fullness of time'. What of before? He provides the standard Augustinian biblical-theological answer: God prefigured the work of Christ in the priestly sacrifices of the Old Testament period, whether those offered before the Law of Moses or according to it. In the providence of God, priestly ministry was exercised prior to Sinai (cf. Exod. 19:22, 24) as well as according to the pattern given at Sinai. By means of the Old Testament priesthood old covenant saints looked forward in faith by way of promise to that priesthood of Christ to which we look back in faith.

Here—it may seem both curiously and unexpectedly—Owen bids farewell to his readers (p. 351). Day to day humanity breaks momentarily interrupts his massive, driving intellect. In essence Owen thinks the excursus is already long enough, although (as ever!) there is still much to say. But—we could not have guessed—

---

3 Owen is using the term in its Latin sense: *virtus*, strength or power.

he is in fact feeling unwell, and the printer is knocking at his door for a complete manuscript. We will—he hopes—excuse him if he leaves further exposition for later!

Indeed we will.

But just before setting out on the reading journey, it may be helpful to provide further orientation—this time to some of the individuals and issues Owen addresses.

PEOPLE TO MEET, ISSUES TO FACE

There are some historical and theological landmarks in *The Priesthood of Christ* that may not be wholly familiar to contemporary readers and a few comments about them may provide helpful orientation to what follows.

Given Owen's context (he is writing in 1668) we might expect him to comment on Roman Catholic teaching.

Owen's grandparents were alive at the time of the Spanish Armada—an invading force calculated to bring England back to subservience to the papacy. He was born less than a hundred years from the date when Luther's *Ninety-Five Theses* exploded onto the church of early sixteenth century Europe. The reign of 'Bloody Mary' (1496–1533) when large numbers of Protestants had been executed, was within living memory. The Stuart monarchy of Owen's own day had taken a decided Rome-ward direction in the eyes of many. Roman Catholicism was not merely a religious issue; it was a political one. So we find here critique of Roman Catholic theology.

Owen also lived during the period when the Quaker movement appeared to be gaining momentum. Here too he had issues (it should not be forgotten that while 'Quaker' today may convey the idea of a pacifism and quietism, the nomenclature was originally expressive of a very different aspect of radical religious life. While by no means a homogeneous group, the nickname 'quakers' was expressive of some of the more radical groups. In addition, such theologically significant figures the Lutheran Andreas Osiander (1498–1552) and the Dutch lawyer-theologian Hugo Grotius (1583–1645) also make cameo appearances in these pages.

But throughout this work (and it is not alone in his corpus of writings) it is Socinianism that Owen chiefly has in his cross hairs.

'Socinianism'?

Socinianism was in some respects similar to Arianism in the early church and Unitarianism today. Its distinctives included denying the eternal deity of Christ, the doctrine of the Trinity, and the centrality of penal substitution. For all practical purposes it saw Jesus as a unique man given supreme authority and (at least in its earlier forms) to be worshiped only as a kind of representative symbol of God. It taught that salvation (insofar as it was necessary for those not totally depraved) came through repentance and good works. Many of its emphases would reappear in developed form in, for example, the teaching of Lord Herbert (1583–1648, elder brother of the great metaphysical pastor-poet, George Herbert).

The rise of this theology at the time of the Reformation is traced back to Lelio Sozzini (Latin: *Laelius Socinus*), an Italian, and his nephew Fausto (Latin: *Faustus Socinus*). Born in Siena in 1525, Lelio was a man of unusual charm and free spirit, with an enquiring but restless mind. Underwritten by his father he was able to travel widely and came into contact with the burgeoning groups of men whose intelligent minds and eager hearts had been captured by the evangelical reformation. Sozzini's attractive personality and inquisitive mind gave him an entreé to such luminaries as Luther's colleague and friend Phillip Melanchthon, Heinrich Bullinger, and John Calvin.

At various times Sozzini questioned Calvin on such matters as predestination, the resurrection of the body, and the grounds of salvation. Calvin's correspondence with him is partially extant, and in it he expresses the two sides of Sozzini he had obviously experienced. Thus he wrote to him in 1551:

> The word of God…is my only guide, and to acquiesce in its plain doctrines shall be my constant rule of wisdom. Would that you also, my dear Lelio, would learn to regulate your powers with the same moderation! You have no reason to expect a reply from me so long as you bring forward those monstrous questions. If you are gratified by floating among these aerial speculations…I am very greatly grieved that the fine talents with which God has endowed you, should be occupied not only with what is vain and fruitless, but that they should also be injured by pernicious figments. What I warned you of long ago, I must again

seriously repeat, that unless you correct in time this itching after investigation, it is to be feared that you will bring upon yourself severe suffering. I should be cruel towards you did I treat with a show of indulgence what I believe to be a very dangerous error…

Adieu, brother very highly esteemed by me; and if this rebuke is harsher than it ought to be, ascribe it to my love to you.

A year or so later, following the trial and death of the anti-trinitarian Michael Servetus, Sozzini's own mind turned to the issue of the trinity itself, which he would likewise come to reject.

Sozzini died in 1562, a couple of years before Calvin. But he had by that time exercised considerable influence on his young nephew Fausto who both imbibed and developed his uncle's thought. More than that, he published his anti-trinitarian views and as a result, Calvin's fears for the uncle were fulfilled in the nephew, who was persecuted and physically abused. From 1579 until his death in 1604 he lived in Poland, and it was there that his influence became virtually institutionalised.

Several of Fausto's leading colleagues seem to have been involved in both 'perfecting' the catechism he had prepared (later published as the *Racovian Catechism*) and disseminating their Unitarian and Socinian views. These included Johannes Crellius (1590–1633) who became Rector of the University of Cracow, Johannes Volkelius (died 1618) who may have acted as an amanuensis to Socinus, and Valentinius Smalcius, all of whom, along with Ludwig Woolzogenius, Owen both mentions and vigorously critiques.

This was not the first time Owen had dealt with Socinianism. In 1652 an Englishman John Biddle[4] had translated and published the *Racovian Catechism* (it was condemned by Parliament in April 1652, and all copies were to be burned). Indeed Parliament had requested Owen's help to deal with Socinianism and in 1655 he published an extensive and devastating critique in *Vindiciae Evangelicae*.

In *The Priesthood of Christ*, however, Owen's central concern with Socinianism is that it reduces the priesthood of Christ to his roles as prophet and king and thus destroys both its centrality and its distinctive significance. In Socinianism Christ's death amounts to

4 Biddle had also translated a *Memoir of the Life of Faustus Socinus* in 1653.

little more than a revelation of God's heart of love; it is not therefore an atoning action of sacrifice made for our sins.

While Owen by no means denies that all of Christ's offices belong together, and may be exercised simultaneously, nor ignore the fact that God does reveal his love at the cross, he insists that something was definitively accomplished on the cross to procure our salvation. Otherwise it does not reveal the heart of God. As in other areas, Owen recognises that behind the Socinian view lies an inadequate view of God, an unbiblical diminution of the gravity of sin and an inevitable downplaying of the reality of the judgment and wrath of God.

Relevance to Today?

But why should Owen's exposition of Christ's priesthood, and his polemic against Socinianism have relevance to today's church? Because we live in currents of theological thought at both the academic and popular levels where echoes of Socinus can be heard.

There is no doubt a very pressing need for us to understand that Christ's ministry was a revelatory one (the prophetic office) and the establishing of a new order in his kingdom (the kingly office). But to see the Christus Victor motif—Christ the Conquering King, or the Lordship of Christ, or even for that matter the kingdom of Christ, as central to the New Testament's gospel without emphasising the central role of his vicarious sacrifice and substitutionary death under the judgment and wrath of God as the heart of our salvation is a fatal blunder for theology, pastoral ministry, and world evangelism.

It will be said that the earliest Christian Confession was 'Jesus is Lord' and not 'Jesus is Priest.' But that is not the point. The point is that it is as Saviour, as Substitute, as Penalty-Bearer, crucified and risen, that he now is Lord—not apart from that. His power to bring deliverance is not naked power but atoning power (as Hebrews 1:1–4; 2: 5–14) clarifies.

Years ago the Swedish Lutheran theologian Gustav Aulén famously argued in his book *Christus Victor*[5] that Martin Luther saw the Kingship of Christ, not his penal substitutionary death (priesthood) as central to the gospel. Aulén's own theology,

---

5 First published in Swedish in 1930 and in English in 1931.

however, made it clear that this was by no means an unbiased conviction. Penal substitution was not central in his own exposition of the work of Christ.[6]

More recently among some adherents of the so-called 'New Perspective on Paul' a similar argument for the central role of Christ's kingship and the centrality of the Christus Victor motif (Jesus is Lord) has been made to the diminution if not exclusion of the gravity of sin as guilt, the righteous judgment of God on sin, and the reality of divine wrath. In emerging and emergent ecclesiastical circles echoes of the same have been heard.

Owen will have none of this. Probably no theologian in the English language has ever rivalled him in stressing the absolute centrality of Christ's penal substitution, and therefore his role as Priest. The point is that Christ is not victor unless he is first substitute. The deliverance he brings requires that he deal with both the guilt of sin and the wrath of God as well as our bondage to the powers of darkness.

> *Probably no theologian in the English language has ever rivalled Owen stressing the absolute centrality of Christ's penal substitution...For that reason alone* The Priesthood of Christ *is worth all the time it takes to read it with humility, care, and reflection.*

For that reason alone *The Priesthood of Christ* is worth all the time it takes to read it with humility, care, and reflection. Written as it was in the mid-seventeenth century, and providing a vigorous theological workout for many readers, there are important points at which it remains a tract for the times.

So, with some quick map reading, and a little warning that you may meet strangers on the way, and have some hard thinking to do, it is time for your journey to begin. I hope that, even if the road sometimes calls for perseverance, the walk will be bracing, and at the end you will be grateful to Owen that you are stronger spiritually and theologically than you were at the beginning.

Sinclair B Ferguson
First Presbyterian Church
Columbia, South Carolina.

6 As his *The Faith of the Christian Church* (Swedish, 1923; English, 1948) demonstrated.

1

THE OFFICE OF PRIESTHOOD

A Unique Emphasis on Christ's Priesthood

Amongst the many excellencies of this Epistle to the Hebrews, which render it as useful to the church as the sun in the firmament is to the world, the revelation that is made therein concerning the nature, singular pre-eminence, and use of the priesthood of our Lord Jesus Christ, may well be esteemed to deserve the first and principal place; for whereas the whole matter of the sacrifice that he offered, and the atonement that he made thereby, with the inestimable benefits which thence redound to them that do believe, depend solely on this, the excellency of the doctrine of this must needs be acknowledged by all who have any interest in these things. It is indeed, in the substance of it, delivered in some other passages of the books of the New Testament, but yet more sparingly and obscurely than any other truth of the same or a like importance. The Holy Ghost reserved it to this as its proper place, where, upon the consideration of the institutions of the Old Testament and their removal out of the church, it might be duly represented, as that which gave an end to them in their accomplishment, and life to those ordinances of evangelical worship which were to succeed in their room.

When our Lord Jesus says that he came to 'give his life a ransom for many' (Matt. 20:28), he had respect to the sacrifice that he had to offer as a priest. The same also is intimated where he is called 'The Lamb of God' (John 1:29); for he was himself both priest and sacrifice. Our apostle also mentions his sacrifice and his offering of himself to God (Eph. 5:2); on the account of which he calls him 'a propitiation' (Rom. 3:25); and mentions also his 'intercession,' with the benefits of that (Rom. 8:34). The clearest testimony to this purpose is that of the apostle John, who puts together both the general acts of his sacerdotal office, and intimates with that their mutual relation (1 John 2:1–2); for his intercession as our 'advocate' with his Father respects his oblation as he was a 'propitiation for our sins.' So the same apostle tells us to the same purpose, that he 'washed us in his own blood' (Rev. 1:5), when he expiated our sins by the sacrifice of himself. These are, if not all, yet the principal places in the New Testament in which immediate respect is had to the priesthood or sacrifice of Christ. But in none of them is he called 'a priest,' or 'an high priest,' nor is he said in any of them to have taken any such office upon him; neither is the nature of his oblation or intercession explained in them, nor the benefits rehearsed which accrue to us from his discharge of this office in a peculiar manner. Of what concernment these things are to our faith, obedience, and consolation—of what use to us in the whole course of our profession, in all our duties and temptations, sins and sufferings— we shall, God assisting, declare in the ensuing exposition. Now, for all the acquaintance we have with these and sundry other evangelical mysteries belonging to them or depending on them, with all the light we have into the nature and use of Mosaic institutions, and the types of the Old Testament, which make so great a part of the Scripture given and continued for our instruction, we are entirely obliged to the revelation made in and by this epistle.

A MYSTERIOUS DOCTRINE

And this doctrine, concerning the priesthood of Christ and the sacrifice that he offered, is on many accounts deep and mysterious. This our apostle plainly intimates in sundry passages of this epistle. With respect to this he says, the discourse he intended was δυσερμήνευτος λέγειν, 'hard to be uttered,' or rather, hard to be understood when uttered (Heb. 5:11); as also another apostle, that there are in this epistle δυσνόητά τινα (2 Pet. 3:16), 'some things hard to be understood,' which relate to this. Hence he requires that those who attend to this doctrine should be past the condition of living on 'milk' only, or being contented with the first rudiments and principles of religion; and that they be able to digest 'strong meat,' by having 'their senses exercised to discern both good and evil' (Heb. 5:12–14). And when he resolves to proceed in the explication of it, he declares that he is leading them 'on to perfection' (Heb. 6:1), or to the highest and most perfect doctrines in the mystery of Christian religion. And several other ways he manifests his judgment, as of the importance of this truth, and how needful it is to be known, so of the difficulty there is in coming to a right and full understanding of it. And all these things do justify an especial and peculiar inquiry into it.

WHY FOCUS ON THIS SUBJECT?

Now, although our apostle, in his excellent order and method, has delivered to us all the material concernments of this sacred office of Christ, yet he has not done it in an entire discourse, but in such a way as his subject-matter and principal design would admit of, and indeed did necessitate. He does not in any one place, nor upon any one occasion, express and teach the whole of the doctrine concerning it, but, as himself speaks in another case, πολυμερῶς καὶ πολυτρόπως, 'by various parts,' or degrees, and 'in sundry ways,' he declares and makes known the several concernments of it: for this he did partly as the Hebrews could bear it; partly as the series of his discourse led him to the mention of it, having another general end in design; and partly as the explanation of the old Aaronic institutions and ordinances, which, for the benefit of them that still adhered to them, he aimed at, required it of him.

For me to have undertaken the discourse of the whole upon any particular occasion, would have lengthened out a digression too much, diverting the reader in his perusal of the exposition; and had I insisted on the several parts and concernments of it as they do occur, I should have been necessitated to a frequent repetition of the same things. Neither way could I have given an entire representation of it, whereby the beauty and the symmetry of the whole might be made evident. This, therefore, inclined my thoughts, in the first place, to comprise a summary of the entire doctrine concerning it in these previous exercitations. From hence, as the reader may take a prospect of it singly by itself, so he may, if he please, carry along much insight with him from it into the most abstruse passages in the whole epistle. And this, added to what we have discoursed on chapter 1:2, concerning the kingly right and power of Christ, will give a more full and complete account of these his two offices than, it may be, has as yet been attempted by any.

NOT THE POPE'S FAVOURITE DOCTRINE

Moreover, the doctrine concerning the priesthood and sacrifice of the Lord Christ has in all ages, by the craft and malice of Satan, been either directly opposed or variously corrupted; for it contains the principal foundation of the faith and consolation of the church, which are by him chiefly maligned. It is known in how many things and by how many ways it has been obscured and depraved in the Papacy. Sundry of them we have occasion to deal about in our exposition of many passages of the epistle; for they have not so much directly opposed the truth of the doctrine, as, disbelieving the use and benefit of the thing itself to the church, they have substituted various false and superstitious observances to effect the end to which this priesthood of Christ and his holy discharge thereof are alone of God designed. These, therefore, I shall no otherwise consider but as their opinions and practices occur occasionally to us, either in these exercitations or in the exposition ensuing.

But there is a generation of men, whom the craft of Satan has stirred up in this and the foregoing age, who have made it a great part of their preposterous and pernicious endeavours in and about religion to overthrow this whole office of the Lord Christ, and the efficacy of the sacrifice of himself depending thereon. This they have attempted with much subtilty and diligence, introducing a metaphorical or imaginary priesthood and sacrifice in their room; so, robbing the church of its principal treasure, they pretend to supply the end of it with their own fancies. They are the Socinians whom I intend. And there are more reasons than one why I could not omit a strict examination of their reasonings and objections against this great part of the mystery of the gospel. The reputation of parts, industry, and learning, which the bold curiosity of some has given to them, makes it necessary, at least upon unavoidable occasions, to obviate the insinuation of their poison, which that opens a way for. Besides, even among ourselves, they are not a few who embrace and do endeavour to propagate their opinions.

And the same course, with their faces seeming to look another way, is steered by the Quakers, who have at last openly espoused almost all their pernicious tenets, although in some things as yet they obscure their sentiments in cloudy expressions, as wanting will or skill to make a more perspicuous declaration of them.

And there are others also, pretending to more sobriety than those before mentioned, who do yet think that these doctrines concerning the offices and mediation of Christ are, if not unintelligible by us, yet not of any great necessity to be insisted on; for of that esteem are the mysteries of the gospel grown to be with some, with many among us. With respect to all these, added to the consideration of the edification of those that are sober and godly, I esteemed it necessary to handle this whole doctrine of the priesthood of Christ distinctly, and previously to our exposition of the uses of it as they occur in the epistle.

A Comprehensive Endeavour

There are also sundry things which may contribute much light to this doctrine, and be useful in the explication of the terms, notions, and expressions, which are applied to the declaration of it, that cannot directly and orderly be reduced under any singular text or passage in the epistle. Many dawnings there were in the world to the rising of this Sun of Righteousness—many preparations for the actual exhibition of this High Priest to the discharge of his office. And some of these were greatly instructive in the nature of this priesthood, as being appointed of God for that purpose. Such was the use of sacrifices, ordained from the foundation of the world, or the first entrance of sin; and the designation of persons in the church to the office of a figurative priesthood, for the performance of that service. By these God intended to instruct the church in the nature and benefit of what he would after accomplish, in and by his Son Jesus Christ. These things, therefore—that is, what belonged to the rite of sacrificing and the Mosaic priesthood—must be taken into consideration, as retaining yet that light in them which God had designed them to be communicative of. And, indeed, our apostle himself reduces many of the instructions which he gives us in the nature of the priesthood and sacrifice of Christ to those institutions which were designed of old to typify and represent them. Besides all these, there may be observed sundry things in the common usages of mankind about this office, and the discharge of it in general, that deserve our consideration; for although all mankind, left out of the church's enclosure, through their own blindness and the craft of him who originally seduced them into an apostasy from God, had, as to their own interest and practice, miserably depraved all sacred things, every thing that belonged to the worship or service of the Divine Being, yet they still carried along with them something that had its first fountain and spring in divine revelation, and a congruity to the inbred principles of nature. In these also—where we can separate the wheat from the chaff, what was from divine revelation or the light of nature from what was of diabolical delusion or vain superstition—we may discover what is useful and helpful to us in our design. By these means may we be enabled to reduce all sacred truth in this matter to its proper principles, and direct it to its proper end.

And these are the reasons why, although we shall have frequent occasion to insist on this office of Christ, with the proper acts and effects of it, in our ensuing exposition, both in that part of it which accompanies these exercitations and those also which, in the goodness and patience of God, may follow, yet I thought meet to handle the whole doctrine of it apart in preliminary discourses. And let not the reader suppose that he shall be imposed on with the same things handled in several ways twice over: for as the design of the exposition is to open the words of the text, to give their sense, with the purpose and arguings of the apostle, applying all to the improvement of our faith and obedience, of which nothing will here fall under our consideration; so what may be here discoursed, historically, philologically, dogmatically, or eristically, will admit of no repetition or rehearsal in the expository part of our endeavours.

These things being premised, as was necessary, we apply ourselves to the work lying before us.

BIBLICAL TERMS FOR 'PRIEST'

Our Lord Jesus Christ is in the Old Testament, as prophesied of, called כֹּהֵן, 'cohen:' (Ps. 110:4) אַתָּה־כֹהֵן לְעוֹלָם—'Thou art cohen for ever.' And Zechariah 6:13, וְהָיָה כֹהֵן עַל־כִּסְאוֹ—'And he shall be cohen upon his throne.' We render it in both places 'a priest;' that is, ἱερεύς, 'sacerdos.' In the New Testament, that is, in this Epistle, he is frequently said to be ἱερεὺς and ἀρχιερεὺς; which we likewise express by 'priest' and 'high priest,'—'pontifex,' 'pontifex maximus.' And the meaning of these words must be first inquired into.

כָּהַן, the verb, is used only in Piel, 'cihen;' and it signifies 'sacerdotio fungi,' or 'munus sacerdotale exercere,'—'to be a priest,' or 'to exercise the office of the priesthood;' ἱερουργέω. The LXX mostly render it by ἱερατεύω, which is 'sacerdotio fungor,'—'to exercise the priestly office;' although it be also used in the inauguration or consecration of a person to the priesthood. Once they translate it by λειτουργέω (2 Chron. 11:14), 'in sacris operari,'—'to serve (or minister) in (or about) sacred things.' Ἱερουργέω is used by our apostle in this sense, and applied to the preaching of the gospel: Εἰς τὸ εἶναί με λειτουργὸν Χριστοῦ Ἰησοῦ εἰς τὰ ἔθνη, ἱερουργοῦντα τὸ εὐαγγέλιον τοῦ θεοῦ (Rom. 15:16);—'Employed in the sacred ministration of the gospel.' He uses both λειτουργός and ἱερουργέω metaphorically, with respect to the προσφορά or sacrifice which he made of the Gentiles, which was also metaphorical. And ἱερατεύω is used by Luke with respect to the Jewish service in the temple (Luke 1:8); for originally both the words have respect to proper sacrifices.

Some would have the word כֹּהֵן to be ambiguous, and to signify 'officio fungi, aut ministrare in sacris aut politicis,'—'to discharge an office, or to minister in things sacred or political.' But no instance can be produced of its use to this purpose. Once it seems to be applied to things not sacred. Isaiah 61:10, כֶּחָתָן יְכַהֵן פְּאֵר—'As a bridegroom decks himself with ornaments;' or, 'adorns himself with beauty;' that is, beautiful garments. If the word did originally and properly signify 'to adorn,' it might be thence translated to the exercise of the office of the priesthood, seeing the priests therein were, by especial institution, to be clothed with garments לְכָבוֹד וּלְתִפְאָרֶת (Exod. 28:40), 'for glory and for beauty.' So the priests of Moloch were called 'chemarims,' from the colour of their garments, or their countenances made black with the soot of their fire and sacrifices. But this is not the proper signification of the word; only, denoting the priesthood to be exercised in beautiful garments and sundry ornaments, it was thence traduced to express adorning. The LXX render it by περιτίθημι, but withal acknowledge somewhat sacerdotal in the expression: Ὡς νυμφίῳ περιέθηκέ μοι μίτραν·—'He has put on me' (restraining the action to God) 'a mitre as on a bridegroom;' which was a sacerdotal ornament. And Aquila, 'as a bridegroom, ἱερατευμένος στεφάνῳ·'—'bearing the crown of the priesthood,' or discharging the priest's office in a crown. And the Targum, observing the peculiar application of the word in this place, adds, וככהנא דכא—'And as an high priest is adorned.' All agree that an allusion is made to the garments and ornaments of the high priest. The place may be tendered, 'As a bridegroom, he' (that is God, the bridegroom of the church) 'does consecrate me with glory,'—'gloriously set me apart for himself.' The word therefore is sacred; and though כֹּהֵן be traduced to signify other persons, as we shall see afterwards, yet כֹּהֵן [properly] is only used in a sacred sense.

DIVINATION AND SOOTHSAYING

The Arabic כהן, 'cahan,' is 'to divine, to prognosticate, to be a soothsayer, to foretell;' and כאהן, 'caahan,' is 'a diviner, a prophet, an astrologer, a figure-caster.' This use of it came up after the priests had generally taken themselves to such arts, partly curious, partly diabolical, by the instigation of the false gods whom they ministered to. Homer puts them together, as they came afterwards mostly to be the same, Iliad. A. 62:

ἀλλ᾽ ἄγε δή τινα μάντιν ἐρείομεν, ἢ ἱερῆα
ἢ καὶ ὀνειροπόλον,

'A prophet, or a priest, or an interpreter of dreams.'

Μάγους καὶ ασστρονόμους τε και θυτας μετεπέμπετο (Herod., lib. 4); 'He sent for magicians, astronomers, and priests,' for θύτης is a priest; for the priests first gave out oracles and divinations in the temples of their gods. From them proceeded a generation of impostors, who exceedingly infatuated the world with a pretense of foretelling things to come, of interpreting dreams, and doing things uncouth and strange, to the amazement of the beholders. And as they all pretended to derive their skill and power from their gods, whose priests they were, so they invented, or had suggested to them by Satan, various ways and means of divination, or of attaining the knowledge of particular future events. According to those ways which in especial any of them attended to were they severally denominated. Generally they were called חֲכָמִים, 'wise men;' as those of Egypt (Gen. 41:8), and of Babylon (Dan. 2:12–13). Hence we render μάγοι, the followers of their arts, 'wise men' (Matt. 2:1). Among the Egyptians they were divided into two sorts, חַרְטֻמִּים and מְכַשְּׁפִים (Exod. 7:11); the head of one sort in the days of Moses being probably Jannes, and of the other Jambres (2 Tim. 3:8). We call them 'magicians and sorcerers.' Among the Babylonians there is mention of these, and two sorts more are added to them, namely, אַשָּׁפִים and כַּשְׂדִים (Dan. 2:2). Of the difference and distinction among these we shall treat afterwards. From this practice of the generality of priests did כָּהַן come to signify 'to soothsay' or 'divine.'

THE PRIESTS OF EGYPT

כֹּהֵן is then a priest; and he who was first called so in the Scripture, probably in the world, was Melchizedek (Gen. 14:18). On what account he was so called shall be afterwards declared. Sometimes, though rarely, it is applied to express a priest of false gods; as of Dagon (1 Sam. 5:5); of Egypt (Gen. 41:45), 'Joseph married the daughter of Poti-pherah, כֹּהֵן אֹן'—'priest of On,' that is, of Heliopolis, the chief seat of the Egyptian religious worship. Nor is there any colour why the word should here be rendered 'prince,' as it is, רבא, by the Targum—the Latin is 'sacerdos,' and the LXX. ἱερεύς—for the dignity of priests, especially of those who were eminent among them, was no less at that time in Egypt, and other parts also of the world, than was that of princes of the second sort; yea, we shall consider instances afterwards in which the kingly and priestly offices were conjoined in the same person, although none ever had the one by virtue of the other but upon special reason. It was therefore, as by Pharaoh intended, an honour to Joseph to be married to the daughter of the priest of On; for the man, according to their esteem, was wise, pious, and honourable, seeing the wisdom of the Egyptians at that time consisted principally in the knowledge of the mysteries of their religion, and from their excellency therein were they exalted and esteemed honourable. Nor can it be pleaded, in bar to this exposition, that Joseph would not marry the daughter of an idolatrous priest, for all the Egyptians were no less idolatrous than their priests, and he might as soon convert one of their daughters to the true God as one of any other; which no doubt he did, whereon she became a matriarch in Israel. In other places, where, by כֹהֵן, an idolatrous priest is intended, the Targum renders it by כּוּמְרָא; 'comara,' whence are chemarims. Yet the Syriac translator of the Epistle to the Hebrews calls a priest and an high priest, even when applied to Christ, כּוּמְרָא and רַב כּוּמְרֵא, though elsewhere in the New Testament he uses כָּהֲנָא, 'chahana,' constantly. The reason for this I have declared elsewhere.

A PRINCELY TITLE

It is confessed that this name is sometimes used to signify secondary princes, those of a second rank or degree, but is never once applied to a chief, supreme prince, or a king, though he that is so was sometimes, by virtue of some special warrant, cohen also. The Jews, therefore, after the Targum, offer violence to the text (Ps. 110:4), where they would have Melchizedek to be called a cohen because he was a prince. But it is said expressly he was a king, of which rank none is, on the account of his office, ever called cohen; but to those of a second rank it is sometimes accommodated: 'Ira the Jairite was כֹהֵן לְדָוִד;'—'a chief ruler', say we, 'about David' (2 Sam. 20:26). A priest he was not, nor could be; for, as Kimchi on the place observes, he is called the 'cohen of David,' but a priest was not a priest to one man, but to all Israel. So David's sons are said to be cohanim: וּבְנֵי דָוִד כֹּהֲנִים הָיוּ—'And the sons of David were cohanim' (2 Sam. 8:18); that is, 'princes,' though the Vulgate renders it 'sacerdotes.' So also Job 12:19, we translate it 'princes.' And in those places the Targum uses רבא,

'rabba;' the LXX sometimes αὐλάρχης, 'a principal courtier,' and sometimes συνετός, 'a counsellor.' It is, then, granted that princes were called כֹּהֲנִים, but not properly, but by way of allusion, with respect to their dignity; for the most ancient dignity was that of the priesthood. And the same name is therefore used metaphorically to express especial dignity: תִּהְיוּ־לִי מַמְלֶכֶת כֹּהֲנִים—'And ye shall be to me a kingdom of priests' (Exod. 19:6), speaking of the whole people. This Peter renders βασίλειον ἱεράτευμα—'A kingly' (or 'royal') 'priesthood' (1 Pet. 2:9). The name of the office is כְּהֻנָּה (Exod. 40:15), ἱεράτευμα, 'pontificatus, sacerdotium,' 'the priesthood.' Allowing, therefore, this application of the word, we may inquire what is the first proper signification of it. I say, therefore, that כֹּהֵן, 'cohen,' is properly θύτης, 'a sacrificer;' nor is it otherwise to be understood or expounded, unless the abuse of the word be obvious, and a metaphorical sense necessary.

MELCHIZEDEK—THE FIRST PRIEST

He who is first mentioned as vested with this office is Melchizedek: וְהוּא כֹהֵן לְאֵל עֶלְיוֹן—'And he was a priest to the most high God' (Gen. 14:18). The Targumists make a great difference in rendering the word כֹּהֵן. Where it intends a priest of God properly, they retain it, כהן and כהנא; where it is applied to a prince or ruler, they render it by רבא, 'rabba;' and where an idolatrous priest, by כומרא. But in this matter of Melchizedek they are peculiar. In this place they use משמש, 'meshamesh:' והוא משמש קדם אל עלאה—'And he was a minister before the high God.' And by this word they express the ministry of the priests: לשמשא קדם יי כהניא דקריבין—'The priests who draw nigh to minister before the Lord' (Exod. 19:22); whereby it is evident that they understood him to be a sacred officer, or a priest to God. But in Psalm 110:4, where the same word occurs again to the same purpose, they render it by רבא, 'a prince,' or great ruler: 'Thou art a great ruler like Melchizedek:' which is a part of their open corruption of that psalm, out of a design to apply it to David; for the author of that Targum lived after they knew full well how the prophecy in that psalm was in our books and by Christians applied to the Messiah, and how the ceasing of their law and worship was from thence invincibly proved in this epistle. This made them maliciously pervert the words in their paraphrase, although they durst not violate the sacred text itself. But the text is plain, 'Melchizedek was cohen to the high God,'—'a priest,' or one that was called to the office of solemn sacrificing to God; for he that offers not sacrifices to God is not a priest to him, for this is the principal duty of his office, from which the whole receives denomination. That he offered sacrifices, those of the church of Rome would prove from these words, הוֹצִיא לֶחֶם וָיַיִן—'He brought forth bread and wine' (Gen. 14:18). But neither the context nor the words will give them countenance herein; nor if they could prove what they intend would it serve their purpose. Coming forth to meet Abraham (as our apostle expounds this passage, Heb. 7), he brought forth bread and wine, as a supply for the relief and refreshment of himself and his servants, supposing them weary of their travel. So dealt Barzillai the Gileadite with David and his men in the wilderness (2 Sam. 17:27–9). They brought out necessary provision for them, for they said, 'The people are hungry, and weary, and thirsty, in the wilderness.' And Gideon punished them of Succoth and Penuel for not doing the like (Judg. 8:5–8, 13–17). But the aim of these men is to reflect some countenance on their pretended sacrifice of the mass; which yet is not of bread and wine, for before the offering they suppose them to be quite changed into the substance of flesh and blood. The weakness of this pretense shall be elsewhere more fully declared. At present it may suffice that הוֹצִיא is no sacred word, or is never used to express the offering of any thing to God. Besides, if it were an offering he brought forth, it was a מִנְחָה, or 'meat-offering,' with a נֶסֶך, or 'drink-offering,' being of bread and wine. Now, this was only an acknowledgment of God the Creator as such, and was not an immediate type of the sacrifice of Christ; which was represented by them alone which, being made by blood, included a propitiation in them. But that Melchizedek was by office a sacrificer appears from Abraham delivering up to him מַעֲשֵׂר מִכֹּל, 'the tenth of all' (Gen. 14:20), that is, as our apostle interprets the place, τῶν ἀκροθινίων, 'of the spoils' he had taken. מַעֲשֵׂר is a sacred word, and denotes God's portion according to the law. So also those who had only the light of nature, and it may be some little fame of what was done in the world of old, whilst God's institutions were of force among men, did devote and sacrifice the tenth of the spoils they took in war.

So Camillus framed his vow to Apollo when he went to destroy the city of Veil: 'By your leadership, Pythian Apollo, and roused by your divine will, I proceed to destroy the city of the Veii, and to you I vow the tenth part of the spoils.' (Liv., lib. 5. cap. 21).

The like instances occur in other authors. 'Ακροθίνια is not used for the spoils themselves anywhere but in this place. In other authors, according to the derivation of the word, as it signifies the top or uppermost part of an heap, it is used only for that part or portion of spoils taken in war which was devoted and made sacred: Εἴτε δὴ ἀκροθίνια ταῦτα καταγιεῖν θεῶν ὀτεῳδή (Herod. lib. 1. cap. 86). And again, Πρῶτα μέν νυν τοῖσι θεοῖσι ἐξεῖλον ἀκροθίνια· (lib. 8. cap. 121); 'They took out the dedicated spoils for the gods.' And the reason why our apostle uses the word for the whole spoils, whence a tenth was given to Melchizedek, is, because the whole spoil was sacred and devoted to God, whence an honourary tenth was taken for Melchizedek, as the priests had afterwards out of the portion of the Levites; for all Levi was now to be tithed in Abraham. Among those spoils there is no question but there were many clean beasts meet for sacrifice; for in their herds of cattle consisted the principal parts of the riches of those days, and these were the principal spoils of war (see Num. 31:32–3). And because Saul knew that part of the spoils taken in lawful war was to be given for sacrifices to God, he made that his pretense of saving the fat cattle of the Amalekites, contrary to the express command of God (1 Sam. 15:15). Abraham therefore delivered these spoils to Melchizedek, as the priest of the most high God, to offer in sacrifice for him. And it may be there was somewhat more in it than the mere pre-eminence of Melchizedek, which was the principal consideration of this, and his being the first and only priest in office, by virtue of especial call from God—namely, that Abraham himself, coming immediately from the slaughter of many kings and their numerous army, was not yet ready or prepared for this sacred service; for even among the heathens they would abstain from their sacred offices after the shedding of blood, until they were, one way or other, purified to their own satisfaction. So in the poet, 'You, father, take in your hand our holy things, our ancestral gods; coming from such a great war and fresh slaughter, it is a sin for me to touch them, until I have washed myself in a living stream.' (Virg. Aeneid. 2:717).

A PRIEST IS A SACRIFICER

The matter is yet made more evident by the solemn election
of a priesthood of old among the people of God, or the church
in the wilderness. Sacrificing from the foundation of the world
had been up to this time left at liberty. Every one who was called
to perform any part of solemn religious worship was allowed to
discharge that duty also. But it pleased God, in the reducing of his
church into an especial peculiar order, to represent in and by it more
conspicuously what he would afterwards really effect in Jesus Christ,
to erect among them a peculiar office of priesthood. And although
this respected in general τὰ πρὸς τὸν θεόν, all things that were to be
done with God on the behalf of the people, yet the especial work
and duty belonging to it was sacrificing. The institution of this office
we have Exodus 28, whereof afterwards. And herein an enclosure
was made of sacrificing to the office of the priests; that is, so soon
as such an office there was by virtue of especial institution. And
these two things belonged to them: (1.) That they were sacrificers;
and, (2.) That they only were so: which answers all that I intend
to evince from this discourse, namely, that a priest is a sacrificer.
Whereas, therefore, it is in prophecy foretold that the Messiah
should be a priest, and he is said so to be, the principal meaning of
it is, that he should be a sacrificer, one that had right and was called
to offer sacrifice to God. This was that for which he was principally
and properly called a priest, and by his undertaking so to be, an
enclosure of sacrificing is made to himself alone.

This is the general notion of a priest amongst all men throughout
the world; and a due consideration of this is of itself sufficient to
discharge all the vain imaginations of the Socinians about this office
of Christ, whereof we shall treat afterwards.

2

THE ORIGIN OF THE PRIESTHOOD OF CHRIST

We have seen that Jesus Christ is a priest, that as such he was prophesied of under the old testament, and declared so to be in the new. The origin of this office is in the next place to be inquired after. This, in the general, all will acknowledge to lie in the eternal counsels of God; for 'known to him are all his works from the beginning of the world' (Acts 15:18). But these counsels, absolutely considered, are hid in God, in the eternal treasures of his own wisdom and will. What we learn of them is by external revelation and effects: 'The secret things belong to the Lord our God: but those things which are revealed belong to us and to our children for ever, that we may do all the words of this law' (Deut. 29:29). God frequently gives bounds to the curiosity of men, like the limits fixed to the people in the station at Sinai, that they should not gaze after his unrevealed glory, nor pry into the things which they have not seen. It was well said, that 'the one who scrutinises majesty is swallowed up by glory.' Our work is, to inquire wherein, how, and whereby, God has revealed his eternal counsels, to the end that we may know his mind, and fear him

> *God frequently gives bounds to the curiosity of men... that they should not gaze after his unrevealed glory, nor pry into the things which they have not seen.*

for our good. And so even the angels desire to bow down and to look into these things (1 Pet. 1:12)—not in a way of condescension, as into things in their nature beneath them; but in a way of humble diligence, as into things in their holy contrivance above them. Our present design, therefore, is to trace those discoveries which God has made of his eternal counsels in this matter, and that through the several degrees of divine revelation whereby he advanced the knowledge of them, until he brought them to their complement in the external exhibition of his Son, clothed in human nature with the glory of this office, and discharging the duties thereof.

Not in Eden

The counsels of God concerning us, with our relation to him and his worship, are suited to the state and condition wherein we are, for they also are effects of those counsels. Our first condition, under the law of creation, was a condition of innocence and natural righteousness. In reference to this estate, God had not ordained an establishment in it of either priest or sacrifice; for as they would have been of no use therein, so there was nothing supposed in that condition which might be prefigured or represented by them. Wherefore God did not pre-ordain the priesthood of Christ with respect to the obedience of man under the law of creation; nor did he appoint either priesthood or sacrifice, properly so called, in that state of things whilst it did continue; nor should any such have been, upon a supposition of its continuance. And this we must confirm against the opposition of some.

No Sacrifices—No Priests

We have declared in our preceding discourse that a priest, properly so called, is a sacrificer. There is, therefore, an indissoluble relation between these two—namely, priesthood and sacrifice—and they do mutually assert or deny each other; and where the one is proper, the other is so also; and where the one is metaphorical, so is the other. Thus, under the old testament, the priests who were properly so by office had proper carnal sacrifices to offer; and under the new testament, believers being made priests to God, that is, spiritually and metaphorically, such also are their sacrifices, spiritual and metaphorical. Wherefore arguments against either of these conclude equally against both. Where there are no priests, there are no sacrifices; and where there are no sacrifices, there are no priests. I intend only those who exercise the office of the priesthood for themselves and others. I shall therefore, first, manifest that there was no priesthood to be in the state of innocency; whence it will follow that therein there could be no sacrifice: and, secondly, that there was to be no sacrifice, properly so called; whence it will equally follow, that there was no priesthood therein. That which ensues on both is, that there was no counsel of God concerning either priesthood or sacrifice in that state or condition.

No Sin—No Sacrifices—No Priests

Πᾶς γὰρ ἀρχιερεὺς ἐξ ἀνθρώπων λαμβανόμενος ὑπὲρ ἀνθρώπων καθίσταται τὰ πρὸς τὸν θεόν, ἵνα προσφέρῃ δῶρά τε καὶ θυσίας ὑπὲρ ἁμαρτιῶν says our apostle (Heb. 5:1). What is here affirmed of the high priest (הַכֹּהֵן הַגָּדוֹל) is true in like manner concerning every priest; only, the high priest is here mentioned by way of eminence, because by him our Lord Christ, as to this office and the discharge of it, was principally represented. Every priest, therefore, is one ἐξ ἀνθρώπων λαμβανόμενος—'taken from amongst men.' He is 'a partaker of human nature,' in common with other men partaker of human nature; and antecedently to his assumption of his office, he is one of the same rank with other men, and he is taken or separated to this office from among them. He is vested with his office by the authority, and according to the will of God. This office, therefore, is not a thing which is common to all, nor can it take place in any state or condition in which the whole performance of divine service is equally incumbent on all individually; for none can be 'taken from among others' to perform that which those others are every one obliged personally to attend to. But every priest, properly so called, καθίσταται ὑπὲρ ἀνθρώπων—'is ordained and appointed to act for other men.' He is set over a work in the behalf of those other men from among whom he is taken; and this is, that he may take care of and perform τὰ πρὸς τὸν θεόν, or do the things that for men are to be done with God; מוּל הָאֱלֹהִים—that is, to pacify, to make atonement and reconciliation (Exod. 18:19). And this he was to do by offering δῶρά τε καὶ θυσίας, various sorts of 'gifts and sacrifices,' according to God's appointment. Now, all slain sacrifices, as we shall manifest afterwards, were for sin. This office, therefore, could have no place in the state of innocency; for it will not bear an accommodation, of any part of this description of one vested therewithal.

PRIESTS WOULD HAVE HINDERED WORSHIP

I do acknowledge, that in the state of uncorrupted nature there should have been some ὑπὲρ τοῦ θεοῦ τὰ πρὸς τὸν ἀνθρώπων, to deal with others for and in the name of God; for some would have been warranted and designed to instruct others in the knowledge of God and his will. This the state and condition of mankind did require; for both the first relation of man and wife, and that which was to ensue thereon of parents and children, include subordination and dependence. 'The head of the woman is the man' (1 Cor. 11:3) — that is, 'the husband' (Eph. 5:23); and the duty of the man it had been to instruct the woman in the things of God. For a pure nescience of many things that might be known to the glory of God and their own advantage was not inconsistent with that estate, and their knowledge was capable of objective enlargements; and the design of God was, gradually to instruct them in the things that might orderly carry them on to the end for which they were created. Herein would he have made use of the man for the instruction of the woman, as the order of nature required: for man was originally 'the head of the woman;' only, upon the curse, natural dependence was turned into troublesome subjection (Gen. 3:16). But the entrance of sin, as it contained in it the seeds of all disorder, so it plainly began in the destruction of this order; for the woman, undertaking to learn the mind of God from herself and the serpent, was deceived, and first in the transgression: 'Adam was first formed, then Eve. And Adam was not deceived, but the woman being deceived was in the transgression' (1 Tim. 2:13–14). From Adam being first formed, and the woman out of him and for him, she should have learned her dependence on him for instruction by divine institution. But going to learn the mind of God of the serpent, she was deceived. She might have learned more than yet she knew, but this she should have done of him who was her head by the law of creation. The case is the same as to the other relation, that would have been between parents and children. Yea, in this the dependence was far greater and more absolute; for although the woman was made out of the man, which argues subordination and dependence, yet she was made by the immediate power of God, man contributing no more to her being than the dust did to his. This gave them in general an equality. But children are so of their parents as to be wholly from them and by them. This makes their dependence and subjection absolute and universal. And whereas parents were in all things to seek their good—which was one of the prime dictates of the law of nature—they were, in the name and stead of God, to rule, govern, and instruct them, and that in the knowledge of God and their duty towards him. They were ὑπὲρ θεοῦ, 'for God,' or in his stead to them, to instruct them in their duty, suitably to the law of their creation and the end thereof.

But every one thus instructed was in his own name and person to attend to the things of God, or what was to be performed on the behalf of men; for in reference to God, there would have been no common root or principle for men to stand upon. Whilst we were all in the loins of Adam we stood all in him, and we also fell all in him, ἐφ' ᾧ πάντες ἥμαρτον (Rom. 5:12). But so soon as any one had been born into this world, and so should have had a personal subsistence of his own, he was to stand by himself, and to be no more, as to his covenant interest, concerned in the obedience of his progenitors; for the covenant with mankind would have been distinct with each individual, as it was with angels. There might have been, there would have been, order, subordination, and subjection, among men, in respect of things from God to them—so probably there is among the angels, although the investigation thereof be neither our duty nor in our power—but, as was said, every one, according to the tenor of the covenant then in force, was in his own person to discharge all duties of worship towards God. Neither could any one be taken out from the residue of men to discharge the works of religion towards God for them, in the way of an office, but it would be to the prejudice of their right and the hinderance of their duty. It follows, therefore, that the office of a priest was impossible in that condition—that is, of one who should be ordained ὑπὲρ ἀνθρώπων καθίσταται τὰ πρὸς τὸν θεόν—and had any such office

been possible, there would not have been in it any prefiguration of
the priesthood of Christ, as will afterwards appear.

No Metaphorical Killing

The same is the state of things with reference to sacrifices. There
is, as was said before, a relation between them and the priesthood.
Hence is that saying in Bereshith Rabba: כהניו כמזבט כן—'As is
the altar for sacrifice, so are the priests that belong to it.' And by
sacrifices in this inquiry, we understand those that are properly
so: for that which is proper in every kind is first; nor is there any
place for that which is improper or metaphorical, unless something
proper from whence the denomination is taken have preceded, for
in allusion to this the metaphor consists. Now, the first possible
instance in this matter being in the state about which we inquire,
there must be proper sacrifices therein, or none at all; for nothing
went before with respect to which any thing might be so called, as
now our spiritual worship and service are, with allusion to them
under the old testament.

And concerning those sacrifices, we may consider their
nature and their end. A sacrifice is זֶבַח, that is, θυσία, 'victima,
sacrificium mactatum,'—'a slain or killed offering;' yea, the first
proper signification of זבח; is 'mactavit, jugulavit, decollavit,
occidit,'—'to kill, to slay by the effusion of blood,' and the like.
Neither is this signification cast upon it from its affinity to טבח,
'to kill or slay' (the change of ט and ז being frequent, as in the
Chaldee almost perpetual), but it is its own native signification:
Genesis 31:54, וַיִּזְבַּח יַעֲקֹב זֶבַח. Say we, 'Jacob offered sacrifices.'
Junius, 'Mactavit animalia,'—'He slew beasts;' which we allow in
the margin, 'He killed beasts.' Targum, ונכס יעקב נכסתא. נכס
is 'to kill or slay,' and is constantly so used; and נכסתא is no more
but 'mactatio,' 'a slaughter;' but because all sacrifices were offered
by slaying, it is applied to signify a sacrifice also (so Isa. 34:6). It
is true, there was a covenant made between Jacob and Laban, and
covenants were sometimes confirmed by sacrifices, with a feast of
the covenanters ensuing thereon; but it is not likely that Jacob and
Laban would agree in the same sacrifice, who scarcely owned the
same God. It is, therefore, only the provision and entertainment

that Jacob made for Laban and his company, for which he slew the cattle, that is intended; otherwise the sacrifice would have been mentioned distinctly from the feast. So are these things expressed (Exod.18:12). And so זָבַח, is rendered by us 'to kill or slay' absolutely (1 Sam. 28:24; Deut. 12:15–16; 1 Kings 1:9, 19:21); and so also ought it to be translated Numbers 22:40, where it is 'offered' in our books. זֶבַח, the substantive, is also 'slaughter, throat-cutting, murder' (so Isa. 34:6; Zeph. 1:7); which James expresses by σφαγή (chap. 5:5). And זְבָחִים are absolutely no more than σφάγια, as from the slaughter of the sacrifices the altar is called מִזְבֵּחַ. Θύω, also, and θυσία, do no otherwise signify but 'to sacrifice,' or sacrifice by mactation or killing.

SACRIFICE MEANS SLAYING

It is therefore evident that there neither is nor can be any sacrifice, properly so called, but what is made by killing or slaying of the thing sacrificed; and the offerings of inanimate things under the law, as of flour or wine, or the fruits of the earth, were improperly so called, in allusion to or by virtue of their conjunction with them that were properly so. They might be עוֹלוֹת, 'offerings' or 'ascensions,' but זְבָחִים, 'sacrifices,' they were not. And the act of sacrificing principally consists in the mactation or slaying of the sacrifices, as shall afterwards be manifested. And whereas the oblation, as it is used to express the general nature of a sacrifice, is commonly apprehended to consist in the actings of the sacrificer after the killing of the sacrifice or victim, it is so far otherwise that it principally consists in bringing of it to be slain, and in the slaying itself, all that follows belonging to the religious manner of testifying faith and obedience thereby. This also discovers the proper and peculiar end of sacrifices, firstly and properly so called, especially such as might prefigure the sacrifice of Christ, to which our present discourse is confined. All such sacrifices must respect sin, and an atonement to be made for it. There never was, nor ever can be, any other end of the effusion of blood in the service of God. This the nature of the action ('which was in his head') and the whole series of divine institutions in this matter do manifest; for to what end should a man take another creature into his power and possession, which also he might use to his advantage, and, slaying it, offer it up to God, if not to confess a guilt of his own, or somewhat for which he deserved to die, and to represent a commutation of the punishment due to him, by the substitution of another in his room and place, according to the will of God? And this casts all such sacrifices as might be any way prefigurative of the sacrifice of Christ out of the verge of paradise, or state of innocency; for as therein there should have been no bloody mactation of our fellow-creatures, so a supposition of sin therein implies an express contradiction.

Sacrifices Require Faith in Divine Revelation

Again, sacrifices require faith in the offerer of them: 'By faith Abel offered a sacrifice' (Heb. 11:4). And faith in the subject respects its proper object, which is divine revelation. Men can believe no more with divine faith than is revealed, and all our actings in faith must answer the doctrines of faith. Now, not to insist upon this particular, that sacrifices were not revealed before the fall (which that they were cannot be proved), I say that there was no doctrine in or belonging to the covenant of creation that should directly or analogically require or intimate an acceptance of any such religious worship as sacrifices. This might be manifested by a just consideration of the principles of that revelation which God made of himself to man under the first covenant, and what was necessary for him to know that he might live to God; but this I have done at large elsewhere, nor have I any thing of moment to add to former discourses to this purpose. And this also renders it impossible that there should be any sacrifices properly so called, and prefigurative of the sacrifice of Christ, in the state of innocency.

Incarnation and the State of Innocence

But these things are opposed, and must be vindicated. And this opposition is made to both the positions laid down, the one concerning a priest, the other concerning sacrifices: for some have been and are of a mind, that 'though man had not sinned, yet the Son of God should have taken our nature on him,' both for the manifestation of the glory of God and the cherishing of the creation; and if so, he should have been in some sense the priest of the world.

And those of this persuasion are of two sorts. First, such as acknowledge a pre-existence of the Lord Christ in a divine nature. These affirm that [even] had not sin entered into the world, he should have been so made flesh by the uniting of our nature to himself in his own person, as now it is come to pass. This some of the ancient schoolmen inclined to, as Alexander ab Ales., Albertus Magnus, Scotus, Rupertus; as it is opposed by Aquinas (p. 3, q. 3); Bonaventure in Sentent. (lib. iii. dist. i. ar. 2, q. 1), and others. Immediately on the Reformation this opinion was revived by Osiander, who maintained that Adam was said to be made in the image of God, because he was made in that nature and shape whereunto the Son of God was designed and destinated. And he also was herein opposed by Calvin (*Instit.* lib. ii. cap. xii., lib. iii. cap. xi); by Wigandus de Osiandrismo (p. 23); and Schlusselburgius (lib. vi). Yet some are still of this judgment, or seem so to be.

The other sort are the Socinians, who contend that God would have given such a head to the creation as they fancy Christ to be; for as they lay no great weight on the first sin, so they hope to evince by this means that the Lord Christ may discharge his whole office without making any atonement for sin by sacrifice. And this, with most of their other opinions, they have traduced from the ancient Pelagians, as an account is given in this particular by Cassianus de Incarnatione (lib. i. p. 1241). Says he of the Pelagians:

> 'It is a fact,' says he of the Pelagians, 'that rushing forth with more monstrous insanity, they say that our Lord Jesus Christ came to this world not to offer redemption to the human race, but to show an example of good deeds; evidently, men following his teaching, as long as they walk along the same path of virtue, may arrive at the rewards of that same virtue.'

Those who assert sacrifices to have been necessary in the state of innocency are the Romanists. Bellarmine, Gregory de Valentia, and others, do expressly contend for it. And these also have their peculiar design in this their peculiar opinion; for they endeavour to establish a general maxim, 'That proper sacrifices are indispensably necessary to all religious worship,' thereby to make way for their missatical oblation. I shall consider the pretences of both sorts, and so proceed with our design.

47

INCARNATION WITHOUT RESPECT TO REDEMPTION REJECTED

As to the first opinion, concerning the incarnation of the Son of God without respect to sin and redemption, there are many pretences given to it, which shall be afterwards particularly considered. They say that 'the manifestation of the glory of God required that he should effect this most perfect way of it, that so he might give a complete expression of his image and likeness. His love and goodness also were so perfectly to be represented, in the union of a created nature with his own. And herein, also, God would satisfy himself in the contemplation of this full communication of himself to our nature. Besides, it was necessary that there should be a head appointed to the whole creation, to conduct and guide it, man especially, to its utmost end.' And sundry other things they allege out of the Bible of their own imaginations. It is granted that even in that state all immediate transactions with the creatures should have been by the Son; for by him, as the power and wisdom of God, were they made (John 1:3; Heb. 1:2; Col. 1:16–17). He, therefore, should have immediately guided and conducted man to his happiness, and that both by confirming him in his obedience and by giving him his reward; an express document whereof we have in the angels that sinned not. But for the opinion of his being incarnate without respect to redemption and a recovery from sin and misery, the whole of it is ἄγραφον, or unwritten, and therefore uncertain and curious; yea, ἀντίγραφον, or contrary to what is written, and therefore false; and ἄλογον, or destitute of any solid spiritual reason for the confirmation of it.

It Is not Written

First, it is unwritten—nowhere revealed, nowhere mentioned in the Scripture; nor can an instance be given of the faith of any one of the saints of God, either under the old testament or the new, in this matter. The first promise, and consequently first revelation, of the incarnation of the Son of God, was after the entrance of sin, and with respect to the recovery of the sinner, to the glory of God. Hereby are all other promises, declarations, and revelations concerning it, as to their end, to be regulated; for that which is the first in any kind, as to an end aimed at, is the rule of all that follows in the same kind. And therefore that which men ground themselves upon in this opinion is indeed neither argument nor testimony, but conjecture and curiosity. They frame to themselves a notional state of things, which they suppose beautiful and comely, (as who are not enamored of the fruits of their own imaginations?) and then assert that it was meet and according to divine wisdom that God should so order things to his own glory as they have fancied! Thus they suppose, that, without respect to sin or grace, God would take to himself the glory of uniting our nature to him. Why so? Because they find how greatly and gloriously he is exalted in his so doing. But is this so absolutely from the thing itself, or is it with respect to the causes, ends, effects, and circumstances of it, as they are stated since the entrance of sin, and revealed in the Scripture? Setting aside the consideration of sin, grace, and redemption, with what attends them, a man may say, in a better compliance with the harmony and testimony of Scripture, that the assumption of human nature into union with the divine, in the person of the Son of God, is no way suited to the exaltation of divine glory, but rather to beget false notions and apprehensions in men of the nature of the Godhead, and to disturb them in their worship thereof; for the assumption of human nature absolutely is expressed as a great condescension, as it was indeed (Phil. 2:5–8), and that which served for a season to obscure the glory of the Deity in him that assumed it (John 17:5). But the glory of it lies in that which caused it, and that which ensued thereon; for in them lay the highest effects and manifestations of divine love, goodness, wisdom, power, and holiness (Rom. 3:24–6). And this is plainly revealed in the gospel, if any thing be so. I fear, therefore, that this curious speculation, that is thus destitute of any scriptural testimony, is but a pretense of being wise above what is written, and a prying into things which men have not seen, nor are they revealed to them.

It Is Contrary to What Is Written

Secondly, this opinion is contradictory to the Scripture, and that in places innumerable. Nothing is more fully and perspicuously revealed in the Scripture than are the causes and ends of the incarnation of Christ; for whereas it is the great theatre of the glory of God, the foundation of all that obedience which we yield to him, and of all our expectation of blessedness with him, and being a thing in itself deep and mysterious, it was necessary that it should be so revealed and declared. It were endless to call over all the testimonies which might be produced to this purpose; some few only shall be instanced in.

First, therefore, on the part of the Father, the sending of the Son to be incarnate is constantly ascribed to his love to mankind, that they might be saved from sin and misery, with a supposition of the ultimate end, or his own glory thereby: 'God so loved the world, that he gave his only-begotten Son, that whosoever believes in him should not perish, but have everlasting life' (John 3:16). 'Whom God has set forth to be a propitiation' (Rom. 3:25). 'God commends his love toward us, in that, while we were yet sinners, Christ, died for us' (5:8). 'For what the law could not do, in that it was weak through the flesh, God sending his own Son in the likeness of sinful flesh, and for sin, condemned sin in the flesh' (8:3). 1 John 4:9; Galatians 4:4–5.

Secondly, on the part of the Son himself, the same causes, the same ends of his taking flesh, are constantly assigned: 'The Son of man is come to seek and to save that which was lost' (Luke 19:10). 'This is a faithful saying, and worthy of all acceptation, that Christ Jesus came into the world to save sinners' (1 Tim. 1:15). 'Forasmuch then as the children are partakers of flesh and blood, he also himself likewise took part of the same; that through death he might destroy him that had the power of death, that is, the devil' (Heb. 2:14). 'To this end was I born, and for this cause came I into the world, that I should bear witness to the truth' (Gal. 2:20; John 18:37) — namely, of the promises of God made to the fathers concerning his coming (Rom. 15:8). See Philippians 2:6–11. And all this is said in pursuit and explication of the first promise concerning him, the sum whereof was, that he should be manifested in the flesh to 'destroy the works of the devil,' as it is expounded (1 John 3:8). This the whole Scripture constantly and uniformly gives testimony to, this is the design and scope of it, the main of what it intends to instruct us in; the contrary whereunto, like the fancying of other worlds, or living wights in the moon or stars, dissolves the whole harmony of it, and frustrates its principal design, and therefore is more carefully to be avoided than what rises up in contradiction to some few testimonies of it. I say, that to ascribe to God a will or purpose of sending his Son to be incarnate, without respect to the redemption and salvation of sinners, is to contradict and enervate the whole design of the revelation of God in the Scripture; as also, it rises up in direct opposition to particular testimonies without number. Origen observed this (Hom. xxiv. in Numer.):

> If there had been no sin, it would not have been necessary for the Son to become the Lamb of God; but he would have remained that which he was in the beginning, the Word of God. Since sin certainly entered this world, sin also requires propitiation. As true propitiation is not without sacrifice, it was necessary to provide a sacrifice for sin.

So Augustine, 'Hence he came into the world to save sinners. There is no other reason why he came into the world.' (Serm. 8 de Verbis Apostoli, tom. x).

It Is Destitute of Spiritual Reason

Thirdly, this opinion is destitute of spiritual reason, yea, is contrary to it. The design of God to glorify himself in the creation and the law or covenant of it, and his design of the same end in a way of grace, are distinct; yea, they are so distinct as, with reference to the same persons and times, to be inconsistent. This our apostle manifests in the instance of justification and salvation by works and grace: 'If it be by grace, then it is no more of works: otherwise grace is no more grace. But if it be of works, then it is no more grace: otherwise work is no more work' (Rom. 11:6). It is impossible that the same man should be justified by works and grace too. Wherefore God, in infinite wisdom, brought the first design, and all the effects of it, into a subordination to the later; and so he decreed to do from eternity. There being, by the entrance of sin, an aberration in the whole creation from that proper end to which it was suited at first, it pleased God to reduce the whole into a subserviency to the design of his wisdom and holiness in a way of grace; for his purpose was to reconcile and gather all things into a new head in his Son, Jesus Christ (Eph. 1:10; Heb. 1:3, 2:7–8). Now, according to this opinion, the incarnation of the Son of God belonged originally to the law of creation, and the design of the glory of God therein. And if this were so, it must, with the whole old creation and all that belonged to this, be brought into a subordination and subserviency to the succedaneous design of the wisdom of God to glorify himself in a way of grace. But this is not so, seeing itself is the fundamental and principal part of that design. 'Known,' indeed, 'unto God are all his works from the beginning.' Therefore, this great projection of the incarnation of his Son lying in the counsel of his will from eternity, he did, in wisdom infinite and holy, order all the concernments of the creation so as they might be disposed into an orderly subjection to his Son incarnate. So that although I deny that any thing was then instituted as a type to represent him—because his coming into the world in our flesh belonged not to that estate—yet I grant things to have been so ordered as that, in the retrieval of all into a new frame by Jesus Christ, there were many things in the works of God in the old creation that were natural types, or things meet to represent much of this to us. So Christ himself is called the 'second Adam,' and compared to the 'tree of life,' whereof we have discoursed in our exposition on the first chapter.

ARGUMENTS FOR INCARNATION IN THE STATE OF INNOCENCE REFUTED

'IT WOULD HAVE PERFECTED CREATION.'

Let us, therefore, now consider the arguments or reasons in particular which they plead who maintain this assertion. The principal of them were invented and made use of by some of the ancient schoolmen; and others have since given some improvement to their conceptions, and added some of their own. Those of the first sort are collected by Thomas (3 p. q. l, a. 3), as traduced from the Pelagians. I shall examine them as by him proposed, omitting his answers, which I judge insufficient in many instances.

His first argument, the substance whereof I have lately heard pleaded with some vehemency, is as follows:

> It belonged to omnipotent power and infinite wisdom to make all his works perfect, and to manifest himself by an infinite effect. But no mere creature can be said to be such infinite effect, because its essence is finite and limited. But in the work of the incarnation of the Son of God alone, an infinite effect of

divine power seems to be manifested, as thereby things infinitely distant are conjoined, God being made man. And herein the universality of things seems to receive its perfection, inasmuch as the last creature, or man, is immediately conjoined to the First Principle, or God.

Answer. This argument has little more in it than curiosity and sophistry; for—

1. That God made all his works 'good,' that is, perfect in their kind, before the incarnation, we have his own testimony. He saw and pronounced of the whole that it was טוֹב מְאֹד, 'valde bonum,' every way good and complete. It was so in itself, without the addition of that work which is fancied necessary to its perfection.

2. It is merely supposed that it was necessary that divine omnipotency should be expressed to the utmost of its perfection. It was enough that it was manifested and declared in the creation of all things out of nothing.

3. It is not possible that any effect in itself infinite should be produced by the power of God: for then would there be two infinites—the producing and the produced; and consequently two Gods—the making God and the made: for that which is in itself absolutely infinite is God, and what is produced is not infinite. Wherefore the work of the incarnation was not of itself an infinite effect, although it was an effect of infinite power, wisdom, and goodness; and so also was the work of the first creation. And although they are all in themselves finite and limited, yet are they the effects of, and do abundantly declare, the infinite power and wisdom whence they were educed (Rom. 1:19–20).

4. The perfection of the universe, or universality of beings, is to be regulated by their state, condition, and end. And this they had in their first creation, without any respect to the incarnation of the Son of God; for the perfection of all things consisted in their relation to God, according to the law and order of their creation, and their mutual regard to one another, with respect to the utmost end, or the manifestation of his glory. And also, their perfection consisted in their subserviency to the bringing

of that creature to the enjoyment of God in blessedness for ever which was capable of it. And herein consisted the conjunction of the last creature to the First Principle, when, by the documents and helps of them that were made before, he was brought to the enjoyment of God.

5. For, that the conjunction of the last creature to the First Principle, by way of personal union, was necessary to the good of the universe, is a fancy that every one may embrace and every one reject at pleasure. But it may be justly conceived that it was more suitable to order that the conjunction mentioned should have been between God and the first creature, namely, the angels; and reasons would have been pleaded for that order had it so come to pass. But the Son of God took not on him their nature, because he designed not to deliver them from sin (Heb. 2:16–17).

'HUMAN NATURE WAS CAPABLE OF THE GRACE OF UNION IN THE STATE OF INNOCENCE.'

Secondly, it is further pleaded:

> That human nature is not become more capacious of grace by sin than it was before; but now, after the entrance of sin, it is capable of the grace of union, which is the greatest grace. Wherefore, if man had not sinned human nature had been capable of this grace, neither would God have withheld any good from human nature whereof it was capable: therefore if man had not sinned God had been incarnate.

Answer.

1. Place angelical nature in the argument, as to that part of it which pleads that it must have all the grace which it is capable of, instead of human nature, and the event will show what force there is in this ratiocination; for angelical nature was capable of the grace of union, and God would not, it is said, withhold any thing from it whereof it was capable. But why, then, is it otherwise come to pass?

2. It must be granted (though, indeed, this argument is not

much concerned therein one way or other) that human nature is both capable of more grace, and actually made partaker of more, after the fall, than it was capable of, or did receive before; for it is capable of mercy, pardon, reconciliation with God, sanctification by the Holy Ghost, all which are graces, or gracious effects of the love and goodness of God; and these things in the state of innocency man was not capable of. Besides, there is no difference in this matter; for the individual nature actually assumed into union was and was considered as pure as in its first original and creation.

3. The ground of this reason lies in a pretense, that whatever any creature was capable of, not in, by, or from itself, but by the power of God, that God was obliged to do in it and for it. And this is plainly to say that God did not communicate of his goodness and of his power to the creatures according to the counsel of his will, but, producing them by the unavoidable destiny of some eternal state, he acted naturally and necessarily, 'to the last man,' in their production. But this is contrary to the nature and being of God, with all the properties thereof. Wherefore, the creation is capable, in every state, of what God pleases, and no more. Its capacity is to be regulated by the will of God; and no more belonged to its capacity in the state of nature than God had assigned to it by the law of creation.

4. It is a presumptuous imagination, to talk of the grace of union being due to our nature in any condition. Why is it not so to the nature of angels? Or did our nature originally excel theirs? Besides, the Scripture everywhere expressly assigns it as an effect of free love, grace, and bounty (John 3:16; 1 John 4:9–10).

5. That there should be an advance made both of the glory of God and the good of the creature itself by the entrance of sin, is an effect of infinite wisdom and grace. Nor did God permit the entrance of sin but with a design to bring about a glory greater and more excellent than the antecedent order of things was capable of. The state of grace exceeded the state of nature. In brief, God permitted that greatest evil, the fall of man, to make way for the introduction of the greatest good, in our restoration by the incarnation and mediation of his Son.

'GOD REVEALED THE MYSTERY OF
THE INCARNATION TO ADAM.'

Thirdly, it is also pleaded:

> That the mystery of the incarnation was revealed to Adam in the
> state of innocency; for upon the bringing of Eve to him, he said,
> 'This is now bone of my bones, and flesh of my flesh.' But 'this,'
> says the apostle, 'is a great mystery;' but he speaks it 'concerning
> Christ and the church' (Eph. 5:32). But man could not foresee or
> foreknow his own fall; no more than the angels could theirs; it
> follows, therefore, that he considered the incarnation as it should
> have been had the state of innocency continued.

Answer.

1. It seems to be supposed in this argument that there was
   indeed a revelation made to Adam (Gen. 2:23), of the
   incarnation of Christ; so that nothing remains to be proved
   but that he did not foreknow his fall, whence it would
   ensue that the pretended revelation belonged to the state of
   innocency. But, indeed, there is no intimation of any such
   revelation; for—
2. I have manifested elsewhere how God, in his infinite wisdom,
   ordered the things of the first creation so as they might be
   laid in a subserviency, in a way of representation, to the new
   creation, or the renovation of all things by Jesus Christ; that
   is, he so made them as that they might be natural types of
   what he would do afterwards. This does not prove that they
   were designed to make any revelation of Christ and his grace,
   or prefigure them, but only were meet to be brought into an
   useful subordination to them, so that from them instructive
   allusions might be taken. Thus was it in the first marriage in
   the law of creation. It had no other nature, use, nor end, but
   to be the bond of individual society of two persons, male and
   female, for the procreation and education of children, with
   all mutual assistances to human life and conversation. And
   the making of woman out of the man, 'bone of his bones,
   and flesh of his flesh,' was intended only for the laying that
   society, whose intimacy was to be unparalleled, in a singular

foundation. But both these things were so ordered, in the wisdom of God, as that they might represent another union, in a state that God would bring in afterwards, namely, of Christ and his church. What Adam spoke concerning the natural condition and relation of himself and Eve, that our apostle speaks concerning the spiritual and supernatural condition and relation of Christ and the church, because of some resemblance between them. Aquinas himself determines this whole matter, with an assertion which would have been to his own advantage to have attended to upon other occasions. Says he, 'We are not able to know that which alone comes forth from the will of God beyond everything which is owed by creatures, except to the extent which it is related in holy Scripture, through which the divine will is known. From this, since everywhere in holy Scripture the reason for the incarnation is assigned to the first sin of man, it is more appropriate to say that the work of the incarnation was ordained by God as suitable against sin, because without the existence of sin there would have been no incarnation.'

'GOD DECREED CHRIST SHOULD ASSUME HUMAN NATURE BEFORE HE DECREED TO SAVE THE ELECT.'

There is yet another argument mentioned by Aquinas, and much improved by the modern Scotists, insisted on also by some divines of our own, which deserves a somewhat fuller consideration; and this is taken from the predestination of the man Christ Jesus. This the schoolmen consider on that of our apostle, 'Concerning Jesus Christ, ὁρισθέντος Υἱοῦ θεοῦ ἐν δυνάμει' (Rom. 1:4): which the Vulgate renders, 'Qui praedestinatus est Filius Dei in virtute;'— 'Predestinate the Son of God with power,' as our Rhemists. But ὁρισθέντος there is no more than ἀποδεδειχθέντος, 'manifested, declared,' as it is well rendered by ours. Nor can expositors fix any tolerable sense to their 'predestinate' in this place. But the thing itself is true. The Lord Christ was predestinated or preordained before the world was. We were 'redeemed with the precious blood of Christ, προεγνωσμένου μὲν πρὸ καταβολῆς κόσμου' (1 Pet. 1:20)—'foreordained' ('predestinated') 'before the foundation of the world.' Now, it is pleaded that 'this predestination of Christ to the grace of union and glory was the first of God's purposes and decrees in order of nature, and antecedent to the predestination of the elect, at least as it should comprise in it a purpose of deliverance from the fall. For God first designed to glorify himself in the assumption of human nature, before he decreed to save the elect by that nature so assumed; for we are said to be 'chosen in him,' that is, as our head (Eph. 1:4), whence it necessarily ensues that he was chosen before us, and so without respect to us. So in all things was he to have the preeminence (Col. 1:19); and thence it is that we are 'predestinated to be conformed to his image' (Rom. 8:29). This preordination, therefore, of the Lord Christ, which was to grace, and glory, was antecedent to the permission of the fall of man; so that he should have been incarnate had that never fallen out.'

These things are by some at large deduced and explained, but this is the sum of what is pleaded in the pursuit of this argument, which shall be as briefly examined as the nature of the matter itself will permit.

The order of the divine eternal decrees, as to their priority one to another in order of nature and reason, so as not the decrees themselves, which are all absolutely free and irrespective, but the things decreed, should be one for another, has been at large discoursed of and discussed by many. But there are yet not a few who suppose those very discourses on all hands to have more of nicety and curious subtilty than of solid truth to edification. And because this is a matter wherein the Scripture is utterly silent, though one opinion may be more agreeable to sound reason than another, yet none is built upon such certain foundations as to become a matter of faith, or the principle of any thing that is so. That which explains this order most conveniently and suitably to divine wisdom, will, and sovereignty, and which best answers the common apprehensions of rational natures and the rules of their actings, is to be preferred before any opinion that includes what is opposite to or alien from any of these things, which that order has respect to. From any such order in the decrees of God no advantage can be drawn to the opinion under consideration; but if men may be allowed to suppose what they will, they may easily infer thereon what they please.

Three Views on the Series of Divine Decrees

Let us, therefore, take a view of the several series of divine decrees, which have been confirmed with a considerable suffrage of learned men, setting aside particular conjectures, which never received entertainment beyond the minds of their authors. And these may be reduced to three:

ACCORDING TO THE ORDER OF THEIR ACCOMPLISHMENT. All agree that the glory of God is the utmost and supreme end that he intends in all his decrees. Although they are free acts of his will and wisdom, yet, on the supposition of them, it is absolutely necessary, from the perfection of his being, that he himself or his glory be their utmost end. His absolute all-sufficiency will not allow that he can in them have any other end. Accordingly, in pursuit of them he makes all for himself (Prov. 16:4); and they serve to declare and make known the perfection of his nature (Ps. 19:1; Rom. 1:19–20). And it is his glory, in the way of justice and mercy, which he ultimately intends in his decrees concerning the salvation of man by Jesus Christ. Whereas many things are ordered by him in a subserviency to this, the decrees of God concerning them are conceived by some in that order which answers the order of their accomplishment; as, first, they say, God decreed to make the world, and man therein upright in his image; secondly, to permit the fall and the consequents thereof, man being to that end left to the liberty of his will; thirdly, he designed to send his Son to be incarnate, for the work of their redemption; fourthly, he decreed to give eternal life to as many as should believe on him and obey him; and, lastly, he determined to bestow effectual grace on some persons in particular, to work faith and obedience in them infallibly, and thereby to bring them to glory, to the praise of his grace and mercy. According to this order of God's decrees, it is plain that in the order of nature the predestination of Christ is antecedent to the election of other particular or individual persons, but withal that it is consequential to the decree concerning the permission of the fall of Adam; and, accordingly, his incarnation does suppose it; which is inconsistent with the opinion under examination.

IN REVERSE ORDER OF THEIR EXECUTION. Others take a contrary course, and, by a misapplication of a common rule, that what is first in intention must be last in execution, they suppose the order of God's decrees, being his intentions or purposes, to be best conceived in a direct retrogradation to the order of their execution. Supposing, therefore, the decree of glorifying himself in the way before mentioned, they judge God's first decree in order of nature to be for the eternal salvation and glory of some certain persons, who are actually at last brought thereunto; for this being the last thing executed must be first intended. Secondly, in subserviency to this, he purposes to give them grace, and faith, and obedience thereby, as the way to bring them to the possession of glory. Thirdly, to these purposes of God they make the decrees concerning the creation and permission of the fall of man, with the incarnation and mediation of Christ, to be subservient, some in one method, some in another. But that all their conceptions must have an inconsistency with the predestination of Christ to his incarnation antecedent to a respect to sin and grace, is plain and evident.

ONLY TWO DECREES HAVE ORDER OF PRIORTY. But whereas both these ways are exposed to insuperable objections and difficulties, some have fixed on another method for the right conception of the order of God's eternal decrees in these things, which has a consistency in itself, and may be fairly brought off from all opposition—which is the utmost that with sobriety can be aimed at in these things—namely, that nothing be ascribed to God in the least unsuited to the infinite perfections of his nature, nor any thing proposed to the minds of men inconsistent with the general principles and rules of reason. And those lay down the general rule before mentioned, namely, that what is first in intention is last in execution. But, secondly, they say withal, that this rule concerns only such things as in their own nature, and in the will of him that designs them, have the relation of end and means to one another; for it has no place among such things as are not capable of that relation. And, moreover, it is required that this end be ultimate and supreme, and not subordinate, which has also the nature of the means. The meaning of it, therefore, is no more but that in all rational purposes there are two things considered—first, the end aimed at, and then the means of its effecting or accomplishment; and that in order of nature, the end, which is the last thing effected, is the first designed, and then the means for it; which things are true, and obvious to the understanding of all men. According to this rule, they ascribe to God but two decrees that have any order of priority between them. The first is concerning his end, which is first intended and last executed; the other concerning all those means which, being in the second place intended for the production of the end, are first accomplished and wrought. The first of these, which is the supreme end of all the dispensations of God towards the things that outwardly are of him, is his own glory, or the declaration of himself in a way of justice and mercy, mixed with infinite wisdom and goodness, as he is the first Being, sovereign Lord and Ruler over all. The second decree, of things subordinate and subservient to this, consists in an intention concerning all intermediate acts of divine wisdom, power, and goodness, which tend to the production of this ultimate end. Such are the creation, the permission of the fall, the pre-ordination of Christ, and others in him, to grace and glory, by the way and means thereunto appointed. Now, although these things are evidently subordinate and subservient to one another, and although there may be apprehended singular decrees concerning them, yet because none of them do lie in the order of the means and ultimate end, there is no priority of one decree before another to be allowed therein; only a decree is supposed of disposing them in their execution, or the things executed, into that order, both in nature and time, as may constitute them all one suitable means of attaining the supreme end intended. Now, it is evident that, according to this order, there cannot be a priority in the pre-ordination of Christ to the decree of the permission of the fall and entrance of sin.

It is true, indeed, Christ was pre-ordained, or [rather] the Son of God was so, to be incarnate before the foundation of the world (1 Pet. 1:20). But how? Even as he was 'manifested in these last times.' As he was preordained to be incarnate, so he was to be so of the blessed Virgin: and this neither was nor could be but with respect to the redemption of mankind; for he took flesh of her in answer to the first promise concerning the seed of the woman, which respected our recovery from sin. As he was born or made of her, he was the Lamb of God that was to take away the sin of the world. Besides, he was not ordained to the grace of union before and without the consideration of glory and exaltation. But this included a supposition of his suffering for sin; for he was first to 'suffer,' and then to 'enter into his glory' (Luke 24:26). Accordingly, he ordered his own prayer, 'I have glorified thee on the earth: I have finished the work which thou gavest me to do. And now, O Father, glorify thou me with thine own self' (John 17:4–5). To fancy a pre-ordination of the Son of God to incarnation not of the blessed Virgin after the entrance of sin, not as the Lamb of God, not as one to be exalted after suffering, is that which neither Scripture nor reason will admit of. It is said, indeed, that we are 'predestinated to be conformed to the image of Christ' (Rom. 8:29), which seems to imply an antecedency in his predestination to ours; but 'the image of Christ' there intended includes his suffering, holiness, and exaltation to glory on his obedience, all which have respect to sin and redemption. And, moreover, the predestination here intended is subordinate to our election to glory, being our designation to the assured and infallible means thereof (Eph. 1:4–5). It is true, it was the design of God that he 'in all things should have the pre-eminence' (Col. 1:18); which, as it denotes excellency, worth, use, dignity, supremacy, nearness to God for the receiving, and to us for the communicating, of all good, so no respect therein is had to such a pre-ordination as should imply his incarnation without an intention of glorifying God in the redemption of sinners thereby, which alone we have undertaken to disprove.

OSIANDER'S ARGUMENTS REFUTED

The arguments of Osiander in this case have been discussed by others, Calvin (*Institut.* lib. 2. cap. 12. sect. 4, etc.); Wigandus de Osiandrismo (p. 23); Tarnovius (in cap. 3. in *Evang. S. Johan*). I shall only touch so far upon them as is necessary to our present design, and that in such instances wherein they have no coincidence with what has been already discussed. And some few things may be premised, which will take away the suppositions on which all his reasonings were founded.

1. The Son was the essential and eternal image of the Father antecedent to all consideration of his incarnation. He is in his divine person 'the image of the invisible God' (Col. 1:15); 'the brightness of his glory, and the express image of his person' (Heb. 1:3): for having his essence and subsistence from the Father by eternal generation, or the communication of the whole divine nature and all its infinite perfections, he is the perfect and essential representation of him.

2. The order of operation in the blessed Trinity, as to outward works, answers to and follows the order of their subsistence. Hence the Son is considered as the next and immediate operator of them. Thus, as he is said to have made all things (John 1:3, Col. 1:16), so the Father is said to make all things by him (Eph. 3:9); not as an inferior, subordinate, instrumental cause, but as acting his wisdom and power in him, to whom they were communicated by eternal generation. Hence, the immediate relation of all things so made is to him; and by and in his person is God even the Father immediately represented to them, as he is his image, and as the brightness of his glory shines forth in him. Hereon follows his rejoicing in the creation, and his delights in the sons of men (Prov. 8:30–31), because of their immediate relation to him.

3. Therefore should he have been the immediate head and ruler of angels and men, had they all persisted in their original integrity and innocency (Col. 1:16); for the representation of God to them, as the cause and end of their being, the object and end of their worship and service, should have been in and by his person, as the image of the Father, and by and through him they should have received all the communications of God to them. He should have been their immediate head, lord, and king, or the divine nature in his person; for this the order of subsistence in the blessed Trinity, and the order of operation thereon depending, did require.

These things being premised, it will not be difficult to remove out of our way the reasons of Osiander for the incarnation of Christ without a supposition of sin and grace; which we would not engage in, after they have been so long ago put into oblivion, but that they are by some revived, and the consideration of them will give occasion to the clearing of some truths not of small importance.

'GOD CREATED ADAM IN CONFORMITY WITH CHRIST'S DESTINED HUMAN NATURE.'

First, His principal plea was taken from the 'image of God' wherein man was created. He says:

> For this was that human nature, consisting of soul and body, in the outward shape, lineaments, and proportion, which it has in our persons, which the Son of God was to take upon him. God having ordained that his Son should take human nature, he created Adam in a conformity to the idea or image thereof.

Answer. This, doubtless, is a better course for the unfolding of our creation in the image of God than that of the old Anthropomorphites, who, in the exposition of this expression, made God in the image of man; but yet is it not therefore according to the truth. The image of God in man was in general those excellencies of his nature wherein he excelled all other creatures here below. In especial, it was that uprightness and rectitude of his soul and all its faculties, as one common principle of moral operations, whereby he was enabled to live to God as his chiefest good and utmost end (Eccles. 7:29). This by our apostle is termed 'righteousness and true holiness,' where he treats of the renovation of it in us by Jesus Christ (Eph. 4:24); to which he adds that which is the principle of them both, in the renovation of our minds (Col. 3:10). Nor does this image of God consist, as some fancy, in moral duties, in distinction from and opposition to any other effect of the grace of Christ in the hearts of men, which acts itself in any duty according to the will of God. 'To pray, to hear the word, to celebrate religious worship,' they say, 'is no part of the image of God; because God does none of these things, and an image must always correspond to the thing it represents.' But our likeness to God does not consist in doing what God does, neither is his image in us in any thing more express than in our universal dependence on him and resignation of ourselves to him, which is a thing the divine nature is incapable of; and when we are commanded to be holy as he is holy, it is not a specificative similitude, but analogical only, that is intended. Wherefore, as the image of God consists in no outward actions of any kind whatever, so the internal grace that is acted in prayer, hearing, and other acts of sacred worship, according to the will of God, does no less belong to the image of God than any other grace, or duty, or virtue whatever. In like manner faith does so also, and that not only as it is an intellectual perfection, but with respect to all its operations and effects, as the Lord Christ himself and the promises of the gospel are in their several considerations the objects of it: for as in our first creation the image of God consisted in the concreated rectitude of our nature, whereby we were disposed and enabled to live to God according to the law of our creation—wherein there was a great representation of His righteousness, or universal, absolute rectitude of his nature, by whom we were made, so whatever is communicated to us by the grace of Jesus Christ, whereby our nature is repaired, disposed, and enabled to live to God, with all acts and duties suitable thereunto, according to the present law of our obedience, belongs to the restoration of the image of God in us; but yet with special respect to that spiritual light, understanding, or knowledge, which is the directive principle of the whole, for 'the new man is renewed in knowledge after the image of him that created him' (Col. 3:10). This, therefore, being the image of God, it is evident that in the creation of man therein there was no respect to the human nature of Christ, which, as the Son of God, he afterwards assumed. Only, it is granted that we are both formed and re-formed immediately in his image; for as he was and is, in his divine person, the express image of the Father, the divine qualifications wherein the image of God originally consisted in us were immediately wrought in us by him, as those wherein he would represent his own perfection. And in the restoration of this image to us, as God implanted in him incarnate all fullness of that grace wherein it consists, who therein absolutely represents the invisible God to us, so we are transformed immediately into his likeness and image, and to that of God by him (2 Cor. 3:18).

It is further pleaded:

> That if the Son of God should not have been incarnate if Adam
> had not sinned, then Adam was not made in the image of Christ,
> but Christ was made in the image of Adam.

Answer. How Adam was made in the image of the Son of God
has been declared—namely, as to the principles of his nature, and
their rectitude with respect to the condition wherein and the end
for which he was made; in which there was a representation of his
righteousness and holiness. And in some sense Christ may be said
to be made in the image of Adam, inasmuch as he was 'made flesh,'
or partaker of the same nature with him: 'Forasmuch as the children
are partakers of flesh and blood, he also himself likewise took part
of the same' (Heb. 2:14). 'He took upon him the form of a servant,
and was made in the likeness of men' (Phil. 2:7). And this he was of
God designed to, even to take on himself that nature wherein Adam
was created, and wherein he sinned. He was to be made like to us in
all things, sin only excepted (Heb. 4:15). Whence, in his genealogy
after the flesh, he is reduced by Luke to the first Adam (3:38); and
he is called not the first, or the exemplar of the creation of men,
but the second Adam (1 Cor. 15:47), being to recover and restore
what was lost by the first. Wherefore, in respect of the substance
and essence of human nature, Christ was made in the image of
Adam; but in respect of the endowments and holy perfections of
that nature, he was made in the image of God.

'THE INCARNATION BECOMES DEPENDENT ON AN ACCIDENT.'

Moreover, it is objected:

> That the incarnation of Christ was a thing decreed for itself, and
> as to its futurition depended only on the immutable counsel of
> God; but this supposition, that it had respect to the fall of man
> and his recovery, makes it to depend on an external accident,
> which, as to the nature of the thing itself, might not have been.

Answer. The resolution of this depends much on what has been
before discoursed concerning the order of the divine decrees, which

need not to be here repeated. Only, we may remember that the foresight of the fall, and the decree of the permission of it, cannot with any reason be supposed to be consequential to the decree concerning the incarnation of the Son of God: for the reparation of man is everywhere in the Scripture declared to be the end of Christ's taking flesh; for 'when the fullness of the time was come, God sent forth his Son, made of a woman, made under the law, to redeem them who were under the law' (Gal. 4:4–5). Neither can his incarnation be properly said either to be 'for itself' on the one side, or by 'accident' on the other; for it was decreed and foreordained for the glory of God. And the way whereby God intended to glorify himself therein was in our redemption, which, in his infinite love to mankind, was the moving cause thereof (John 3:16). Of the same importance is it, 'That if the Son of God had not been incarnate, neither angels nor men could have had their proper head and king;' for, as we have premised, the Son of God should have been the immediate head of the whole creation, ruling every thing in its subordination to God, suitably to its own nature, state, and condition. For as he was 'the image of the invisible God,' so he was 'the first-born of every creature' (Col. 1:15); that is, the Lord, ruler, and inheritor of them, as we have at large elsewhere declared.

'Man in Innocence Needed a Way to Heaven.'

It is pleaded in the last place:

> That had men continued in their integrity, there should have been a season when they were to be changed and translated into heaven. Now, this being to be done by the Son of God, it was necessary that he should be incarnate for that purpose.

And so far is this consideration urged by Osiander. But this is carried on by the Socinians, and improved on another supposition of their own (Vid. Smal. Refut. Thes. Franzii Disput. xii. p. 429).

Man, they tell us, was created absolutely mortal, and should have actually died, although he had never sinned. That he might be raised again from the dead, God would have sent a Messiah, or one that should have been the means, example, and instrumental cause of our resurrection.

Answer. All persons of sobriety will acknowledge that there is nothing in these reasonings but groundless curiosities and vain speculations, countenanced with false suppositions; for as God alone knows what would have been the eternal condition of Adam had he persisted in the covenant of his nature, so whatever change was to be wrought concerning him as the reward of his obedience, God could have effected it by his infinite wisdom and power, without any such instrumental cause as these men imagine. 'Secret things belong to the LORD our God;' nor are we to be 'wise above what is written.' The Socinians' superfetation, that man should have died naturally, though not penally, is a figment of their own, that has been elsewhere discussed, and is very unmeet to be laid as the foundation of new assertions that cannot otherwise be proved.

From what has been discoursed it appears that there was no revelation of the incarnation of the Son of God in the state of innocency; neither did it belong to that state, but was designed in order to his priesthood, which could therein have no place nor use.

ARGUMENTS THAT SACRIFICE IS VITAL TO ALL RELIGION REFUTED

Our next inquiry is concerning sacrifices, and whether they were to have had either place or use in the state of innocency. This being determined, way will be made for the fixing of the original of the priesthood of Christ, whereof we are in the investigation, upon its right foundation. And this inquiry is made necessary to us by some of the Roman church, particularly Bellarmine and Gregory de Valentia. They have not, indeed, fixed any special controversy in this inquiry, whether there should have been any sacrifices in the state of innocency; but, in an attempt to serve a principal concern of their own, they assert and contend for that which determines the necessity of sacrifices in that state and condition of things between God and men; for they plead in general, 'That there neither is, nor ever was in the world, nor can be, any religion without a true and real sacrifice.' Their design herein is only to hedge in the necessity of their sacrifice of the mass; for on this supposition it must be esteemed to be of the very essence of Christian religion, which some, on the contrary, judge to be overthrown thereby. Now, it is certain that there was and should have been religion in the state of innocency, continued if that state had continued; yea, therein all religion and religious worship were founded, being inlaid in our nature, and requisite to our condition in this world, with respect to the end for which we were made. Herein, therefore, on this supposition, sacrifices were necessary, which Bellarmine includes in that 'syllogism,' as he calls it, whereby he attempts the proof of the necessity of his missatical sacrifice in the church of Christ (*De Missa*, lib. i. cap. 20):

> There is such a conjunction between the law or religion and a sacrifice, external and properly so called, that it is altogether necessary either that there is no law or religion truly and properly to be found in the church of Christ, or there is a sacrifice, external and properly so called, to be found therein; but take away the mass, and there is none: wherefore the mass is an external sacrifice, properly so called.

The invalidity of this argument to his especial purpose may easily be laid open; for setting aside all consideration of his mass, Christian religion has not only in it a proper sacrifice, but that alone and single sacrifice with respect to which any services of men in the worship of the church formerly were so called, and whereby they were animated and rendered useful. For all the sacrifices of the law were but obscure representations of, nor had any other end or use but to prefigure, that sacrifice which we enjoy in Christian religion, and to exhibit the benefits thereof to the worshippers. This is the sacrifice of Christ himself, which was external, visible, proper, yea, the only true, real, substantial sacrifice, and that offered once for all. And it is merely ἐξ ἀμετρίας ἀνθολκῆς, or an immeasurable concern in a corrupt imagination, which carried Bellarmine to put in his frivolous and captious exception to the sufficiency of this sacrifice in and to Christian religion—for he pretends and pleads that 'this sacrifice did not belong to the Christian church, which was founded in the resurrection of Christ, before which Christ had offered himself;' as also, that 'this sacrifice was but once offered,' and now ceases so to be, so that if we have no other sacrifice but this, we have none at all: for notwithstanding these bold and sophistical exceptions, our apostle sufficiently instructs us that we have yet an high priest, and an altar, and a sacrifice and the blood of sprinkling, all in heavenly things and places. And, on purpose to prevent this cavil about the ceasing of this sacrifice as to be offered again, he tells us that it is always ζῶσα καὶ πρόσφατος—'living and new-slain.' And, beyond all contradiction, he determined either this one sacrifice of Christ to be insufficient, or that of the mass to be useless; for he shows that where any sacrifices will make perfect them that come to God by them, there no more will be offered. And it is an undoubted evidence that no sacrifice has obtained its end perfectly, so as to making reconciliation for sin, where any other sacrifice, properly so called, does come after it. Nor does he prove the insufficiency of the Aaronic sacrifices to this purpose by any other argument but that they were often offered from year to year, and that another was to succeed in their room when they were over (Heb. 10:1–5); and this, upon the supposition of the Romanists, and the necessity of their missatical sacrifice, falls as heavily on the sacrifice of Christ as on those of the law. It is apparent, therefore, that they must either let go the sacrifice of Christ as insufficient, or that of their mass as useless, for they can have no consistency in the same religion. Wherefore they leave out the sacrifice of Christ, as that which was offered before the church was founded. But the truth is, the church was founded therein. And I desire to know of these men whether it be the outward act of sacrificing or the efficacy of a sacrifice that is so necessary to all religion? If it be the outward act that is of such use and necessity, how great was the privilege of the church of the Jews above that of the Romanists! For whereas these pretend but to one sacrifice, and that one so dark, obscure, and unintelligible, that the principal μύσται and ἐπόπται of their 'sacra' cannot possibly agree amongst themselves what it is, nor wherein it does consist, they had many plain, express, visible sacrifices, which the whole church looked on and consented in. But this whole pretense is vain. Nor is any thing of the least account or worth in religion but upon the account of its efficacy to its end. And that we have with us the continual efficacy of the sacrifice of Christ in all our religious worship and approaches to God, the Scripture is full and express. But these things are not of our present concernment; the consideration of them will elsewhere occur.

No Propitiatory Sacrifices Before the Fall

As to our present purpose, I deny the major proposition of Bellarmine's syllogism, if taken absolutely and universally, as it must be if any way serviceable to his end. This, therefore, he proves.

> It is proved from hence, that almost all religion, whether true or false, in all places and times, has made use of sacrifices in the worship of God; for hence it is gathered that this proceeds from the light and instinct of nature, being a certain principle inbred in us from God himself.

And hereon he proceeds to confute Chemnitius, who assigned the original of sacrificing among the heathen to an instinct of corrupt nature, which is the root of all superstition. I shall not now inquire expressly into the original of all sacrifices; it must be done elsewhere. We here only discourse concerning those that are properly so called, and not only so, but propitiatory also; for such he contends his mass to be. It is, indeed, suitable to the light of nature that of what we have left in our possession we should offer to the service of God, when he has appointed a way for us so to do; but it is denied that in the state of innocency he had appointed that to be by the way of sacrificing sensible things. All eucharistical offerings should then have been moral and spiritual, in pure acts of the mind and its devotion in them. Sacrifices of or for atonement were first instituted, and other offerings had their name from thence, by reason of some kind of analogy. And so far as thank-offerings were materially the same with them that were propitiatory, in the death and blood of any creature, they had in them the nature of a propitiation also. That these were instituted after the fall I have elsewhere sufficiently proved. Being therefore at first enjoined to all mankind in general, as tokens of the recovery promised, they were retained and perpetuated amongst all sorts of men, even when they had lost all notion and remembrance of the promise to which they were originally annexed; for they had a double advantage for the perpetuating themselves: first, a suitableness to the general principle of giving an acknowledgment to God, in a return of a portion of that all which comes from him.

Secondly, they had a compliance with the accusation of conscience for sin, by an endeavour to transfer the guilt of it to another. But their first original was pure divine and supernatural revelation, and not the light or conduct of nature, nor any such innate principle as Bellarmine imagines. No such inseparable conjunction as is pretended between sacrifices and religion can hence be proved, seeing they were originally an arbitrary institution, and that after there had been religion in the world. He proceeds, therefore, further to confirm his first proposition: 'Sacrificing was born with religion, and dies with it; there is, therefore, between them a plain necessary conjunction.' So he. This is only a repetition of the proposition in other words; for to say that there is such a conjunction between sacrifices and religion that the one cannot be without the other, and to say they are born and die together, is to say the same thing twice over. He adds, therefore, his proof of the whole: 'Nam primi homines qui Deum coluisse leguntur filii Adami fuerunt, Cain et Abel, illi autem sacrificia obtulisse dicuntur' (Gen. 4); whereon he proceeds to other instances under the Old Testament. Now, it is plain that by this instance he has overthrown his general assertion; for he excludes from proof the state of innocency, wherein there was unquestionably religion in the world, and that without sacrifices, if Cain and Abel were the first that offered them. He does, therefore, by his instances neither prove what himself intends, nor touch upon our cause, that there were no sacrifices in the state of innocency, though that state is necessarily included in his general assertion.

Priesthood Presupposes Sin

From what has been spoken it appears that there was no decree, no counsel of God, concerning either priest or sacrifice, with respect to the law of creation and the state of innocency. A supposition of the entrance of sin, and what ensued thereon in the curse of the law, lie at the foundation of the designation of the priesthood and sacrifice of Christ. Now, concerning the fall of man, the nature of that sin whereby he fell, the propagation of it to all mankind, the distress, misery, and ruin of the world thereby, I have at large discoursed in our former exercitations, prefixed to the exposition of the first two chapters of this Epistle. I have also in them evinced in general, that it was not the will, purpose, or counsel of God, that all mankind should utterly perish in that condition, as he had determined concerning the angels that sinned, but from the very beginning he gave not only sundry intimations but express testimonies of a contrary design. That, therefore, he would provide a relief for fallen man, that this relief was by the Messiah, whose coming and work he declared in a promise immediately upon the entrance of sin, has been also demonstrated in those exercitations. Building on these foundations, and having now removed some objections out of our way, it remains that we proceed to declare the especial original of the priesthood of Christ in the counsel of God, with respect to the especial manner of deliverance from sin and wrath designed therein.

3

THE PRIESTHOOD OF CHRIST—
ITS ORIGIN IN THE COUNSEL OF GOD

From what has been discoursed, it is manifest that the counsel of God concerning the priesthood and sacrifice of his Son, to be incarnate for that purpose, had respect to sin, and the deliverance of the elect from it, with all the consequents thereof; and the same truth has also been particularly discussed and confirmed in our exposition of the second chapter of this Epistle. That which now lies before us is to inquire more expressly into the nature of the counsels of God in this matter, and their progress in execution. And as in this endeavour we shall carefully avoid all curiosity, or vain attempts to be wise above what is written, so, on the other hand, we shall study with sober diligence to declare and give light to what is revealed herein, to the end that we should so increase in knowledge as to be established in faith and obedience. To this end are our ensuing discourses designed.

GOD, IN THE CREATION OF MAN,
GLORIFIED HIMSELF IN THREE DISTINCT PERSONS

God, in the creation of all things, intended to manifest his nature, in its being, existence, and essential properties; and therein to satisfy his wisdom and goodness. Accordingly, we find his expressions of and concerning himself in the work of creation suited to declare these things (see Isa. 40:12–17). Also, that the things themselves that were made had in their nature and order such an impress of divine wisdom, goodness, and power upon them, as made manifest the original cause from whence they did proceed. To this purpose discourses our apostle (Rom. 1:19–21), Τὸ γνωστὸν τοῦ θεοῦ φανερόν ἐστιν ἐν αὐτοῖς· (Ps. 19:1–2); as do sundry other divine writers also. Wherefore the visible works of God, man only excepted, were designed for no other end but to declare in general the nature, being, and existence of God. But in this nature there are three persons distinctly subsisting; and herein consists the most incomprehensible and sublime perfection of the divine being. This, therefore, was designed to manifestation and glory in the creation of man; for therein God would glorify himself as subsisting in three distinct persons, and himself in each of those persons distinctly. This was not designed immediately in other parts of the visible creation, but in this, which was the complement and perfection of them. And therefore the first express mention of a plurality of persons in the divine nature is in the creation of man; and therein also are personal transactions intimated concerning his present and future condition. This, therefore, is that which in the first place we shall evince, namely, 'That there were from all eternity personal transactions in the holy Trinity concerning mankind in their temporal and eternal condition, which first manifested themselves in our creation.'

'LET US MAKE MAN'

The first revelation of the counsels of God concerning the glorifying of himself in the making and disposal of man is declared וַיֹּאמֶר אֱלֹהִים נַעֲשֶׂה אָדָם בְּצַלְמֵנוּ כִּדְמוּתֵנוּ וְיִרְדּוּ בִדְגַת הַיָּם, 'And God said, Let us make man in our image, according to our likeness, and let them have dominion' (Gen. 1:26). This was the counsel of God concerning the making of אָדָם [man]; that is, not of that particular individual person who was first created and so called, but of the species or kind of creature which in him he now proceeded to create. For the word Adam is used in this and the next chapter in a threefold sense:

1. For the name of the individual man who was first created. He was called Adam from *adamah*, 'the ground,' from whence he was taken (Gen. 2:19–21); ἄνθρωπος ἐκ γῆς χοϊκός, 'of the earth, earthy' (1 Cor. 15:47).
2. It is taken indefinitely for the man spoken of (Gen. 2:7), וַיִּיצֶר יְהוָה אֱלֹהִים אֶת־הָאָדָם עָפָר מִן־הָאֲדָמָה;—'And the Lord God created man;' not him whose name was Adam, for 'He hajediah' [He emphatic] is never prefixed to any proper name, but the man indefinitely of whom he speaks.
3. It denotes the species of mankind. So is it used in this place, for the reddition is in the plural number, 'And let them have dominion,' the multitude of individuals being included in the expression of the species. Hence it is added (Gen. 1:27), 'So God created man in his own image, in the image of God created he him, male and female created he them;' which is not spoken with respect to Eve, who was not then made, but to the kind or race, wherein both sexes were included.

PLURALITY OF PERSONS IN THE CREATOR

Concerning them God says, נַעֲשֶׂה, 'Let US make,' in the plural number; and so are the following expressions of God in the same work: בְּצַלְמֵנוּ, 'In OUR image;' כִּדְמוּתֵנוּ, 'According to OUR likeness.' This is the first time that God so expresses himself, and the only occasion whereon he does so in the story of the creation. As to all other things, we hear no more but וַיֹּאמֶר אֱלֹהִים, 'And God said;' in which word also I will not deny but respect may be had to the plurality of persons in the divine essence, as the Spirit is expressly mentioned (Gen. 1:2). But here the mystery of it is clearly revealed. The Jews constantly affirm that the elders, who translated the Law on the request of Ptolemy king of Egypt, changed or corrupted the text in thirteen places, whereof this was the first; for נַעֲשֶׂה, 'Let us make,' they rendered by Ποιήσω, 'I will make,' and not Ποιήσωμεν, in the plural number. And this, they say, they did lest they should give occasion to the king or others to imagine that their law allowed of any more Gods than one, or on any account departed from the singularity of the divine nature. Whether this were so or no I know not, and have sufficient reason not to be too forward in giving credit to their testimony, if nothing else be given in evidence of what they affirm; for no footsteps or impressions of any such corruptions remain in any copies or memorials of the translation intended by them which are come down to us. But this is sufficiently evident, that the reporter of this story apprehended an unanswerable appearance of a plurality of subsistences in the Deity, which they by whom the Trinity is denied, as we shall see immediately, know not what to make of or how to solve.

No Mere Kingly Speech

It is an easy way which some have taken, in the exposition this place, to solve the difficulty which appears in it. God, they say, in it speaks 'more regio,' 'in a kingly manner,' by the plural number. 'It is,' says Grotius, 'the manner of the Hebrews to speak of God as of a king; and kings do great things on the counsel of the chief about them, (I Reg. 12:6, 2 Paral. 10:9; sic et Deus, I Reg. 22:20).' But the question is not about the manner of speaking among the Hebrews (whereof yet no instance can be given to this purpose of their speaking in the first person, as here), but of the words of God himself concerning himself, and of the reason of the change of the expression constantly used before. God is king of all the world, of the whole creation; and if he had spoken 'more regio' therein, he would have done it with respect to the whole equally, and not signally with respect to man. Besides, this 'mos regius' is a custom of a much later date, and that which then was not, was not alluded to. And the reason added why this form of speech is used, namely, 'because kings do great things on the counsel of their principal attendants,' requires, in the application, that God should consult with some created princes about the creation of man; which is an antiscriptural figment, and shall be immediately disproved. Least of all is any countenance given to this interpretation from the place alleged (1 Kings 22:20)—the application whereof to this purpose is borrowed from Aben Ezra on this place, in his attempt to avoid this testimony given to the Trinity—'Who shall persuade Ahab, that he may go up and fall at Ramoth-gilead?' for as there is nothing spoken in the plural number to parallel this expression, so if that allegorical declaration of God's providential rule be literally pressed, Satan or a lying spirit must be esteemed to be one of the chiefs with whom he consulted. But 'who has directed the Spirit of the LORD, or being the man of his counsel has taught him? With whom took he counsel, and who made him understand?' (Is. 40:13–14).

The ancients unanimously agree that a plurality of persons in the Deity is here revealed and asserted; yea, the council of Sirmium, though dubious, yea, Arianising in their confession of faith, yet denounces anathema to any that shall deny these words, 'Let us make man,' to be the words of the Father to the Son (Socrat. lib. ii. cap. 26). Chrysostom lays the weight of his argument for it upon the change in the manner of expression before used; as he may do justly and solidly. 'It is evident,' says Ambrose, 'that man was created by the council of the Trinity.' Neither have any of those who of late have espoused this evasion answered any of the arguments of the ancients for the sense we plead for, nor replied with any likelihood of reason to their exceptions against that interpretation, which they took notice of as invented long ago. Theodoret, in his *Quæst in Gen.*, quæst. 20, urges, 'That if God used this manner of speech concerning himself merely to declare his mind "*more regio*," he would have done it always, at least he would have done it often.' However, it would unavoidably have been the form of speech used in that kingly act of giving the law at Sinai, for that, if any thing, required the kingly style pretended; but the absolute contrary is observed. God, in that whole transaction with his peculiar people and subjects, speaks of himself constantly in the singular number.

Woeful Mistakes & Foolish Conjectures

But there are two sorts of persons who, with all their strength and artifices, oppose our exposition of this place—namely, the Jews and the Socinians, with whom we have to do perpetually in whatever concerns the person and offices of Christ the Messiah, and in what any way relates thereunto. We shall, therefore, first consider what they offer to secure themselves from this testimony against their infidelity, and then further improve the words to the end peculiarly designed. And although there is a great coincidence in their pretensions, yet I shall handle them distinctly, that it may the better appear wherein the one receives aid and assistance from the other.

The Jews are at no small loss as to the intention of the Holy Ghost in this expression, and, if we may believe some of them, have been so from of old; for, as we observed before, they all affirm that these words were changed in the translation of the LXX because they could not understand how they might be properly expressed without giving countenance to polytheism. Philo, *de Opificio Mundi*, knows not on what to fix, but after a pretense of some reason for satisfaction, adds, Τὴν μὲν οὖν ἀληθεστάτην αἰτίαν Θεὸν ἀνάγκη μόνον εἰδέναι·—'The true reason hereof is known to God alone.' The reason which he esteems most probable is taken out of Plato in his Timaeus. 'For whereas,' he says, 'there was to be in the nature of man a principle of vice and evil, it was necessary that it should be from another author, and not from the most high God.' But as the misadventure of such woeful mistakes may be passed over in Plato, who had no infallible rule to guide him in his disquisition after truth, so in him, who had the advantage of the scriptures of the Old Testament, it cannot be excused, seeing this figment rises up in opposition to the whole design of them. Some seek an evasion in the word נַעֲשֶׂה, which they would have to be the first person singular in Niphal, and not the first person plural in Kal. Having, therefore, a passive signification, the meaning is, that 'homo factus est;' man, or Adam, was made in our image and likeness—that is, of Moses and other men. Of this exposition of the words Aben Ezra says plainly, זה פירוש חסר לב—'It is an interpretation for a fool;' and well refutes it from these words of God himself, 'Whoso sheds man's blood, by man shall his blood be shed; for in the image of God made he man' (Gen. 9:6), with other considerations of the text. R. Saadias would have it that God spoke these words על מנהג מלכים, 'secundum consuetudinem regum;' or לשון רבי שכן מנהג המלכים, as Aben Ezra, 'the plural number, which is the custom of kings.' This we have already rejected, and must yet further call it into examination as it is managed by the Socinians.

But plainly the introduction of this style is comparatively modern, and which nothing but usage or custom has given reverence or majesty to. Joseph Kimchi would have it that God speaks to himself, or the earth, or the four elements; for as the soul of man was to be immediately created by God, so his body was to be from the earth, by a contemperation of the principles and qualities of it. And this man falls on the rock which he principally aims to avoid—namely, an appearance of polytheism; for he makes the earth itself to be a god, that has a principle of operation in itself, with a will and understanding whereby to exert it. Some of them affirm that in these words God consulted בפמליא של מעלה, 'with his family above,' that is, the angels; which Aben Ezra on the place principally inclines to. This must afterwards be distinctly examined. Others say it is God and בית דינו, 'his house of judgment.' בית דינו אלא עם עצמו ואם כתב אעשה אדם לא למדנו שהיא מדבר עם, says Kishi on the place; 'If it had been written, 'Let me,' or 'I will make man,' he had not taught us that he spoke to his house of judgment, but to himself;' whereof he shows the danger, from the expressions in the plural number. Hence some learned men have supposed that of old by 'God and his house of judgment,' they intended the persons of the holy Trinity, the Father, Word, and Spirit; but the explication which they frequently give of their minds herein will not allow us so to judge, at least as to any of their post-Talmudic masters.

Other vain and foolish conjectures of theirs in this matter I shall not repeat. These instances are sufficient as to my present intention; for hence it is evident into what uncertainties they cast themselves who are resolved upon an opposition to the truth. They know not what to fix upon, nor wherewith to relieve themselves. Although they all aim at the same end, yet what one embraces another condemns, and those that are wisest reckon up all the conjectures they can think of together, but fix on no one as true or as deserving to be preferred before others; for error is nowhere stable or certain, but fluctuates like the isle of Delos, beyond the skill of men or devils to give it a fixation. And thus much also of their sense was necessary to be expressed, that it might appear whence and from whom the Socinians and those who syncretize with them in an opposition to these testimonies given to the Trinity do borrow their exceptions. Little or nothing have they to offer for the support of their cause but what they have borrowed from those avowed enemies of our Lord Jesus Christ.

The Socinian Arguments of Enjedinus

I shall not in this instance collect the sentiments of the Socinians out of several of their writers, but take up with him who was one of the first that made it his professed design to elude all the testimonies of the Scriptures which are usually pleaded in the defence of the doctrine of the Trinity. This is Georgius Enjedinus [György Enyedi, a Hungarian Unitarian, 1555–97], whose writings, indeed, gave the first countenance to the Anti-trinitarian cause. And I shall the rather deal with him, because his perverse discourses, which were almost worn out of the world, are lately revived by a new edition, and are become common in the hands of many. Besides, indeed, there is little or nothing material added in this cause by his followers to his sophistical evasions and exceptions, though what he came short of in the New Testament, being prevented by death, is pursued in his method by Felbinger. The title of his book is, *Explicationes locorum Veteris et Novi Testamenti, ex quibus Trinitatis dogma stabiliri solet* [Explanations of the places in the Old and New Testaments from which the doctrine of the Trinity is usually established]; whereof this under consideration is the second. To the argument from hence for a plurality of persons in the same divine essence, he gives sundry exceptions, mostly borrowed from the Jews, invented by them out of their hatred to the Christian faith. And both sorts of these men do always think it sufficient to their cause to give in cavilling exceptions to the clearest evidence of any divine testimony, not regarding to give any sense of their own which they will abide by as the true exposition of them. He therefore first pleads:

> If from this discussion the number and nature of God is sought and collected, we first of all say that this saying no more establishes the Trinity from three persons of the deity, than tribes and every idolatry by their multiplicity and number confirm a lack of God. As for that 'Let us make for ourselves…' it could just as well refer to ten, one hundred, one thousand, as to three, and there is nothing more worthless and foolish than this argument. There are said to be many, therefore there are three, but it could be twenty, thirty, forty etc. Therefore even if there is any strength in this argument, it hardly implies that God is many. But let *this notion* be far from us, as certainly such prophanity that there

are many gods is far from Moses and the witness of the sacred writings, as we will introduce and establish.

But these things are sophistical and vain. The vanity of the divine nature is always supposed in our disquisitions concerning the persons subsisting therein. And this is so clearly and positively asserted in the Scripture, particularly by Moses (Deut. 6:4), besides that any apprehensions to the contrary are directly repugnant to the light of nature, that no expressions can be observed to give the least countenance to any other notion without ascribing direct contradictions to it; which, if certain and evident, were a sufficient ground to reject the whole. No pretense, therefore, to any imagination of a plurality of Gods can be made use of from these words. And the whole remaining sophistry of this exception lies in a supposition that we plead for three distinct persons in the Trinity from this place; which is false. That there is a plurality of subsistences in the divine nature we plead from hence; that these are three, neither more nor less, we prove from other places of Scripture without number. Many of these I have elsewhere vindicated from the exceptions of these men. Without a supposition of this plurality of persons, we say no tolerable account can be given of the reason of this assertion by them who acknowledge the unity of the divine nature; and we design no more but that therein there is mutual counsel—which without a distinction of persons cannot be fancied. This whole pretense, therefore, founded on a vain and false supposition, that this testimony is used to prove a certain number of persons in the Deity, is altogether vain and frivolous. He adds:

> In the second place, whatever this means when weighed carefully, it does not follow from these words of Moses that God who said, 'Let us make' is many, or that there was not one speaker, but rather one so great that these words are openly enlarged by the plural. Therefore there was one who was speaking, but he was speaking to others present. From this however, it does not immediately follow that there were many creators of man. For this conclusion is the work of much progression of thought. For they are without doubt searching for those to whom God was speaking. Then, was it to creatures or to the uncreated *that he spoke*? Moreover, was it to those who were working equally with God in the forming of man?

Although he only here proposes in general what he intends afterwards to pursue in particular, yet something must be observed thereon, to keep upright the state of our inquiry, which he endeavours perpetually to wrest to his advantage.

1. The invidious expressions which he makes use of, as 'a multiple God,' and the like, are devoid of ingenuity and charity, nothing that answers them being owned by those whom he opposes.

2. It follows not from our exposition of these words, nor is it by us asserted, that man had many creators; which he need not pretend that there is need of many consequences to prove, seeing none was ever so fond as to attempt the proof of it. I confess that expression in Job 35:10, אַיֵּה אֱלוֹהַּ עֹשָׂי, 'Where is God my creators?' does prove that he is in some sense many who made us. But whereas creation is a work proceeding from and an effect of the infinite properties of the one divine nature, our Creator is but one, although that one be equally Father, Son, and Spirit.

3. It is granted that one speaks these words, not more together; but he so speaks them that he takes those to whom he speaks into the society of the same work with himself; neither is the speaker more or otherwise concerned in 'Let US make,' and 'in OUR image,' than are those to whom he speaks. Neither, indeed, is it the speaking of these words before many concerned that Moses expresses, but it is the concurrence of many to the same work, with the same interest and concernment in it. And whosoever is concerned, speaking or spoken to, in the first words, 'Let us make,' is no less respected in the following words, 'in our image and likeness.' They must, therefore, be of one and the same nature; which was to be represented in the creature to be made in their image.

These things being premised, we may take a view of the pursuit and management of his particular exceptions:

> And if one delays on the first point, who then (certainly) were those to whom God spoke? First of all we are able to say that

it is not necessary, on account of this form of speech, to decide that there were many individuals. For often writers bring in some deliberation or debate with themselves. From this it does not immediately follow that many are present in consultation, but that he is so great that he scrupulously and carefully considers and weighs up everything. So therefore the Living God, Creator of everything most excellent, is introduced by Moses consulting like a man [lit. anthropomorphically] as is the custom of the Scriptures. Yet it does not follow from that that God is consulting with others about that plan.

Herein this author exceeds the confidence of the Jews, for they constantly grant that somewhat more than one individual person must be intended in these words, or no proper sense can be elicited from them. But the whole of this discourse, and what he would insinuate by it, is merely *petitio principii* accompanied with a neglect of the argument which he pretends to answer: for he only says that 'one may be introduced, as it were, deliberating and consulting with himself,' whereof yet he gives no instance, either from the Scripture or other sober writer, nor can give any parallel to this discourse here used; but he takes no notice that the words directly introduce more than one consulting and deliberating among themselves about the creating of man in their image. And of a form of speech answering to this, where one only and absolutely is concerned, no instance can be given in any approved author.

Again, what he concludes from his arbitrary supposition—namely, that hence 'it does not follow that God took counsel with others besides himself,'—is nothing to the argument in hand; for we prove not hence that God consulted with others besides himself, nor would it be to our purpose so to do. But this the words evince, that he who thus consulted with himself is in some respect more than one. But will this author abide by it, that this is the sense of the place, and that thus the words are to be interpreted? This he has not the least thought of, nor will maintain that it is according to truth: for so they can invent exceptions against our interpretation of any testimony of Scripture, they never care to give one of their own which they will adhere to and defend; which way of dealing in sacred things of so great importance is very perverse and froward. Thus our author, here relinquishing this conjecture, proceeds:

But finally *we say* this: if God is here addressing others, we ask who that might be? Our opponents assert that they must be capable of speech and reason. For why would God speak to those who were neither able to speak nor think? But that is not convincing enough. For we know that God often also sets up those lacking speech *as having* with sense and reason, as in Isaiah 1, 'Hear, heavens.'

Rather than this man would omit any cavil, he will make use of such as are sapless and ridiculous. God does not here speak to others that are not himself, but by speaking as he does, he declares himself to exist in a plurality of persons, capable of mutual consultation and joint operation. But here he must be supposed, as some of the Jews fancied before him, to speak to the inanimate parts of the creation, as he speaks in the first of Isaiah, 'Hear, O heavens, and give ear, O earth.' But in such rhetorical apostrophes they are in truth men that are spoken to, and that scheme of speech is used merely to make an impression on them of the things that are spoken. Apply this to the words of God in the circumstance of the creation of man, and it will appear shamefully ridiculous. Wherefore he trusts not to this subterfuge, but proceeds to another:

But finally *we say* this also, if those present with God were rational beings, what comes next? They say in addition that they could not have been created beings, since God is not accustomed to consulting with created beings in his plans; it is therefore necessary that they were creators, the Son and the Spirit. We certainly ought to remember that holy Scripture nowhere sets up God as without companions, but always assigns those attendants and crowds of angels, that are well known from the visions of the prophets. However, it does not portray creatures as being in consultation with God; this is also refuted by the same visions. For although it is true that God does not consult with anyone in particular, nor does he need anyone for counsel, yet the prophets represent him *as being* in consultation with spirits, 1 Kings 22; Isaiah 6; Job 1. Now in truth, the history of Moses teaches that Adam was formed with care, following the existence of angels. Therefore, they were able to serve God by consultation with regard to the making of man, and God was able to mention them openly.

This man seems willing to grant any thing but the truth. That which this whole discourse amounts to is, that 'God spoke these words to the angels,' as the Jews pretend. So Jarchi says that God spoke to them בדרך מׁשל, 'by way of condescension,' that they should not be troubled to see a creature made little less excellent than themselves. Others of them say that God spoke to them as he is attended with them, or as they wait upon his throne, which they call his 'house of judgment;' and this sense Enjedinus and those that follow him fence withal. But this we have disproved already, so that it need not here be much insisted on. The Scripture expressly denies that God took counsel with any besides himself in the whole work of the creation (Is. 40:12–14). Creation is a pure act of infinite monarchical sovereignty, wherein there was no use of any intermediate, instrumental causes, as there is in the government of the world. Wherefore, in the course of providence, God may be introduced as speaking with or to the creatures whom he will employ in the execution thereof, and who attend his throne to receive his commands; but in the work of creation, wherein none were to be employed, this can have no place, nor can God be represented as consulting with any creatures in the creation without a disturbance of the true notion and apprehension of it. Besides, nothing of this nature can be proved, no not even with respect to providential dispensations, from the places alleged. For Isaiah 6, it is the prophet only whom God in vision speaks to, calling out his faith and obedience, 'Whom shall I send, and who will go for us?' (v. 8); but whereas he speaks both in the singular and plural number, 'Whom shall I send, and who will go for us ?' there is also a plurality of persons in the same individual essence expressed; and to the other persons besides the Father is this place applied by the Holy Ghost (John 12:41; Acts 28:26). In the other two places (1 Kings 22, Job 1), God is introduced speaking to the devil; which it is some marvel to find cited to this purpose by persons of more sobriety and modesty than Enjedinus.

Again, man was made in the image and likeness of him that speaks and all that are as it were conferred with: 'Let us make man in our image.' But man was not made in the image and likeness of angels, but in the image and likeness of God—that is, of God alone, as it is expressed in the next verse. And the image here mentioned does not denote that which is made to answer another thing, but that which another is to answer to: 'Let us make man in our image,' that is, conformable to our nature. Now, God and angels have not one common nature, that should be the exemplar and prototype in the creation of man. Their natures and properties are infinitely distant. And that likeness which is between angels and men does no way prove that man was made in the image of angels, although angels should be supposed to be made before them; for more is required to this than a mere similitude and likeness, as one egg is like another, but not the image of another. A design of conforming one to another, with its dependence on that other, is required to this; so was man made in the image of God alone. But he further excepts:

> But what then if, finally in all respects, God was not with created beings at hand, nor did he speak these words to them? Does it surely follow that those with whom he spoke were the same as him in nature and essence? For this is the point they labour. It is certainly foolish to assert that the one who spoke and those who were addressed are of the same essence. For in the same way was the serpent Eve and man the devil and so forth?

At whose door the censure of folly will rest, a little examination of this sophism will discover. For, whatever this man may imagine, it will certainly follow, that if God spoke to any, and they were not creatures, those to whom he spoke were of the same nature and essence with him that spoke; for God and creatures divide the whole nature of beings, and therefore if any be spoken to that is not a creature, he is God—unless he can discover a middle sort of being, that is not God nor a creature, neither the Maker nor made. Again, it is a wondrous vain supposition, that our argument from hence is taken from such a general proposition, 'He that speaks and he that is spoken to are of the same nature;' the absurdity of which is obvious to children. But here is such a speaking of one as declares him in some respect to be more than one; and they are all assumed into the same society in the forming of man in the likeness of that one nature of which they are equally partakers. All these pretences, therefore, are at last deserted by our author, who betakes himself to that which is inconsistent with them:—

> But perhaps they will respond that Moses is signifying something so great as God not only speaking to others present, but also summoning them to the joint pursuit of his work and to be

participators in creation. 'Let us make,' he says. But the one who is the Creator of man, is also the Creator of the whole world; the who is the Creator of the whole world, is the only true God. This therefore must now be carefully examined. Can it be that God by these words, 'Let us make,' includes others with himself, and even discusses the creation of man with others? For we say that even though the form and voice of this 'Let us make' are plural, yet the meaning and force are singular; and this understanding is not from anyone else except the speaker alone, from God.

As he here at once overthrows all his former pretences, with some others also that he adds from the Jews in the close of his discourse, sufficiently manifesting that it is not truth, or the true sense of the words, which he inquires after, but merely how he may multiply captious exceptions to the sense by us pleaded for, so now, when he comes to own a direct opposition to it, his discourse, wherein he states the matter in difference, is composed of sophistical expressions; for whereas he pretends that our judgment is, that 'God by these words calls in others besides himself to himself into the society of this work,' whereby it is proved that both he that speaks and they that are spoken to are of the same nature, he does but attempt to deceive the unwary reader. For we say not that God speaks to others besides himself, nor calls in others to the work of creation; but God alone speaks in himself and to himself, because as he is one in essence, so as to personal subsistence there are three in one, as many other places of the Scripture do testify. And these three are each of them intelligent operators, though all working by that nature, which is one, and common to or in them all. Therefore are they expressed as speaking thus in the plural number, which could not be, in any congruity of speech, were he that speaks but one person as well as one in nature. And were not the doctrine of the Trinity clearly revealed in other places of Scripture, there could be no proper interpretation given of these words, so as to give no countenance to polytheism; but that being so revealed and taught elsewhere, the interpretation of this place is facile and plain, according to the analogy thereof. But that one person alone is intended in these words, he proceeds to prove:—

For first it is common in all languages everywhere without distinction for people to use the plural, although referring to themselves or other singular things. In such a way Christ spoke, although concerning himself alone, when he said in John 3:11, 'We speak of what we know, and bear witness to what we have seen.' The words which follow make it clear that Christ is speaking of himself in the plural. He says, 'If I have told you earthly things…'. In such a way God speaks of himself alone in Isaiah 41:22, 'Let them come near and tell us what is going to happen, and let us place in our heart and consider the new things, and let them tell us what is going to happen.' Moreover it is possible to observe that the same (unique) singular is mixed in with now the singular being used and now the plural. And in Isaiah 6:8, God says, 'Whom shall I send, and who shall go for us?' It is evident from these verses and similar places, and from common speech, that it is possible for a plural word to refer to one only, if I understand and speak correctly. Therefore, although God said (this) 'Let us make', yet it is just as though he had said, 'Let me make.'

What he says is so usual in all languages, that one speaking of himself should speak in the plural number, having respect to no more than himself, nor letting any others into a concernment with himself in the things spoken, he can give no instance of in any language, out of any ancient approved author.

1. That phrase of speech is a novice in the use of speaking. Particularly it is a stranger to the Scripture. As this author could not, no more can any of his successors, produce any one instance out of the Old Testament of any one, unless it were God alone, were he never so great or powerful, that spoke of himself in the first person in the plural number. Aben Ezra himself on this place grants that no such instance can be given. He is therefore at once deprived of the Hebrew language, wherein yet alone his instances ought to be given, if he will argue from the use of speaking.

2. The places he cites relieve him not. Our Saviour's words respect not himself only, but his disciples also, who taught and baptized in his name, whose doctrine he would vindicate as his own (John 3:11). And as for what he adds afterwards, 'If I have told you earthly things,' it relates directly to that discourse which in his own person he had with Nicodemus, with respect to which he changes his phrase of speech to the

singular number; which overthrows his pretensions. The words of the prophet (Isa. 41:22), are either spoken of God alone, or of God and the church, whom he called and joined with himself in bearing witness against idols and idolaters; and he may take his choice in whether sense he will admit of them. If they are spoken of God alone, we have another testimony to confirm our doctrine, that there must be, and is, a plurality of persons in the one singular, undivided nature of God; if of the church also, there is no exception in them to our rule, that one person speaks of himself in the Scripture only in the singular number.

3. His other instance out of the same prophet, 'Whom shall I send, and who will go for us?' (Is. 6:8), is home to his purpose of proving that the singular and plural numbers are used mixedly or promiscuously of one and the same. But who is that one? It is God alone. No such instance can be given in any other. And why are things so expressed by him and concerning him? Who can give any tolerable reason but this alone, namely, because his nature is one and singular, but subsisting in more persons than one? And indeed this place, considered with its circumstances, and the allegations of it in the New Testament, does infallibly confirm the truth we contend for. He has not yet, therefore, attained to a proof that the word may be so used as he pretends; which, with these men, is enough to secure them from the force of any Scripture testimony.

He adds, therefore:

Second, it is not only possible but entirely necessary that this 'Let us make' denotes a singular person which is thus proven. Because if that voice included a multitude in itself, the Holy Scriptures would never dare change it and turn it into a singular number. But the prophets, Christ himself, and the apostles, whenever they speak of this creation they assign it to be one and indeed use the singular voice. For immediately Moses himself adds below, 'And God created man in his own image and likeness.' In so far as he had nearby said, 'Let us make,' he here explains it by writing 'God created', because there it says 'in our images', here it says in the singular 'in his image'. In the same way in chapter 6:7 he writes, 'I will wipe out man whom I have created.' And Christ says in

Matthew 19:4, 'He who made man in the beginning, made them male and female.' And in Mark 10:6: 'God made them male and female'. Paul writes in Acts 17:26, 'God made from one man every race of man.' And in Colossians 3:10 he writes 'putting on the new man which is renewed in knowledge after the image of him who created him.' Since all then bear witness to the one who created man being unique/singular, it also follows that in the first place the words, 'Let us make' signify only one. For we have now demonstrated that it is possible to signify one by the plural.

Nothing can be more effectually pleaded in the behalf of the cause opposed by this man than what is here alleged by him in opposition thereunto; for it is certain that the holy writers would never have ascribed the creation of all to one, and expressed it in the singular number, as they do most frequently, had it not been one God, one Creator, by whom all things were made. This is the position which he lays down as the foundation of his exception; and he was not so brutish as once to imagine that we believed there were more Creators, and so consequently more Gods, than one. But take this assertion also on the other side, namely, that the holy writers would never have ascribed the creation to more than one, unless that one in some sense or other had been more than so. Wherefore, they do not change, as is pretended, the plural expression into a singular; but the Holy Ghost, expressing the same thing, of making man in the image of God, sometimes expresses it in the singular number, by reason of the singularity of the nature of God, which is the original of all divine operations, for God works by his nature; and sometimes in the plural, because of the plurality of persons in that nature: on which supposition these different expressions are reconciled, without which they cannot so be.

And all these exceptions or cavils are managed merely against the necessary use and signification of the word 'Faciamus,' 'Let us make,' in the plural number. What is alleged by the ancients and others, to clear the intention of the expression in this place particularly, he takes no notice of; for he makes no inquiry why, seeing, in the whole antecedent account of the work of creation, God is introduced speaking constantly in the singular number, here the phrase of speech is changed, and God speaks as consulting or deliberating, in the plural number. And he says not only, 'Let US make,' but adds, 'In OUR image, and after OUR likeness.' To imagine this to be done without some peculiar reason, is to dream rather than to inquire into the sense of Scripture. And other reason besides what we have assigned, with any tolerable congruity to the common use of speaking, cannot be given. But supposing that he has sufficiently evinced his intention, he proceeds to give a reason of the use of this kind of speech, where one is spoken of in the plural number:

> With regard to reasons why it is allowed to signify one using the plural, and when it is usually done, carious reasons are usually given. Some think it is done *to show* honour and esteem, so that eminent and excellent persons are spoken of in the plural. Experts note this use in the Hebrew language. Among these is Cevellerius who discusses this rule in his Grammar. This signifies dignity using the plural to intensify honour. So in Joshua 24:19, 'He *is* a holy God'; in Exodus 21:29, 'His masters' instead of master; in Isaiah 19:4, 'into the hand of harsh masters' instead of master; in Genesis 42:30, 'Lords of the land' instead of lord. Indeed, this use is not only in Hebrew but also in other languages. Well known among scholars is Sophocles, who in Oedipus at Colonus (line 1490), annotates the poet to say, δοῦναί σφιν, for δοῦναι αὐτῷ, and adds a note that it is κατὰ τιμὴν πληθυντικῶς, on account of honour or dignity being spoken of in the plural.

We also grant that it is one who is here intended, only we say, he is not spoken of under that consideration, of being one. Nor is it enough to prove that the word may in the plural number be used in a singular sense, but that it is so in this place, seeing the proper importance of it is otherwise. Neither can that expression concerning God (Josh. 24:19), אֱלֹהִים קְדֹשִׁים הוּא, 'Dii sancti ipse,' be used *honouris gratia*, seeing it is no honour to God to be spoken of as many Gods, for his glory is that he is one only. It has, therefore, another respect, namely, to the persons in the unity of the same nature. I could easily give the reasons of all his other instances in particular, wherein men are spoken of, and manifest that they will yield him no relief; but this may suffice in general, that they are all speeches concerning others in the third person, and all our inquiry is concerning any one thus speaking of himself in the first person, of which no one can be given. Wherefore our author, not confiding to this his last refuge, betakes himself to foolish imaginations of 'God's speaking to the superior parts of the world, whence the soul of man was to be taken, and the inferior, whence his body was to be made;' to 'a design for the instruction of men, how to use counsel and deliberation in great undertakings; to 'a double knowledge in God, universal and particular'—which are all of them rabbinical fopperies, evidently manifesting that he knew not what to confide in or rest upon as to the true cause of this expression, after he had resolved to reject that alone which is so.

Personal Transactions in the Trinity

The foundation of our intention from this place being thus cleared, we may safely build upon it. And that which hence we intend to prove is, that in the framing and producing the things which concern mankind, there were peculiar, internal, personal transactions between the Father, Son, and Spirit. The scheme of speech here used is in *genere deliberativo*—by way of consultation. But whereas this cannot directly and properly be ascribed to God, an anthropopathy must be allowed in the words. The mutual distinct actings and concurrence of the several persons in the Trinity are expressed by way of deliberation, and that because we can no otherwise determine or act. And this was peculiar in the work of the creation of man, because of an especial designation of him to the glory of God as three in one. Neither could he have been created in the accidental image of God but with immediate respect to the Son, as he was the essential image of the Father. The distinct personal actings of the Trinity, wherein the priesthood of Christ is founded, are not, I confess, contained herein; for these things preceded the consideration of the fall, whereby the image now proposed and resolved to be communicated to man in his creation was lost, which Christ was designed to recover. But there is enough to confirm our general assertion, that such distinct actings there were with respect to mankind; and the application of this to our present purpose will be directed in the ensuing testimonies. This, therefore, I have only laid down and proved, as the general principle which we proceed upon. Man was peculiarly created to the glory of the Trinity, or of God as three in one. Hence in all things concerning him there is not only an intimation of those distinct subsistences, but also of their distinct actings with respect to him. So it was eminently in his creation; his making was the effect of special counsel. Much more shall we find this fully expressed with respect to his restoration by the Son of God.

From the Beginning

The same truth is further revealed and confirmed:

> The LORD possessed me
>> in the beginning of his way,
> before his works of old.
> I was set up from everlasting,
>> from the beginning,
>> or ever the earth was.
> When there were no depths,
>> I was brought forth;
> when there were no fountains
>> abounding with water.
> Before the mountains were settled,
>> before the hills was I brought forth:
> while as yet he had not made the earth,
>> nor the fields,
>> nor the highest part of the dust of the world.
> When he prepared the heavens,
>> I was there:
> when he set a compass
>> upon the face of the depth:
> when he established the clouds above:
> when he strengthened
>> the fountains of the deep:
> when he gave to the sea his decree,
>> that the waters
>> should not pass his commandment:
> when he appointed
>> the foundations of the earth:
> then was I by him,
>> as one brought up with him:
> and I was daily his delight,
> rejoicing always before him;
> rejoicing in the habitable part of his earth;
> and my delights were with the sons of men.

Prov. 8:22–31

Arian Distortions

We must first secure this testimony against those who have attempted to deprive the church of God of its use and advantage, and then improve it to our present purpose. In the ancient church none questioned but that the Wisdom which here discourses is the Son of God; only the Arians greatly endeavoured to corrupt the sense of one passage in it, and thereby to wrest the whole to give countenance to their heresy. Those of late who agree with them in an opposition to the same truth, upon other principles, observing how they failed in their attempt, do leave the sense of particular passages unquestioned, and call into question the whole subject of the discourse; wherein, if they prevail, the sense of particular places must be accommodated to what they substitute in the room thereof.

It is Wisdom that speaks and is spoken of. This we believe to be him who is the Wisdom of God, even his eternal Son. This they will not grant, although they are not agreed what it is that is intended. A property, say some, of the divine nature; the exercise of divine wisdom in making the world, say others; the wisdom that is in the law, say the Jews; or, as some of them, the wisdom that was given to Solomon—and of their mind have been some of late. With the Arians I shall not much contend, because their heresy seems to be much buried in the world, although some of late have endeavoured to give countenance to their opinions, or to them who maintained them (*Sand. Hist. Ecclesiastes Enucl.* lib. 3). It was the 22nd verse which they principally insisted on; for whereas it was granted between them and the Homoousians that it is the Son of God which is here spoken of, they hence pleaded for his creation before the world, or his production ἐξ οὐκ ὄντων, and that there was [a time] when he was not. This they did from these words, יְהֹוָה קָנָנִי רֵאשִׁית דַּרְכּוֹ; which words were rendered by the LXX, or the Greek translation then in common use, Ὁ Κύριος ἔκτισέ με, ἀρχὴν ὁδῶν αὐτοῦ·—'Dominus condidit me initium viarum suarum.' And this is followed by all the old translations. בראני, says the Targum; and the Syriac, 'Creavit me;' and the Arabic follows them; only the Vulgar Latin reads, 'Possedit,' 'Possessed me.' On this corrupt translation the Arians bare themselves so high as to provoke their adversaries to a decision of the whole controversy between them by the sentence of this one testimony. But the corruption of the common translation is long since confessed. Aquila and Theodotion both render the word by ἐκτήσατο, 'he possessed.' Nor does קָנָה in any place, or on any occasion, signify to make or create, or any thing of the like importance. Its constant use is either to acquire and obtain, or to possess and enjoy. That which any one has, which is with him, which belongs to him and is his own, he is קֹנֵה, the possessor of. So is the Father said to possess Wisdom, because it was his, with him, even his eternal Word or Son. No more is intended hereby but what the apostle more clearly declares (John 1:1–2), Ἐν ἀρχῇ ὁ Λόγος ἦν πρὸς τὸν Θεόν·—'In the beginning the Word was with God.' But with these I shall not contend.

Jewish & Socinian Distortions

The Jews, and those who in the things concerning the person of Christ derive from them, and who borrow their weapons to combat his deity, we must not pass by; for an examination of their pretences and sophisms in this cause, at least occasionally as they occur to us, I do not guess, but know to be necessary.

Grotius on this place tells us, 'The Hebrews expound these things of that wisdom which is seen in the law.' And as to many of them this information is true. Whereunto he adds of his own, 'And thereunto, indeed, the things here attributed to wisdom do agree, if not only, yet principally;' which whether it be so or no, the ensuing examination will evince.

The Jews, then, affirm that the wisdom here intended is the wisdom of the law, as in the law, or the wisdom that God used in giving the law; but how the things here ascribed to Wisdom can belong to the law given on Sinai is hard to conceive. To take off this difficulty, they tell us that the law was one of the seven things which God made before the creation of the world; which they prove from this place, verse 22, 'The LORD possessed me in the beginning of his way,' yea, and that, as they say, two thousand years before creation, signified by the two alephs in that sentence; Midrash Bamidmar, in cap. 8. But Aben Ezra, in his preface to his *Annotations on the Bible*, tells us that they are mystical allegories, and not true in their literal sense; as does also the author of *Nizachon*, Sec. Beresh. sect. 3, who likewise informs us that these things are said to be made before the world, לפי גדולות וטובות, 'because of their excellency and worth,' whence they were first thought upon. But these figments we need not trouble ourselves about. Their apprehension that the wisdom intended is that of the law, which Grotius gives countenance to, shall be examined. The Socinians are not solicitous what the things mentioned are ascribed to, so they can satisfy themselves in their exceptions to our ascription of them to the Son of God. I shall, therefore, first confirm our exposition of the place, and then remove their exceptions out of our way.

Proverbs Speaks of A Divine Person

First, it is an intelligent person that is here intended; for all sorts of personal properties are ascribed to it. It cannot, therefore, be a mere essential property of the divine nature, nor can the things spoken concerning it with respect to God be any way verified in his essential attributes. Much less is it wisdom in general, or wisdom in man, as by some it is expounded, no one thing here mentioned being in any tolerable sense applicable thereunto.

1. In the whole discourse Wisdom speaks as an intelligent person, of which almost every verse in the whole chapter is an instance.
2. Personal authority and power are assumed by it: 'By me kings reign, and princes decree justice. By me princes rule, and nobles, even all the judges of the earth' (v. 15–16).
3. Personal promises upon duties to be performed towards it, due to God himself: 'I love them that love me, and those that seek me early shall find me;' (v. 17) which is our respect to God, 'O God, thou art my God; early will I seek thee' (Ps. 63:1), and which is elsewhere often expressed.
4. Personal divine actions: 'I lead in the way of righteousness, in the midst of the paths of judgment: that I may cause those that love me to inherit substance; and I will fill their treasures' (v. 20–21). 'I was daily his delight, rejoicing always before him...and my delights were with the sons of men' (v. 30–31).
5. Personal properties; as eternity, 'I was set up from everlasting, from the beginning, or ever the earth was' (v. 23–5); wisdom, 'Counsel is mine, and sound wisdom; I am understanding; I have strength' (v. 14).

Secondly, the name of Wisdom is the name of the Son, who is the wisdom of God. For the Wisdom mentioned (Prov. 9:1), the Jews themselves confess that it is one of the מדות, or distinct properties that are in the divine ישׁות, that is, substance or essence; whereby the Son of God alone can be intended.

Thirdly, the things here spoken of Wisdom are all of them, or at least the principal, expressly elsewhere attributed to the Son (v. 11, Phil. 3:8; v. 15, Rev. 19:16; v. 22, John 1:1–3; v. 23–4, Col. 1:15–17; v. 30, John 1:14; v. 32, Rev. 22:14).

Fourthly, the relation of the Wisdom that speaks to God declares it to be his eternal Word or Son: 'I was daily his delight, rejoicing always before him;' as he did in whom his soul is always well pleased.

And, lastly, as we shall further see, they are the eternal transactions of the Father and Son that are here described, which are capable of no other interpretation.

Enjedinus' Objections Show Why Proverbs 8 Applies to the Son of God

It is not my design to plead here the eternal existence of the Son of God antecedent to his incarnation. I have done it also at large elsewhere. But because the faith thereof is the foundation of what I shall further offer concerning the original of his priesthood, the testimonies produced to that purpose must be vindicated from the exceptions of the professed adversaries of that fundamental truth; and these, as to this place, are summed up and put together by Enjedinus. And his manner is, as was before observed (wherein also he is followed by all those of his way and persuasion), to multiply sophistical exceptions, that so by any means they may distract the mind of the reader and render him uncertain; and therefore they consider not whether what they offer be true or no, but commonly their evasions contradict and overthrow one another. But so the truth may be rejected, they regard not what is received. First, therefore, he lays his exception to the whole matter, and affirms that it is not wisdom, but prudence, that speaks these words, and is the subject of the whole discourse: —

> One must first keep in mind, so that there will indeed be no doubt, that direct speech is spoken by Wisdom. For if one consults the version of Pagninus or Mercerus, and the Hebrew text, it will be

apparent that these words are spoken by Intelligence or Discretion, which in this chapter are sometimes linked, at other times separate, when placed with Wisdom, as is apparent from verse 1 and 14, in the following part of which Intelligence begins to speak concerning herself. For verse 14, according to Pagninus, has this meaning, 'Belonging to me is judgment and wisdom;' and from this point on Wisdom speaks regarding or herself. After this follows, 'I am Intelligence, strength is mine.' etc. Therefore when Paul calls Christ not Intelligence but Wisdom, and the direct speech is spoken by Intelligence, it follows that this passage does not relate to Christ.

What those names of Pagnin, Mercer, and the Hebrew text, are produced for, I cannot well conjecture. Both in the original and in the versions of those learned men the context is as clear to our purpose as in any other translation whatever. And the view of the text will ease us of this forlorn exception. The comparing of the first verse with the fourteenth gives no countenance to it:

1. In verse 1, the mention of תְּבוּנָה is not the introduction of a new person or thing, but another name of the same person or thing, as all expositors agree, whatever they apply the words to.

2. The words תְּבוּנָה (v. 1) and בִינָה (v. 14) both rendered 'understanding,' and both from the same root, are yet not absolutely the same, so that several things may be intended by them.

3. The whole context makes it plain that it is Wisdom which speaks those words, לִי־עֵצָה וְתוּשִׁיָּה אֲנִי בִינָה לִי גְבוּרָה (v. 14). The preceding words are, 'I wisdom dwell with prudence...and the evil way, and the froward mouth, do I hate' (v. 12–13); whereon it follows, 'Counsel is mine, and sound wisdom' (or 'substance'): 'I am understanding; I have strength' As in the beginning Wisdom says, לִי־עֵצָה, so in the close, by a continuation of the same form of speech, אֲנִי בִינָה לִי גְבוּרָה is a defective expression, and there is no verb following to be regulated by בִינָה. Wherefore, according to the perpetual use of that language, the verb substantive is to be supplied, as it is in our translation, 'I am understanding.' Understanding, therefore, cannot be the person speaking, but a descriptive adjunct of him that speaks. There is the same expression concerning Wisdom, verse 12,

אֲנִי־חָכְמָה, 'I wisdom;' but it is not defective because of the verb following, שָׁכַנְתִּי, 'have dwelt,' or 'do dwell.' Supply the verb substantive here, where there is no defect, and the whole sense will be corrupted; but in this place, if it be omitted, there will be no sense remaining. Neither is אֲנִי בִינָה of any other signification than לִי גְּבוּרָה, 'I have' (or 'am') 'understanding,' and 'I have strength.' This plea, therefore, evinces nothing but the boldness of them that use it. He proceeds to another:

Then we accept that Wisdom is here portrayed as self-existent and personal, and here is described as speaking and shouting and has actions attibuted to it, although one cannot nor is accustomed to prove this from elsewhere. But it is extremely common in the Holy Scriptures also to write about actions or events through personification. In the same way mercy and peace are said to watch from the heavens and to exchange a kiss with one another. But let us not digress too much; this Discretion or Intelligence is said to cry out, to stand in the streets, and to shout in the city gates. There is however no one so stupid that he does not understand that Mercy, Peace and Discretion are events and does not recognise personification in the manner of speaking.

How we prove a person to be here intended, that is, the eternal Word of God, has been declared. There are other considerations which evince it besides that here mentioned. But this prosopopoeia, or fiction of a person, is of great use to the Antitrinitarians. By this one engine they presume they can despoil the Holy Ghost of his deity and personality. Whatever is spoken of him in the Scripture, they say it is by a prosopopoeia, or the fiction of a person, those things being assigned to a quality or an accident which really belong to a person only. But as to what concerns the Holy Spirit, I have elsewhere taken this engine out of their hands, and cast it to the ground, so that none of them alive will erect it again. Here they make use of it against the deity of Christ, as they do also on other occasions. I do acknowledge there is such a scheme of speech used by rhetoricians and orators, of which some examples occur in the Scripture. To a thing which is not a person, that is sometimes ascribed which is indeed proper only to a person; or a person who is dead or absent may be introduced as present and speaking. But yet Quintilian, the great master of the art of oratory, denies that by this figure speech can be ascribed to that which never had it. 'For certainly,' says he, 'one is not able to imagine speech, that is not imagined as speech of a person.' If you feign speech, you must feign it to be the speech of a person, or one endowed with a power of speaking. And it is hard to find an instance of such an attribution of speech to things inanimate in good authors, unless it be where, by another figure, they introduce countries or cities speaking or pleading for themselves; wherein, by a metonymy, the inhabitants of them are intended. But such an ascription is not to be found in the Scripture at all; for a prosopopoeia, or fiction of a person, is a figure quite distinct from all sorts of allegories, pure or mixed, apologues, fables, parables; wherein, when the scheme is evident, any thing may be introduced speaking—like the trees in the discourse of Jotham (Judg. 9). The instance of mercy and peace looking down from heaven and kissing each other, is mixedly figurative. The foundation is a metonymy of the cause for the effect, or rather of the adjunct for the cause, and the prosopopoeia is evident. But that a person should be introduced speaking in a continued discourse, ascribing to himself all personal properties, absolute and relative, all sorts of personal actions, and those the very same which in sundry other places are ascribed to one certain person, as all the things here mentioned are to the Son of God, who yet is no person, never was a person, nor represents any person, without the least intimation of any figure therein, or any thing inconsistent with the nature of things and persons treated of, and that in a discourse didactical and prophetical, is such an enormous, monstrous fiction, as nothing in any author, much less in the Old or New Testament, will give the least countenance to.

There are in the Scripture, allegories, apologues, parables, but all of them so plainly, evidently, and professedly such, and so unavoidably requiring a figurative exposition from the nature of the things themselves (as where stones are said to hear, and trees to speak), that there is no danger of any mistake about them, nor difference concerning their figurative acceptation. And the only safe rule of ascribing a figurative sense to any thing or expression in the Scripture, is when the nature of things will not bear that which is proper; as where the Lord Christ calls himself a door and a vine, and says that bread is his body. But to make allegories of such discourses as this, founded in the fiction of persons, is a ready way to turn the whole Bible into an allegory—which may be done with as much ease and probability of truth. He further excepts:—

> When in the second place they contend that this is not figurative, but that everything asserted is literal, it is utterly absurd. For although we admit that this Wisdom was a great person, which they call the Word himself, yet it is certain that in the time of Solomon he did not shout in the streets, nor live cheerfully with men, nor build a house, nor destroy the seven columns, nor offer sacrifices, nor mix wine, nor the rest of the deeds which are here recorded as having been performed. They should then confess that Christ was incarnate from eternity, since actions could not have happened unless he had been born to men. And therefore it is shameless and unlearned to deny that this speech of Solomon is figurative.

He names not who they are who say no expressions in this discourse are figurative. Neither does this follow upon a denial that the whole is founded in the fiction of a person; for a true and real person may speak things figuratively, and sometimes it is necessary that so he should do. These men will not deny God to be a person, nor yet that he often speaks of himself and his works figuratively. The same does Wisdom also here, in the declaration of some of his works. But that which animates this exception is a false supposition, that the eternal Word cannot be said to do or act any thing but what he does immediately in his own person, and that as incarnate. What God does by the ministry of others, that he also does himself. When he gave the law by the ministry of angels, he gave the law himself; and when he speaks by the prophets, he is everywhere said to speak himself. That, therefore, which was done in the days of Solomon by the command, appointment, authority, and assistance of Wisdom, was done then by Wisdom itself. And so all things here ascribed to it, some properly, some figuratively, were done by the Word in the means by him appointed. In the ministry of the priests, Levites, prophets, teachers of the law, inviting all sorts of persons to the fear of the Lord, he performed the most of them; and the remainder of the things intended he effected in his ordinances and institutions of divine worship. Besides, there is a prophetical scheme in these words. It is here declared not only what Wisdom then did, but especially what it should do, namely, in the days of the gospel; for the manner of the prophets is to express things future as present or past, because of the certainty of their accomplishment. And these things they spoke of the coming of Christ in the flesh. See 1 Peter 1:11–12, 3:19.

But utterly to remove this pretense of prosopopoeias and figures, it need only to be observed, which none will deny, that the Wisdom that speaks here, chap. 8, is the same that speaks, chap. 1, from verse 20 to the end. And if Wisdom there be not a person, and that a divine person, there is none in heaven; for to whom or what else can those words be ascribed which Wisdom speaks (vv. 23–6, 28): 'Turn you at my reproof: behold, I will pour out my Spirit to you, I will make known my words to you. Because I have called, and ye refused; I have stretched out my hand, and no man regarded; but ye have set at nought all my counsel, and would none of my reproof: I also will laugh at your calamity; I will mock when your fear cometh. Then shall they call upon me, but I will not answer; they shall seek me early, but they shall not find me.' If these things express not a person, and that a divine person, the Scripture gives us no due apprehension of any thing whatever. Who is it that pours out the Holy Spirit? Whom is it that men sin against in refusing to be obedient? Whom is it that in their distress they call upon, and seek early in their trouble? The whole Scripture declares to whom, and to whom alone, these things belong and may be ascribed.

After an interposition of some things nothing to the purpose, he yet puts in three more exceptions to this testimony to the eternal personal existence of this Wisdom; as—

> In addition this is the wisdom concerning which Solomon communicated, spoke, taught and established to men. Be Jesus Christ only spoke to men in the last days, according to the apostolic testimony in Hebrews 1; therefore, it was not of the era of Solomon.

The apostle says not that Jesus Christ spoke only in the latter days, Hebrews 1, but that God in the last days spoke to us in his Son. And the immediate speaking to us by the Son in the last days, as he was incarnate, hinders not but that he spoke before by his Spirit in the prophets, as the apostle Peter affirms him to have done (1 Pet. 1:11). And by this Spirit did he speak—that is, teach and instruct men—in the days of Solomon, and from the foundation of the world (1 Pet. 3:18–20).

> Finally this prophecy, Isaiah 42:1–2, 'Behold my servant whom I have chosen will not shout out, nor will his voice nor will anyone hear his voice in the streets,' is applied to Christ in Matthew 12:18–19. But this wisdom is said to shout in the streets. Therefore it is wrong that this wisdom of Solomon is Jesus Christ.

A man of gravity and learning ought to have been ashamed of such a puerile cavil. The prophet Isaiah, setting out the meekness and peaceableness of the Lord Christ in the discharge of his office, with his tenderness and condescension towards the poorest and meanest that come to him, expresses it, among others, by these words, 'He shall not cry, nor lift up, nor cause his voice to be heard in the street;' intending no more but that he should do nothing by way of strife, contention, or violence, in private or public places. And this prophecy is applied to him by Matthew at that very season when 'great multitudes followed him' in the streets and fields, whom he taught and healed (Matt. 12:15–17). Hence this man would conclude, that because Wisdom is said to cry in the streets—that is, to instruct men in public places, which he did formerly by his Spirit, and in the days of his flesh in his own person—the Son of God cannot be intended. Yet he further adds:—

> Finally, concerning this wisdom, it is not said that it was begotten from eternity; but only that in Hebrew it was considered fashioned by the world; it signifies another a long way off, who was begotten from eternity. And it is able to come some extent from the world, and be one who existed from the creation of the world, and even also before it; from this however it does not follow that it is eternal.

He tells us not where in the Hebrew text wisdom is said to be *'formata a seculo;'* nor is there any such passage in the context. It says, indeed, verse 23, מֵעוֹלָם נִסַּכְתִּי; which words of themselves do not absolutely and necessarily declare eternity, though no other expression or antecedent eternity be commonly made use of; but as this מֵעוֹלָם is here particularly explained to denote the existence of Wisdom before the whole creation or any part of it, as it is at large in the whole ensuing discourse, especially verses 25, 26, it does necessarily denote eternity, nor can it be otherwise expressed. And although we do not particularly prove the relation of the Son to the Father by eternal generation from this place, yet as Wisdom is not said here to be formed or created, so the word used verse 25, חוֹלָלְתִּי, which we have rendered, 'I was brought forth,' does more than intimate that generation.

This being the whole of what the enemies of the sacred Trinity have to object to our application of this discourse to the eternal Word or Son of God, we may upon its removal proceed to the improvement of this testimony to our present design.

CHRIST WAS BESIDE THE FATHER

A personal transaction, before the creation of the world, between the Father and the Son, acting mutually by their one Spirit, concerning the state and condition of mankind, with respect to divine love and favor, is that which we inquire after, and which is here fully expressed; for the Wisdom or Word of God having declared his eternal existence with the Father and distinction from him, manifests withal his joint creation of all things, especially his presence with God when he made רֹאשׁ עַפְרוֹת תֵּבֵל (v. 26), 'the highest part of the dusts of the habitable world ;' that is, הָרִיאשׁוּן אָדָם, 'The first Adam,' as Jarchi interprets it, and that not improbably. Then he declares that he was אֶצְלוֹ, 'by him,' with him, before him (v. 30); that is, πρὸς τὸν θεόν, John 1:1–2. And he was with him, אָמוֹן, 'Nutricius,' 'One brought up with him.' The word seems to be of a passive signification, or the participle Pahul, and is of the masculine gender, though referring to חָכְמָה, Wisdom, which speaks of itself and is of the feminine, and that because it is a person which is intended; such constructions being not infrequent in the Hebrew, where the adjunct agrees with and respects the nature of the subject, rather than the name or some other name of the same thing. See Genesis 4:7. The word may have various significations, and is accordingly variously rendered by interpreters. The Chaldee render it מהימן, that is, 'faithful,' 'I was faithful with him;' and the LXX, ἁρμόζουσα, 'framing, forming,' that is, all things with him. So also Ralbag on the place expounds it actively, 'One nourishing all

things,' as Jarchi does passively, עִמּוֹ גְדֵלָה, brought up with him;'
which sense of the words our translation follows. And it is used to
that purpose, הָאֱמֻנִים עֲלֵי תוֹלָע, 'brought up in scarlet' (Lam. 4:5).
And although it may be not undecently taken in an active sense,
yet I rather judge it to be used passively, 'nutricius, alumnus,' one
that is in the care and love of another, and to be disposed by him.

And we may inquire in what sense this is spoken of the Son
with respect to the Father. The foundation of the allusion lies in
the eternal mutual love that is between the Father and the Son.
Thereunto is added the consideration of the natural dependence
of the Son on the Father—compared to the love of a father
to a son, and the dependence of a son on his father. Therefore
most translations, with respect to this allusion, supply 'as' to the
words, 'As one brought up.' Again, אָמוֹן, 'alumnus,' 'one brought
up,' is always so with and to some especial end or purpose, or to
some work and service. And this is principally here intended. It is
with respect to the work that he had to accomplish that he is called
'Alumnus Patris,' 'One brought up of the Father.' And this was no
other but the work of the redemption and salvation of mankind,
the counsel whereof was then between the Father and the Son. In
the carrying on of that work the Lord Christ everywhere commits
himself and his undertaking to the care, love, assistance, and
faithfulness of the Father, whose especial grace was the original
thereof (Ps. 22:9–11, 19–20; Isa. 50:7–9). And in answer to this, the
Father promises him, as we shall see afterwards, to stand by him,
and to carry him through the whole of it; and that because it was
to be accomplished in such a nature as stood in need of help and
assistance. Wherefore, with respect to this work, he is said to be
אָמוֹן אֶצְלוֹ, 'before him,' as one whom he would take care of, and
stand by with love and faithfulness, in the prosecution of the work
which was in their mutual counsel, when he should be clothed with
that nature which stood in need of it.

Jesus Is the Father's Joy; the Father Is Christ's Delight

With respect to this he adds, וָאֶהְיֶה שַׁעֲשֻׁעִים יוֹם יוֹם;—'And was
delights every day.' There are ineffable mutual delights and joys in
and between the persons of the sacred Trinity, arising from that
infinite satisfaction and complacency which they have in each other

from their respective in-being, by the participation of the same nature; in which no small part of the blessedness of God consists. And by this word that peculiar delight which a father has in a son is expressed: יֶלֶד שַׁעֲשֻׁעִים; 'A pleasant child, a child of delights' (Jer. 31:20). But the delights here intended have respect to the works of God *ad extra*, as a fruit of that eternal satisfaction which arises from the counsels of God concerning the sons of men. This the next verse makes manifest, 'Rejoicing in the habitable part of his earth, and my delights with the sons of men;' for after he had declared the presence of Wisdom with God before the first creation (which is a notation of eternity), and its cooperation with him in that, he descends to manifest the especial design of God and Wisdom with respect to the children of men. And here such an undertaking on the part of the Son is intimated, as that the Father undertakes the care of him and his protection when he was to be humbled into the form of a servant; in the prospect of which he delighted in him continually.

So he expresses it in Isaiah 42:1–7 (רָצְתָה נַפְשִׁי, the same with שַׁעֲשׁוּעִים לוֹ יוֹם יוֹם. See Matt. 12:18, 17:5; Eph. 1:6):

> Behold my servant, whom I uphold; my elect, in whom my soul delights. I have put my Spirit upon him: he shall bring forth judgment to the Gentiles. He shall not cry, nor lift up, nor cause his voice to be heard in the street. A bruised reed shall he not break, and the smoking flax shall he not quench: he shall bring forth judgment to truth. He shall not fail nor be discouraged, till he have set judgment in the earth: and the isles shall wait for his law. Thus says God the LORD, he that created the heavens, and stretched them out; he that spread forth the earth, and that which comes out of it; he that gives breath to the people upon it, and spirit to them that walk therein: I the LORD have called thee in righteousness, and will hold thine hand, and will keep thee, and give thee for a covenant of the people, for a light of the Gentiles; to open the blind eyes, to bring out the prisoners from the prison, and them that sit in darkness out of the prisonhouse.

This is the delight of the Father, and [such is] his presence with the Son in his work, of which an eternal prospect is here presented. In answer to which the Son delights in him, whose delight he was, מְשַׂחֶקֶת לְפָנָיו בְּכָל־עֵת, 'rejoicing with exultation,' with all manner of expressions of joy; for the word properly signifies an outward expression of an inward delight—the natural overflowings of an abounding joy. And what is this delight of the Son in answering the delight of the Father in him, with respect to the work he had to do, the psalmist declares, 'Then said I, Lo, I come: in the volume of the book it is written of me, I delight to do thy will, O my God: yea, thy law is within my heart' (Ps. 40:7–8). This מְגִלַּת־סֵפֶר, this 'volume of the book,' which our apostle calls κεφαλίδι βιβλίου, 'the beginning' (or 'head') 'of the book' (Heb. 10:7), is no other but the counsel of God concerning the salvation of the elect by Jesus Christ, enrolled as it were in the book of life, and thence transcribed into the beginning of the book of truth, in the first promise given to Adam after the fall. This counsel being established between Father and Son, the Son with respect to this rejoices continually before God, on the account of that delight which he had to do and accomplish his will, and in our nature assumed to answer the law of mediation which was prescribed to him.

The Mutual Delight of the Father and the Son in the Work of Redemption

For, this being declared to be the mutual frame of God and his Wisdom towards one another, Wisdom proceeds to manifest with what respect towards outward things it was that they were so mutually affected: 'Rejoicing in the habitable part of his earth, and my delights were with the sons of men' (v. 31). That the things here spoken of were transacted in eternity, or before the creation, is evident in the context. The eternal counsels, therefore, and purposes of God and Wisdom, with respect to the sons of men, are here expressed. The Word was now 'foreordained,' even 'before the foundation of the world,' to the work of mediation and redemption (1 Pet. 1:20); and many of the sons of men were 'chosen in him' to grace and glory (Eph. 1:4); and the bringing of them to that glory to which they were chosen was committed to him, as the captain of their salvation. This work, and the contemplation of it, he now delights in, because of that eternity of divine glory which was to ensue thereon. And because he was designed of the Father to this, and the work which he had to accomplish was principally the work of the Father, or the fulfilling of his will and the making effectual of his grace, in which he sought his glory and not his own primarily (John 7:18), he speaks of him as a distinct person, and the sovereign Lord of the whole. He did it בְּתֵבֵל אַרְצוֹ, 'in the world of his earth.' And the same word which he used to express his frame towards God, מְשַׂחֶקֶת (v. 30), 'rejoicing, exulting,' he uses here in reference to his work, to intimate that it was on the same account that he is said to rejoice before the Father and in the habitable part of his earth; that is, on account of the work he had undertaken. So also he expresses his delight in the children of men, because of the concernment of the glory of God therein, by שַׁעֲשׁוּעִים, the same word whereby he declares the Father's delight in himself with respect to his work.

And these things cannot refer to the first creation, seeing they regard בְּנֵי אָדָם, 'the children of men,' the sons or posterity of him who was at first singly created. And these things are revealed for our consolation and the strengthening of our faith, whereunto they may be improved; for if there were such mutual delights between the Father and the Son in the counsel and contrivance of the work of our redemption and salvation, and if the Son so rejoiced in the prospect of his own undertaking to that end, we need not doubt but that he will powerfully and effectually accomplish it. For all the difficulties of it lay open and naked under his eye, yet he rejoiced in the thoughts of his engagement for their removal and conquest. He now saw the law of God established and fulfilled, the justice of God satisfied, his glory repaired, Satan under his feet, his works destroyed, sin put an end to, with all the confusion and misery which it brought into the world—all matters of everlasting joy. Here we place the first spring of the priesthood of Christ, the first actings of God towards man for his reparation. And it is expressed by the mutual delight of the Father and Son in the work and effect of it, to which the Son was designed; and this was intimate love, grace, complacency, and infinite wisdom. God foreseeing how the designed effect of love and grace in the recovery of mankind by the interposition of his Son would issue in his own eternal glory, was pleased therewith and rejoiced therein; and the Son, considering the object of his love and the peculiar glory set before him, delighted in the counsel of the Father. Wherefore the foundation of Christ's priesthood, herein designed, was in love, grace, and wisdom, though in its exercise it respect holiness and justice also.

Jews and Muslims Stumble Over Psalm 2

And this also seems to be expressed by the psalmist, 'I will declare the decree: the LORD has said to me, Thou art my Son; this day have I begotten thee' (Ps. 2:7). The direct sense and importance of these words has been declared in our Exposition on Hebrews 1:5–6; and the testimony that is given in them to the divine nature of Jesus Christ I have also formerly vindicated, *Vindiciae Evangelicae*; and I have in like manner elsewhere declared the perverse iniquity of some of the later Jewish masters, who would apply this psalm singly to David, without any respect to the Messiah. This Rashi confesses that they do on purpose to oppose the 'heretics' or Christians. But this is contrary to the conceptions and expositions of all their ancient doctors, and the express faith of their church whilst it continued; for from this place they constantly acknowledged that the Messiah was to be the Son of God—or rather, that the Son of God was to be the Messiah. Hence was that inquiry of the high priest, 'I adjure thee by the living God, that thou tell us whether thou be the Christ, the Son of God' (Matt. 26:63).

According to the faith of their church, he takes it for granted that 'the Christ' and 'the Son of God' were the same. The same confession on the same principle made Nathanael, 'Thou art the Son of God; thou art the King of Israel' (John 1:49). And Peter's confession, 'Thou art the Christ, the Son of the living God' (Matt. 16:16; John 6:69) was nothing but a due application of the faith of the Judaical church to the person of our Saviour; which was all that he then called for. 'Unless,' says he, 'you believe that I am he, you shall die in your sins.' And this faith of the church was principally built on this testimony, where God expressly calls the Messiah his Son, and that on the account of his eternal generation.

So Maimonides, Jarchi himself, and Kimchi, do all confess that their ancients interpreted this psalm of the Messiah. The words of Jarchi are plain: את הענין על מלך המשיח ולפי משמעו ולתשובת המינים נכון לפותרו על דוד עצמו רבותינו דרשו—'Our masters expounded this psalm' (or, 'the construction of it') 'concerning the King Messiah; but as the words sound, and that an answer may be returned to the heretics, it is expedient to interpret it of David himself.' His confession is plain, that their ancient doctors looked on this psalm as a prophecy of the Messiah, as is also expressly acknowledged by Maimonides and Kimchi in their expositions. But as to these words, ולתשובת המינים, 'and for an answer to the heretics,' the reader will not find them either in the edition of Basil or of Venice—that is, of the Bible with their Masoretical criticisms and rabbinical annotations—being expunged by such as had the oversight of those editions, or before razed out of the copies they made use of.

A great number of instances of this sort, to excellent advantage, are collected by the learned Dr. Pococke, *Notae Miscellan*, (cap. 8). And in the same place, that we go no farther for it, the same learned author gives us an account of the evasions invented by some of the Mohammedans against the force of this testimony, which yet they allow to respect Jesus Christ, whom they will by no means grant to be the Son of God. A prophet, if we please, he shall be; but that none may believe him to be the Son of God, the impostor himself laid in provision in the close of his Koran, in that summary of his Mussulman confession, 'He is one God, God eternal, who neither begets nor is begotten, and to whom none is equal.' The reasons of their infidelity are putid and ridiculous, as is commonly known, and their evasion of this testimony a violent escape: for they tell us the text is corrupted, and instead of 'My Son,' it should be 'My prophet;' and instead of 'I have begotten thee,' it should be 'I have cherished thee;' the former words in the Arabic language consisting of the same letters transposed, and the latter differing in one letter only; and the fancied allusion between or change of the words is not much more distant in the Hebrew. But it is ridiculous to suppose that the Jews have corrupted their own text, to the ruinous disadvantage of their own infidelity.

Enjedinus' Perverse Arguments

There is, therefore, an illustrious testimony in these words given to the eternal pre-existence of the Lord Christ in his divine nature before his incarnation; and this causes the adversaries of that sacred truth to turn themselves into all shapes to avoid the force of it. He with whom we have before concerned ourselves raises himself to that confidence as to deny that the things mentioned in this psalm had any direct accomplishment in Jesus Christ; and his next attempt is to prove that these words, 'They pierced my hands and my feet'

(Psalm 22:16), had no respect to him. To this purpose does he here discourse:

> If one insists on the words spoken here as being literal, they were never fulfilled in Jesus Christ. For it is clear that this does not agree with his divinity. For I deny that he had been born of Mary when these events happened historically. For who, I ask, were these people, these nations, these kings who rose up together against the now king Jesus? Certainly not Pilate, who was not even a king, nor Herod who had this name, but whom they deprived of his throne and royal rank. Neither of them were troublesome. They did not conspire against his reign, nor rally troups. No indeed, even though Pilate heard him say he was a king, he was prepared to release and dismiss him. And Herod did not rage against him, but looked down on him, and sent him away uninjured since he had that in his power. In John 18:35, Pilate admits, 'It was your people and priests who handed you over to me.' Therefore, it was the Jews alone who were the enemies of Jesus, and they did not form a plan against him; but when the desired goal was achieved, the opposite of this is here recounted. In summary, since the bull has charged, such great pursuit, such great clash of arms and apparatus of war, as the words of this psalm indicate, were never used against Jesus. Besides, these kings and people say, 'Let us break their bonds,' etc. But Jesus did not govern the Jews or the Gentiles, nor throw them into chains, nor impose tribute, nor prescribe laws, which held them constricted and from which they longed to free themselves. For if these things are to be applied to the teaching about Jesus, they must be introduced in a spiritual and mystical sense.

Having elsewhere handled, expounded, and vindicated this testimony, I should not here have diverted to the consideration of this discourse, had it not been to give an instance of that extreme confidence which this sort of men betake themselves to when they are pressed with plain Scripture testimonies; for not any of the Jews themselves, who despise the application of this prophecy to Christ in the New Testament, do more perversely argue against his concernment therein than this man does. He tells us, in the entrance of his discourse on this psalm, that all the Hebrews, whose authority in the interpretation of the Scripture no sober man will despise, are against the application of this psalm to Christ. But as he is deceived if he thought that they all agree in denying this psalm to be a prophecy of the Messiah (for, as we have showed, the elder masters were of that mind), so he that shall be moved with the authority of the later doctors in the interpretation of those places of Scripture which concern the promised Messiah, that is, Jesus Christ, and yet pretend himself to be a Christian, will scarce retain the reputation of a sober person among such as are not stark mad. However, no Jew of them all can more perversely oppose the gospel than this man here does, as will appear in the examination of what he says.

First, that the things spoken in this psalm regard the Lord Christ with respect to his divine nature alone, or as absolutely considered, none ever affirmed or taught; for they all regard him as incarnate, or as he was to be incarnate, and as exalted, or as he was to be exalted to his kingly rule and throne. But yet some things here spoken are distinctly verified in his divine nature, some in his human, as I have elsewhere declared. In general, they all regard his person with respect to his kingly office. But what ensues in this author, namely, that these things belong none of them properly to Jesus Christ, is above the rate of ordinary confidence. All the apostles do not only jointly and with one accord apply the things here spoken to the Lord Jesus, but also give a clear exposition of the words, as a ground of that application — a thing seldom done by the sacred writers (Acts 4:24–8):

> They lifted up their voice to God with one accord, and said, Lord, thou art God, which hast made heaven, and earth, and the sea, and all that in them is: who by the mouth of thy servant David hast said, Why did the heathen rage and the people imagine vain things? The kings of the earth stood up, and the rulers were gathered together against the Lord, and against his Christ. For of a truth against thy holy child Jesus, whom thou hast anointed, both Herod, and Pontius Pilate, with the Gentiles, and the people of Israel, were gathered together, for to do whatsoever thy hand and thy counsel determined before to be done.

In their judgment, Herod and Pontius Pilate, with their adherents — as exercising supreme rule and power in and over that people, with respect to them on whom they depended, and whose authority they exerted, namely, the Romans, the great rulers over the world — were the 'kings' and 'rulers' intended in this psalm. And so also the גּוֹיִם, or 'heathen,' they took to be the 'Gentiles,' who adhered to Pilate in the execution of his Gentile power, and the לְאֻמִּים mentioned to be 'the people of Israel.' Let us, therefore, consider what this man excepts against the exposition and application of these words made by the apostles, and which they expressed as the solemn profession of their faith, and we shall quickly find that all his exceptions are miserably weak and sophistical. 'Pilate,' he says, 'was not a king.' But he acted regal power, the power of a supreme magistrate among them, and such are everywhere called kings in the Scripture. Besides, he acted the power of the great rulers of the world, who made use of kings as instruments of their rule; so that in and by him the power of the Gentile world was acted against Christ. Herod he grants to have been a king, who yet was inferior in power and jurisdiction to Pilate, and received what authority he had by delegation from the same monarch with Pilate himself.

Secondly, he denies that these or either of them opposed Christ as to his kingdom; for 'Pilate moved once for his delivery, and Herod rather scorned him than raged against his kingdom.' But this unbridled confidence would much better become a Jew than one professing himself to be a Christian. Did they not oppose the Lord Christ? Did they not rage against him? Who persecuted him? Who reviled him? Who apprehended him as a thief or murderer? Who mocked him, spit upon him, scourged him, crucified him, if not with their hands, yet with their power? Did they not oppose him as to his kingdom, who by all ways possible endeavoured to hinder all the ways and means whatsoever whereby it was erected and established? Certainly never had prophecy a more sensible accomplishment.

Thirdly, and for what he adds in reference to the Jews, that 'their counsels were not in vain against Christ, as those were that are here mentioned, but obtained their wished end,' I cannot see how it can be excused from a great outrage and excess of blasphemy. They did, indeed, whatever the hand and counsel of God determined before to be done; but that their own counsels were not vain, that they accomplished what they designed and aimed at, is the highest blasphemy to imagine. They took counsel against him as a seducer and a blasphemer; they designed to put an end to his work, that none ever should esteem him or believe in him as the Messiah, the

Saviour of the world, the Son of God. Was this counsel of theirs not in vain? Did they accomplish what they aimed at? Then say there is not a word of truth in the gospel or Christian religion.

Fourthly, for that 'concourse of people, consultations, and noise and preparation for war,' which though, as he says, 'mentioned in the text, he cannot find in the actings of men against the Lord Christ,' it is all an imagination of the same folly; for there is no mention of any such preparation for war in the text as he dreams of. Rage and consultation, with a resolution to oppose the spiritual rule of the Son of God, are indeed described, and were all actually made use of, originally against the person of Christ immediately, and afterwards against him in his gospel, with the professors and publishers of it.

Fifthly, he adds to this that: 'Christ ruled neither Jews nor Gentiles; that he made no laws, nor put any bonds upon them, that they might be said to break.' So answers Kimchi the testimony from Micah 5:2, where Christ is called the ruler of Israel. 'Answer them,' says he, לא משל בישראל אבל הם משלו בו—'that Jesus ruled not over Israel, but they ruled over him, and crucified him.' But notwithstanding all this petulancy, his enemies shall all of them one day know that God has made him both Lord and Christ; that he is a king and a lawgiver for ever; that he came to put the holy bands and chains of his laws on the world, which they in vain strive to reject and cast out of the earth, for he must reign until all his enemies are made his footstool. It is granted that in some of these words spiritual things are figuratively expressed, but their literal sense is that which the figure intends; so that no mystic or allegorical sense is here to be inquired after, it being the Lord Christ the Son of God, with respect to his kingly office, who is here treated of primarily and directly, however any of the concernments of his kingdom might be typed out in David; and he it is who says, 'I will declare the decree: the LORD has said to me, Thou art my Son, this day have I begotten thee.'

Eternal Transactions Between the Father and Son Confirmed

The foundation of this expression is laid in the divine and eternal filiation of the Son of God, as I have elsewhere evinced; but the thing directly expressed is spoken in reference to the manifestation of this in and after his incarnation. He that speaks the words is the

Son himself; and he is the person spoken to, as Psalm 110:1, 'The LORD said to my Lord,' in which the same eternal transaction between the Father and Son is declared. So here, 'The LORD,' that is the Father, 'has said to me.' How? By the way of an eternal statute, law, or decree. As he was the Son of God, so God declares to him that in the work he had to do he should be his Son, and he would be his Father, and make him his firstborn, higher than the kings of the earth. And therefore are these words applied several ways to the manifestation of his divine filiation. For instance, he was 'declared to be the Son of God with power, by the resurrection from the dead' (Rom. 1:4). And this very decree, 'Thou art my Son, this day have I begotten thee,' is used by our apostle to prove the priesthood of Christ, which was confirmed to him therein (Heb. 5:5); and this could no otherwise be but that God declared therein to him, that in the discharge of that office, as also of his kingdom and rule, he would manifest and declare him so to be. It appears, therefore, that there were eternal transactions between the Father and Son concerning the redemption of mankind by his interposition or mediation.

4

FEDERAL TRANSACTIONS
BETWEEN THE FATHER AND THE SON

Our next inquiry is after the nature of those eternal transactions which, in general, we have declared from the Scripture in our foregoing exercitation. And these were carried on *'per modum foederis,'* 'by way of covenant,' compact, and mutual agreement, between the Father and the Son; for although it should seem that because they are single acts of the same divine understanding and will, they cannot be properly federal, yet because those properties of the divine nature are acted distinctly in the distinct persons, they have in them the nature of a covenant. Besides, there is in them a supposition of the susception of our human nature into personal union with the Son. On the consideration of this he comes to have an absolute distinct interest, and to undertake for that which is his own work peculiarly. And therefore are those counsels of the will of God, wherein lies the foundation of the priesthood of Christ, expressly declared as a covenant in the Scripture; for there is in them a respect to various objects and various effects, disposed into a federal relation one to another. I shall therefore, in the first place, manifest that such a covenant there was between the Father and the Son, in order to the work of his mediation, called therefore the covenant of the Mediator or Redeemer; and afterwards I shall insist on that in it in particular which is the original of his priesthood.

Covenants Between God and Man

First, we must distinguish between the covenant that God made with men concerning Christ, and the covenant that he made with his Son concerning men. That God created man in and under the terms and law of a covenant, with a prescription of duties and promise of reward, is by all acknowledged. After the fall he entered into another covenant with mankind, which, from the principle, nature, and end of it, is commonly called the covenant of grace. This, under several forms of external administration, has continued ever since in force, and shall do so to the consummation of all things. And the nature of this covenant, as being among the principal concernments of religion, has been abundantly declared and explained by many. The consideration of it is not our present business. That the Lord Jesus Christ was the principal subject-matter of this covenant, the undertaker in it and surety of it, the Scriptures expressly declare: for the great promise of it was concerning him and his mediation, with the benefits that should redound to mankind thereby in grace and glory; and the preceptive part of it required obedience in and to him new and distinct from that which was exacted by the law of creation, although enwrapping all the commands thereof also. And he was the surety of it, in that he undertook to God whatever by the terms of the covenant was to be done for man, to accomplish it in his own person, and whatever was to be done in and by man, to effect it by his own Spirit and grace; that so the covenant on every side might be firm and stable, and the ends of it fulfilled. This is not that which at present we inquire into; but it is the personal compact that was between the Father and the Son before the world was, as it is revealed in the Scripture, that is to be declared.

Terms for Covenant

To clear things in our way, we must treat somewhat of the name and nature of a covenant in general. The Hebrews call a covenant בְּרִית, the Greeks συνθήκη, and the Latins 'fœdus;' the consideration of which words may be of some use, because of the original and most famous translations of the Scripture.

Latin—'Fœdus'

'Fœdus' some deduce 'a feriendo,' from 'striking.' And this was from the manner of making covenants, by the striking of the beast to be sacrificed in their confirmation; for all solemn covenants were always confirmed by sacrifice, especially between God and his people. Hence are they said to 'make a covenant with him by sacrifice' (Ps. 50:5), offering sacrifice in the solemn confirmation of it. And when God solemnly confirmed his covenant with Abraham, he did it by causing a token of his presence to pass between the pieces of the beasts provided for sacrifice (Gen. 15:17–18). So when he made a covenant with Noah, it was ratified by sacrifice (Gen. 8:20–22, 9:9–10). And to look backwards, it is not improbable but that, upon the giving of the first promise, and laying the foundation of the new covenant therein, Adam offered the beasts in sacrifice with whose skins he was clothed. And how the old covenant at Horeb was dedicated with the blood of sacrifices, our apostle declares (Heb. 9:18–20, from Exod. 24:5–8). And all this was to let us know that no covenant could ever be made between God and man, after the entrance of sin, but upon the account of that great sacrifice of our High Priest which by those others was represented. Hence is the phrase, 'fœdera ferire,' 'to strike a covenant':

> Cicero pro Coelio (or 'For Coelius'), 'Have I therefore cut off peace with Pyrrhus, so that every day you will strike treaties of shameful love?' 'Treaties', 'strike [as in strike a bargain]' and 'strike' have the same rise and occasion. And the Hebrews also express the making of a covenant by striking hands, though with respect to another ceremony. Some derive the word 'from a pig horribly cut;' for a hog was clean in the devil's sacrifices:- 'They were uniting (in) treaties by cutting pigs.' – Virgil, Aeneid, 8:641.

And hence was the ancient formula of ratifying covenants by the striking and therewith killing of a hog, mentioned by the Roman historian, 'If one first rebels by public resolution or by evil fraud, then you, Jupiter, so strike him, just as today I will strike this pig; and strike him so much more, as you more able and more powerful'

(Liv. 1:24); upon the pronouncing of which words he killed the hog with a stone. And there was the same intention among them who, in making a covenant, cut a beast in pieces, laying one equal part against another, and so passing between them; for they imprecated as it were upon themselves that they might be so destroyed and cut into pieces if they stood not to the terms of the covenant. See Jeremiah 34:18–20, where respect is had to the covenant made with the king of Babylon. But in the use and signification of this word we are not much concerned.

Greek—συνθήκη

The Greek word is συνθήκη, and so it is constantly used in all good authors for a solemn covenant between nations and persons. Only the translation of the LXX. takes no notice of it; for observing that בְּרִית, 'berith,' in the Hebrew was of a larger signification, applied to things of another nature than συνθήκη (denoting a precise compact or convention) could be extended to, they rendered it constantly by διαθήκη, whereof we must treat elsewhere. Genesis 14:13, they render בַּעֲלֵי בְרִית, 'covenanters,' by συνωμόται, 'confederati,' or 'conjurati,' 'confederates sworn together.' Wherefore of the word συνθήκη there is no use in this matter; and the nature of the thing intended must be inquired into.

Hebrew—בְּרִית

בְּרִית is largely and variously used in the Old Testament, nor are learned men agreed from what original it is derived. בָּרָא, and בָּרַה, and בָּרַר, are considered to this purpose.

Sometimes it intends no more but peace and agreement, although there were no compact or convention to that purpose: for this is the end of all covenants, which are of three sorts, as the Macedonian ambassador declared to the Romans; for either they are between the conqueror and the conquered, or between enemies in equal power, or between those who were never engaged in enmity. The end of all these sorts of covenants is mutual peace and security. Hence they are expressed by בְּרִית, 'a covenant.' So Job 5:23, עִם־אַבְנֵי הַשָּׂדֶה בְרִיתֶךָ—'Thy covenant shall be with the stones of the field.' Say we, 'Thy league shall be;' that is, 'Thou shalt have no hurt from them.' And, Hosea 2:18, a covenant is said to be made with the beasts of the field, and the fowls of heaven, and the creeping things of the earth. Security from damage by them, and their quiet use, is called a covenant metonymically and metaphorically, because peace and agreement are the end of covenants.

Secondly, synecdochically, the law written on the two tables of stone was called the covenant: 'He wrote upon the tables the words of the covenant, the ten commandments' (Exod. 34:28). Now, this law was purely preceptive, and an effect of sovereign authority, yet is it called a covenant. But this it is not absolutely in its own nature, seeing no mere precept, nor system of precepts as such, nor any mere promise, can be a covenant properly so called; but it was a principal part of God's covenant with the people, when accepted by them as the rule of their obedience, with respect to the promises wherewith it was accompanied. Hence the tables of stone whereon this law was written are called 'The tables of the covenant:'—אֶת־שְׁנֵי לֻחֹת הָאֲבָנִים לֻחוֹת הַבְּרִית—'The two tables of stone, the tables of the covenant' (Deut. 9:11). These tables were first made by God himself (Exod. 31:18), and given into the hands of Moses; and when they were broken, he was commanded פְּסָל; to effigiate them, or cut stones after their image, into their likeness, for the first were seen only by himself (Deut. 10:11; Exod. 34:1). And when they were broken, whereby their use and signification ceased, they were not kept as relics, though cut and written by the finger or divine power of God—which doubtless the superstition of succeeding ages would have attempted; but the true measure of the sacredness of any thing external is use by divine appointment. And also the ark was hence called 'the ark of the covenant,' and sometimes 'the covenant' itself, because the two tables of stone, the tables of the covenant, were in it (1 Kings 8:9).

So among the Grecians, the tables or rolls wherein covenants were written, engraven, or enrolled, were called συνθῆκαι. So Demosthenes, Κατὰ Ὀλυμπιοδ. κεφ. ιβ΄: Συγχωρῶ ἀνοιχθῆναι τὰς ἐνταυθοῖ ἐπὶ τοῦ δικαστηρίου·—'I require that the covenants may be opened here in the court,' or 'before the judgment-seat;' that is, the rolls wherein the agreement was written. And Aristot. Rhetor. lib. i.: Ὁποῖοι γὰρ ἄν τινες ὦσιν οἱ ἐπιγεγραμμένοι, ἢ φυλάστοντες, τούτοις αἱ συνθῆκαι πισταί εἰσι·—'Covenants are of the same credit with those that wrote and keep them;' that is, the writings wherein such conventions are contained. For covenants that were solemnly entered into between nations were engraven in brass, as the league and covenant made between the Romans and Jews in the days of Judas Maccabeus (1 Mac. 8:22); or in marble, as that of the Magnesians and Smyrnians, illustrated by the learned Selden; and other covenants were enrolled in parchment by public notaries.

Thirdly, an absolute promise is also called בְּרִית, 'a covenant,' the covenant of God: 'As for me, this is my covenant with them, says the LORD; My Spirit that is upon thee, and my words which I have put in thy mouth, shall not depart out of thy mouth' (Isa. 59:21). And God also calls his decree constitutive of the law of nature and its continuance his covenant, 'Thus says the LORD; If ye can break my covenant of the day, and my covenant of the night, that there should not be day and night in their season' (Jer. 33:20).

It is therefore certain that where God speaks of his covenant, we cannot conclude that whatever belongs to a perfect, complete covenant is therein intended. And they do but deceive themselves who, from the name of a covenant between God and man, do conclude always to the nature and conditions of it; for the word is used in great variety, and what is intended by it must be learned from the subject-matter treated of, seeing there is no precept or promise of God but may be so called.

COVENANT SIGNS

In the making of covenants between men, yea, in the covenant of God with men, besides that they were always conceived 'verbis expressis,' there was some sign and token added, for their confirmation. This was generally the slaying of some creature, and the dividing of it into parts, before mentioned. Hence 'sancire fœdus' and 'sanctio fœderis' are 'a sanguine,' from the blood shed in their confirmation. Of the slaying of a beast there is mention in all who have spoken of ancient covenants. So was it in that between the Romans and Albans, whose form is reported by Livy, as that whose tradition was of greatest antiquity among them. And there are likewise instances of the division of the slain beasts into two parts, like what we observed before concerning Abraham, and the princes of Judah in Jeremiah: Οἱ Μολοττοὶ ἐν τοῖς ὁρκωμοσίαις κατακόπτοντες εἰς μικρὰ τοὺς Βοῦς τὰς συνθήκας ἐποιούντο; 'The Molossians in their confederations cut oxen into small pieces, and so entered into covenants' (Herod.). And how these pieces or parts were disposed Livy declares: 'While the first part stood out on the right, the latter part was placed on the left-hand side of the road; between this divided sacrifice the armed forces were processed.' (lib. 39). And hence it is that כָּרַת, which signifies 'to cut' or 'divide,' is used in the Scripture absolutely for the making of a covenant, without any addition of בְּרִית (1 Sam. 20:16; 1 Kgs 8:9). And although such outward things did never belong to the essence of a covenant, yet were they useful significations of fidelity, intended and accepted in the performance of what was engaged in it; and therefore God himself never made a covenant with men but he always gave them a token and visible pledge thereof. And whosoever is interested in the covenant itself has thereby a right to and is obliged to the use of the sign or token, according to God's appointment.

COVENANT ESSENTIALS

An absolutely complete covenant is a voluntary convention, pact, or agreement, between distinct persons, about the ordering and disposal of things in their power, to their mutual concern and advantage.

Distinct Persons

Distinct persons are required to a covenant, for it is a mutual compact. As 'a mediator is not of one,' that is, there must be several parties, and those at variance, or there is no room for the interposition of a mediator, Galatians 3:20—so a covenant, properly so called, is not of one. In the large sense wherein בְּרִית is taken, a man's resolution in himself with respect to any especial end or purpose may be called his covenant, as Job 31:1, 'I made a covenant with my eyes.' And so God calls his purpose or decree concerning the orderly course of nature in the instance before given. But a covenant, properly so called, is the convention or agreement of two persons or more.

Not Coerced

This agreement must be voluntary and of choice upon the election of the terms convented about. Hence בְּרִית is by some derived from בָּרָא, which signifies 'to choose' or 'elect;' for such choice is the foundation of all solemn covenants. What is properly so is founded on a free election of the terms of it, upon due consideration and a right judgment made of them. Hence, when one people is broken in war or subdued by another, who prescribe terms to them, which they are forced as it were to accept for the present necessity, it is but an imperfect covenant, and, as things are in the world, not like to be firm or stable. So some legates answered in the senate of Rome when their people were subdued, 'You will have the kind of peace you desire; if good, (it will be) firm and stable, but if not then shortlived.'

Power to Fulfill

The matter of every righteous and complete covenant must be of things in the power of them who convent and agree about them; otherwise any, yea the most solemn compact, is vain and ineffectual. A son or daughter in their father's house, and under his care, making a vow or covenant for the disposal of themselves, can give no force to it, because they are not in their own power. Hence, when God invites and takes men into the covenant of grace, to which belongs a restipulation of faith and obedience, which are not absolutely in their own power, that the covenant may be firm and stable he takes upon himself to enable them thereunto; and the efficacy of his grace to that purpose is of the nature of the covenant. Hence, when men enter into any compact wherein one party takes on itself the performance of that which the other thinks to be, but is not, really in its power, there is *dolus malus* in it, which enervates and disannuls the covenant itself. And many such compacts were rescinded by the senate and people of Rome, which were made by their generals without their consent; as those with the Gauls who besieged the Capitol, and with the Samnites, at the *Furcæ Caudinæ*.

Mutual Satisfaction

Lastly, the end of a covenant is the disposal of the things about which the covenant is made to the mutual content and satisfaction of all persons concerned. Hence was the ancient form, 'That this and that people might be happy and prosperous.' If either party be absolutely and finally detrimented by it, it is no absolute, free, or voluntary covenant, but an agreement of a mixed nature, where the consent of one party is given only for the avoiding of a greater inconvenience. And these things we shall find of use in our progress.

INEQUALITY & SUBORDINATION IN COVENANTERS

As all these things concur in every equal compact, so there is an especial kind of covenant, depending solely on the personal undertakings and services of one party in order to the common ends of the covenant, or the mutual satisfaction of the covenanters. So it is in all agreements where any thing is distinctly and peculiarly required of one party. And such covenants have three things in them:

1. A proposal of service;
2. A promise of reward;
3. An acceptance of the proposal, with a restipulation of obedience out of respect to the reward.

And this indispensably introduces an inequality and subordination in the covenanters as to the common ends of the covenant, however on other accounts they may be equal; for he who prescribes the duties which are required in the covenant, and gives the promises of either assistance in them or a reward upon them, is therein and so far superior to him, or greater than he who observes his prescriptions and trusts to his promises. Of this nature is that divine transaction that was between the Father and Son about the redemption of mankind. There was in it a prescription of personal services, with a promise of reward; and all the other conditions, also, of a complete covenant before laid down are observed therein. And this we must inquire into, as that wherein does lie the foundation and original of the priesthood of Christ.

The Covenant between the Father and the Son

First, to a proper covenant it is required that it be made between distinct persons. Such have I elsewhere proved the Father and Son to be, and in this discourse I do take that fundamental principle of our profession as granted. That there were eternal transactions in general between those distinct persons, with respect to the salvation of mankind, has been evinced in the foregoing exercitation. That these were federal, or had in them the nature of a covenant, is now further to be manifested.

Subordination in the Covenant

And in general this is that which the Scripture intends, where God, that is the Father, is called by the Son his God, and where he says that he will be to him a God and a Father; for this expression of being a God to any one is declarative of a covenant, and is the word whereby God constantly declares his relation to any in a way of covenant (Jer. 31:33, 32:38; Hos. 2:23).

For God, declaring that he will be a God to any, engages himself to the exercise of his holy properties, which belong to him as God, in their behalf and for their good; and this is not without an engagement of obedience from them. Now, this declaration the Scripture abounds in: 'Thou hast said to the LORD, Thou art my Lord' (Psa. 16:2).

These are the words of the Son to the Father, as is evident from verses 9–11. 'My God, my God' (Psa. 22:1), 'I delight to do thy will, O my God' (Psa. 40:8), 'God, thy God, has anointed thee' (Psa. 45:7), 'He shall stand and feed in the strength of the LORD, in the majesty of the name of the LORD his God' (Mic. 5:4), 'I ascend to my Father and your Father, and to my God and your God' (John 20:17), 'I will make him a pillar in the temple of my God...and I will write upon him the name of my God, and the name of the city of my God' (Rev. 3:12). All which expressions argue both a covenant and a subordination therein.

And on this account it is that our Saviour says his Father is greater than he, John 14:28. This place, I confess, the ancients expound unanimously of the human nature only, to obviate the Arians, who ascribed to him a divine nature, but made, and absolutely in itself inferior to the nature of God. But the inferiority of the human nature to God or the Father is a thing so unquestionable as needed no declaration or solemn attestation, and the mention of it is no way suited to the design of the place. But our Saviour speaks with respect to the covenant engagement that was between the Father and himself as to the work which he had to do: for therein, as we shall further manifest, the Father was the prescriber, the promiser, and lawgiver; and the Son was the undertaker upon his prescription, law, and promises. He is, indeed, in respect of his divine personality, said to be 'God of God.' No more is intended hereby but that the person of the Son, as to his personality, was of the person of the Father, who communicated his nature and life to him by eternal generation. But the Father on that account is not said to be his God, or to be a God to him, which includes the acting of divine properties on his behalf, and a dependence on the other side on him who is so a God to him. And this has its sole foundation on that covenant and the execution of it which we are in the consideration of.

ACCORDING TO THEIR OWN COUNSEL

Again; the transactions before insisted on and declared are proposed to have been by the way of 'counsel,' for the accomplishment of the end designed in a covenant: תִּהְיֶה בֵּין שְׁנֵיהֶם וַעֲצַת שָׁלוֹם (Zech. 6:13). The counsel about peace-making between God and man was 'between them both;' that is, the two persons spoken of—namely, the Lord Jehovah, and he who was to be צֶמַח, 'The Branch.' And this was not spoken of him absolutely as he was a man, or was to be a man, for so there was not properly עֵצָה, or 'counsel,' between God and him; 'for who has known the mind of the Lord? or who has been his counsellor?' (Rom. 11:34). And, besides, the Son in his human nature was merely the servant of the Father to do his will (Isa. 42:1). But God takes this counsel with him as he was his eternal Wisdom, only with respect to his future incarnation; for therein he was to be both the 'Branch of the LORD' and 'the fruit of the earth' (Isa. 4:2). To this regard also is had in his name: 'He shall be called Wonderful, Counsellor' (Isa. 9:6); for these titles, with those that follow, do not absolutely denote properties of the divine nature, though they are such divine titles and attributes as cannot be ascribed to any but to him who is God; but there is in them a respect to the work which he had to do as he was to be a 'child born' and 'a son given' to us. And on the same account is he called 'The everlasting Father,' a name not proper to the person of the Son with mere respect to his personality. There is, therefore, a regard in it to the work he had to do, which was to be a father to all the elect of God. And therein also was he 'The Prince of Peace'—he who is the procurer and establisher of peace between God and mankind. On the same account God speaking of him, says that he is רֹעִי גֶּבֶר עֲמִיתִי —'My shepherd, and the man my fellow' (Zech. 13:7); such an one as with whom he had sweetened and rejoiced in secret counsel, as Psalm 55:14, according to what was before declared on Proverbs 8:30–31.

NOT NECESSARY TO GOD

Particularly, the will of the Father and Son concurred in this matter; which was necessary, that the covenant might be voluntary and of choice.

And the original of the whole is referred to the will of the Father constantly. Hence our Lord Jesus Christ on all occasions declares solemnly that he came to do the will of the Father: 'Lo, I come to do thy will, O God' (Psa. 40:6–8; Heb. 10:5–10); for in this agreement the part of the enjoiner, prescriber, and promiser, whose will in all things is to be attended to, is on the Father. And his will was naturally at a perfect liberty from engaging in that way of salvation which he accomplished by Christ. He was at liberty to have left all mankind under sin and the curse, as he did all the angels that fell; he was at liberty utterly to have destroyed the race of mankind that sprang from Adam in his fallen estate, either in the root of them, or in the branches when multiplied, as he almost did in the flood, and have created another stock or race of them to his glory. And hence the acting of his will herein is expressed by grace—which is free, or it is not grace—and is said to proceed from love acting by choice; all arguing the highest liberty in the will of the Father (John 3:16; Eph. 1:6).

And the same is further evidenced by the exercise of his authority, both in the commission and commands that he gave to the Son, as incarnate, for the discharge of the work that he had undertaken; for none puts forth his authority but voluntarily, or by and according to his own will. Now, he both sent the Son, and sealed him, and gave him commands; which are all acts of choice and liberty, proceeding from sovereignty. Let none, then, once imagine that this work of entering into covenant about the salvation of mankind was any way necessary to God, or that it was required by virtue of any of the essential properties of his nature, so that he must have done against them in doing otherwise. God was herein absolutely free, as he was also in his making of all things out of nothing. He could have left it undone without the least disadvantage to his essential glory or contrariety to his holy nature. Whatever, therefore, we may afterwards assert concerning the necessity of satisfaction to be given to his justice, upon the supposition of this covenant, yet the entering into this covenant, and consequently all that ensued thereon, is absolutely resolved into the mere will and grace of God.

AN ACT OF PERFECT LIBERTY FOR THE SON

The will of the Son also was distinct herein. In his divine nature and will he undertook voluntarily for the work of his person when the human nature should be united thereunto, which he determined to assume; for what is spoken of the second person is spoken with respect to his purpose to assume our nature, for the obedience whereof, in all that was to be done upon it or by it, he undertook. This the Scripture fully declares, and that for a double end. First, to demonstrate that the things which he underwent in his human nature were just and equal, inasmuch as himself whose it was voluntarily consented to this. Secondly, to manifest that those very acts which he had in command from his Father were no less the acts of his own will. Wherefore, as it is said that the Father loved us, and gave his Son to die for us; so also it is said that the Son loved us, and gave himself for us, and washed us in his own blood. These things proceeded from and were founded in the will of the Son of God; and it was an act of perfect liberty in him to engage into his peculiar concernments in this covenant. What he did, he did by choice, in a way of condescension and love. And this his voluntary susception of the discharge of what he was to perform, according to the nature and terms of this covenant, was the ground of the authoritative mission, sealing, and commanding, of the Father towards him. See Psalm 60:7–8; Hebrews 10:5; John 10:17–18. And whatever is expressed in the Scripture concerning the will of the human nature of Christ, as it was engaged in and bent upon its work, it is but a representation of the will of the Son of God when he engaged into this work from eternity. So then he freely undertook to do and suffer whatever on his part was required; and therein owns himself the servant of the Father, because he would obey his will and serve his purposes in the nature which he would assume for that end (Isa. 42:1, 6, 49:8–9; Zech. 13:7); and therein acknowledges him to be his Lord (Psa. 16:2), to whom he owed all homage and obedience: for this mind was in him, that whereas he was in the form of God, he humbled himself to this work (Phil. 2:5–8), and by his own voluntary consent was engaged therein. Whereas, therefore, he had a sovereign and absolute power over his own human nature when assumed, whatever he submitted to, it was no injury to him, nor injustice in God to lay it on him.

ONE WILL ACTS DISTINCTLY IN THE FATHER AND THE SON

But this sacred truth must be cleared from an objection to which it seems obnoxious, before we do proceed. 'The will is a natural property, and therefore in the divine essence it is but one. The Father, Son, and Spirit, have not distinct wills. They are one God, and God's will is one, as being an essential property of his nature; and therefore are there two wills in the one person of Christ, whereas there is but one will in the three persons of the Trinity. How, then, can it be said that the will of the Father and the will of the Son did concur distinctly in the making of this covenant?'

This difficulty may be solved from what has been already declared; for such is the distinction of the persons in the unity of the divine essence, as that they act in natural and essential acts reciprocally one towards another—namely, in understanding, love, and the like; they know and mutually love each other. And as they subsist distinctly, so they also act distinctly in those works which are of external operation. And whereas all these acts and operations, whether reciprocal or external, are either with a will or from a freedom of will and choice, the will of God in each person, as to the peculiar acts ascribed to him, is his will therein peculiarly and eminently, though not exclusively to the other persons, by reason of their mutual in-being. The will of God as to the peculiar actings of the Father in this matter is the will of the Father, and the will of God with regard to the peculiar actings of the Son is the will of the Son; not by a distinction of sundry wills, but by the distinct application of the same will to its distinct acts in the persons of the Father and the Son. And in this respect the covenant whereof we treat differs from a pure decree; for from these distinct actings of the will of God in the Father and the Son there does arise a new habitude or relation, which is not natural or necessary to them, but freely taken on them. And by virtue of this were all believers saved from the foundation of the world, upon the account of the interposition of the Son of God antecedently to his exhibition in the flesh; for hence was he esteemed to have done and suffered what he had undertaken so to do, and which, through faith, was imputed to them that did believe.

THEY HAVE POWER TO FULFILL THE COVENANT

Moreover, a covenant must be about the disposal of things in the power of them that enter into it, otherwise it is null or fraudulent. And thus things may be two ways. First, absolutely; secondly, by virtue of some condition or something in the nature of the covenant itself.

1. Things are absolutely in the power of persons, when they are completely at their disposal antecedently to the consideration of any covenant or agreement about them; as in the covenant of marriage, where the several persons engaging are *sui juris*—they have an absolute power in themselves to dispose of their own persons with respect to the ends of marriage. So it is in all covenants. When the things to be disposed of according to the limitations of the covenant are lawful and good antecedently to any agreement made about them, and

because they are in the power of the covenanters, they may be disposed of according to the terms of the compact. So was it in this covenant. To do good to mankind, to bring them to the enjoyment of himself, was absolutely in the power of the Father. And it was in the power of the Son to assume human nature, which becoming thereby peculiarly his own, he might dispose of it to what end he pleased, saving the union which ensued on its assumption, for this was indissoluble.

2. Again, some things are made lawful or good, or suited to the glory, honour, or satisfaction and complacency, of them that make the covenant, by virtue of somewhat arising in or from the covenant itself. And of this sort are most of the things that are disposed in the covenant between the Father and the Son under consideration. They become good and desirable, and suited to their glory and honour, not as considered absolutely and in themselves, but with respect to that order, dependence, and mutual relation, that they are cast into by and in the covenant.

Such was the penal suffering of the human nature of Christ under the sentence and curse of the law. This in itself absolutely considered, without respect to the ends of the covenant, would neither have been good in itself, nor have had any tendency to the glory of God; for what excellency of the nature of God could have been demonstrated in the penal sufferings of one absolutely and in all respects innocent? Nay, it was utterly impossible that an innocent person, considered absolutely as such, should suffer penally under the sentence and curse of the law; for the law denounces punishment to no such person. Guilt and punishment are related; and where the one is not, real, or supposed, or imputed, the other cannot be. But now, in the terms of this covenant, leading to the limitations and use of these sufferings, they are made good, and tend to the glory of God, as we shall see. So the pardoning and saving of sinners absolutely could have had no tendency to the glory of God; for what evidence of righteousness would there have been therein, that the great Ruler of all the world should pass by the offenses of men without animadverting upon them? What justice would have appeared, or what demonstration of the holiness of the nature of God would there have been therein? Besides, it was impossible, seeing it is the judgment of God that they who commit sin are worthy of death. But, as we shall see, through the terms and conditions of this covenant, this is rendered righteous, holy, and good, and eminently conducing to the glory of God.

THE MATTER OF THE COVENANT—TO SAVE SINNERS

The matter of this covenant, or the things and ends about which and for which it was entered into, are next to be considered. These are the things which, as we observed before, are to be disposed of to the honour, and as it were mutual advantage, of them that make the covenant. And the matter of this covenant in general is the saving of sinners, in and by ways and means suited to the manifestation of the glory of God. So it is compendiously expressed where the execution of it is declared, 'God so loved the world, that he gave his only-begotten Son, that whosoever believes in him should not perish, but have everlasting life' (John 3:16).

And upon the coming of the Son into the world he was called Jesus, because he was to 'save his people from their sins' (Matt. 1:21); even Jesus the deliverer, who saves us from the wrath to come (1 Thess. 1:10). To declare this design of God, or his will and purpose in and by Jesus Christ to save his elect from sin and death, to bring his many sons to glory, or the full enjoyment of himself to eternity, is the principal design of the whole Scripture, and to which the whole revelation of God to men may be reduced. This was that on the prospect of which the Son or Wisdom of God rejoiced before him, and had his delights with the children of men before the foundation of the world (Prov. 8:30–31). Man having utterly lost himself by sin, coming short thereby of the glory of God, and being made obnoxious to everlasting destruction, the prevision of which was in order of nature antecedent to this covenant, as has been declared, the Father and Son do enter into a holy mutual agreement concerning the recovery and salvation of the elect in a way of grace. This we place as the matter of this covenant, the thing contracted and agreed about. The distinction of the parts of it into persons and things, the order and respect in it of one thing to another, are not of our present consideration; the explanation of them belongs to the covenant of grace which God is pleased to enter into with believers by Jesus Christ. But this was that in

THE PRIESTHOOD OF CHRIST

general that was to be disposed of to the mutual complacency and satisfaction of Father and Son.

THE END OF THE COVENANT—GOD'S GLORY

The end of these things, both of the covenant and the disposition of all things made thereby, was the especial glory both of the one and the other.

God does all things for himself. He can have no ultimate end in any thing but himself alone, unless there should be any thing better than himself or above himself. But yet in himself he is not capable of any accession of glory by any thing that he intends or does. He is absolutely, infinitely, eternally perfect, in himself and all his glorious properties, so that nothing can be added to him. His end therefore must be, not the obtaining of glory to himself, but the manifestation of the glory that is in himself.

When the holy properties of his nature are exercised in external works, and are thereby expressed, declared, and made known, then is God glorified.

The end therefore in general of this covenant, which regulated the disposal of the whole matter of it, was the exercise, exaltation, and manifestation, of the glorious properties of the divine nature; other supreme end and ultimate it could have none, as has been declared. Now, such is the mutual respect of all the holy properties of God in their exercise, and such their oneness in the same divine being, that if any one of them be exerted, manifested, and thereby glorified, the residue of them must be therein and thereby glorified also, because that nature is glorified in which they are, and to which they do belong. But yet, in several particular works of God, his design is firstly, immediately, and directly, to exercise in a peculiarly eminent manner, and therein to advance and glorify, one or more of his glorious properties, and the rest consequentially in and by them. So in some of his works he does peculiarly glorify justice, in some mercy, in some his power. We may therefore, as to the end of this holy, eternal compact, consider what are those properties of the divine nature which were peculiarly engaged in it, and are peculiarly exerted in its execution, and were therefore designed to be exalted in a peculiar manner. Now these are three: wisdom, attended with sovereignty; justice, springing from holiness; grace, mercy, goodness, love, which are various denominations of the same divine excellency.

That this covenant sprang from these properties of the divine nature, that the execution of it is the work and effect of them all, and that it is designed to manifest and glorify them, or God in and by them, to eternity, the Scripture does fully declare.

Wisdom

The infinite, sovereign wisdom of God, even the Father, exerted itself:

1. In passing by the angels in their fallen condition, and fixing on the recovery of man (Heb. 2:16; 2 Pet. 2:4; Jude 6).
2. In the projection or provision of the way in general to bring about the salvation of man, by the interposition of his Son, with what he did and suffered in the pursuit of this (Acts 2:23, 4:28).
3. In the disposal of all things in that way in such a holy and glorious order, as that marks and footsteps of infinite divine wisdom should be imprinted on every part and passage of it (1 Cor. 1:23–31; Rom. 11:33–6; Eph. 3:10–11).

Justice

His justice, accompanied with or springing from holiness, gave as it were the especial determination to the way to be insisted on for the accomplishment of the end aimed at, and it was effectually exerted in the execution of it; for upon a supposition that God would pardon and save sinners, it was his eternal justice which required that it should be brought about by the sufferings of the Son, and it was itself expressed and exercised in those sufferings, as we shall afterwards more fully declare (Rom. 3:25–6, 8:3; Gal. 3:13; 2 Cor. 5:21).

Grace

Grace, love, goodness, or mercy, chiefly induced to the whole. And these the Scriptures most commonly cast the work upon, or resolve it into (See John 3:16–17; Rom. 5:8, 11:6; 1 Cor. 1:29–31; Eph. 1:5–7, 3:7–8).

In these things, in the exercise, manifestation, and exaltation, of these glorious excellencies of the divine nature, with their effects in and upon the obedience of angels and men, does consist that peculiar glory which God, even the Father, aims at in this covenant, and which supplies the place of that security or advantage which amongst men is intended in such compacts.

The Son Uniquely Honoured

There must also, moreover, be an especial and peculiar honour of the Son, the other party covenanting, intended therein; and was so accordingly, and is in like manner accomplished. And this was twofold:

First, what he had conjunctly with the Father, as he is of the same nature with him, 'over all, God blessed for ever;' for on this account the divine excellencies before mentioned belong to him, or are his, and in their exaltation is he exalted. But as his undertaking herein was peculiar, so he was to have a peculiar honour and glory thereby, not as God, but as the Mediator of the covenant of grace, which sprang from hence. For the accomplishment of the ends of this covenant, as we shall see, he parted for a season with the glory of his interest in those divine perfections, emptying himself, or making himself of no reputation (Phil. 2:5-9). And he was to have an illustrious recovery of the glory of his interest in them, when he was 'declared to be the Son of God with power, by the resurrection from the dead' (Rom. 1:4), when he was again glorified with the Father, with that glory which he had with him before the world was (John 17:5)—namely, that peculiar glory which he had and assumed upon his undertaking to be a Saviour and Redeemer to mankind, then when his delights were with the sons of men, and he rejoiced before the Father, and was his delight on that account.

And this, secondly, was attended with that peculiar glorious exaltation which in his human nature he received upon the accomplishment of the terms and conditions of this covenant. What this glory was, and wherein it does consist, I have manifested at large in the Exposition on Hebrews 1:3 (See Isa. 53:12; Ps. 110:1, 6, 2:8-9; Zech. 9:10; Ps. 72:8; Rom. 14:11; Isa. 45:23; Matt. 28:18; Phil. 2:10; Heb. 12:2, etc.).

PROMISES OF REWARD

The manner how these things were to be accomplished—that is, the condition and limitation of this covenant, as it had respect to a prescription of personal obedience and promises of reward—is lastly to be considered; for herein lies the occasion and spring of the priesthood of Christ, which we are inquiring after. And this sort of covenants has most affinity to those relations which are constituted by the law of nature; for every natural relation, such as that of father and children, of man and wife, contains in it a covenant with respect to personal services and rewards. Now, things were so disposed in this covenant, that on the account of bringing sinners to obedience and glory, to the honour of God the Father, and of the peculiar and especial honour or glory that was proposed to himself, he, the Son, should do and undergo in his own person all and every thing which, in the wisdom, righteousness, holiness, and grace of God, was requisite or necessary to that end, provided that the presence and assistance of the Father were with him, and that he accepted of him and his works.

I shall a little invert the order of these things, that I may not have occasion to return again to them after we are engaged in our more peculiar design.

We may therefore, in the first place, consider the promises that in this compact or covenant were made to the Son upon his undertaking this work, although they more naturally depend on the prescription of duty and work made to him. But we may consider them as encouragements to the susception of the work. And these promises were of two sorts: such as concerned his person; such as concerned the prosperity of the work which he undertook. Those also which concerned his person immediately were of two sorts: 1. Such as concerned his assistance in his work; 2. Such as concerned his acceptance and glory after his work.

About the Son's Person

The person of the Son of God, not absolutely considered, but with respect to his future incarnation, is a proper object of divine promises; and so was he now considered, even as an undertaker for

139

the execution and establishment of this covenant, or as he became the minister of God to confirm the truth of the promises made afterwards to the fathers (Rom. 15:8).

And herein he had promises as to his assistance. The work he undertook to accomplish, as it was great and glorious, so also it was difficult and arduous. It is known from the gospel what he did and what he suffered—what straits, perplexities, and agonies of soul, he was reduced to in his work. All this he foresaw in his first engagement, and thereon by his Spirit foretold what should befall him (Ps. 22, Isa. 53; 1 Pet. 1:11). Whatever opposition hell and the world—which were to prevail to the bruising of his heel—could make against the Son of God acting in the frail nature of man, he was to encounter withal; whatever the law and the curse of it could bring on offenders, he was to undergo it. Hence in that nature he stood in need of the presence of God with him and of his divine assistance. This, therefore, was promised to him; in respect whereunto he placed his trust and confidence in God, even the Father, and called upon him in all his distresses (See Isa. 42:4, 6; Ps. 16:10–11, 22:1–31, 89:28; Isa. 50:5–9). This God promised him, and gave him that assurance of, which at all times he might safely trust to—namely, that he would not leave him under his troubles, but stand by and assist him to the utmost of what had a consistency with the design itself whose execution he had undertaken.

Promises were given to him concerning his exaltation, his kingdom, and power, with all that glory which was to ensue upon the accomplishment of his work (See Isa. 53:12; Ps. 110:1, 6, 2:8–9; Zech. 9:10; Ps. 72:8; Dan. 7:14; Rom. 14:11; Isa. 45:23; Phil. 2:10). And these promises the Lord Christ had a constant eye to in his whole work; and upon the accomplishment of it, made his request, and expected that they should be made good and fulfilled—as well he might, being made to him and confirmed with the 'oath of God' (Luke 24:26; John 17:5; Heb. 12:2). And these are an essential part of the covenant that he was engaged by.

About the Prosperity of the Son's Work

The second sort of promises made to him are such as concern his work, and the acceptance of it with God. By them was he assured that the children whom he undertook for should be delivered and saved, should be made partakers of grace and glory (See Heb. 2:9–11, etc., and our Exposition thereon). And this is that which gives the nature of merit to the obedience and suffering of Christ. Merit is such an adjunct of obedience as whereon a reward is reckoned of debt. Now, there was in the nature of the things themselves a proportion between the obedience of Christ the mediator and the salvation of believers. But this is not the next foundation of merit, though it be an indispensable condition thereof; for there must not only be a proportion, but a relation also, between the things of which the one is the merit of the other. And the relation in this case is not natural or necessary, arising from the nature of the things themselves. This, therefore; arose from the compact or covenant that was between the Father and Son to this purpose, and the promises wherewith it was confirmed. Suppose, then, a proportion in distributive justice between the obedience of Christ and the salvation of believers (which wherein it does consist shall be declared afterwards); then add the respect and relation that they have one to another by virtue of this covenant, and in particular that our salvation is engaged by promise to Christ; and it gives us the true nature of his merit. Such promises were given him, and do belong to this covenant, the accomplishment of which he pleads on the discharge of his work (Isa. 53:10–11; Ps. 22:30–31; John 17:1, 4–6, 9, 12–17; Heb. 7:26; Isa. 49:5–9; Ps. 2:7; Acts 13:33).

PRESCRIPTIONS OF OBEDIENCE

The conditions required of, or prescriptions made to, the undertaker in this covenant, for the end mentioned, and under the promises directed to, do complete it. And these may be reduced to three heads.

He Should Take on Human Nature

That he should assume or take on him the nature of those whom, according to the terms of this covenant, he was to bring to God. This was prescribed to him (Heb. 2:9, 10:5); which, by an act of infinite grace and condescension, he complied withal (Phil. 2:6–8, Heb. 2:14). And therein, although he was with God, and was God, and made all things in the glory of the only-begotten Son of God, yet he was 'made flesh' (John 1:14). And this condescension, which was the foundation of all his obedience, gave the nature of merit and purchase to what he did. This he did upon the prescription of the Father; who is therefore said to 'send forth his Son, made of a woman' (Gal. 4:4); and to 'send forth his Son in the likeness of sinful flesh' (Rom. 8:3): in answer to which act of the will of the Father he says, 'Lo, I come to do thy will' (Heb. 10:7). And this assumption of our nature was indispensably necessary to the work which he had to do. He could no otherwise have exalted the glory of God in the salvation of sinners, nor been himself in our nature exalted to his mediatory kingdom, which are the principal ends of this covenant.

He Should Be the Father's Servant

That in this nature so assumed he should be the servant of the Father, and yield universal obedience to him, both according to the general law of God obliging all mankind, and according to the especial law of the church under which he was born and made, and according to the singular law of that compact or agreement which we have described (Isa. 42:1, 49:5; Phil. 2:7). He came to do, to answer and fulfill, the whole will of God, all that on any account was required of him. This he calls the 'commandment' of his Father, the commands which he received of him, which extend themselves to all the prescriptions of this covenant.

He Should Suffer for Sinners

That whereas God was highly incensed with and provoked against all and every one of those whom he was to save and bring to glory, they having all by sin come short thereof, and rendered themselves obnoxious to the law and its curse, he should, as the servant of the Father to the ends of this covenant, make an atonement for sin in and by our nature assumed, and answer the justice of God by suffering and undergoing what was due to them; without which it was not possible they should be delivered or saved, to the glory of God (Isa. 53:11–12). And as all the other terms of the covenant, so this in particular he undertook to make good, namely, that he would interpose himself between the law and sinners, by undergoing the penalty thereof, and between divine justice itself and sinners, to make atonement for them. And so are we come to the well-head or the fountain of salvation. Here lies the immediate sacred spring and fountain of the priesthood of Christ, and of the sacrifice of himself, which in the discharge of that office he offered to God.

A Sacrifice to Satisfy Divine Justice

Man having sinned, the justice of God, as the supreme Lord, Ruler, and Governor over all, was violated thereby, and his law broken and disannulled. Every sin personally added to the first sin, which was the sin of our nature in Adam, does so far partake of the nature thereof as to have the same consequents with respect to the justice and law of God. In one or both these ways all men had sinned and come short of the glory of God, or were apostatized from the end of their creation, without power, hope, or possibility in themselves for the retrieval thereof. Neither was there any way for our recovery, unless God were propitiated, his justice atoned, and his law repaired or fulfilled. This now was that which in this eternal covenant the Son of God, as he was to be incarnate, did undertake to perform. And this could no otherwise be done but by the obedience and suffering of the nature that had offended; whereby greater glory should redound to God, in the exaltation of the glorious properties of his nature, through their eminent and peculiar exercise, than dishonour could be reflected on him or his rule by sin committed in that nature. This was done by the death and blood-shedding of the Son of God under the sentence and curse of the law. To this, in this covenant, he voluntarily and of choice gave himself up to the will of God, to undergo the penalty due to sinners, according to the terms and for the ends of the law: for inasmuch as the sufferings of Christ were absolutely from his own will, the obedience of his will therein giving them virtue and efficacy; and seeing he did in them and by them interpose himself between God and sinners, to make atonement and reconciliation for them; and seeing that to this end he offered up himself to the will of God, to do and suffer whatever he required in justice and grace for the accomplishment of the ends of this compact and agreement; which having effected, he would persist to make effectual to those for whom he so undertook all the benefits of his undertaking, by a continual glorious interposition with God on their behalf; he so became the high priest of his people, and offered himself a sacrifice for them.

ACCORDING TO THE HEAVENLY TRANSCRIPT

For when God came to reveal this counsel of his will, this branch and part of the eternal compact between him and his Son, and to represent to the church what had been transacted within the veil, for their faith and edification, as also to give them some previous insight into the manner of the accomplishment of these his holy counsels, he did it by the institution of a priesthood and sacrifices, or a sacred office and sacred kind of worship, suited and adapted to be a resemblance of this heavenly transaction between the Father and the Son; for the priesthood and sacrifices of the law were not the original exemplar of these things, but a transcript and copy of what was done in heaven itself, in counsel, design, and covenant, as they were a type of what should be afterwards accomplished in the earth. Now, although the names of priests and sacrifices are first applied to the office mentioned under the law and their work, from whence they are traduced under the new testament and transferred to Jesus Christ, that we may learn thereby what God of old instructed his church in, yet the things themselves intended and signified by these names belong properly and firstly to Jesus Christ, upon the account of this his undertaking; and the very names of priests and sacrifices were but improperly ascribed to them who were so called, to be obscure representations of what was past, and types of what was to come.

INDISPENSABLY NECESSARY

The sum is, the Son of God, in infinite love, grace, and condescension, undertaking freely, in and of his own will, to interpose himself between the wrath of God and sinners, that they might be delivered from sin with all its consequents, and saved, to the glory of God, according to the terms of the covenant explained, his offering and giving up of himself to the will of God in suffering and dying, in answer to his holiness, righteousness, and law, was, in the revelation of this counsel of God to the church, represented by his institution of a sacred office of men, to offer up, by slaying and other rites of his own appointment, the best of other creatures, called by him a priesthood and sacrifices; these things in the first place belonging properly to the accomplishment of the forementioned holy undertaking in and by the person of that Son of God. And if it be inquired wherefore things were thus ordered in the wisdom and counsel of God, we answer, that, with respect to the holiness, righteousness, and veracity of God, it was absolutely and indispensably necessary that they should be so disposed; for on the supposition of the sin of man, and the grace of God to save them who had sinned, the interposition of the Son of God described on their behalf was indispensably necessary, as shall be proved in the ensuing Exercitation.

5

THE PRIESTHOOD OF CHRIST—ITS NECESSITY
ON THE SUPPOSITION OF SIN AND GRACE

It appears from the precedent discourse that the priesthood of Christ was founded in sundry free acts of the will of God. Into that, therefore, is it principally to be resolved. The actual appointing of him also to this office was a free act of the sovereign will and pleasure of God, which might not have been. The redeeming of man was no more necessary on the part of God than his creation. Howbeit on this supposition, that God, in his infinite grace and love, would save sinners by the interposition of his Son, there was something in the manner of it indispensable and necessary; and this was, that he should do it by undergoing the punishment that was due to them or their sins who should be saved, or offer himself a sacrifice to make atonement and reconciliation for them. This God did require; nor could it have been ordered otherwise, but that an inconsistency with the glory of his holiness, righteousness, and veracity, would have ensued thereon. The priesthood of the Son of God was necessary, not absolutely and in itself, but on the supposition of the law and entrance of sin, with the grace of God to save sinners.

This being a matter of great importance, and without a due

stating whereof the doctrine concerning the priesthood of Christ, or the nature and use of this office of his, cannot be rightly conceived or apprehended, I must somewhat largely insist upon it. And I shall do it the rather because the truth in this matter is strenuously opposed by the Socinians, and the defense of it deserted by some otherwise adhering to sound doctrine in the main of our cause: for I shall not mention them who in these things are not wise beyond the writings of two or three whom they admire; nor those who, being utter strangers to the true reasons and grounds of truth herein, do boldly and confidently vent their own imaginations, and that with the contempt of all who are not satisfied to be as ignorant as themselves.

THE NATURE OF RIGHTEOUSNESS

Whereas we assert the necessity of the priesthood of Christ to depend on the righteousness of God, it is requisite that some things should be premised concerning the nature of righteousness in general, and in particular of the righteousness of God. Aristotle divides justice into that which is universal and that which is particular; and he makes the former to be the same with virtue in general; only it has, as he supposes, a respect to others, and is not merely for itself (Ethic. lib. 5 cap. 1:2). Particular justice is either distributive or commutative; and in its exercise it consists in words or deeds. That justice which consists in words, respects either commands, and it is called equity; or promises and assertions, and is veracity or truth. And both these, even equity in his commands, and truth or faithfulness in his promises, are frequently in the Scripture called the 'righteousness of God' (See Ezra 9:15; Neh. 9:8; Ps. 31:1; Rom. 1:17, 3:21; 2 Tim. 4:8). And this is the righteousness of God which David and other holy men so often plead and appeal to, whilst in the meantime they plainly acknowledge that in the strictness of God's justice they could neither stand before him nor find acceptance with him (Ps. 130:3, 143:1–2). The righteousness which consists or is exercised in works or actions is either the righteousness of rule in general, or of judgment in particular. And this latter is either remunerative or corrective; and this also is either chastening or avenging. And all these are subordinate to distributive justice; for commutative has no place between God and man. 'Who has given first to him, that it should be recompensed to him again?'

And these distinctions are of use in the declaration of the various acceptations of the 'righteousness of God' in the Scripture. But their explication and further illustration is not at present necessary to us; for I shall take up with a more general consideration of the righteousness of God and distribution of it, to which whatever is ascribed to it in the Scripture may be reduced. Wherefore, the righteousness of God is taken two ways: first, absolutely in itself, as it is resident in the divine nature; secondly, with respect to its exercise, or the actings of God suitably to that holy property of his nature.

THE RIGHTEOUSNESS OF GOD IN ITSELF

In the first sense or acceptation it is nothing but the universal rectitude of the divine nature, whereby it is necessary to God to do all things rightly, justly, equally, answerably to his own wisdom, goodness, holiness, and right of dominion: 'The just LORD is in the midst thereof; he will not do iniquity: morning by morning does he bring his judgment to light' (Zeph. 3:5). I say it is the essential, natural readiness and disposition of the holy nature of God to do all things justly and decently, according to the rule of his wisdom and the nature of things, with their relation one to another. And this virtue of the divine nature, considered absolutely, is not πρὸς ἕτερον with respect to others, as all justice in men does, but is the infinite, essential rectitude of God in his being. Hence it does so preside in and over all the works of God, that there is none of them, though proceeding immediately from mercy and goodness on the one hand, or from severity or faithfulness on the other, but that God is said to be righteous therein, and they are all represented as acts of righteousness in God; and this not only because they are his acts and works who will do no evil, who can do none, but also because they proceed from and are suited to that holy, absolute, universal rectitude of his nature, wherein true righteousness does consist. So are we said to obtain faith 'through the righteousness of God' (2 Pet. 1:1) — the same with 'abundant mercy' (1 Pet. 1:3); 'My salvation shall be for ever, and my righteousness shall not be abolished' (Isa. 51:6); that is, 'my faithfulness.' See the description of it in general (Job 34:10–15). The absolute rectitude of the nature of God, acted in and by his sovereignty, is his righteousness (Rom. 9:8, 14–15).

God's Right to Rule by His Righteousness

For between the consideration of this righteousness of God and the actual exercise of it, which must respect somewhat without him, to be made by him, somewhat in his creatures, there must be interposed a consideration of the right of God, or that which we call 'jus dominii,' a right, power, and liberty of rule or government; for it is not enough that any one be righteous to enable him to act righteously in all that he does or may do with respect to others, but, moreover, he must have a right to act in such and those cases wherein he does so. And this right, which justice supposes, is or may be twofold: (a) supreme and absolute; (b) subordinate. For we speak of justice and right only with respect to public actings, or actings of rule, which belong to righteousness as it is distributive; for that which is commutative, and may have place in private transactions among private persons, we have here no consideration of. Now, for that which is subordinate, it is a right to distribute justice or things equal to others, according to the direction and by the authority of a superior: and this superior may be either real only, as is a law—in which sense the law of nature is a superior to all rulers on the earth, and the respective laws of nations to most; or personal also, which is that which is denied, where any one is acknowledged as a supreme governor. That this right has no place in God is evident. He has no greater whereby he may swear, and therefore swears by himself (Heb. 6:13).

The right, therefore, which God has to act his righteousness, or to act righteously towards others, is supreme and sovereign, arising naturally and necessarily from the relation of all things to himself; for hereby—namely, by their relation to him as his creatures— they are all placed in an universal, indispensable, and absolutely unchangeable dependence on him, according to their natures and capacities. The right of God to rule over us is wholly of another kind and nature than any thing is or can be among the sons of men, that which is paternal having the nearest resemblance of it, but it is not of the same kind; for it does not arise from the benefits we receive from him, nor has any respect to our consent, for he rules over the most against their wills, but depends merely on our relation to him as his creatures, with the nature, order, and condition of our existence, wherein we are placed by his sovereignty. This in him is unavoidably accompanied with a right to act towards us according to the counsel of his will and the rectitude of his nature. The state and condition, I say, of our being and end, with the relation which we have to him and to his other works, or the order wherein we are set and placed in the universe, being the product or effect of his power, wisdom, will, and goodness, he has an unchangeable, sovereign right to deal with us and act towards us according to the infinite, eternal rectitude of his nature. And as he has a right so to do, so he cannot do otherwise. Supposing the state and condition wherein we are made and placed, with the nature of our relation to and dependence on God, and God can act no otherwise towards us but according to what the essential rectitude of his nature does direct and require; which is the foundation of what we plead in the case before us concerning the necessity of the priesthood of Christ.

The Righteousness of God in Operation

Secondly, the righteousness of God may be considered with respect to its exercise, which is so frequently expressed in the Scripture, and whereon depends the rule and government of the world. This supposes the right of God before declared, as that right itself is no absolute but a relative property of God, supposing the creation of all things, in their nature, order, and mutual respects, according to his wisdom and by his power. On this supposition it follows naturally and necessarily, not as a new thing in God, but as a natural and necessary respect which his nature and being has to all creatures upon their production; for suppose the creation of all things, and it is as natural and essential to God to be the ruler of them and over them as it is to be God. Now, the exercise of the righteousness of God, in pursuit of his right of rule, is either absolute and antecedent, or respective and consequential. As it is absolute and acted antecedently to the consideration of our obedience or disobedience, so it is put forth and exercised in his laws and promises; for they are acts or effects of righteousness disposing things equally, according to their nature and the will of God. God's ways are equal. His justice in legislation is universal equity; for all things being created in order by divine wisdom, there arose from thence a τὸ πρέπον, a meetness and condecency, to which respect was had in God's legislation, whereby his law or the commandment became equal, holy, meet, just, and good. And whereas it was necessary that the law of God should be accompanied with promises and threatenings, the eternal rectitude of God's nature acting righteously in their execution or accomplishment is his truth. Hence truth and righteousness are in the Scripture frequently used to express the same thing.

The Administration of Divine Justice

Again, there is a respective righteousness in actions, which also is either of rule or of judgment. First, there is *'justitia regiminis,'* or the particular righteousness of actual rule. I do not place this as though it were absolutely consequential to that of legislation before mentioned; for take the righteousness of rule or government in its whole latitude, and it comprehends in it the righteousness of legislation also as a part thereof. For so it is the virtue or power of the nature of God, whereby he guides all his actions or works in disposing and governing of the things created by him, in their several kinds and orders, according to the rule of his own eternal rectitude and wisdom; for righteousness of government must consist in an attendance to and observation of some rule. Now, this in God is the absolute righteousness of his nature, with his natural right to rule over all, in conjunction with his infinitely wise and holy will, which is that to him which equity or law is to supreme rulers among men. And therefore God, in the exercise of this righteousness, sometimes resolves the faith and obedience of men into his sovereign right over all (Job 41:11, 33:12, 13, 34:12–15; Jer. 19:1–6; Isa. 45:9; Rom. 9:20, 11:32–3)—sometimes into the holiness of his nature (Zeph. 3:5; Ps. 47:8)—sometimes into the equity and equality of his ways and works themselves (Ezek. 18:25). But there is a particular exercise of this righteousness of rule which has respect to the law, any law given to men immediately by God, as confirmed with promises and threatenings. The ruling and disposing of the temporal and eternal states or conditions of men, according to the tenor and sentence of the law given to them, belongs to this. And as this is actually executed, it is called '*justitia judicialis*,' or the righteousness of God whereby he distributes rewards and punishments to his creatures according to their works. Hereof one part consists in the punishing of sin as it is a transgression of his law; and this is that wherein at present we are concerned, for we say that the righteousness of God, as he is the supreme ruler of the world, does require necessarily that sin be punished, or the transgression of that law which is the instrument of his rule be avenged.

Foundations of Divine Justice

The exercise of this righteousness in God presupposes sundry things:

1. The creation of all things, in their kind, order, state, and condition, by a free act of the will and power of God, regulated by his goodness and infinite wisdom: for our God does whatever he pleases; he works all things according to the counsel of his own will.

2. In particular, the creation of intelligent, rational creatures in a moral dependence on himself, capable of being ruled by a law, in order to his glory and their own blessedness. The being and nature of mankind, their rational constitution, their ability for obedience, their capacity of eternal blessedness or misery, depend all on a sovereign free act of the will of God.

3. The nature of the law given to these creatures, as the means and instrument of their moral, orderly dependence on God; of which the breach of that law would be a disturbance.

4. The eternal, natural, unchangeable right that God has to govern these creatures according to the tenor of that law which he has so appointed for the instrument of his rule. This is no less necessary to God than his being.

5. The sin of those creatures, which was destructive of all that order of things, which ensued on the creation and giving of the law. For it was so

    (a) Of the principal end of the creation, which could be no

other but the glory of God from the obedience of his creatures, preserving all things in the order and state wherein he had made and placed them;

(b) Of the dependence of the creature on God, which consisted in his moral obedience to him according to the law; and,

(c) It was introductory of a state of things utterly opposite to the universal rectitude of the nature of God. Only the right of God to rule the sinning creature to his own glory abode with him, because it belongs to him as God.

And this represents the state of things between God and the sinning creature; wherein we say, that upon a supposition of all these antecedaneous free acts, and of the necessary continuance of God's righteousness of rule and judgment, it was necessary that the sinning creature should be punished according to the sentence of the law. Only observe, that I say not that this righteousness of judgment, as to the punitive part or quality of it, is a peculiar righteousness in God, or an especial virtue in the divine nature, or an especial distinct righteousness, which the schoolmen generally incline to; for it is only the universal rectitude of the nature of God, sometimes called his righteousness, sometimes his holiness, sometimes his purity, exercising itself not absolutely, but on the suppositions before laid down.

DIVINE RIGHTEOUSNESS DEFINES CHRIST'S PRIESTHOOD

On this state of things, on the necessary exercise of this righteousness of God upon the supposition mentioned, depend both the necessity and especial nature of the priesthood of Christ. Designed it was in grace, as we have before proved, on supposition that God would save sinners. But it was this justice that made it necessary, and determined its especial nature; for this was that which indispensably required the punishment of sin, and therefore was it necessary that he who would save sinners should undergo for them the punishment that was due to them. This was therefore to be done by the Son of God, in the interposition that he made with God on the behalf of sinners. He was to answer the justice of God for their sin. But because this could not be done by mere suffering or enduring punishment, which is a thing in its own nature indifferent, the will and obedience of Christ in the manner of undergoing it was also required. This made his priesthood necessary, whereby whilst he underwent the punishment due to our sins, he offered himself an acceptable sacrifice for their expiation. This is that, therefore, which is now distinctly proposed to confirmation, namely, that the justice or righteousness of God, as exercised in the rule and government of his rational creatures, did indispensably and necessarily require that sin committed should be punished, whence arises the especial nature of the priesthood of Christ. And this I shall do, first, by premising some observations making way to the true stating and explication of the truth; secondly, by relating the judgment or opinion of the Socinians, our professed adversaries in and about these things; thirdly, by producing the arguments and testimonies whereby the truth contended for is established, wherewithal the exceptions of the adversaries to them shall be removed out of the way.

THE ATTRIBUTES OF GOD IN OPERATION

There are some attributes of God which, as to their first exercise *ad extra*, require no object antecedently existing to their acting of themselves, much less objects qualified with any sort of conditions. Such are the wisdom and power of God, which do not find but produce the objects of their first actings *ad extra*. These, therefore, in their actings must needs be absolutely and every way free, being limited and directed only by the sovereign will and pleasure of God; for it was absolutely free to God whether he would act any thing outwardly or no, whether he would make a world or no, or of what kind. But on the supposition of the determination of his will so to act in producing things without himself, it could not be but he must of necessity, by the necessity of his own nature, act according to those properties, that is, infinitely powerfully and infinitely wisely. But herein were they no way limited by their first objects, for they were produced and had being given to them by themselves. But there are properties of the divine nature which cannot act according to their nature without a supposition of an antecedent object, and that qualified in such or such a manner. Such are his vindictive justice and his pardoning mercy; for if there be no sinners, none can be punished or pardoned. Yet are they not therefore to be esteemed only as free acts of the will of God; for not their existence in him, but their outward exercise only, depends on and is limited by the qualification of their objects. So then—

God Does not Punish Sin for His Mere Good Pleasure

The rule of God's acting from or by his vindictive justice is not a mere free act of his will, but the natural dominion and rule which he has over sinning creatures, in answer to the rectitude and holiness of his own nature; that is, he does not punish sin because he will do so merely, as he made the world because he would, and for his pleasure, but because he is just and righteous and holy in his rule, and can be no otherwise, because of the holiness and rectitude of his nature. Neither does he punish sin as he can, that is, to the utmost of his power, but as the rule of his government and the order of things in the universe, disposed to his glory, do require.

Divine Justice Required Penal Law

This justice exerted itself in one signal act antecedent to the sin of man, namely, in the prescription of a penal law; that is, in the annexing of the penalty of death to the transgression of the law. This God did not merely because he would do so, nor because he could do so, but because the order of all things, with respect to their dependence on himself as the supreme ruler of all, did so require. For had God only given men a law of the rule of their dependence on him and subjection to him, and not inseparably annexed a penalty to its transgression, it was possible that man by sin might have cast off all his moral dependence on God, and set himself at liberty from his rule, as it was some such thing that was aimed at in the first sin, whereby man foolishly hoped that he should make himself like to God; for having broke and disannulled the sole law of his dependence on God, what should he have had more to do with him? But this case was obviated by the justice of God, in predisposing the order of punishment to succeed in the room of the order of obedience, if that were broken. And that this provision should be made, the nature of God did require.

God Determines the Circumstances of Punishment

The justice of God required a punishment of sin as a punishment. To this do belong the way and degree, the time, season, and manner of it; but these things are not necessarily stated in the justice of God. The assignation and determination of them belong to his sovereign will and wisdom. So would things have been ordered in the execution of the sentence of the law on Adam, had it not been taken off by the interposition of the Mediator. Whatever, therefore, God does in this kind, when he hastens or defers deserved punishments, in the aggravation or diminution of penalties, it is all in the disposal of his holy will.

God Punishes Freely, yet Necessarily, but not Indifferently

Whereas, upon the suppositions mentioned, I do affirm that it is necessary, on the consideration of the nature of God and his natural right to govern his creatures, that sin should be punished, yet I say not that God punishes sin necessarily; which would express the manner of his operation, and not the reason of it. He does not punish sin as the sun gives out light and heat, or as the fire burns, or as heavy things tend downwards, by a necessity of nature. He does it freely, exerting his power by a free act of his will. For the necessity asserted does only exclude an antecedent indifferency, upon all the suppositions laid down. It denies that, on these respects, it is absolutely indifferent with God whether sin be punished or no. Such an indifferency, I say, is opposite to the nature, law, truth, and rule of God, and therefore such a necessity as excludes it must herein be asserted. It is not, then, indifferent with God whether sin, or the transgression of his law, be punished or no, and that because his justice requires that it should be punished; so far, therefore, it is necessary that so it should be. But herein is God a free agent, and acts freely in what he does, which is a necessary mode of all divine actings *ad extra*; for God does all things according to the counsel of his own will, and his will is the original of all freedom. But suppose the determination of his will, and the divine nature necessarily requires an acting suitable to itself. It is altogether free to God whether he will speak to any of his creatures or no: but supposing the determination of his will that he will so speak, it is absolutely necessary that he speak truly; for truth is an essential property of his nature, whence he is 'God that cannot lie.' It was absolutely free to God whether he would create this world or no: but on supposition that so he would do, he could not but create it omnipotently and infinitely wisely; for so his nature does require, because he is essentially omnipotent and infinitely wise. So there was no necessity absolute in the nature of God that he should punish sin: but on supposition that he would create man, and would permit him to sin, it was necessary that his 'sin should be avenged;' for this his righteousness and dominion over his creatures did require.

Justice Resists Pardon without Satisfaction

It is objected:

> That on the same suppositions it will be no less necessary that God should pardon sin than that he should punish it. For mercy is no less an essential property of his nature than justice; and if, on supposition of the proper object of justice and its qualification, it is necessary that it should be exercised—that is, that where sin is there also should be punishment—why then, on the supposition of the proper object of mercy and its qualification, is it not necessary that it also should be exercised—that is, that where there is sin and misery there should be pity and pardon? And whereas one of these must give place to the other, or else God can act nothing at all towards sinners, why may we not rather think that justice should yield as it were to mercy, and so all be pardoned, than that mercy should so far give place to justice as that all should be punished?'

ANSWER. We shall make it fully appear that God has, in infinite wisdom and grace, so ordered all things in this matter that no disadvantage does redound either to his justice or his mercy, but that both of them are gloriously exercised, manifested, and exerted. That this was done by the substitution of the Son of God in their stead, to answer divine justice, who were to be pardoned by mercy, and that it could be done no otherwise, is that which we are in the confirmation of. And those by whom this is denied can give

THE NECESSITY OF THE PRIESTHOOD OF CHRIST

no tolerable account why all are not condemned, seeing God is infinitely righteous, or all are not pardoned, seeing he is infinitely merciful. For what they fancy concerning impenitency will not relieve them; for if God can forgive sin without any satisfaction to his justice, he may forgive every sin, and will do so, because he is infinitely merciful; for what should hinder or stand in the way, if justice do not?

But there is not the same reason of the actual exercise of justice and mercy; for upon the entrance of sin, as it respects the rule of God, the first thing that respects it is justice, whose part it is to preserve all things in their dependence on God; which without the punishment of sin cannot be done. But God is not obliged to the exercise of mercy, nor does the forbearance of such an exercise any way intrench upon the holiness of his nature or the glory of his rule. It is true, mercy is no less an essential property of God than justice; but neither the law, nor the state and order of things wherein they were created, nor their dependence on God as the supreme governor of the whole creation, raises any natural respect or obligation between mercy and its object. God, therefore, can execute the punishment which his justice requires without the least impeachment of his mercy; for no act of justice is contrary to mercy. But absolutely to pardon where the interest of justice is to punish, is contrary to the nature of God.

It is denied that sin and misery do constitute the proper object of mercy. It is required that every thing contrary to the nature of God in sin and the sinner be taken out of the way, or there is no proper object for mercy. Such is the guilt of sin unsatisfied for. And moreover, faith and repentance are required to the same purpose. Socinus himself acknowledges that it is contrary to the nature of God to pardon impenitent sinners. These [faith and repentance] none can have but on the account of an antecedent reconciliation, as is evident in the fallen angels. And on these suppositions even mercy itself will be justly exercised, nor can it be otherwise.

ANSWERING SOCINIAN OBJECTIONS TO THE JUSTICE OF GOD

These things are premised to give a right understanding of the truth which we assert and contend for. It remains that we briefly represent what is the opinion which the Socinians advance in opposition to this foundation of the priesthood and sacrifice of Christ; for they are awake to their concerns herein, and there is none of them but in one place or other attempts an opposition to this justice of God, and the necessity of its exercise upon the supposition of sin, though the defense of it has been unhappily and causelessly by some deserted. The sum of what they all plead is,[1] that there is no such thing as justice in God, requiring that sin be punished; that the cause and fountain of punishment in God is anger, wrath, or fury; that these denote free acts of the will of God, which he may exercise or omit at his pleasure. If he punish sin, he does nothing against justice, nor if he omit so to do. In all these things he is absolutely free. Such a governor of his creatures do they fancy him to be! Hence it follows that there was no necessity, no just or cogent reason, why the punishment of our sin or the chastisement of our peace should be laid on Christ; for there was neither need nor possibility that any satisfaction should be made to the justice of God. Only he has freely determined to punish impenitent sinners, and as freely determined to pardon them that repent and believe the gospel. For this has he sent the Lord Christ to testify and declare to us; with respect to which he is called and to be esteemed our Saviour. The words of Socinus are express to this purpose, *De Christo Servatore*, lib. 1 cap. 2:

> If anyone asks how it happens that we who deserve eternal death come into eternal life, it is not an adequate answer to say since we have Christ as Saviour: but the myrrh of eternal supplication is according to his own indescribable benevolence as is our forgiveness from God. By his free will and decree we have deserved eternal death and he has given us in its place the prize of inward life, provided that we come to our senses and, rejecting all impiety, busy ourselves with an innocent and pure life thereafter. With respect to this if it is asked by which reasoning this was made known to us, when we do not ever see God, nor hear his speech, then such great divine generosity has provided

---

[1] The judgment of these men is expressed by Socinus, *Praelec. Theol.* cap. 16 lib. 1, *de Jesu Christo Servator.*, lib. 3 cap. 1; *Catech. Racov.*, cap. 8 quest. 19; *Ostorod. Institut.* cap. 31; *Volk. de Ver. Relig.* lib. 5 cap. 21; Crellius, *Lib. de Deo*, cap. 28; *Vindic. Socin. ad Grot.* cap. 1; *de Causis Mortis Christi*, cap. 16; *Smalcius adv. Franzium, Disputat.* Quarta; *Gitichius ad Lucium.* Woolzogen.; *Compend. Relig. Christianae*, sect, 48.

us with no uncertain faith and this ought to explain Jesus Christ
to us and strengthen us in many ways.

This is the substance of the persuasion of these men in this matter;
which how contradictory it is to the whole mystery and design of
the gospel, and contains a complete renunciation of the mediation
of Christ, will in our ensuing discourse be made to appear.

That, therefore, which we are engaged in the confirmation of may
be reduced to two heads:

First, that the justice of God, whereby he governs the world
and rules over all, is an essential property of the divine nature,
whence God is denominated 'just' or 'righteous;' and that on the
account of this it is necessary that sin should be punished, or not
be absolutely pardoned without respect to satisfaction given to
that justice of God.

Secondly, that hence it became necessary, that in the designation
of the Lord Jesus Christ, the Son of God, to his office of priesthood,
he should make his soul an offering for sin, to make an atonement
thereby for it; without which there could have been no remission,
because without it there could be no satisfaction given or
reconciliation made.

The Holy God Cannot But Punish Sin

Our first argument is taken from the consideration of the nature
of God and his holiness. Whatever is spoken of the purity and
holiness of God, with his hatred of and aversation from sin and
sinners on the account thereof, confirms our assertion; for we
intend no more thereby but that God, the great ruler of the world,
is of so holy a nature as that he cannot but hate and punish sin,
and that so to do belongs to his absolute perfection; for the purity
and holiness of God is nothing but the universal perfection of his
nature, which is accompanied with a displicency in and a hatred
of sin, whence he will punish it according to its desert. So is it
expressed, 'Thou art of purer eyes than to behold evil, and canst not
look on iniquity' (Hab. 1:13). Not to be able to look on or behold
iniquity, expresses the most inconceivable detestation of it. God
is טְהוֹר עֵינַיִם; which expresses the infinite holiness of his nature,

with what respect therein he has, and cannot but have, towards that which is perverse and evil. So when the prophet had made his inference from hence, namely, that he was holy, מֵרְאוֹת רָע, that any look or aspect unsuitable to this towards sin or evil is not to be expected from him, he adds expressly, תוּכָל וְהַבִּיט אֶל־עָמָל לֹא; and he cannot (that is, because of the holiness

God can do…every thing that is not contrary to himself; that is, to the essential properties of his nature. He can do nothing that is contrary to or inconsistent with his truth, holiness, or righteousness.

of his nature, which such an action would be contrary to) 'look on,' that is, pass by, spare, or connive at, 'iniquity.' For that is the rule of what God can do or cannot do. He can do every thing that is not contrary to himself; that is, to the essential properties of his nature. He can do nothing that is contrary to or inconsistent with his truth, holiness, or righteousness. Wherefore, whereas not to look on sin, not to behold it, do include in them, and by the negation of contrary acts express, the punishing of sin—that is, all sin, or sin as sin—and these are resolved into the nature of God, or his essential holiness, this testimony declares that the punishment of sin is thence necessary to God, as he is the holy, supreme governor of the world.

Hence this holiness of God is sometimes expressed by jealousy, or has jealousy joined with it, or accompanying it: 'He is an holy God; he is a jealous God: he will not forgive your transgressions nor your sins' (Josh. 24:19). And God makes mention of this his jealousy, when he would instruct men in his severity in the punishing of sin: for the nature of jealousy is not to spare (Exod. 20:5); nothing but the executing of vengeance will satisfy it (Prov. 6:34). And this is that which God intended in the revelation of himself which he made by the proclamation of his name before Moses, 'That will by no means clear' (or 'acquit') 'the guilty'—namely, for whom no atonement is made (Exod. 34:7).

And it is to instruct us herein that this holiness of God is expressed by fire, 'Our God is a consuming fire,'—'devouring fire' and 'everlasting burnings' (Heb. 12:29); and that 'a fiery stream' is said to proceed from him (Isa. 33:14), and that his throne is like 'a fiery flame' (Dan. 7:9–10). Now it is certain that God acts not in any external work by a mere and absolute necessity of nature, as fire burns. This, therefore, we are not taught by this representation of the holiness of God.

But if we may not learn thence, that as eventually fire will burn any combustible thing that is put into it, so the holiness of God requires that all sin be assuredly punished, we know not what to learn from it; and it is certainly not made use of merely for our amazement.

An account of the nature and holiness of God is given us to the same purpose

> For thou art not a God that has pleasure in wickedness: neither shall evil dwell with thee. The foolish shall not stand in thy sight: thou hatest all workers of iniquity. Thou shalt destroy them that speak lies: the LORD will abhor the bloody and deceitful man.
>
> Ps. 5:4–6

All the actings of God in the hatred and punishing of sin proceed from his nature; and what is natural to God is necessary. The negative expression; 'Thou art not a God that has pleasure' (v. 4), includes strongly the affirmative, expressed, 'Thou hatest all workers of iniquity' (v. 5).

And this he does because he is such a God as he is—that is, infinitely holy and righteous. And that hatred which is here ascribed to God contains two things in it:

1. A natural displicency; he cannot like it, he cannot approve it, he cannot but have an aversation from it.
2. A will of punishing it proceeding therefrom, and which is therefore necessary, because required by the nature of God.

Expressions are here multiplied, to manifest that sin is contrary to the nature of God, and that it is inconsistent therewith to pass it by unpunished. But if the punishing of sin depend upon a mere free act of the will of God, which might or might not be without any disadvantage to his nature, there is no reason why his holiness or righteousness should be made mention of, as those which induce him to this and indispensably require it. This is that which from this consideration is confirmed to us—namely, that such is the holiness of the nature of God, that he cannot pass by sin absolutely unpunished: for it is contrary to his holiness, and therefore he cannot do it; for he cannot deny himself.

God is the Supreme Judge and Governor

Again, God in the Scripture is proposed to us as the supreme judge of all, acting in rewards and punishments according to his own righteousness, or what the rectitude and holy properties of his own nature do require and make just, good, and holy. Although his kingdom, dominion, government, and rule, be supreme and absolute, yet he rules not as it were arbitrarily, without respect to any rule or law. That God should have any external rule or law in his government of the world, is absolutely and infinitely impossible; but his law and rule is the holiness and righteousness of his own nature, with respect to that order of all things which, in his will and wisdom, he has given and assigned to the whole creation. In respect to this he is said to do right as a ruler and a judge: 'Shall not the Judge of all the earth do right?' (Gen. 18:25). הֲשֹׁפֵט כָּל־הָאָרֶץ expresses that σχέσις of the divine nature, and that office as it were of God, which in this matter he represents himself by to us as vested withal. He is that supreme rector or governor of all the world, who uses and is to use righteousness in his government, or to govern righteously. Before such a one the just and the unjust cannot, ought not to be treated or dealt withal in the same manner; for although none be absolutely righteous in his sight, yet some may be so comparatively, with respect to some kind of guilt and guilty persons. According as the distance is between persons, so the righteousness of God requires that they be differently dealt withal.

But it is pleaded, 'That the intention of the expression here used is to plead for mercy, that the just should not be utterly destroyed with the unjust; and that we improve the testimony to a contrary end, namely, to prove that God must punish all sin.' But all that is hence aimed at is no more but that God is denominated just and righteous from that righteousness whereby he punishes sin; which therefore can be no free act of his will, but is an essential property of his nature. And if so, then does that righteousness of his require that sin be punished; for God does right as a judge, and a judge cannot acquit the guilty without injustice. And what an external law is to a subordinate judge, that God's righteousness and holiness is to him, as he is the judge of all the earth. And this appeal of Abraham to the righteousness of God as he is a judge is founded in a principle of the light of nature, and as such is repeated by our apostle (Rom. 3:5–6). And to this end is God, as the ruler of the world, represented as on a throne, executing justice and judgment; the introduction of which solemnity is of no use unless it instruct us that God governs the world as a righteous judge, and that justice requires that he inflict punishment on sinners: 'Justice and judgment are the habitation of thy throne' (Psalm 9:7, 16; 97:2–3; 89:14); that is, they always dwell and reside there, because God on his throne acts according to the justice and righteousness of his nature. And hence he is both denominated righteous, and declared so to be, in and by the punishment of sin (Rev. 16:5–6). See Romans 1:32; 2 Thessalonians 1:6; Exodus 9:27; which places I have to the same purpose pleaded and vindicated elsewhere.

Summary

The whole of what has been thus far pleaded may be reduced to the ensuing heads:

1. God is naturally and necessarily the supreme governor of his rational creatures with respect to their utmost end, which is his own glory. Upon the supposition of his being and theirs, an imagination to the contrary would imply all sorts of contradictions.

2. The law of obedience in and to such creatures arises naturally and necessarily from the nature of God and their own; for this original law is nothing but that respect which a finite, limited, dependent creature has to an absolute, infinitely wise, holy, and good Creator, suited to the principles of the nature which it is endued withal. Therefore it is indispensably necessary.

3. The annexing of a penalty to the transgression of this law was nothing but what the righteousness of God, as the supreme ruler of his creatures, did make necessary, as that without which the glory and holiness of his rule could not be preserved upon the entrance of sin.

4. The institution of punishment, answerable to the sanction of the law, is an act of justice in God, and necessary to him as the supreme governor of the universe.

ANSWERING SOCINIAN OBJECTIONS
TO THE RIGHTEOUSNESS OF GOD

And this is the first ground whereon the necessity of the satisfaction of Christ, and of the atonement he was to make as our high priest, is founded; for on supposition that God, in infinite grace and mercy, would eternally save sinners, the punishment due to their sins was to be undergone by him who interposed himself between them and the justice of God which required it. Now, as there are some who believe the satisfaction of Christ, on the abundant testimonies given to it in the Scripture, and yet resolve the reason of it into the infinite wisdom and sovereign pleasure of God only—with whom I do not now expressly deal, because although we differ about the way, we agree in the end—so the Socinians employ the chief of their strength in opposition to this righteousness of God, as knowing that if it be maintained, they are cast in their whole cause. I shall therefore remove all those objections which they principally fortify themselves with against the evidence of the truth asserted, and their exceptions also which they put in to the testimonies and arguments wherewith it is confirmed, and thereby put an end to this Exercitation.

Justice Is not Opposed to Mercy

He whom I shall first begin withal is Socinus himself, who in all these things laid that foundation which his followers have built upon. And as in almost all his other works he casually reflects on this righteousness of God, so in that, *De Jesu Christo Servatore*, he directly opposes it in two chapters at large (lib. 1 cap. 1, lib. 3 cap. 1). In the first place he designs to answer the arguments produced by his adversary for it, and in the latter he levies his objections against it. And in the first place, he proceeds solely on the supposition that the righteousness which we here plead for, and that mercy whereby God forgives sins, are contrary and opposite to one another, so that they cannot be properties of his nature, but only external acts of his will and power.

This is the foundation of his whole discourse in that place, which he asserts as a thing evident, but undertakes not at all to prove. But this supposition is openly false; for the justice and mercy of God may be considered either in themselves or with respect to their effects. In neither sense are they contrary or opposite to each other. For in themselves, being essential properties of the nature of God, as they must be, in that they are perfections of an intelligent Being, they differ not from the universal rectitude of his holy nature, but only add a various respect to external things; so that in themselves they are so far from being opposite, as that God is denominated just from the exercising the perfections of his nature in a way of justice, and merciful from a like exercise in a way of mercy. Absolutely, therefore, and essentially they are the same. Neither are their effects contrary or opposite to each other, only they are diverse, or not of the same kind; nor are the effects of the one contrary to the other. To punish, where punishment is deserved, is not contrary to mercy; but where punishment is not deserved there it is so, for then it is cruelty. And yet also in that case, the part of wrong, namely, in punishing without desert, is more opposite to justice itself than the cruel part is to mercy. And so is it where punishment exceeds guilt, or where proceedings are not according to an equal measure or standard. Nor is to spare through or by mercy contrary to justice; for if to spare and pardon be not for the good of the whole, for the preservation of order and the end of rule, it is not mercy to pardon or spare, but facility, remissness in government, or foolish pity. Secure those things in rule and government which justice takes care of and provides for, and then to spare in mercy is no way contrary to it. If these things be not provided for, to spare is not an act of mercy, but a defect in justice. And if these things were not so, it would be impossible that any one could be just and merciful also, yea, or do any act either of justice or mercy: for if he punish he is unmerciful, that is, wicked, if punishment be contrary to mercy; and if he spare he is not just, if sparing be opposite to justice. There is therefore nothing solid or sound, nothing but an outward appearance of reason, really contrary to the highest evidence of right reason indeed, in this sophism, which is laid as the foundation of the opposition made to the righteousness of God pleaded for.

The Righteousness of God Is not Twofold

On this false supposition Socinus grants a twofold righteousness in God with respect to sin and the punishment thereof—one which he perpetually uses whilst he destroys obstinate, impenitent, and contumacious sinners; the other whereby sometimes he punishes sinners according to his law, which yet are not obstinate, without any expectation of their repentance. And these several sorts of justice in God he confirms by sundry instances in the place before alleged. But it is plain that these things belong not to the question under debate; for they respect only the external manner and acts of punishing, and nothing is more fond than thence to feign various righteousnesses in God, or to conclude that therefore every transgression of the law does not require a just recompense of reward. Nor is it supposed that the justice of God does so exact the punishment of sin as that all sin must be immediately punished, in the same manner, especially as to temporal punishments, which respect this life. It belongs to the sovereign authority and infinite wisdom of God, as the governor of the world, so to dispose of the time, season, manner, and measure of the punishment due to sin, as may most conduce to the end aimed at in the whole. Thus he cuts off some in their entrance into a course of sin; others he 'endures with much longsuffering,' though 'vessels of wrath fitted to destruction' (Rom. 9:22). And this he does because he is willing so to do, or so it pleases him. But hence it follows not that finally he pardons or spares some, or punishes others, merely because he will.

That, therefore, whereby he deceives himself and others in this matter, is the exclusion of the satisfaction of Christ from having the place of any cause, or from being of any consideration, in the matter of pardoning sin; for this he expressly pleads and contends for in this place, as is evident from the words before cited, wherein he allows no more to Christ and his mediation but only that he came to declare that God would forgive us our sins. His whole proof, therefore, is but a begging of the thing in question. For the reason why God constantly punishes them who are obstinate in their sins and impenitent, is really because their sins deserve, in his justice and according to his law, so to be punished; and they are not spared, because they obstinately refuse the remedy or relief provided for them, in that they fulfill not the condition whereby they might be interested in the sufferings of Christ for sin. 'He that believes not shall be damned;' that is, shall personally be left to the justice of God and sentence of the law. [As to] those whom God spares and punishes not, it is not because their sins do not deserve punishment, or because the justice of God does not require that their sins should be punished, but because they are interested by faith in the satisfaction made by Christ when he underwent the punishment due to their sins by the will of God. And this is the rule of punishment and sparing, as they are final and decretory, according to a sentence never to be repealed nor altered. As for temporary punishments, whether they are corrective only or vindictive, their dispensation depends absolutely on the will and pleasure of God, who will so order and dispose them as that they may be subordinate to his final determination of the eternal condition of sinners. But this exclusion of the consideration of the interposition of Christ, in a way of suffering punishment for the procuring of the pardon of sin, is that which disturbs the whole harmony of what is taught us concerning the justice and mercy of God in the Scripture.

And the venom of this has so infected the minds of many, in these latter days, that they have even rejected the whole mystery of the gospel, and taken up with a religion which has more of Judaism, Mohammedanism, and Gentilism in it, than of Christianity. And indeed if it be so, that in the remission of sins there is no respect to the Lord Christ, but only that he has declared it, and showed the way whereby we may attain it, it must be acknowledged that there is no righteousness in God requiring the punishment of sin; as also, that it was merely from an act of the will and pleasure of God that by any sins we deserve everlasting punishment. For neither, then, was the sanction of the law, or the constitution of the penalty of its transgression, any act of justice in God, but of his will absolutely, which might not have been; and so, notwithstanding the state and condition wherein we were created, and our moral dependence on God, and God's government over us, man might have sinned, and sinned a thousand times, and broken the whole law, and yet have been no way liable to punishment—namely, if

God had so pleased; and it was as free to him to reward sin as to punish it. For if you allow any reason to the contrary from the nature and order of things themselves, and our relation to God as rational creatures, made meet to be subject to him in a way of moral obedience, you introduce a necessity of punishment from the righteousness of God, which is denied. And on this supposition, upon an alike act of the will of God, sin might have been made to be virtue, and obedience sin, and so it might have been the duty of man to have hated God, and to have opposed him to the uttermost of his power; for all the merely free acts of God's will might have been otherwise, and contrary to what they are. And if you say it could not be so in this case, because the nature of God and his righteousness required it should be otherwise, you grant all that is contended for. This false supposition made way for the twofold righteousness which Socinus feigns in God; and the instances which he gives in the confirmation of it respect only God's actual punishing of sin and sinners in this world, some sooner, and some after more forbearance, which none deny to proceed from his sovereign will and pleasure.

Wrath Is the Effect of Justice

The same author in the same place betakes himself to another plea, and will not allow that God does at all punish sin because he is just, or that his so doing is an act of justice in him; for so he speaks: 'When speaking about God, what is placed in opposition to his mercy is not called 'justice' but rather 'severity', or 'anger', or 'indignation', or 'fury', or 'vengeance', or expressed by some other similar term' (lib. 1 cap. 1 p. 1).

ANSWER. There are no things in God that are opposite or contrary one to another; and this sophism was before discovered. Nay, anger and fury, though they denote not any thing in God, but outward effects from that which is in him, are not opposed to mercy; for mercy being a virtue and a divine perfection, whatever is contrary to it is evil. Only, as they denote effects of justice, they are diverse from the outward effects of mercy. This therefore proves not that that, from whence it is that God punishes sin, is not justice; which must be proved, or this man's cause is lost. I do acknowledge that both אֶדֶק and δικαιοσύνη are variously used in the Scripture when applied to God, or do signify things of a distinct consideration; for upon the supposition of the rectitude of the divine nature in all things, righteousness may be variously exercised, yea, it is so in all that God does. Hence Socinus gives sundry instances where God is said to be righteous in acts of mercy and goodness, as very many may be given; for besides that the rectitude, equality, and holiness, which are in all his ways, are known from his righteousness in the declaration that he makes of himself and his dealings with men, in a way of goodness, kindness, benignity, and mercy, there is universally a supposition of his promise of grace in Jesus Christ, the accomplishment of which depends on his righteousness; which therefore may be pleaded, even when we pray for mercy, as it is often by David. For the faithfulness of God in fulfilling his promises, whether in the pardon of our sins or the rewarding of our obedience, is his righteousness in his word. Thence is he 'justified in his sayings' (Rom. 3:4); that is, he is declared righteous in the fulfilling his promises and threatenings. Yet this hinders not but that God is just when he 'takes vengeance;' that is, when he does so and in his so doing (Rom. 3:5).

That anger and fury are not properly in God all do acknowledge. The outward effects of the righteousness of God in the punishing of sin are so expressed, to declare the certainty and severity of his judgments. To say that God prescribes a penalty to the transgression of his law, and executes accordingly, merely in anger, wrath, or fury, is to ascribe that to him which ought not to be done to any wise law-maker or governor among men. Nor will it follow that because God is said to punish sin in anger and wrath, therefore he punishes sin only because he will, and not because he is just, or that his justice does not require that sin be punished. Yea, it thence follows that the justice of God is the cause of the punishment of sin; for to act in anger and fury any otherwise than as they are effects of justice is vicious and evil. God does not, therefore, punish sin because he is angry; but to show the severity of his justice, he makes an appearance of anger and wrath in punishing. These things belong to the outward manner, and not the inward principle of inflicting punishment.

Justice Does Reside in God

In the first chapter of his third book he again attempts an opposition to this righteousness of God. 'This justice,' says he, 'to which you altogether rush to give attention to, does not reside in God but is effected by his own will. For when God punishes sin, so that we call this work of his by some appropriate name, we then say he is employing justice.' Therefore it seems do we deal benignly with God; and what he does only in anger and fury we give it a worthy name, and say he does it in righteousness! But what shall we say when God himself ascribes his punishing of sin to his justice and judgment in governing the world? This he does plainly (Ps. 9:7–8, 50:6, 98:9; Rom. 1:32, 3:5). Shall he also be said to find out a worthy name for what he does, though he do it on such accounts as wherein the thing signified by that name is not concerned? It is a hard task, doubtless, to prove that God does not 'judge the world in righteousness.' But he has reason, as he supposes, for his assertion; for he adds:

> Because, however, this justice does not reside in God, it is especially able to be evident outside of him, because if it resided in God he would never be able to pardon even anyone's smallest transgression; for God never does nor is able to do that which is against his own character. By way of example, since wisdom and equity reside in God, he never does, nor is able to do anything foolish nor unfair.

So he. But he seems not to observe that herein he pleads our cause more forcibly than his own: for we say, that because this justice is a natural property of God, he can do nothing against it, and so cannot forgive any sin absolutely without respect to satisfaction made to that righteousness; and when this is done, to pardon and forgive sin is no way adverse or contrary to it. This whole difficulty is reconciled in the cross of Christ, and can be so no otherwise; for God set him forth to be a propitiation, εἰς ἔνδειξιν τῆς δικαιοσύνης (Rom. 3:25); which when it is done, as pardon is a fruit or effect of mercy, so it is consistent with the severity of justice (see 1 Cor. 5:21; Rom. 8:3; Gal. 3:13–14; Heb. 9:13–15). And the whole ensuing discourse of Socinus in that chapter may be reduced to these two heads:

1. A supposition that Christ did not nor could undergo the punishment due to our sins; which is to beg the matter in question, contrary to Scripture testimonies innumerable, many of which I have elsewhere vindicated from the exceptions of himself and his followers. For let this be granted, and all his discourse about the impossibility of pardoning any sin, upon the supposition of such a righteousness in God, falls to the ground. And if he will not grant it, yet may he not be allowed to make a supposition on the contrary to be the ground of his argument whereby he endeavours to overthrow it.

2. He confounds the habits of justice and mercy with the acts of them. Hence would he prove an inequality betwixt justice and mercy, because there is so between punishing and pardoning. And so also God declares that he delights in mercy, but is slow to anger. But actually to pardon is no way opposite to justice, where satisfaction is made; nor to punish [opposite] to mercy, where the law of obtaining an interest in that satisfaction is not observed. And all that God declares in the Scripture concerning his justice and mercy, with the exercise of them towards sinners, is grounded on the supposition of the interposition and satisfaction of Christ. Where that is not, as in the case of the angels which sinned, no mention is made of mercy, more or less, but only of judgment according to their desert.

In the Racovian Catechism

The author of the Racovian Catechism manages the same plea against the vindictive justice of God, and gathers the objections to a head, which Socinus more largely debated on (cap. 8. *De Morte Christi*). And although little be added therein to what I have already cited, yet it containing the substance of what they are able to plead in this cause, I shall take a view of it in the words of these catechists:

> These opponents wish to grant on mercy and justice of such a kind that we deny inherently belongs to God. For, as far as one considers mercy, it is not therefore so clearly part of his character as they perceive it to be; because if by his character God is not able utterly to punish any sin; and again if they

suppose that that justice is in God's character, God is never able to forgive sin. For God is never able to do anything which is against his character.

By way of example, since wisdom is part of God's character, he never does anything contrary to it – truly, if he does anything, he does everything wisely. Certainly, since it is evident that God forgives and punishes sins when he wishes, it is clear that the kind of mercy and justice, which they imagine, are not part of the character of God, but are effected by his will. This which they mark with the name of justice, they truly call the anger and fury of God. On the contrary, this justice is attributed to God in the Sciptures, when he forgives sins (1 John 1:9; Rom. 3:25–6).

And hereon they conclude that there was no need, nor can there be any use, of the satisfaction of Christ.

ANSWER. First, the design of this discourse is to prove that justice and mercy are not properties of the divine nature; for if they be, it cannot be denied but that the sufferings of Christ were necessary that sin might be pardoned. Now, herein we have against our adversaries the light of nature, and that not only as teaching us, by the conduct of right reason, that there is a singular perfection in these things, which must therefore be found in Him who is so the author of all goodness and limited perfections to others as to contain essentially and eminently all goodness and perfection in himself, but also it is not difficult to evince the actual consent of all mankind who acknowledge a Deity to this principle, that God is just and merciful, with that justice and mercy which have respect to the sins and offenses of men. There is, indeed, this difference betwixt them, that justice is ascribed to God properly, as a habit or a habitual perfection; mercy analogically and reductively, as an affection. And therefore mercy in God is not accompanied with that sympathy and condolency which are mixed with it in our human nature. But that natural goodness and benignity whence God is ready to relieve, whereof his sparing and pardoning are proper effects, are that mercy of God which he represents to us under the highest expressions of tenderness and compassion (see

Ps. 103:8–14). And in such declarations of himself he instructs us in what apprehensions we ought to have of his nature; which if it be not gracious and merciful, we are taught by him to err and mistake. So when God showed to Moses his glory, and made a declaration of himself by his name, he did it not by calling over the free acts of his will, or showing what he would or could do, if so be he pleased, but he described his nature to him by the essential properties of it, that the people might know who and what he was with whom they had to do (Exod. 34:6–7). And yet among them is that mercy reckoned which is exerted in the pardoning of iniquity, transgression, and sin. The same is to be said concerning the justice of God; for this vindictive justice is nothing but the absolute rectitude of the nature of God with respect to some outward objects, namely, sin and sinners. Had there, indeed, never been any sin or sinners, God could not in any outward acts have exercised either vindictive justice or sparing mercy; but yet he had been notwithstanding eternally just and merciful

And there is this difference between the justice and mercy of God on the one hand, and his power and wisdom on the other, that these latter, being absolute properties of the divine nature, without respect to any other thing, do constitute their own objects; so that in all the works of God he does not only not act against them, but he cannot act without them, for all that he does must necessarily be done with infinite power and wisdom. But for the other, they cannot outwardly exert or act themselves but towards objects antecedently qualified; whence it is enough that God neither does nor can do any thing against them. And this he cannot do; for, secondly, it is weakly pleaded that if God be merciful, he cannot punish any sin. For to punish sin absolutely is no way contrary to mercy. If it were, then every one who corrects or punishes any for sin must needs be unmerciful. Nor is it contrary to justice to pardon sin when satisfaction is made for it; without which God neither does nor can pardon any sin, and that for this reason, namely, that it is contrary to his justice so to do. Thirdly, whence God is said to pardon sin in his righteousness, or because he is righteous, has been declared before. His faithfulness in his promises with respect to the mediation of Jesus Christ is so called, which our adversaries cannot deny.

In the Writings of Crellius

Crellius in almost all his writings opposes this justice of God, ofttimes repeating the same things; which it were tedious to pursue—besides, I have long since answered all his principal arguments and objections, in my *Diatriba de Justitia Divina*. I shall therefore here only call one of his reasons to an account, whereby he would prove that there was no necessity for making any satisfaction to God for sin, because I find it to prevail among many who are less skilled in disputations of this nature. And this is that which he insists on (*Lib. de Deo*, cap. 3 *de Potestate Dei*). He lays down this as a principle: 'God has power to inflict punishment, and not to inflict it; but it is by no means repugnant to divine justice to pardon sins which he could justly punish.' He is treating in that place about the supreme dominion and free power of God. And to this he says it belongs to inflict punishment, or to spare and pardon. But he is herein evidently mistaken: for although he who is absolutely supreme over all may punish and spare, yet it belongs not to him as such so to do: for punishing and sparing are the acts of a governor or judge as such; and to God as such are they constantly ascribed in the Scripture (James 4:12; Ps. 9:8–9; Gen. 18:25; Ps. 50:6, 94:2; Heb. 12:23). Now, it is one thing what may be done by virtue of absolute sovereignty and dominion, setting aside the consideration of rule and government, and another what ought to be done by a righteous ruler or judge. And whereas he says it is not contrary to justice to spare one who might *de jure* be punished, if he means by 'a ruler may punish him by right,' no more but that he may do so and do him no wrong, were there no more in the case it might be true. But it is not thus at any time with sinners; for not only may God punish them and do them no wrong, but his own holiness and righteousness requires that they should be punished. And therefore the assertion, if accommodated to the cause in hand, must be this, 'It is no wrong to justice to spare them who ought to be punished;' which is manifestly false. And Crellius himself grants that there are sins and sinners which not only God may punish *de jure*, but that he ought so to do, and that it would be contrary to his justice not to punish them (*Adv. Grot.* ad cap. 1 p. 98):

Next, we do not deny that God's uprightness and justice sometimes move him to punish sins. Of course, as it is not only very consistent with his fairness, but also with what in divine decrees we are told what ought to be, they would not condone pardon to the kind of men who never come to their senses and who stubbornly perservere in their sins; especially if the sort of sin in which they persist breathes out conspicuous wickedness of mind, or open contempt of divine majesty; for if pardon is given to such men the majesty of the Supreme Ruler is diminished, and it cheapens his expansive law and his own glory, which is the particular goal of all his deeds.

What here he grants concerning some sins, we contend to be true concerning all. Neither do that justice, equity, and rule which require these sins of contumacy and impenitency to be punished, depend on a free decree or act of the will of God only, for then no sin of itself or in its own nature deserves punishment. And it implies a contradiction to say that it does so, and yet that it depends merely on the will of God. And in that book *De Deo* he has other conceptions to this purpose: 'It is somehow an honest reasoning, concerning which God cannot dispense justice rightly' (Cap. 23 p. 180); and 'To God it is unworthy and contumacious to dismiss sins with impunity' (p. 186); and 'Neither the holiness nor the majesty of God considers every conceivable situation when his commands are violated with impunity' (ch. 28). If it be thus with respect to some sins, it must not be because of sin, but only of some degrees of sin, if it be not so with all sin whatever. And who can believe that the nature of sin is not contrary to the holiness and majesty of God, but that some certain degrees only of it are so? And who shall give in that degree of sin when it becomes so inconsistent with God's holiness and majesty? It is said that this is stubbornness and impenitency. But whoever sins once against God will be impenitent therein, unless relieved by the grace of Jesus Christ, which supposes his satisfaction. And this is evident in the instance of the angels that sinned.

The defense which he makes of his former assertion, containing the substance of what remains of their plea against the necessity of the satisfaction of Christ, I shall particularly examine, and put an end to this exercitation. He therefore pleads:

Whether he punishes or does not punish, he administers injustice
to no one; accordingly, he is only driven by his own justice; for
punishment is not owed to the guilty but he owes it; and indeed
he owes it to those whose wrong to all overflows the most, and
who are absent in our distress. However, justice allows that he
enacts vengeance upon those who watch a matter, and not to
enact vengeance, and to forgive whatever pleases him the most.
For this is part of his own justice and lordly character.

ANSWER. 'Jus Dei,' δικαίωμα τοῦ Θεοῦ, 'the right of God,' in this
matter, is neither 'jus proprium,' which answers the right of every
private person, nor 'jus dominicum,' or the right of absolute
dominion, but the right of a ruler or supreme judge, to which
the things here ascribed to the right of God in this matter do not
belong, as we shall see. For whereas he says, first, 'That whether
he punish or do not punish, he does wrong to none,' it is granted
that no wrong is done to men; for, by reason of his sovereignty,
he can do them none. But where punishment is due to any sin, it
cannot be absolutely spared, without the wrong or impeachment
of that justice in whose nature it is to require its punishment. It is
not, then, properly said that if God should not punish sin he should
wrong any, for that he cannot do, do he what he will; but not to
punish sin is contrary to his own holiness and righteousness. And
for what he adds, secondly, 'That punishment is not due to the
offender, but that he owes his punishment to him against whom
the injury is done, who in this case is God;' I say, certainly no man
ever imagined that punishment is so due to the offender, or is so
far his right, as that he should be injured if he were not punished,
or that he might claim it as his right. Few offenders will pursue
such a right. And whereas it is said that the injury in sin is done to
God, it must be rightly understood; for the injury that is done to
him has no analogy with that which is done by one private man
to another. Neither does our goodness add any thing to him, nor
our sin take any thing from him (Job 35:6–8):

> If thou sinnest, what doest thou against him?
> Or if thy transgressions be multiplied,
>   what doest thou to him?
> If thou be righteous, what givest thou him?
>   Or what receives he of thine hand?

Thy wickedness may hurt a man as thou art;
and thy righteousness
may profit the son of man.

But that which is here called 'injury,' is the transgression of the law of the righteous Judge of all the world; and shall he not do right? Shall he not recompense to men according to their ways? And therefore that falls to the ground which he adds as the proof of the whole: 'For as it is lawful for every one to prosecute his own right, so every one may forego it, remit of it, or not prosecute it, at his pleasure.' And this is that which is principally insisted on by them in this cause, namely, that the right of punishing being in God only, he may forego it if he please, seeing every one may recede from or not pursue his own right at his pleasure. But a person may have a double right. First, that which arises from a debt, or a personal injury. This every man may pursue, so as that hereby he wrongs not any unconcerned therein, nor transgresses any rule of duty prescribed to himself; and every one may at his pleasure remit, so as no prejudice redound thereby to others. But our sins in respect of God have neither the nature of debts properly, nor of personal injuries, though they are metaphorically so called. And there is a right of rule or government, which is either positive or natural. Of the first sort is that which magistrates have over their subjects. To this belongs the fight of exacting punishment according to the law. Now, this is such a right as has duty inseparably annexed to it. This, therefore, a righteous magistrate cannot forego without destroying the end of magistracy in the public good. For a magistrate to say, 'I have, indeed, a right to punish offenders in the commonwealth, but I will forego it, seeing all its exercise depends upon my will,' is a rejection of his duty, and an abrenunciation of his authority. But, lastly, the right of God to rule over all is natural and necessary to him: so therefore is our obligation to obedience, or obnoxiousness to punishment. To say that God may forego this right, or remit of it, is to say that he may at his pleasure cease to be our Lord and God; for the same nature of God which necessarily requires our obedience does indispensably require the punishment of our disobedience. And so have we closed our first argument in this cause, with our vindication of it.

6

DID CHRIST SUFFER

WHAT SINNERS SHOULD HAVE SUFFERED?

Unto what we have argued in the foregoing exercitation it is generally objected, 'That if the justice of God did thus indispensably require the punishment of sin, which was the ground of the satisfaction made by Christ, then it was necessary that Christ should undergo the same punishment that the sinners themselves should have done, namely, that which the justice of God did require. But this was impossible,' as is pretended. And to overthrow this apprehension, that the Lord Christ underwent the same punishment in kind which we should have done, or as was due to us, they have thus stated the opinion of them whom they do oppose. 'Some,' they say, 'do maintain that our sins are to be looked on as our debts, or under the notion of debts, and God as the creditor, requiring the payment of them. Wherefore our Lord Jesus Christ, by his death and sufferings, paid this debt; so that his death was '*solutio ejusdem*,' or the payment of what was due in the same kind. This, say some learned men, gave great advantage to Socinus; who easily proved that there was no necessity for a mere creditor to exact his debt, but that he might at his pleasure '*cedere jure suo*,' or forego his own right. And this must needs be supposed of God in this matter, whose love, and grace, and pardoning mercy, are so celebrated therein.' And to confirm this argument it is usually added—which is the main thing pleaded by Socinus and Crellius themselves—'That the Lord Christ neither did nor could undergo the penalty due to us, because that was eternal death. And to plead that either Christ should have undergone it, if he could not have delivered himself from it, or that what was wanting to his sufferings as to their duration was compensated by the dignity of his person, is to acknowledge that indeed he did not undergo the same punishment that we are obnoxious to.'

The Doctrine of the Satistfaction of Christ

Learned men, and those sound in the substance of the doctrine of the satisfaction of Christ, being differently minded, either in the thing itself or about the sense of the terms whereby it is expressed, I shall endeavour to state right conceptions about it, or at least express my own, without a design to contradict those of any others.

Our Criminal Indebtedness

For the consideration of our sins under the notion of debts, and God as a creditor, it is generally known that before the rising of any heresy, the most learned men had expressed themselves with such a liberty as advantage has been thence taken by such adversaries of the truth as afterwards arose. Thus the Scripture having called our sins our debts, and made mention of the payment made by Christ, and compared God to a creditor, before Socinus called the whole matter of the satisfaction of Christ into question, it is no wonder if the truth were commonly expressed under these notions, without such distinctions as were necessary to secure them from unforeseen exceptions. He with whom Socinus first disputed on this subject was Covetus; and he does indeed make use of this argument to prove the satisfaction of Christ, namely, 'That our sins being our debts, justice required that there should be payment made of them, or for them.' But the truth is, he does not take his argument from the nature of debts in general, but from the especial nature of these debts, as the Scripture calls them: for he made it appear that these debts are such as are crimes, or transgressions of the law of God; on the account of which the persons that had contracted these debts, or were guilty of these crimes, became liable and obnoxious to punishment in the judgment of God, who is the sovereign ruler over all. There is, therefore, a distinction to be put between such debts as are civil or pecuniary only, and those which are criminal also. And when the Scripture sets out our sins as debts, with such circumstances as allude to pecuniary debts and their payment, it is to make the thing treated of obvious to our understandings by a similitude exposed to the acquaintance of all men; but as our sins are really intended, the expression is metaphorical. And Socinus, in his disputation about the nature of debts, creditors, and payments, had no advantage but what he took by a supposition that the terms which were used by his adversary metaphorically (his argument being taken from the thing intended) were urged by him in their proper sense; which indeed they were not. And so, whereas all his dispute respects civil or pecuniary debts only, he was far enough from triumphing over his adversary, who intended such as were criminal. Wherefore, as this notion, of debts, creditors, and payments, need not yet be forborne in a popular way of teaching, because it is made use of in the Scripture to give us a sense of our condition upon the account of our sins, especially a declaration being made that these debts will be exacted of us; so in a disputation about the truth, it is necessary to declare of what nature these debts are, as all generally do, asserting them to be criminal.

CHRIST UNDERWENT OUR PUNISHMENT

There is much ambiguity in that expression, of 'Christ's paying the same which was due from us.' For that term, 'the same,' may be variously modified, from divers respects. Consider the punishment suffered, it may be it was the same; consider the person suffering, and it was not the same. And therefore it may be said, as far as it was a penalty it was the same; as it was a payment it was not the same; or it was not the same as it was a satisfaction. For it was only what the law required, and the law required no satisfaction as formally such. Punishment and satisfaction differ formally, though materially they may be the same. I judge, therefore, that Christ was to undergo, and did undergo, that very punishment, in the kind of it, which those for whom he suffered should have undergone, and that, among others, for the reasons ensuing.

He Suffered What Justice Required

Christ underwent the punishment which, in the justice or judgment of God, was due to sin. That the justice of God did require that sin should be punished with a meet and due recompense of reward, we have proved already, and shall afterwards further confirm. To answer and satisfy this justice it was that Christ suffered; and therefore he suffered what that justice required. And this is what is pleaded for, and all. We should have undergone no more but what in the justice of God was due to sin. This Christ underwent—namely, what in the justice of God was due to sin, and therefore what we should have undergone. Nor can it be supposed that, in the justice of God, there might be two sorts of penalties due to sin, one of one kind, and another of another. If it be said that because it was undergone by another it was not the same, I grant it was payment, which our suffering could never have been; it was satisfaction, which we by undergoing any penalty could not make; but he yet suffered the same penalty which we should have done. No more is intended but that the Lord Christ underwent that punishment which was due to our sins; which I cannot see how it can well be denied by those who grant that he underwent any punishment at all, seeing the justice of God required no other.

Only One Kind of Punishment

That which was due to sin was all of it, whatever it was, contained and comprehended in the curse of the law; for in the curse God threatened the breach of the law with that punishment which in his justice was due to it, and all that was so. I suppose this will not be denied. For the curse of the law is nothing but an expression of that punishment which is due to the breach of it, delivered in a way of threatening. But now Jesus Christ underwent the curse of the law; by which I know not what to understand but that very punishment which the transgressors of the law should have undergone. Hence our apostle says that he was 'made a curse for us' (Gal. 3:13) because he underwent the penal sentence of the law. And there were not two kinds of punishment contained in the curse of the law, one that the sinner himself should undergo, another that should fall on the Mediator; for neither the law nor its curse had any respect to a mediator. Only every transgressor was cursed thereby. The interposition of a mediator depends on other principles and reasons than any the law was acquainted withal. It was therefore the same punishment, in the kind of it, which was due to us, that the Lord Christ was to undergo, or it was that which neither the justice nor the law of God required.

Scripture May Be Understood No Other Way

It is said expressly that God caused all our iniquities to meet on him (Isa. 53:6), or 'has laid on him the iniquity of us all;' that he bare our sins (v. 11), or 'bare our sins in his own body on the tree' (1 Pet. 2:24); whereby he who knew no sin was made sin for us (2 Cor. 5:21)—the sense of all which places I have elsewhere pleaded and vindicated. Now, unless we will betake ourselves to the metaphorical sense of our adversaries, and grant that all these, and the like expressions in the Scripture innumerable, signify no more but that Christ took away our sins, by declaring and confirming to us the way of faith and obedience, whereby we may obtain the pardon of them, and have them so taken away, we can assign no sense to them but that the Lord Christ underwent the punishment due to our sins in the judgment of God, and according to the sentence of the law; for how did God make our sins to meet on him, how did he bear them, if he did not suffer the penalty due to them, or if he underwent some other inconvenience, but not the exact demerit of sin? And there is no other sense given of these places by them who plead for the satisfaction of Christ but this, that he bare the punishment due to our sins; which is all that is contended for.

He Was Our Substitute

Christ suffered in our stead. He was our Ἀντίψυχος. And it is usual with all learned men to illustrate his being so by the instances of such as have been renowned in the world on that account; which they have clear warranty for from our apostle (Rom. 5:7). When one would substitute himself in

Ἀντίψυχος: a ransom (cf. 4 Mac. 6:29).

the room of another who was obnoxious to punishment, he that was so substituted was always to undergo that very penalty, whether by loss of limb, liberty, or life, that the other should have undergone. And in like manner, if the Lord Christ suffered in our stead, as our Ἀντίψυχος, he suffered what we should have done. And to conclude, if a certain punishment of sin be required indispensably, on the account of the holiness and essential righteousness of God, I know not on what ground we can suppose that several sorts or kinds of punishment might be inflicted for it at pleasure.

OBJECTIONS TO THE DOCTRINE

It remains that we consider the principal objections that are usually leveled against the truth asserted, and either answer them, or show how that which we maintain is not concerned in them nor opposed by them.

'CHRIST COULD NOT UNDERGO ETERNAL DEATH.'

First, therefore, it is objected, 'That the punishment which we should have undergone was death eternal, but this Christ did not, nor could undergo; so that he underwent not the same punishment that we should have done.'

ANSWER. Death as eternal was in the punishment due to our sin, not directly, but consequentially; and that '*a natura subjecti*,' not '*a natura causae*.' For, that the punishment of sin should be eternal arose not from the nature and order of all things, namely, of God, the law, and the sinner, but from the nature and condition of the sinner only. This was such as that it could no otherwise undergo a punishment proportionable to the demerit of sin but by an eternal continuance under it. This, therefore, was not a necessary consequent of guilt absolutely, but of guilt in or upon such a subject as a sinner is, who is no more but a finite limited creature. But when, by God's appointment, the same punishment fell on Him whose person, upon another consideration, was infinitely distanced from those of the sinners themselves, eternity was not of the nature of it.

But then it may be said, 'That the admission of one to pay or suffer for another, who could discharge the debt in much less time than the other or offender could, is not the same that the law required; for the law takes no notice of any other than the person who had offended. And if a mediator could have paid the same, the original law must have been distinctive—that either the offender must suffer or another for him.'

ANSWER. These things are for the most part true, but not contrary to our assertion, as is pretended, through a misapprehension of it. For the law requires no such thing as one to suffer for another, nor, absolutely considered, does admit of it. This was from God's gracious dispensation of or with the law, as the supreme Lord and ruler over all. The law itself takes notice only of offenders, nor has any such supposition included in it as that the offenders must suffer or a mediator in their stead. But this the law has in it, and inseparable from it, namely, that this kind of punishment is due to the transgressor of it. And by God's gracious substitution of Christ in the room of sinners, there was no relaxation made of the law as to the punishment it required; nor is there any word in the Scripture giving countenance to such an apprehension. That there was a dispensation with the law so far as that one person should undergo the punishment (namely, the Son of God) which others did deserve, he becoming a mediator for them, the Scripture everywhere declares. Upon the supposition of his substitution in the place and stead of sinners, could there be any word of Scripture produced intimating such a relaxation of the law as that it should not require of him the whole punishment due to sin, but only some part of it, or not the punishment which was due to sinners, but somewhat else of another kind that was not in the original sanction and curse of it, there would be an end of this difference. But this appears not, nor is there any thing of sound reason in it, that one should suffer for another, in the stead of another, and thereby answer the law whereby that other was bound over to punishment, and yet not suffer what he should have done. Nor is it pleaded, in this case, that the dignity of the person makes up what was wanting in the kind or degree of punishment; whence it is supposed that it would follow that then he who so suffered, suffered not what others should have done who were not so worthy. It is only said, that from the dignity of the person undergoing the same kind of punishment that others should have done, that respect of it which consisted in its duration, and arose from the disability of the persons liable to it otherwise to undergo it, could have here no place.

It is yet further pleaded, 'That if the same be paid in a strict sense, then deliverance would have followed *ipso facto*, for the release immediately follows the payment of the same; and it had been injustice to have required any thing further of the offenders when strict and full payment had been made of what was in the obligation.'

ANSWER. To discuss these things at large would require a larger discourse than I shall now divert to. But—

1. It has been showed already, howsoever we allow of that expression of 'paying the same,' it is only suffering the same for which we contend. Christ underwent the same punishment that the law required, but that his so doing should be a payment for us depended on God's sovereign dispensation, yet so that, when it was paid, it was the same which was due from us.

2. This payment, therefore, as such, and the deliverance that ensued thereon, depended on a previous compact and agreement, as must all satisfaction of one for another. This compact, as it concerned the person requiring satisfaction and the person making it, we have before described and explained; and as it concerns them who are to be partakers of the benefit of it, it is declared in the covenant of grace. Deliverance, therefore, does not naturally follow on this satisfaction, but *jure fœderis*; and therefore was not to ensue *ipso facto*, but in the way and order disposed in that covenant.

3. The actual deliverance of all the persons for whom Christ suffered, to ensue *ipso facto* upon his suffering, was absolutely impossible; for they were not [in being], the most of them, when he suffered. And that the whole of the time, way, and manner of this deliverance depends on compact, is evident from them who were delivered actually from the penalty long before the actual sufferings of Christ, merely upon the account of his sufferings which should afterwards ensue.

4. Deliverance is no end of punishment, considered merely as such;

none is punished properly that he may be delivered; however, the cessation of punishment may be called a deliverance.

5. Mere deliverance was not the whole end of Christ's sufferings for us, but such a deliverance as is attended with a state and condition of superadded blessedness. And the duties of faith, repentance, and obedience, which are prescribed to us, are not enjoined only or principally with respect to deliverance from punishment, but with respect to the attaining of those other ends of the mediation of Christ, in a new spiritual life here and eternal life hereafter. And with respect to them may they justly be required of us, though Christ suffered and paid the same which we ought.

6. No deliverance *ipso facto*, upon a supposition of suffering or paying of the same, was necessary, but only the actual discharge of him who made the payment, and that under the notion and capacity of an undertaker for others: which in this case did ensue; for the Lord Christ immediately on his sufferings was discharged, and that as our surety and representative.

But it may be further objected, 'That it is impossible to reconcile the freeness of remission with the full payment of the very same that was in the obligation; for it is impossible that the same debt should be fully paid and freely forgiven.'

ANSWER. It is well if those who make use of this objection, because they suppose it of force and weight, are satisfied with their own answers to the Socinians when it is much urged and insisted on by them. For it seems at first view that if the freedom of pardon to us exclude any kind of satisfaction to be made by another for us, that it excludes all; for as to the freedom of pardon, wherein soever that freedom does consist, it is asserted in the Scripture to be absolute, without any respects or restrictions. It is not said that God will so freely pardon us that he will not require all that was due, the same that was due, but somewhat he may and will. It is not said that he will not have a suffering of this kind of punishment, but the suffering of another kind of punishment he will. And so to suppose is a thing unworthy of the grace and righteousness of God. To say that God freely remitted our sins, abrogating the law and the curse of it, requiring no punishment, no satisfaction for them, neither from ourselves nor from the Mediator, has, at first view, an appearance of royal grace and clemency, until, being examined, it is found inconsistent with the truth and holiness of God. To say that God required the execution of the sentence and curse of the law, in the undergoing of the punishment due to sin, but yet, out of his love and infinite grace, sent his Son to undergo it for us, so to comply with his holiness, to satisfy his justice, and fulfill his truth and law, that he might freely pardon sinners—this the Scripture everywhere declares, and the so doing is consistent with all the perfections of the divine nature. But to say that he would neither absolutely pardon us without any satisfaction, nor yet have the same penalty undergone by Christ which his justice and law required as due to sin, but somewhat else, seems to be unworthy of the holiness of God on the one side, which is but partially complied withal, and of his grace on the other, which is not exalted by it, and is a conceit that has no countenance given to it in the Scripture. Wherefore, the absolute freedom of pardon to us is absolutely consistent with Christ suffering the same penalty which was due to our sins.

'PAYMENT AND REMISSION MUST RESPECT THE SAME PERSON.'

And whereas it is pleaded, 'That satisfaction and remission must respect the same person, for Christ did not pay for himself, but for us, neither could the remission be to him; so that what was exactly paid by him, it is all one as if it had been paid by us;' unless it be cautiously explained, it has a disadvantageous aspect towards the whole truth pleaded for. The Scripture is clear that God pardons us for Christ's sake; and no less clear that he spared not him for our sakes. And if what Christ did be so accounted as done by ourselves as that payment and remission respect immediately the same person, then be it what it will, more or less, that was so paid or so satisfied for, we are not freely pardoned, but are esteemed to have suffered or paid so much, though not the whole. This is not that which we do believe. But satisfaction was made by Christ, and remission is made to us. He suffered, the just for the unjust, that we may go free. In brief, Christ's undergoing the punishment due to our sins, the same that we should have undergone—or, to speak with respect to that improper notion, his paying the same debts which we owed—does not in the least take off from the freedom of our pardon; yet it much consists therein, or at least depends thereon. I say not that pardon itself does so, but the freedom of it in God, and with respect to us, does so.

For God is said to do that freely for us which he does of grace; and whatever he does of grace is done for us freely. Thus the love and grace of God in sending Jesus Christ to die for us were free; and therein lay the foundation of free remission to us. His constitution of his suffering of the same punishment which was due to our sins, as the surety and mediator of the new covenant, was free and of mere grace, depending on the compact or covenant between the Father and Son, before explained.

In our own persons we make no satisfaction, nor pay one farthing of our debt; we did nothing toward the procurement of another to do it; we bring neither money nor price to obtain a pardon; but are absolved by the mere free grace of God by Jesus Christ.

The imputation of our sin to him, or the making him to be sin for us, by his own voluntary choice and consent, was in like manner free. The constitution of the new covenant, and therein of the way and law of the participation of the benefits of the sufferings of Christ, was also free and of grace. The communication of the Holy Spirit to us, enabling us to believe and to fulfill the condition of the covenant, is absolutely free. And other instances of the freedom of God's grace, with respect to the remission of sin, might be given to us it is every way free. In our own persons we make no satisfaction, nor pay one farthing of our debt; we did nothing toward the procurement of another to do it; we bring neither money nor price to obtain a pardon; but are absolved by the mere free grace of God by Jesus Christ. And there is nothing here inconsistent with Christ suffering the same that we should have done, or his paying the same debt which we owed, in the sense before explained.

7

THE NECESSITY OF THE PRIESTHOOD OF CHRIST

There yet remain some other arguments whereby the truth of this is confirmed, which I shall only briefly represent, that we be not too long detained on this particular head of our design. Besides, I have both urged and vindicated these arguments already in another way.

All Men Know that Sin Requires Punishment

In the next place, therefore, to what has been insisted on, we may plead the common suffrage of mankind in this matter: for what all men have a presumption of is not free, but necessary, nor can be otherwise; for it is from a principle which knows only what is, and not what may be or may not be. Of such things there can be no common or innate persuasion among men. Such are all the free acts of the will of God. They are of things that might be or might not be; otherwise were they not free acts. If, therefore, God's punishing of sin were merely an effect of a free act of his will, without respect to any essential property of his nature, there could never have been any general presumption or apprehension of it in the minds of men. But this there is, namely, that God is righteous with that kind of righteousness which requires that sin be punished; and he therefore does punish it accordingly. Hence our apostle, speaking of the generality of the heathen, affirms that they knew that it was 'the judgment of God that they who committed sin were worthy of death' (Rom. 1:32).

They are enormous sins indeed, mostly, which he instances in; but his inference is from the nature, and not the degree of any sin. 'They who commit sin are worthy of death;' that is, obnoxious to it on the account of their guilt, and which shall therefore be inflicted on them. And death is the punishment due to sin. And this is 'the judgment of God'—that which his justice requires, which, because he is just, he judges meet to be done; or, this is that right which God excercises in the government of all.

And this was known to the Gentiles by the light and instinct of nature, for other instruction herein they had not. And this natural conception of their minds they variously expressed, as has been elsewhere declared. Thus, when the barbarians saw Paul bound with a chain, whence they supposed him to be a malefactor, they presently concluded, upon the viper's leaping on his hand, that vengeance from God was fallen on him, which he should not escape notwithstanding the deliverance which he had had at sea; for this δίκη, or 'vengeance' they thought to be peculiarly designed to find out sinners that had seemed to have made an escape from punishment justly deserved (Acts 28:4). That such punishment is due to sin they were sufficiently convinced of by the testimony of their own consciences (Rom. 2:14–15); and whereas conscience is nothing but the judgment which a man makes concerning himself and his actions, with respect to the superior judgment of God, a sense of the eternal righteousness of God was therein included.

DEMONSTRATED IN SACRIFICES

And this sense of avenging justice they expressed in all their sacrifices, wherein they attempted to make some atonement for the guilt of sin. And this in an especial manner evidenced itself, partly in that horrid custom of sacrificing of other men, and partly in the occasional devoting of themselves to destruction to the same end; as also in their more solemn and public lustrations and expiations of cities and countries, in the time of public calamities and judgments.

For, what was the voice of nature in those actings, wherein it offered violence to its own inbred principles and inclinations? It was this alone: 'The Governor over all is just and righteous; we are guilty. He will not suffer us to live, vengeance will overtake us, if some way or other some course be not found out to appease him, to satisfy his justice, and to divert his judgments' (Mic. 6:6–7). This they thought to be the most probable way to bring about this end, namely, to take another of the same nature with themselves, and it may be dear to them, and to bring him to death, the worst that could be feared or suffered, in their own stead, with an imprecation *'quod in ejus caput sit'* upon him.

GOD'S ANGER DECLARES HIS JUSTICE

Again; what is affirmed in the Scripture concerning the anger, wrath, and fury of God against sin, and in the punishment of sinners, confirms what we affirm (see Rom. 1:18; Num. 25:4; Deut. 13:17; Josh. 7:26; Ps. 78:49; Isa. 13:9; Hab. 3:8).

Now, this anger and wrath, especially in the signification of the original words, do denote such commotions and alterations as the divine nature is no way subject to; for with God there is neither variableness nor shadow of change (Jas. 1:17). Yet our apostle says that this anger is 'revealed from heaven'—namely, in the acts of divine providence in the world. Nothing, therefore, can be intended hereby but the effects of anger; that is, punishment. And so it is declared (Rom. 3:5; Eph. 5:6; Rom. 2:5): for the anger or wrath of God is said to come upon men when they are punished by him for their sins. Yet something in God is declared hereby; and this can be nothing but a constant and unchangeable will of rendering to sin a meet recompense of reward (Rom. 9:22).

And this is justice, the justice pleaded for, which is inseparable from the nature of God. Hence God is said to judge and punish in his anger (Ps. 56:7). And if any thing but this vindictive justice be therein intended, that is assigned to him which ought not to be assigned to a man that is honest and wise. And this does God no less manifest in the works of his providence than he does his goodness and patience; though the instances of it neither are nor ought to be continual, because of the future general judgment, to which all things and persons are reserved.

Why Should Sin Be Punished?

It will be granted by some that there is such a natural property in God as that which we contend for; 'But it does not thence follow,' they say, 'that it is necessary that God should punish all sin; but he does it, and may do it, by an absolute free act of his will. There is, therefore, no cogent argument to be taken from the consideration of this for the necessity of the sufferings of Christ.' The heads of some few arguments to the contrary shall put a close to this whole discourse

God Hates Sin

God hates sin, he hates every sin; he cannot otherwise do. Let any man assert the contrary—namely, that God does not hate sin, or that it is not necessary to him, on the account of his own nature, that he should hate sin—and the consequence thereof will quickly be discerned. For to say that God may not hate sin, is at once to take away all natural and necessary difference between moral good and evil; for if he may not hate it, he may love it. The mere acts of God's will which are not regulated by any thing in his nature but only wisdom and liberty, are not determined to this or that object, but he may so will any thing, or the contrary. And then if God may love sin, he may approve it; and if he approve sin, it is not sin, which is a plain contradiction. That God hates sin (see Ps. 5:4–5, 11:5, 14:1, 53:1; Lev. 26:30; Deut. 16:22; Kings 21:26; Prov. 15:9; Hab. 1:13). And this hatred of sin in God can be nothing but the displicency in or contrariety of his nature to it, with an immutable will of punishing it thence arising; for, to have a natural displicency against sin, and not an immutable will of punishing it, is unworthy of God, for it must arise from impotency. To punish sin, therefore, according to its demerit is necessary to him.

God Is a Consuming Fire

God with respect to sin and sinners is called 'a consuming fire' (Heb. 12:29; Deut. 4:24; Isa. 5:24, 33:14, 66:15–16). Something we are taught by the allusion in this expression. This is not the manner of God's operation. God works freely; the fire burns necessarily.

God, I say, always works freely, with a freedom accompanying his operation; though in some cases, on some suppositions, it is necessary that he should work as he does. It is free to him to speak to us or not; but on the supposition that he will do so, it is necessary that he speak truly, for God cannot lie. Fire, therefore, acts by brute inclination, according to its form and principle. God acts by his understanding and will, with a freedom accompanying all his operations. This, therefore, we are not taught by this allusion. The comparison, therefore, must hold with respect to the event, or we are deceived, not instructed by it. As, therefore, the fire necessarily burns and consumes all combustible things to which it is applied, in its way of operation, which is natural; so does God necessarily punish sin when it lies before him in judgment, in his way of operation, which is free and intellectual.

GOD CANNOT ALLOW HIS GLORY TO BE IMPEACHED

It is necessary that God should do every thing that is requisite to his own glory. This the perfection of his nature and existence does require. So he does all things for himself. It is necessary, therefore, that nothing fall out in the universe which should absolutely impeach the glory of God, or contradict his design of its manifestation. Now, suppose that God would and should let sin go unpunished, where would be the glory of his righteousness as he is the supreme ruler over all? For, to omit what justice requires is no less a disparagement to it than to do what it forbids (Prov. 17:15). And where would be the glory of his holiness, supposing the description given of it (Hab. 1:13)—where would be that fear and reverence which is due to him, where that sense of his terror, where that secret awe of him which ought to be in the hearts and thoughts of men—if once he were looked on as such a God, as such a Governor, as to whom it is a matter of mere freedom, choice, and liberty, whether he will punish sin or no, as being not concerned in point of righteousness or holiness so to do? Nothing can tend more than such a persuasion to ingenerate an apprehension in men that God is such an one as themselves, and that he is so little concerned in their sins that they need not themselves be much concerned in them. Such thoughts they are apt to conceive, if he do but hold his peace for a season, and not reprove them for their sins (Ps. 50:21). And if their hearts are fully set in them to do evil, because in some signal instances judgment is not speedily executed (Eccles. 8:11), how much more will such pernicious consequences ensue, if they are persuaded that it may be God will never punish them for their sins, seeing it is absolutely at his pleasure whether he will do so or no!—that neither his righteousness, nor his holiness, nor his glory, requires any such thing at his hands! This is not the language of the law; no, nor yet of the consciences of men, unless they are debauched. Is it not, with most Christians, certain that eventually God lets no sinners go unpunished? Do they not believe that all who are not interested by faith in the sufferings of Christ, or at least that are not saved on the account of his undergoing the punishment due to sin, must perish eternally? And if this be the absolute rule of God's proceeding towards sinners, if he never went out of the way of it in any one instance, whence should it proceed but from what his nature does require?

God Is the Righteous Judge of All

Lastly, God is, as we have showed, the righteous judge of all the world. What law is to another judge, who is to proceed by it, that is the infinite rectitude of his own nature to him. And it is necessary to a judge to punish where the law requires him so to do; and if he do not, he is not just. And because God is righteous by an essential righteousness, it is necessary for him to punish sin as it is contrary to that, and not to acquit the guilty. And what is sin cannot but be sin, neither can God order it otherwise; for what is contrary to his nature cannot by any act of his will be rendered otherwise. And if sin be sin necessarily, because of its contrariety to the nature of God, on the supposition of the order of all things by himself created, the punishment of it is on the same ground necessary also.

Why Christ's Priesthood Is Necessary

On the grounds insisted on, argued and proved it is, that on the supposition before also laid down and explained—namely, that God would glorify himself and his grace in the recovery and salvation of sinners, which proceeded alone from the free counsel of his will—it was, with respect to the holiness and righteousness of God, absolutely necessary that the Son of God, in his interposition for them, should be a priest, and offer himself for a sacrifice; seeing therein and thereby he could and did undergo the punishment which, in the judgment of God, was due to the sins of them that were to be saved by him.

His Death Is Useless Otherwise

Hereon we lay the necessity of the death and suffering of Jesus Christ; as also our apostle does declare (Heb. 2:10–11). And they who are otherwise minded are not able to assign so much as a sufficient cause or just and peculiar reason for it; which yet to think it had not is highly injurious to the wisdom and grace of God. The reason assigned by the Socinians is, that by his death he might confirm the doctrine that he taught, and our faith in himself, as also to set us an example of patient suffering.

But these things were not highly necessary if considered alone, nor peculiar, and such there must be, or no man can satisfy himself why the Son of God should suffer and die; for God sent many before to reveal his will—Moses, for instance, whose declarations thereof all men were bound to believe—and yet caused them not to die violent, bloody, and cursed deaths, in the confirmation of them. So the death of Moses was concealed from all the world, only it was known that he died; his doctrine was not confirmed by his death. Besides, our Lord had such a power of working miracles as to give an uncontrollable evidence to his being sent of God, and of God's approbation of what he taught. Nor can it be pretended that it was necessary that he should die that he might rise again, and so confirm his doctrine by his resurrection; for he might have died for this end any other way, and not by a shameful and cursed death—not by a death in the view whereof he cried out that he was forsaken of God.

Besides, on the supposition that Christ died only to confirm his doctrine, his resurrection was not of any more virtue to ingenerate, strengthen, or increase faith in us, than any other miracle that he wrought; for himself tells us that the rising of any one from the dead absolutely is not accompanied with such a peculiar efficacy to that purpose (Luke 16:31).

But on supposition that he died for our sins, or underwent the punishment due to them, his resurrection from the dead is the principal foundation of our faith and hope. Neither was his being an example to us indispensably necessary; for God has given us other examples to the same purpose, which he obliges us to conform ourselves to (James 5:10–11). Whereas, therefore, all acknowledge that Christ was the Son of God, and there must be some peculiar reason why the Son of God should die a shameful and painful death, this cannot be assigned by them by whom the indispensable necessity of punishing is denied.

Others say it was needful the Lord Christ should suffer, for the declaration of the righteousness of God, with his hatred of and severity against sin. So indeed the Scripture says, but it says so on the suppositions before laid down and proved. How they can say so, with any congruity to or consistency with reason, by whom these are denied, I cannot understand; for if there be no such justice in God as necessarily requires that sin be punished, how can it be exalted or manifested in the punishment of it? If the punishment of sin be a mere free act of the will of God, which he may exert or the contrary, the pleasure of his will is manifested indeed therein, but how his justice is made known I see not.

Suppose, as the men of this persuasion do, that it was easy with God to pardon the sins of men freely, without any satisfaction or compensation; that there was nothing in his nature which required of him to do otherwise; that had he done so, he had done it without the least disadvantage to his own glory—that is, he had acted therein as became his holiness and righteousness, as he is the supreme governor over all—on these suppositions, I say, who can give a reasonable account why he should cast all our sins on his Son, and punish them all in his person, according as if justice had required him so to do? To say that all this was done for the satisfaction of that justice which required no such thing to be done, is not satisfactory.

CONCLUSION

That which is proposed to confirmation in these exercitations is, that the justice or righteousness from whence it is that God punishes sin, and which he excercises in so doing, is an essential property of his nature.

From what has been discoursed, both the original and necessity of the priesthood of Christ are evidently demonstrated. There was no respect in the designation of it to the state of innocency. Upon the supposition and consideration of the fall, the entrance of sin, and the ruin of mankind thereby, there were personal transactions in the holy Trinity with respect to their recovery, as there had been before in their creation. Herein the Son undertook to be our deliverer, in and by the assumption of our nature, wherein alone it could be wrought, into personal union with himself; because, for this end, the justice and holiness of God required that the penalty due and threatened to sin should be undergone and suffered.

This the Son willingly undertook to do in that nature which he assumed to himself. And because the things themselves to be suffered were not only or so much indeed considered as his will and obedience in suffering—being an instance of obedience, in compliance with the will and law of God, outbalancing the disobedience of the first, and all our sins in opposition to this— therefore was he, in all his sufferings to offer himself up freely to the will of God; which offering up of himself was his sacrifice: to which end he was called, anointed, ordained of God a high priest; for this office consists in a power, right, and faculty, given him of God to offer up himself in sacrifice, in, by, and under his suffering of the penalty due to sin, so as thereby to make expiation of sin and reconciliation for sinners, as we shall prove in our next discourse.

8

THE NATURE OF THE PRIESTHOOD OF CHRIST

That our Lord Jesus Christ is the true and only high priest of the church has been before declared, and it is in words acknowledged by all in some sense or other. The general nature also of that office has been fully manifested, from what we have discoursed concerning its original, with the ends thereof, and his designation thereunto. Without the utter overthrow of those foundations in the first place, all the attempts of men against the true and proper nature of this office as vested in him are weak and impotent. The sacrifice that he offered as a priest, the nature, use, and end thereof, must be considered apart afterwards, in its proper place. The qualifications of his person, with the love, care, and grace, which he excercises in the discharge of this office, must all be distinctly spoken to, as they are represented to us by the apostle in the epistle itself.

ATTEMPTS TO SET ASIDE CHRIST'S SACRIFICE

Wherefore there would be no necessity of handling the nature of this office here apart, were it not for the opposition that is made to it, and that depravation of the doctrine of the gospel concerning it which some have attempted; for whereas the principal design of the Socinians in these things is to overthrow the sacrifice that he offered as a priest, they lay the foundation of their attempt in an opposition to the office itself. It is therefore principally with respect to them that I have here proposed the nature of that office to consideration; and I shall be more conversant in its vindication than in its declaration; which most Christians are acquainted withal. And I shall proceed in this method herein: first, I shall declare what are in general their conceptions about this office; in opposition to which the truth declared in the Scripture shall be taught and vindicated. Secondly, I shall more particularly declare their opinions as to the several concernments of it, and consider as well their explanation of their own sense, with their confirmation of it, as their opposition and exceptions to the faith of the church of God.

In the first place, they grant that the Lord Christ is our high priest—that is, that he is so called in the Scripture; but that he is so really they deny. For this name, they say, is ascribed to him not properly or directly, to denote what he is or does, but by reason of some kind of allusion that there is between what he does for us and what was done by the priests of old amongst the Jews, or under the old testament. He is therefore, in their judgment, improperly and metaphorically called a priest, as believers are said to be kings and priests, though after somewhat a more excellent manner; for he is so termed because of the good offices that he does for the church, and not that he is or ever was a priest indeed.

Hereon they say, secondly, that he then entered on this office, or then began to do that work with reference to which—because of its allusion to the work of the priests under the law—he is called a priest, when, upon his ascension into heaven and appearance in the holy place, he received power from God to help, and relieve, and assist the church, in all its occasions. What he did and suffered before in the world, in his death and bloodshedding, was, by virtue of God's decree, a necessary preparation to his discharge of this office, but belonged not to this, nor did he there offer any sacrifice to God.

Wherefore they also affirm, thirdly, that this priesthood of Christ is indeed of the same nature with his kingly office, both of them consisting in a power, ability, authority, and readiness, to do good to the church. Only herein there seems some difference between them, that as a king he is able to help and save us, but as a priest he is willing and ready so to do.

Fourthly, that the object of the acts of the priesthood of Christ is firstly and principally man, yea, it is only so, none of them having God for their object, no more than the acts of his kingly power have; for it is his care of the church, his love towards it, with the supply of his grace and mercy which from God he bestows upon it, on the account of which he is said to be a priest, and his so doing is called the exercise of his priesthood.

This in general is the substance of what they affirm and teach concerning this office of Christ, as we shall more particularly manifest and evince in the ensuing exercitation. Now, if these things are so, I confess all our exposition of this epistle, at least the principal parts of it, must fall to the ground, as being built on the sandy foundation of many false suppositions. And not only so, but the faith of the whole church of God in this thing is overthrown; and so are also all the common notions of mankind about the office of the priesthood and its exercise that ever prevailed in the world. And, to lay the whole fabric of truth in all instances level with the earth, the instructive relation or analogy that is between the types of the old testament and the substance of things declared in the new is taken away and destroyed. Wherefore it is necessary that we should diligently assert and confirm the truth in this matter in opposition to all their bold assertions, and vindicate it from their exceptions, whereby we shall fully declare the nature of this blessed office of Christ.

THE HIGH PRIEST OF THE CHURCH

Our first difference is about the name and title, as to the signification of it when applied to Jesus Christ. And we affirm that he is properly the high priest of the church, and not metaphorically only. When I say he is properly the high priest of the church, my meaning is, that he is so the high priest as he is the king and prophet of the church. And look, by what means or arguments it may be proved that Christ is the true, real king and prophet of the church, and not metaphorically called so only, by the same may it be proved that he is in like manner the high priest of the church also; for both the name is in a like manner assigned to him, and the office, and the acts of it, yea, they are so more fully and expressly than the other. And he may as well be said to be metaphorical in his person as in his offices. But I shall distinctly manage these arguments, which I challenge all the Socinians in the world to return a direct answer to, and not by long digressions and tergiversations; a precedent for which is given them by Crellius in this case, whose sophistical evasions shall be called to a particular account afterwards.

First, he to whom all things whatever properly belonging to a priest are ascribed, and to whom belongs the description of a priest in all things essential to him, such ascription and accommodation being made by the Holy Ghost himself, or persons divinely inspired by him, he is a high priest properly so called. And that things are so with reference to the priesthood of Christ will appear in the ensuing instances.

By Name

As to the name itself, this is so ascribed to him. No man durst have so called him had he not been first called so by the Holy Ghost. And this he is both in the Old Testament and in the New. He is expressly said to be the כֹּהֵן, ἱερεύς, ἀρχιερεύς, 'a priest', 'an high priest', without the least intimation on any occasion of impropriety or a metaphor in the expression. And as he is thus called frequently, so constantly with respect to those acts and duties which are proper to the office of the priesthood. Now, whatever colour may be given to the metaphorical use of a word or a name where it is but once or rarely used, and that with respect to such things as answer not to the proper signification, there can be none where it is used frequently, and in the same case invariably, and constantly with respect to things that suit its proper signification.

A Real and Proper Priest

The description of a high priest properly so called is given by our apostle, Hebrews 5:1: Πᾶς γὰρ ἀρχιερεὺς ἐξ ἀνθρώπων λαμζανόμενος, ὑπὲρ ἀνθρώπων καθίσταται τὰ πρὸς τὸν Θεὸν, ἵνα προσφέρῃ δῶρά τε καὶ θυσίας ὑπὲρ ἁμαρτιῶν. A priest is one who is taken from

among other men by the call and appointment of God, and is
appointed in the stead, or on the behalf of other men, in things
pertaining to God; that is, to offer to him gifts and sacrifices for
sins. See this description explained in our exposition of the place.
Now this is the description of a priest properly so called; for it is
the priesthood of Aaron which the apostle intends to express in the
first place, as is evident in verse 4. But Aaron was a priest properly
so called—that is, within his own sphere of typicalness; at least he
was not so only metaphorically. To say he was, is to destroy the
thing itself of the priesthood, and thereby to destroy the metaphor
also; for a metaphor cannot be of nothing. But now whatever is
contained in this description, and whatever in answer to it was
found in Aaron, as belonging to his office, and not adhering to him
individually from the infirmity of his person, is all ascribed by the
apostle to Jesus Christ; as is undeniably evinced in our exposition
of the place, to which I refer the reader. In brief, he was taken by
the call and appointment of God from amongst men (Deut. 18:18,
Heb. 7:13–14). He was appointed for men, or to act in their behalf
(1 John 2:1–2); and that τὰ πρὸς τὸν Θεόν, 'in things pertaining to
God' (Heb. 7:25–6, 9:14–15), particularly 'to offer gifts and sacrifices'
for sin (Heb. 8:3). If this were all that was required to constitute
Aaron a priest properly so called, then the ascription of these things
to Jesus Christ by the Holy Ghost is sufficient to declare him a priest
properly so called. And there is strength added to this argument
from what the apostle discourses concerning the necessity of a call
from God to this office; for he tells us that 'no man takes this honour
to himself'—that is, to be a priest—'but he that is called of God,
as was Aaron' (Heb. 5:4). And thence he shows and proves that
Christ did not take this honour to himself, but in like manner was
called of God (v. 5). Now, if not the honour of a real and proper
priesthood with respect to Christ be intended, but somewhat
else, metaphorically so called, then is the apostle's way of arguing
utterly impertinent, as from an instance of one kind arguing the
necessity of a thing of another. And it may be replied to him, that
although a man must be called of God to a priesthood that is real
and proper, such as was that of Aaron, yet it does not thence follow
that such a call is necessary to that which is so metaphorically only;
for so all believers are made priests to God, but yet none of them
have any especial call from God to this.

The discourse of our apostle (Heb. 7:11–16), gives further evidence to the same truth:

> If therefore perfection were by the Levitical priesthood (for under it the people received the law) what further need was there that another priest should rise after the order of Melchizedek, and not be called after the order of Aaron? For the priesthood being changed, there is made of necessity a change also of the law. For he of whom these things are spoken pertains to another tribe, of which no man gave attendance at the altar. For it is evident that our Lord sprang out of Judah; of which tribe Moses spoke nothing concerning the priesthood. And it is yet far more evident: for that after the similitude of Melchizedek there arises another priest etc.

For we may observe:

1. That as Aaron was a priest, so there was a necessity, from the prophecy of Psalm 110:4, that there should be another priest. Now, if this other priest were not a priest properly so called, as Aaron was, there is no consequence in the apostle's discourse, it proceeding on terms equivocal.
2. The priesthood, according to this prophecy and our apostle's interpretation of it, was only to be changed. But if, after the removal of the law, there was no other proper priesthood to succeed, it was not changed, but abolished. And it is more true that there was none than that there was any; for properly there was none, though metaphorically there was.
3. On this supposition all the circumstances insisted on by our apostle as exceedingly observable to his purpose—namely, that our Lord was of the tribe of Judah, and not of Levi; that he was constituted a priest in an especial way, and not like to that of old—are of no use: for there is nothing peculiar in these things, if he intend not a priest properly so called.
4. It utterly enervates that invincible argument whereby the apostle proves the necessary cessation of the law and legal or Mosaic institutions; for he builds on this supposition, that the priesthood being changed, the law of divine worship or service must be so also. And this unavoidably follows because of the inseparable relation that was between the Aaronic priesthood

and all the worship of the tabernacle. But if this other priest whom he intends was not properly, but only metaphorically so, there might be a thousand of them, and yet no necessity for the change of the law of worship ensue. For two priests, one of which is proper and the other metaphorically so only, are consistent at the same time, but two that are properly so are not; whence our apostle says that the Lord Christ could not be a proper priest of the same nature with those of the order of Aaron whilst they continued (Heb. 8:4).

5. He is expressly said to be a priest 'after the order of Melchizedek.' But this Melchizedek was a priest properly so called. He therefore must be so who is a priest according to the same order; for priests of several sorts and kinds, as real and nominal only, or proper and metaphorical, cannot be said to be after the same order, for no orders can be more different than those of which one is proper, the other metaphorical. This difference is not in some property and adjunct, but in the whole kind; as real and painted fire differ, or a man and his image. Besides, he is said to be a priest 'after the order of Melchizedek,' so as that withal he is denied to be a priest 'after the order of Aaron.' But if he were not properly so called, but only metaphorically, by reason of some allusion to a proper priesthood in what he did, the direct contrary might much rather be asserted; for there was more allusion between Aaron in his priesthood and him, and our apostle gives more instances of it, than between him and Melchizedek. And if it be false that Christ was a high priest according to the order of Aaron, notwithstanding the great allusion between what he did and what was done by Aaron in that office, and the great representation made of him and his actings thereby, then is it not true that Christ was called a priest 'after the order of Melchizedek,' by reason of some allusion to the office of the priesthood.

6. This conception would utterly enervate the sense of the general argument that the apostle manages towards these Hebrews, as well as that especial one about the cessation of the law. For he is pressing them to stability and constancy in the profession of the gospel, that they fall not back to their old Judaism which they had deserted. To enforce his exhortation to this

purpose, the principal argument he insists on is taken from the excellency and glory of the priesthood under the new testament—incomparably exalted above that of the old, which yet was the most glorious and useful part of their worship. But that which is metaphorical in any kind is evidently less than that which is properly so. It is replied by Crellius, 'That what is only metaphorically so may yet be more excellent than that which is properly;' of which he gives some instances. And it is true it may be so. But it cannot be so in that instance wherein the metaphor consists. Suppose the Lord Christ to be only metaphorically a priest, yet he may, on many other accounts, be far more excellent and glorious than Aaron. But yet the priesthood of Aaron being properly so, and his only metaphorically so, the priesthood of Aaron was more excellent than his; which is directly contrary to the scope of the apostle. Suppose the Lord Christ were only metaphorically a prophet or a king, he may yet on many other considerations be more excellent than either Moses or David, yet they must, on this supposition, be granted to have had the offices of prophet and king more eminently than he. So also must it be with his priesthood, on this supposition, with respect to that of Aaron.

7. Add to all these particular instances to the contrary, that this Socinian fiction of the Lord Christ being not a priest, but only called so, by reason of some similitude between what he does for the church and what was done by the priests of the law—which indeed, as by them explained, is none at all—is directly opposite to the whole design and discourse of the apostle in this epistle. For, treating of the priesthood of Christ, he constantly calls him a priest in the sense which they had of that expression to whom he wrote, or he spoke not to their understandings; he assigns all sorts of sacerdotal actions to him, in all instances of duties belonging to a priest as such, and that in competition with, and by way of preference above, the priests of the order of Aaron; nor does he in any place, either directly or indirectly, give the least intimation that all these expressions of his were only tropical or metaphorical, not indeed signifying those things which those to whom he wrote understood by them. This had not been to instruct the Hebrews, but to deceive them, nor will be granted by those

who have a greater reverence for the sacred writings than to wrest them at their pleasure into a compliance with their own preconceived opinions.

And this is the first thing which we are to consider in the investigation and vindication of the true nature of the priesthood of Christ. It was such as that on the account thereof he was a priest properly so called; which as it gives a rule to the interpretation of the nature of the sacrifice which as a priest he offered, so is the truth of it confirmed by all other things which are ascribed to him under that qualification, as we shall see afterwards.

And what remains for the further confirmation of this will be added in our ensuing consideration of the attempt of our adversaries to establish the contrary assertion.

GOD—THE PRIMARY OBJECT

'Christ being come an high priest of good things to come, by a greater and more perfect tabernacle,' his actings in that office do in the first place respect God himself—τὰ πρὸς τὸν Θεόν. He did the things that were to be performed with God on the behalf of the people. And this further manifests the nature of his office. He came as a priest εἰς τὸ ἱλάσκεσθαι τὰς ἀμαρτίας τοῦ λαοῦ (Heb. 2:17); that is, ἱλάσκεσθαι τὸν Θεὸν περὶ τῶν ἀμαρτιῶν, as has been observed by many, 'to make reconciliation with God for the sins of the people.' For sins cannot be the immediate object of reconciliation, but he alone is so who was displeased with them, and by whom, on

For sins cannot be the immediate object of reconciliation, but he alone is so who was displeased with them, and by whom, on that reconciliation, they are pardoned and the sinner acquitted.

that reconciliation, they are pardoned and the sinner acquitted. But yet neither can we carry this without control. This also is denied by our adversaries in this cause, although therein they offer violence not only to all that we are taught in the Scripture about these things, but also to all the common sentiments of mankind, putting such senses on these expressions as are absolutely contrary to them and inconsistent with them. What are those senses we shall afterwards examine. For the present, it suffices to our purpose to take notice of their denial that the sacerdotal actings of Christ—that is, his oblation and intercession—do respect God in the first place; the contrary to which we shall now teach and confirm.

The Scripture instructs us, as we have proved, that the Lord Christ was and is our high priest; and, moreover, that as such he offered himself to God once for all, to make reconciliation for the sins of the people, as a propitiatory, expiatory sacrifice (Isa. 53:10; Heb. 1:3, 2:17, 5:5, 7:27, 10:10; Eph. 5:2; 1 John 2:2). What the Holy Ghost intends hereby, and what is the meaning of these expressions, he had before instructed the church in, by those institutions under the old testament whereby he foresignified and represented what was intended in them and by them. To suppose these expressions to have one signification under the old testament, and another quite of a different nature under the new, whereas the things signified by the one were appointed only to teach and instruct us in the nature of the other, is to take away all certainty from what we are taught in the Scripture. We may therefore positively conclude, that if the actings of the priests under the old testament did respect God in the first place, then those of Christ did so also, or there is no similitude or analogy between these things; which to affirm is to overthrow both the old testament and the new. This, therefore, we must in the first place confirm.

The principal duty and work of the priests under the law was to offer sacrifices. As the whole law speaks thus, so our apostle expressly confirms it, making that work the great end of the priesthood. Sacrifices had respect to sin. Priests were appointed to offer θυσίας περὶ ἁμαρτιῶν, 'sacrifices for sin.' And when God called them to the work, he said it was לְכַהֲנוֹ־לִי, that they should exercise the priesthood towards him (Exod. 28:1). Had there been no sin, there had been no sacrifices properly so called, as we have proved before. There might have been a dedication of any thing in our power to God, as an acknowledgment of his sovereignty and bounty. But sacrifices by blood had all respect to sin, as the nature of them does declare. Wherefore, God appointing priests to offer sacrifices for sin, and therein to minister to him, he must be the first object of their actings as such. Sacrifices by blood, to be offered by these priests, and by them only, God appointed of various kinds, with respect to various occasions, of bulls, goats, sheep, fowls; whose nature and differences I have explained in our former exercitations (Exerc. 24). The principal end of all these sacrifices, was to make atonement for sin. This is so express in their institution as that it is all one to deny that there were any sacrifices appointed of God as to deny that they were appointed to make atonement (see Lev. 1:4, 5:5, 6, 6:7, 16:6, 34, etc). Now, the nature, use, and end of atonement, was to avert the anger of God due to sin, and so to pacify him that the sinner might be pardoned. This is the importance of the word, and this was the end of those sacrifices whereby atonement was made. The word is sometimes used where no sacrifice was implied, but is never used in any other sense than that declared. So Moses spoke to the people upon their making of the calf: 'Ye have sinned a great sin: and now I will go up to the LORD; peradventure I shall make an atonement for your sin' (Exod. 32:30). He hoped that he should by his interposition turn away the wrath of God, and obtain pardon for them; which he calls making an atonement, because of its respect to the great future sacrifice, by virtue of which alone we may prevail with God on such occasions. In Leviticus 5:5-6, as in many other places, this is appropriated to sacrifices: 'When a man shall be guilty in one of these things, he shall confess that he has sinned in that thing: and he shall bring his trespass offering to the LORD for his sin which he has sinned...and the priest shall make an atonement for him concerning his sin' (so also verses 17-18, Lev. 6:6-7, etc). The sin committed was against the Lord; the guilt contracted was confessed to the Lord; the sacrifice or offering was brought to the Lord; the atonement was made by the priest before the Lord—all which give it the nature before described, and admit of no other. In some instances the sins committed were to be confessed over the head of the sacrifice wherewith the atonement was to be made; which rendered the whole action more pregnant with representation. A person guilty of sin, convicted in his own conscience, condemned by the sentence of the law, by God's allowance and appointment brought a clean beast, assigned in general for that use, and, bringing it to the altar, confessed over it his sin and guilt, laying them legally upon it, so delivering it up into the hands of the priest, by whom it was slain, and the blood poured out, as suffering under the guilt laid upon it; wherein, with some other ensuing acts, it was offered to God to make atonement for the sin committed and confessed. Thus was blood given to the people to make atonement for their souls, because the life of the beast was in the blood, which was destroyed in the shedding thereof (Lev. 17:11).

Certainly no man can ever arrive to so much confidence as to question whether the actings of the priests in those sacrifices whereby atonement was made, did not in the first place respect God himself; nor, indeed, do I know that it is by any positively and directly denied: for the sense we plead for depends not on the use of any one single word, or the signification of it in these or other places, but upon the whole nature and express ends of those institutions. And herein all mankind are agreed, namely, that the divine Power was the immediate object of sacerdotal actings—that they were done with God on the behalf of men, and not actings towards men on the behalf of God.

By all these terms and expressions does our apostle describe the sacerdotal actings of Christ. For having declared him to be a high priest, he affirms that he offered a sacrifice to God—a sacrifice to make reconciliation for sin: as also, that therein God made all our sins to meet upon him; which 'he bare in his own body on the tree.' The question now is, what is intended thereby? Our adversaries say it is the merciful and powerful actings of Christ towards us, giving out help, assistance, grace, and mercy, from God to us; so delivering us from all evil, the whole punishment due to sin, and eternal death. But why are these things called his offering of himself to God a sacrifice to make reconciliation for sin? They say it is because of an allusion and similitude that is between what he so does for us, and what was done by the priests of old in their sacrifices. But it is plain, from what has been declared concerning the sacerdotal actings of the priests of old in their sacrifices, that there is no allusion nor similitude between these things, nor can they assign wherein it should consist. Their actings were immediately towards God on our behalf, his, it is said, are towards us on God's behalf; theirs were to make atonement for sin, his to testify love and mercy to sinners; theirs by shedding of blood, wherein was life, his in power and glory. Wherefore I say, if we have any instruction given us in these things—if the office of the priesthood, or any duties of it, any sacrifices offered by the priests, were instituted to typify, prefigure, and represent Jesus Christ as the great high priest of the church—it cannot be but that his sacerdotal actings do justly and immediately respect God himself; which shall now be further confirmed.

The Plain Sense of Christ's Offices

There are (as is out of controversy) three offices which the Lord Christ, as the mediator and surety of the new covenant, bears and excercises towards the church, namely, those of king, prophet, and priest. And these, as they are distinctly assigned to him, so they are distinct among themselves, and are names of diverse things, as really, so in the common notions and sense of mankind. And in these offices, where there is an affinity between them, or any seeming coincidence, in their powers, duties, and acts, the kingly and prophetical do make a nearer pass to each other than either of them do to the sacerdotal, as shall afterwards be more fully evinced; for the nature of these two offices requires that the object of their exercise be men. As in general it does so, so in particular in those of Christ. He acts in them in the name of God, and for God, towards men. For although a king be the name of one who is invested with power absolute and supreme, yet is it so only with respect to them towards and over whom he is a king. As denoting an infinite, absolute, independent power, of necessity it belongs to God alone essentially considered. This office in Christ is considered as delegated by the Father, and exercised in his name: 'The head of every man is Christ;' but 'the head of Christ is God.' He anoints him king on his holy hill of Zion (Ps. 2:6); and he rules in the name and majesty of his God (Mic. 5:4). Wherefore the whole exercise of the power and duty of this office is from God, and for God towards men. In his name he rules his subjects and subdues his enemies. None can fancy God to be the object of any of the acts of this office.

It is so in like manner with his prophetic office. God raised him up from among his brethren to be the prophet of his church, to reveal his will; and by him he spoke to us (see *Exposition on Hebrews* 1:1–2). His whole work as a prophet is to reveal the will of God, and therein to teach and instruct us. Men, therefore, are the immediate object of the powers, duties, and acts of this office.

And that which we further observe from hence is this, that there is no one thing that the Lord Christ acts immediately towards the church, but that it belongs to and proceeds from one or the other of these powers or offices. If anyone be otherwise minded, let him prove the contrary by instances, if he be able. The Scripture affords none to that purpose. It follows hence, therefore, that God is the object of the actings of Christ in his priestly office. For if he be not so, then:

1. There is no room nor place in his whole mediation for any such office, seeing all he performs towards us belongs to the other. And therefore those by whom this is denied do upon the matter at length contend that indeed he has no such office. And if this be so—

2. It does not belong to Christ as mediator to deal with God in any of the concerns of his people; for he must do so as a priest, or not at all. And then we have no advocate with the Father; which is utterly abhorrent from the common faith of Christianity. And this absurd supposition shall be afterwards removed by express testimonies to the contrary. Take away this fundamental principle, that Christ as mediator deals with God for us, and you overthrow the faith of all Christians.

3. This would render the whole instruction intended for the church in the Aaronic priesthood and sacrifices useless and impertinent, nothing of the like nature being signified thereby; for that, as we have proved, openly respected God in the first place. And on this supposition the accommodation of it to the priesthood of Christ by our apostle would be altogether vain.

4. It is contrary to the common notion of the nature of the priesthood amongst mankind; for none yet ever owned such an office in things religious, but apprehended the use of it to be in doing the things with God that were to be done on the behalf of men.

And hereby, as was observed, would the faith and consolation of all believers, which are resolved into what the Lord Christ has done and does for them with God, be utterly overthrown.

The Obvious Nature of Priestly Acts and Duties

Again; the same truth is undeniably evinced from the nature of sacerdotal acts and duties. These are, as it is stated by common consent, those two of oblation and intercession. And both these are expressly ascribed to the Lord Jesus Christ as he is a high priest, and nothing else immediately as he is so. The actual help and aid which he gives us is the fruit and effect of these sacerdotal actings. The sole inquiry, therefore, in this matter is, what or who is the immediate object of oblation and intercession? Is this God, or man? Did Christ offer himself as a sacrifice to God, or to us? Does he intercede with God for us, or with us only? A man would suppose that the absurdity of these imaginations, so expressly contrary to the Scripture and the common sense of mankind, should even shame our adversaries from the defense of them. But they are not so obtuse or so barren in their invention as to want evasions at any time. 'What if they are taken at their plain meaning? — they will slip away like an eel!' They therefore tell us, 'It is true, if you take oblation and intercession in their proper sense, then God, and none other, must be their immediate object; but as they are ascribed to Christ they are used only metaphorically, and do indeed denote such actions of his towards the church as have some allusion to oblation and intercession properly so called.' But I say —

1. There was never such a metaphor heard of before, as that one thing should be called by the name of another, between which there is no peculiar similitude, as there is none between offering to God and giving grace to men.
2. Who has given them this authority to turn what they please into metaphors; by which means they may, when they have a mind to it, make an allegory, and consequently a fable, of the whole Scripture? It is expressly affirmed that the Lord Christ is a high priest. Nothing is in the notion of that office, taken properly, that is unworthy of him, no more than in those of king and prophet. No intimation is given us, directly or indirectly, that this office is ascribed to him metaphorically. As such he is said to make oblation and intercession to God — the things wherein the exercise of the priestly office does consist.

What confidence is it, now, to deny that he does these things properly and immediately with God as a high priest, by an arbitrary introduction of a metaphor which the Scripture gives not the least countenance to!

CHRIST HAD SOMETHING TO OFFER

We might, moreover, plead the use and end of the sacrifice which he offered as a high priest, which was to make expiation of sin and atonement for it. But because we differ with our adversaries about the sense of these expressions also, I shall not make use of them as the medium of an argument until the precise signification of them be evinced and determined; which shall be done, God willing, in our consideration of the nature of the sacrifice itself. Wherefore I shall close this head of our disputation with some express testimonies confirming the truth in hand.

To this purpose speaks our apostle, 'For every high priest is ordained to offer gifts and sacrifices: wherefore it is of necessity that this man have somewhat also to offer' (Heb. 8:3). The things which the high priests had of old to offer as gifts and sacrifices, they offered to God. This I presume is unquestionable; for God commanded them that all their gifts and sacrifices should be offered to him upon his altar, consecrated for that purpose. To have done otherwise had been the highest idolatry. But Christ, if he be a high priest, must, says the apostle, of necessity have somewhat to offer, as they did, and after the same manner; that is, to God. If this he did not, there is nothing of reason or sense in the apostle's inference; for what necessity can there be, because the high priests of old did offer sacrifices to God, that then if Jesus Christ be a high priest he must do something of another kind? They have nothing to say upon these instances, but to confess the words and deny the thing, and then tell us that they agree to the words, but differ about their interpretation—the interpretation they suggest being a direct denial of the thing itself; of which more afterwards.

To the same purpose speaks our apostle (Heb. 5:1); which place has been before vindicated, and is so fully in the ensuing exposition, to which the reader is referred. And this consideration discovers much of the general nature, use, and end, of the priesthood of Christ, which we inquire after; for it is hence evident that it is the power, office, and duty, whereby he makes an interposition between God and us—that is, with God on our behalf. And there are two general ends of this interposition, as the Scripture testifies, and which the common faith of Christians relies upon. And these are—

1. *'Averruncatio mali,'* the removal of all sorts of evil from us, every thing that did or might befall us in a way of evil, hurt, damage, or punishment, on the account of our sins and apostasy from God.
2. *'Acquisitio boni,'* the procuring and obtaining for us every thing that is good, with respect to our reconciliation to God, peace with him, and the enjoyment of him.

And these are intended in the general acts of his office; for—first, his oblation principally and firstly respects the making atonement for sin, and the turning away of the wrath that was due to us as sinners; wherein he was Jesus, the deliverer, who saves us from the wrath to come. And this is all that is included in the nature of oblation as absolutely considered: but as the oblation of Christ was founded on the covenant before described, it had a further prospect. For with respect to the obedience which therein he yielded to God, according to the terms of that covenant, it was not only satisfactory, but meritorious; that is, by the sacrifice of himself he did not only turn away the wrath which was due to us, but also obtained for us 'eternal redemption,' with all the grace and glory belonging to this. There remains nothing to be done on our behalf, after the once offering of himself, whereby he 'perfected for ever them that are sanctified,' but only the actual application of these good things to us, or our actual instating in the possession of them. To this is his intercession, the second duty of his priestly office, designed; the especial nature of which must be elsewhere declared and vindicated.

CHRIST'S CALL TO THE PRIESTHOOD

For the further clearing of the whole subject of our inquiry, we must yet consider both the call of Christ to this office, his actual inauguration, and his discharge of it, both when and where; for all these belong to its nature.

The call of the Lord Christ to this office is expressly asserted by our apostle (Heb. 5:4–6):

> And no man takes this honour to himself, but he that is called of God, as was Aaron. So also Christ glorified not himself to be made an high priest; but he that said to him, Thou art my Son, today have I begotten thee. As he says also in another place, Thou art a priest for ever after the order of Melchizedek.

If the reader desire to see the particulars wherein the call of Christ consisted, its comparison with the call of Aaron, preference before it, or exaltation above it, he may consult our exposition on that place, from whence I shall repeat nothing here. In general I say, that the call of Christ to the office of the priesthood consisted in that eternal covenant which was between the Father and him concerning his undertaking the work of our recovery and salvation, which I have at large before described. He was not made a priest by virtue of any vocal command, as Aaron was called by a command given to Moses to that purpose (Exod. 28:1); nor by virtue of any established law, which gave the posterity of Aaron their succession to that office; but he was called by an immediate transaction between him and the Father before the world was. This call of his, therefore, may be considered either with respect to designation or manifestation. As it intends the designation of Christ to his office, so it is expressed in these words of God the Father to him, 'Thou art my Son, this day have I begotten thee;' which what they import in the covenant transactions between the Father and the Son has been before declared.

The manifestation of this call consisted originally in the first promise given concerning his incarnation and undertaking of the work of our redemption (Gen. 3:15). With respect to this he says, Ps. 40:8–9, הִנֵּה־בָאתִי בִּמְגִלַּת־סֵפֶר כָּתוּב עָלָי לַעֲשׂוֹת־רְצוֹנְךָ אֱלֹהַי אָז אָמַרְתִּי—'Then said I, Lo, I come: in the volume of the book'— that is, בִּרֹאשׁ מְגִלַּת, 'in the beginning of the sacred volume,' as our apostle renders it, ἐν κεφαλίδι, 'in the head' of it (Heb. 10:7); that is, in that first promise, recorded in the beginning of the Scripture, wherein his own consent was tacitly included, and the virtue of his office and sacrifice established, whence he became the 'Lamb slain from the foundation of the world.' And more need not be added in this place concerning this call of Christ to the office of the priesthood.

HIS INAUGURATION TO THE PRIESTLY OFFICE

His actual inauguration into it, and susception of it, is next to be considered. And he was vested with all his offices from his conception and nativity. There was no time wherein he was, as to his human nature, and was not the king, priest, and prophet of his church; for he received all his offices by the unction of the Spirit, when God 'anointed him with the oil of gladness above his fellows.' And this was done fundamentally in his incarnation, when he was conceived and sanctified by the Holy Spirit, communicated to him not by measure. And so he was born 'Christ the Lord' (Luke 2:11). He was born one anointed by the Holy Ghost, Lord, and consequently priest and prophet—all which offices were communicated by unction. Together with those graces, gifts, and abilities, which were necessary to their discharge, right, title, and authority for their exercise in their proper seasons were conveyed to him thereby. And in these two does all office and power consist.

The actual exercise of all the offices of Christ was regulated by the will of the Father, his own wisdom and compliance therewith, with the order and nature of the things themselves about which he was to be conversant therein. He was anointed to be the great prophet of the church from the womb; yet he entered not upon the public discharge of that office until after his baptism, when his commission and call to this were proclaimed from heaven (Matt. 3:17). So also was he 'Christ the Lord'—that is, the king of the church; yet began he not visibly to exercise that office in his own person until the mission of his apostles with authority from him to preach the gospel (Matt. 10). So had God disposed of things, and so did the nature of the work which he had to do require. And as to his priestly office, he neither did nor could enter upon the exercise and discharge of it until the end of his prophetical ministry; for he could not do it but by his death, which was to put an end to that ministry here on the earth, excepting only the instructions which he gave to his apostles after his resurrection (Acts 1:3).

But to propose the whole matter somewhat more distinctly, there are three things that concurred to the inauguration of the Lord Christ to this office, or there were degrees of it:

1. His real unction by the Holy Ghost with an all-fullness of gifts and graces, at his incarnation. This whole work of the Spirit, with its effects, I have elsewhere at large discussed, and shall not further insist upon it.
2. His declarative unction at his baptism, when the Spirit descended upon him, and filled him with power for the exercise of all the gifts and graces he had received for the discharge of his whole office.
3. To both these there succeeded an especial dedication to the actual performance of the duties of this office. And this was his own act, which he had power for from God. This himself expresses, John 17:19, Ὑπὲρ αὐτῶν ἐγὼ ἁγιάζω ἐμαυτόν·— 'I sanctify,' that is, I consecrate or dedicate, 'myself.' For of real sanctification, by purification and further infusion of grace, he was not capable: and the communication of real grace to the human nature was the work of the Holy Ghost; he did not so sanctify himself. But he did dedicate, separate, and consecrate himself to God, in the discharge of this office. It does also respect the sacrifice which he was to offer: 'I consecrate and give up myself to be a sacrifice.' But he who was to be the sacrifice was also to be the sacrificer. This consecration, therefore, respected his person, and what he was to do as the sacrificer, no less than what he was to suffer as a sacrifice; for this also was necessary, and every high priest was so consecrated.

In that prayer, therefore, of our Saviour (John 17) do I place the beginning and entrance of the exercise of his priestly office. Whatever he did after this to the moment of his death belonged principally to that. Sundry things, I confess, fell in occasionally afterwards, wherein he acted his prophetic office in bearing witness to the truth; but the scope of all his ensuing actions and passions respect his priestly office only: for although his sacrifice, precisely considered, consisted in his actual offering of himself on the cross, yet his sacerdotal actings with reference to it are not to be confined to this. And what these actings were, without an inquiry into the nature of his sacrifice, which I have designed for the subject of another discourse, I shall briefly recount.

HIS DISCHARGE OF THE PRIESTLY OFFICE

Sundry things were considerable in the sacrifices of old, which, although they did not all belong to the essence of them, yet they did to their completeness and perfection, being all types and resemblances of what was afterwards to be done by Christ himself. Some of these we shall call over, to give an illustration to this.

Features of Ancient Sacrifice

First, there was required thereunto the adduction of the sacrifice, or of the beast to be sacrificed, to the priest, or the priest's provision of it, which was incumbent on him with respect to the תָּמִיד, or daily sacrifice in the temple. This belonged to the sacrifice, and is expressed by a sacred word, אָדָם כִּי־יַקְרִיב קָרְבָּן (Lev. 1:2). The bringing or adduction of it made it a 'corban', a gift brought, sacred, dedicated to God. For there was in it—

1. *'Animus offerentis,'* the mind and intention of the offerer to devote it to God; which was the foundation, and gave life to the sacrifice. Hence it was a principle even among the heathen that no sacrifice was accepted that proceeded not *'a libenti animo,'* 'from a willing mind.' And this the apostle seems to allude to, Εἰ γὰρ προθυμία πρόκειται (2 Cor. 8:12), 'If there be a free determination or purpose of mind,' namely, in offering any thing to God, καθὸ ἐὰν ἔχῃ τις, εὐπρόσδεκτος, οὐ καθὸ οὐκ ἔχει, 'it is accepted according to what a man has, and not according to what he has not.' It is the mind, and not the matter; that gives measure and acceptance to an offering.
2. There was in it loss and damage in the charge of it. The offerer parted with it *'e peculio suo.'* He gave it up to make expiation for his sin.
3. The care of providing it according to the law belonged also to this. The offerer was to take care that it was of clean beasts, a male or female, as the law required, without blemish. It is true, the priest was also to make judgment concerning

223

this after its bringing to him; but he that brought it was to use his utmost skill and diligence in the choice of a meat-offering out of his flock, or he fell under the curse of the deceiver (Mal. 1:13–14).

4. The act of adduction itself belonged to the holy service, with a testification of a desire, in a way of faith and obedience, to have it offered to God. These things, indeed, were no essential parts of the sacrifice, but they were necessarily antecedent to it and preparatory for it. And all these things, in some cases, were left to the people, although they signified what was to be done by Christ in his sacrifice, to manifest the imperfection of the Levitical priesthood, which could not comprise nor answer all that was to be prefigured by sacrifices.

Secondly, there was mactation, or the killing of the beast by the priests at the altar. And herein consisted the essence, all that followed being instituted in testification of its direction and dedication to God. Hence to slay and to sacrifice in this matter are the same. 'And you will sacrifice the black sheep, and revisit the sacred grove' (Virg. Georg. 4.546). See our second Exercitation for the confirmation of this. And the substance of the sacrifice is to be thought principally to consist herein, though the offering of it was also necessary to its completeness and perfection; for—

1. Herein the intention of the sacrificer and sacrificed, in that solemn formula which was understood in all expiatory sacrifices, 'Which was in his head,' was effected or accomplished. And as the common sense of all nations agreed in a commutation in such sacrifices, as I have proved elsewhere, so we are plainly taught it in the Scripture; for besides that this is the open sense and meaning of all institutions about them, so the especial rite of confessing sin over the head of the scape-goat, thereby laying it on him, yea, and the command that he who brought his sin or trespass-offering should therewith confess his own guilt, do make it evident. Now this, as is manifest, was accomplished only in the mactation and death of the sacrifice.

2. It was the blood whereby atonement was made, and that as it was the life of the creature; and the reason why it was given

to make atonement was, because the life was in it, wherefore that act whereby the blood of the creature was so taken away as that thereby the life of it was destroyed, was the principal thing in the sacrifice itself. It is true, atonement on the altar was to be made with the blood after the effusion of it; but it was with it whilst it was yet warm, before the animal spirits were utterly departed from it, and that because its virtue for expiation depended on its being poured out in death. And no blood could have been offered but that which was taken away in the mactation or total destruction of the life of the sacrifice. And the pouring of the blood at the altar, with the sprinkling of it variously, belonged to the appropriation of the sacrifice to God, to whose sanctified altar it was brought.

Thirdly, there was the burning of the sacrifice, or in some cases the principal parts of it, on the altar. This finished or completed the sacrifice. For whereas, in the great anniversary of expiation, some part of the blood of the sacrifice was carried into the most holy place, it was no part of the sacrifice itself, but a consequent of it, in a holy improvement of what was finished before, as to the duty itself. And this was appointed for no other end but because it was the only way whereby the perpetual efficacy of the blood of Christ in heaven, which was shed on the earth, might be represented. In these things did the discharge of the priestly office in those of the order of Aaron principally consist. And all these things were exactly answered and fulfilled, in a spiritual and glorious manner, by our Lord Jesus Christ, the great high priest of the church, who was himself to be all and to do all after he had solemnly dedicated and consecrated himself to this work, as we shall see by a review and application of the particulars recounted.

Features of Ancient Sacrifice Fulfilled in Christ

First, there was the adduction, or his bringing himself to be an offering or sacrifice to God. And this consisted in all those sacred actions of his which were previously preparatory to his death; as—

1. His going up to Jerusalem to the passover. He went on purpose to offer himself to God. And in his way he acquainted

his disciples with what would befall him therein (Luke 18:31–3; Matt. 20:17–19); which when one of them would have dissuaded him from, he gave him that vehement and severe reproof, 'Get thee behind me, Satan: thou art an offense to me: for thou savorest not the things that be of God' (Matt. 16:23). Peter, considering only the outward part of his sufferings, with the shame and scandal wherewith it was attended, would have prevailed with him to have avoided it; which he knew was in his power to do. But withal, which he knew not, he dissuaded him from going to offer himself to God, for which cause principally he came into the world, and so fell under this sacred rebuke; for this great and weighty work of obedience was so fully implanted in the heart of Christ, that he could not bear with any thing that had the appearance of a diversion from it. With such intention, freedom, willingness, and readiness of mind, did he go to offer himself, according to the will of God; which gave life, virtue, and merit, to his oblation.

2. His going into the garden the night before his suffering. What was it but as it were the bringing of himself to the door of the tabernacle to offer himself to God, or to make his soul an offering for sin, according to the will of God?

3. He offered up to God prayers and supplications; which, because they had respect to his sacrifice, are reckoned by our apostle as sacerdotal acts (Heb. 5:7). Principally his prayers in the garden are intended; for his supplications there, with the manner of them, the apostle expresses and declares; see our exposition of the place. For all sacrifices were accompanied with supplications for grace and pardon. And herein did our Saviour actually give up himself to God to be a sacrifice; which was to be done by expressions of his obedience, and supplications for that issue thereof which was promised to him.

4. His propassion or foresuffering in the garden, in the anguish of his soul, the agony of his mind, and bloody sweat, belongs to this. Hereon, indeed, succeeded an external shame, which was necessary for the leading and bringing of him 'as a lamb to the slaughter' (Isa. 53:7), but his own mind and will it was that brought him to be a sacrifice to God. The offering himself

was his own act, from first to last, and is constantly ascribed to him.

Secondly, there was mactation or slaying of the sacrifice, which was in his death as it was bloody. Herein consisted the essence and substance of the sacrifice; herein he offered himself to God. For although the other acts, of sprinkling the blood and burning the carcass of the sacrifice, or its oblation, were in the typical sacrifices distinct from the slaying of it, yet this was by reason of the imperfection of all persons and things that were made use of in that sacred service. Hence many distinct acts succeeding one to another among them were necessary. In the Lord Christ, by reason of the perfection of his person, and that he himself was both priest and sacrifice, things were done at once which were separately by them represented. Wherefore in the very death of Christ, in and by his bloodshedding, he offered himself to God.

It is fondly excepted, 'That if his death was a sacrifice, the Jews and the soldiers who crucified him were the priests.' The violence which was offered to him by all sorts of persons was necessary on other accounts; so also were the assaults which he then conflicted with from the prince and power of darkness: for they belonged to the curse of the law, which was now upon him. But his being a sacrifice depended only on his own will, he offering himself in obedience to the will of God, according to the compact before described. The soldiers were no more but as the cords that bound the sacrifice to the horns of the altar; nor did they so take away his life but that he laid it down of his own mere will, in compliance with the commandment of the Father (John 10:18).

In the pouring out of his blood, the heavenly altar of his body was sprinkled, and all heavenly things purified, even with this 'better sacrifice' (Heb. 9:23). Thus is he said to 'pour out his soul to death' (Isa. 53:12). That expression contains the whole nature of a sacrifice: for his soul is said to be poured out to death with respect to the pouring out of the blood; for in it was the life poured out, the blood being given to make atonement because the life was in it.

Thirdly, there was the oblation itself. This in those sacrifices, the sacred performance of which was accomplished πολυμερῶς, by many parts and degrees, by reason of the imperfection of the sacrificer and sacrificed, followed after the mactation, with the shedding and sprinkling of blood. In this absolutely perfect sacrifice of Christ it was not so. His oblation was at the same time and in the same action with his blood-shedding; for it was his holy, obediential giving up himself to the will of God, in undergoing what was due to our sins, making atonement for them thereby. He 'offered himself to God through the eternal Spirit' (Heb. 9:14).

The holy and eternal Spirit of God dwelling in him in all fullness, supporting his faith, confirming his obedience, kindled in him that fire of zeal to the glory of God and the reparation of his honour, from the reflection cast upon it by the sin, apostasy, disobedience, and rebellion of mankind, with that flame of love to their salvation, which as it were consumed this sacrifice in its oblation to God. Thus in and by his 'giving himself for us'—that is, in and by his death, which is constantly intended by that expression—he made himself 'an offering and a sacrifice to God for a sweet-smelling savour' (Eph. 5:2).

Fourthly, hereon ensued the representation of the whole, in answer to the high priest's entering into the most holy place with a token, part, representation, and remembrance of the blood that was offered on the altar. This was done by Christ when he entered into the holy place not made with hands, as it were sprinkled with his own blood, or accompanied with the efficacy and merit of his sacerdotal offering, 'to appear in the presence of God for us.' This was consequential to that offering of himself whereby he made atonement for us; for 'he entered into the holy place'—αἰωίαν λύτρωσιν εὑράμενος—'having obtained eternal redemption' (Heb. 9:12). His obtaining eternal redemption was by the sacrifice of himself in his death; for redemption was by price and exchange, and the Lord Christ paid no other price for sin and sinners but his own blood (1 Pet. 1:18–19). And this was antecedent to his entering into the holy place; for he did so 'having obtained eternal redemption.' And it is in vain to except that sometimes things present are expressed by verbs and participles of a preterit signification, or in those tenses which denote things past, seeing they are not to be construed so unless the matter spoken of do enforce such a construction, of which here there is no pretense;

nor can any one instance be given of the use of εὑρίσκω in that way in the whole New Testament (see Heb. 9:24).

Complete Accomplishment

This brief account of the analogy that was between the sacerdotal actings in sacrificing under the law and those of the Lord Christ in offering himself as our high priest to God, does fully evince the time, place, and manner of his discharge of this office; whereby the nature of it is also manifested. The sacrifice of Christ, indeed, was not carried on by those distinct, separate steps and degrees which the sacrifices of old were, by reason of the imperfection of the offerer and what was offered, and the necessity of many circumstances in those things which were carnal in themselves and appointed to be carnally visible; yet on the whole, in the transactions that were invisibly carried on between Christ the high priest and God, to whom he offered himself, every thing that belonged to the nature of a true and real sacrifice, or which as such was represented by them of old, was, in its proper place, order, and manner, actually accomplished. And I must needs say, that I look upon it as one of the boldest attempts on religion that ever was made by men pretending to any sobriety, namely, to deny that the Lord Christ was a priest whilst he was on the earth, or that he offered himself a sacrifice to God in his death; and those who have the confidence to stand and persist in that opinion, against all that light which the nature of the thing itself and the testimonies of Scripture do give to the truth in this matter, need not fear that on any occasion they shall be wanting to themselves therein. But of these things I must treat more fully in our ensuing exercitation.

SCRIPTURAL CONFIRMATION

I have only in this place taught the doctrine concerning the nature of the priesthood of Christ, and his discharge of that office, as my design did necessarily require I should do. The testimonies whereby the truth of it is confirmed I have long since urged and vindicated from the exceptions of our adversaries in another treatise. Here, therefore, I shall only briefly represent some of them.

He 'Loved Us and Gave Himself for Us'

Ὁ Χριστὸς ἠγάπησεν ἡμᾶς, καὶ παρέδωκεν ἑαυτὸν ὑπὲρ ἡμῶν προσφορὰν καὶ θυσίαν, τῷ Θεῷ εἰς ὀσμὴν εὐωδίας (Eph. 5:2). It is unavoidable that those expressions, he 'loved us and gave himself for us,' should signify nothing but what he did in his death; for they are never used in any other sense. So are they repeated, verse 25 of this chapter, Ἠγάπησε τὴν ἐκκλησίαν, καὶ ἑαυτὸν παρέδωκεν ὑπὲρ αὐτῆς—that is, to die for it; for this was that whereby Christ expressed his love to his church (John 10:15; Phil. 2:6–8). So also speaks our apostle expressly, 'Christ loved me, and gave himself for me' (Gal. 2:20); the same with that of John, 'Who loved us, and washed us from our sins in his own blood' (Rev. 1:5), which he did when he was 'delivered for our offenses' (Rom. 4:25). Παρεδόθη διὰ τὰ παραπτώματα ἡμῶν is the expression of what was done when παρέδωκεν ἑαυτὸν ὑπὲρ ἡμῶν. The subject, therefore, spoken of is agreed on, or cannot be questioned. Concerning this, the apostle says that it was προσφορά καὶ θυσία, 'an offering and a sacrifice;' or that in giving himself for us he offered himself to God an offering and a sacrifice. By these two words our apostle expresses all sorts of sacrifices under the law (Heb. 10:5, from Ps. 40:7), where they are expressed by זֶבַח וּמִנְחָה; for although 'mincha' be usually applied to a peculiar thank-offering of meat and drink, yet where these two are joined together, 'zebach and mincha,' they denote all sorts of expiatory sacrifices: 'The iniquity of Eli's house shall not be purged'—בְּזֶבַח וּבְמִנְחָה—'by any sort of expiatory sacrifices' (1 Sam. 3:14). And θυσία, or זֶבַח, is such a sacrifice as consisted in mactation or killing, as we have proved before. This Christ offered in his death or when out of his love to us, in obedience to the will of God, he gave up himself to death for us. This love and obedience, the Socinians say, is the sacrifice intended in this place, which is therefore metaphorical; but that Christ offered himself a sacrifice in his death they deny that the apostle here asserts. But—

1. In all other places where there is any mention of the offering of Christ, it is expressly said that he offered 'himself,' or his 'soul,' or his 'body' (Isa. 53:10; Heb. 9:14, 10:10); yea, as here he is said to offer sacrifice in his death, so his suffering therein is affirmed to be necessary to his sacrifice of himself (Heb.

9:25–6). He 'gave himself for us a sacrifice,' is no more but that he suffered when he offered himself, as the apostle expressly affirms.

2. Although προσφορά may be used for a metaphorical sacrifice, and so possibly may θυσία also, yet whenever they are conjoined in the Scripture, they denote all sorts of proper sacrifices, as is evident from the place before cited; and therefore they can intend here nothing but that sacrifice which all those proper sacrifices prefigured. Besides, θυσία, unless the metaphor be evident and cogent, does signify nothing but a sacrifice by immolation or killing. Θύειν, as we have showed, is but σφάττειν, 'to kill,' only it is to slay in sacred services; with respect to which also the other word is used in good authors. So Plutarch affirms of the Gauls, that they believed θεοὺς εἶναι ξαίροντας ἀνθρώπων σφαττωμένων αἵματι, καὶ ταύτην τελειοτάτην θυσίαν—'that the gods delighted in the blood of slain men, and that this was the most perfect sacrifice.' Ἀνθρωποσφαγία, if it respect things sacred, is the same with ἀνθρωποθυσία. So, whereas the Lord Christ was ἀμνίον ἐσφαγισμένον, 'a Lamb slain' (Rev. 5:12, 13:8)—being called 'a Lamb,' and 'the Lamb of God,' as all acknowledge, with respect to the paschal lamb—it is said πάσχα ἡμῶν ἐθύθη Χριστὸς, 'Christ our passover,' our paschal lamb, 'is sacrificed for us.' Θυσία, therefore, being used to express the nature of the death of Christ with respect to God, nothing can be intended thereby but a proper and bloody sacrifice.

3. Our adversaries acknowledge that the Lord Christ did offer himself as a complete expiatory sacrifice to God. I ask, then, when he is positively and directly affirmed to offer himself an offering and sacrifice to God, why is not that the expiatory sacrifice which he offered? They have not any thing to reply, but only that he offered not that sacrifice in his death, but upon his entrance into heaven; which is only in favor of their own hypothesis, to contradict the apostle to his face.

4. Προσφορὰν καὶ θυσίαν are regulated by the same verb with ἑαυτόν, Παρεδώκεν ἑαυτὸν Προσφορὰν καὶ θυσίαν: so that there can be no other sense of the words but 'Christ offered himself a sacrifice,' or 'gave himself a sacrifice.' And whereas it is objected that παραδίδωμι is not used for sacrificing, or

offering sacrifice, besides that it is false, as may be seen in Micah 6:7, where יִתֵּן in the original is rendered by παραδίδωμι, so here was a peculiar reason for the use of this word, because the apostle included in the same expression both his giving himself for us and the manner of it, namely, by giving himself a sacrifice to God for us.

5. Whereas it is said that this sacrifice was 'a sweet-smelling savor to God,' it does not advantage our adversaries, as I shall elsewhere manifest, from the rise, nature, and first use of that expression. At present it may suffice that it is used expressly concerning expiatory sacrifices (Lev. 4:31), and whole burnt-offerings, which were of the same nature (Lev. 1:9). And whereas this is the first kind of sacrifice appointed under the law, and is said expressly to 'make atonement' (Lev. 1:4), and therein, to be 'an offering of a sweet savor to the LORD,' it plainly declares that all other sacrifices which made atonement were in like manner a sweet savor to the Lord; on the account whereof that of Christ, wherein God rested and was well pleased, is so called. But of these things we must treat elsewhere more at large.

He 'Offered' to God

'As he says also in another place, Thou art a priest for ever after the order of Melchizedek. Who in the days of his flesh, when he had offered up prayers and supplications with strong crying and tears to him that was able to save him from death' (Heb. 5:6–7). The reader may consult the exposition of this place, wherein the difficulties of it are removed, and the intention of the Holy Ghost in it is truly explained. At present I shall only observe some few passages in confirmation of the truth under consideration; as—

1. The works, acts, or duties, here assigned to Christ, are assigned to him expressly as he was a high priest, as is undeniably manifest in the context; wherefore they are sacerdotal acts, or acts of Christ as a priest.

2. He performed them 'in the days of his flesh,' and that when he was in great distress, standing in need of aid and assistance from God; that is, at the time of his death.

3. It is therefore here plainly affirmed, that our Lord Jesus Christ, as a high priest, did, in his dying for us, offer to God.

If we inquire in other places what he offered, it is expressly said that it was 'himself,' his 'soul,' his 'body,' as we have proved. And that Christ, as a high priest, in the days of his flesh offered himself to God, is all that we need for the confirmation of what we assert concerning the time, place, and nature, of the exercise of his priesthood. It will be excepted that Christ is not said in this place to offer himself, but only to offer up 'prayers and supplications;' which are a metaphorical and not a real sacrifice. But the apostle did not solemnly introduce him as called to the office of a high priest, and acting the powers of that office, merely with respect to prayers and supplications considered by themselves, and to instance in those only at his death, when he might have mentioned those when, in the course of his life, he continued mighty by himself. What he offered he intended afterwards to declare, and does so expressly; here he designed only to assert, that, being called to be a high priest, he offered to God; and that as to the manner of that offering, it was with prayers and supplications, cries and tears, wherein he describes his offering of himself by those adjuncts of it which were also sacerdotal.

He 'Purged Our Sins'

Δι' ἑαυτοῦ καθαρισμὸν ποιησάμενος τῶν ἁμαρτιῶν ἡμῶν ἐκάθισεν ἐν δεξιᾷ τοῦ θρόνου τῆς μεγαλωσύνης ἐν ὑψηλοῖς—'When he had by himself purged our sins, he sat down on the right hand of the Majesty on high' (Heb. 1:3). It is agreed between us and our adversaries that this purging of our sins was the effect of that expiatory sacrifice which the Lord Christ offered to God as our high priest. The whole question that can remain is when he offered it. And the apostle here expressly declares that this was done before he sat down at the right hand of God; and this is so plain in the words as that no exception can be invented against it. That alone which they have invented for an evasion is, that Christ indeed offered himself at his first entrance into heaven, and on his appearance in the presence of God for us, before he sat down at the right hand of God. This Crellius insists upon (cap. 10. part. 31, 537–8). But this will yield them no relief, neither according to the truth nor according to their own principles; for—

1. Although we may have distinct apprehensions of Christ's entering into heaven and his sitting at the right hand of God, yet it is but one state of Christ that is intended in both, his entrance into heaven being only the means of his sitting down at the right hand of God; and therefore they are never mentioned together, but sometimes the one, sometimes the other, is made use of to express the same state. So his sitting down at the right hand of God is expressed as immediately ensuing his suffering, it being that state to which his resurrection, ascension, and entrance into heaven, were subservient: 'He endured the cross, despising the shame, and is set down at the right hand of the throne of God' (Heb. 12:2). The whole is, that he 'passed through the heavens' (Heb. 4:14), and was thereon 'made higher than the heavens' (Heb. 7:26); that is, he 'suffered,' and so 'entered into his glory' (Luke 24:26). Nor does the Scripture anywhere give the least intimation of any mediatorial act of Christ interposing between his entrance into heaven and sitting down at the right hand of God.

2. This answer has no consistency with their own principles in this matter: for they contend that the expiation of our sins consists in the taking of them away, by freeing us from the punishment which is due to them. And this must be done by virtue of the power which Christ received of God after his obedience; but this his receiving of power belongs to his sitting at the right hand of God, so as he can in no sense be said to have purged or expiated our sins before it. And if they will allow that Christ expiated our sins anywhere in heaven or earth antecedently to our actual freedom in present pardon or future complete deliverance, then does not the expiation of sins consist in our actual deliverance from them, as they contend that it does.

He 'Entered' the Holy Place

To the same purpose speaks the apostle, Διὰ τοῦ ἰδίου αἵματος εἰσῆλθεν ἐφάπαξ εἰς τὰ ἅγια, αἰωνίαν λύτρωσιν εὑράμενος· —'By his own blood he entered in once into the holy place, having obtained eternal redemption' (Heb. 9:12). This entrance of Christ 'into the holy place' was his entrance into heaven. Antecedently to this he is said to have 'obtained eternal redemption.' This 'redemption we have through his blood, even the forgiveness of sins' (Eph. 1:7); and this forgiveness, or the putting away of sin, was 'by the sacrifice of himself' (Heb. 9:26). Wherefore, the sacrifice of Christ, whereby he obtained redemption, or put away sin, was by his blood-shedding. And this was, as it is here expressed, antecedent to his entrance into the holy place. Crellius, in answer to this testimony (p. 536), engages into a long discourse to prove that things present, or not perfectly past, are sometimes expressed by the aorist, or sign of the time past; as if our argument from hence were built merely on that form of the word, on supposition of a general maxim that all words in that tense do necessarily signify the time past. But we proceed on no such supposition. We say, indeed, and contend, that there must be, some cogent reason to interpret that of the time present or to come which is expressed as past and done. For this we say there is none in this place, nor is any pretended but the false hypothesis of our adversaries, that Christ offered not himself until his entrance into heaven, which they judge sufficient to oppose to the clearest testimonies to the contrary. For whereas the words of the apostle signify directly that the Lord Christ first obtained eternal redemption, and then entered into heaven, or the holy place not made with hands, they will have his intention to be the direct contrary—that he first entered into heaven, and then obtained eternal redemption; for that offering of himself which they suppose was consequential to his entrance into the holy place. But we argue from the scope of the words. It is said that 'Christ by his own blood entered in once into the holy place, having obtained eternal redemption.' I desire to know how or by what means he did so obtain, or find, or acquire it. Is it not plain that it was 'by his own blood,' and that which he shed before he entered into the sanctuary?

He Offered Himself Once

Moreover, Christ is said to 'offer himself once' (Heb. 7:27, 9:28, 10:10, 12, 14). His offering was one, and once offered. An action once performed, and then ceasing to be performed, however it continues in its virtue and efficacy, is so expressed. The high priest entered into the most holy place once in the year; that is, his so doing was an act that was at once performed, and after that was not for that year. Hence the apostle proves the excellency of this sacrifice of Christ above those of the Aaronic priests, because they, by reason of their weakness and imperfection, were often offered; this of Christ, being every way complete, and of infinite efficacy, was offered but once, and at once (Heb. 10:1-4, etc). What sacrifice, therefore, can this be, that was then but once offered? Does this seem to express the continual appearance of Christ in heaven? which, if a sacrifice, is always offering, and not once offered, and so would be inferior to them which were offered only once a year. For that which effects its design by being performed once a year, is more efficacious than that which must be always effecting. Besides, our apostle says expressly that the Lord Christ was 'once offered to bear the sins of many' (Heb. 9:28). But this he did then, and only then, when he 'bare our sins in his own body on the tree' (1 Pet. 2:24); which irrefragably proves that then he was offered to God.

No Sacrifice without Suffering

Add yet to this that the offering of Christ, which the apostle insists upon as his great sacerdotal act and duty, was necessarily accompanied with suffering, and therefore was on the earth and not in heaven: 'Nor yet that he should offer himself often…for then must he often have suffered since the foundation of the world' (Heb. 9:25-6).The argument of the apostle is built upon a general principle, that all sacrifice was in and by suffering. The sacrificed beast was slain, and had his blood poured out. Without this there could be no sacrifice. Therefore if Christ himself had been to be often offered, he must have often suffered. It is excepted, 'That although his offering did not consist in his sufferings, nor did they both concur at the same time, yet his suffering was previously necessary, as an antecedent condition to his offering of himself in heaven; and on that account the apostle might well conclude that if he were often to be offered, he must have often suffered.' But—

1. There can be no reason given, on the opinion of our adversaries, why the suffering of Christ was antecedently necessary to that

offering of himself which they imagine. At best they refer it to an absolute free act of the will of God, which might have been otherwise, and Christ might have often offered and yet not often suffered.

2. Christ is said not only to 'offer himself,' but to be 'offered:' 'Christ was once offered to bear the sins of many' (v. 28). Now, though the offering of himself may be accommodated to that presentation which he made of himself in heaven, yet his being offered to bear sins plainly includes a suffering in what he did.

3. There were many typical sacrifices, which nothing belonging to went beyond their suffering. Such were all the expiatory sacrifices, or sacrifices to make atonement, whose blood was not carried into the sanctuary. For their slaying, the pouring out of their blood, the consumption on the altar, were all destructive to their beings. And these sacrifices were types of the sacrifice of Christ, as our apostle testifies, 'Who needs not daily'—καθ' ἡμέραν—'to offer up sacrifice, first for his own sins, and then for the people's: for this he did once, when he offered up himself' (Heb. 7:27). Had he intended only the sacrifice of the high priest, he could not have said that he was to offer it καθ' ἡμέραν, 'daily,' when he was to do so only κατ' ἐνιαυτόν, 'yearly' (Heb. 10:1). It is therefore תָּמִיד, or 'daily sacrifice,' that he intends, and this was not carried on beyond suffering.

And this is yet more plainly expressed, 'And every priest stands daily ministering and offering oftentimes the same sacrifices, which can never take away sins: but this man, after he had offered one sacrifice for sins, for ever sat down on the right hand of God' (Heb. 10:11–12). Comparing the sacrifice of Christ with these sacrifices, he declares that they were types and representations thereof, or there would be no foundation for such a comparison, nor for the exaltation of his above them, as to its efficacy and its consequents. But there was nothing of these sacrifices carried into the holy place, nor any representation made of them therein, but in their suffering and destruction they were consummated; for they were the sacrifices which every priest who ministered at the altar did offer either daily or on all occasions. Wherefore, if the sacrifice of Christ answered to them, as the apostle teaches us that it did, he offered it in his suffering, his death, and blood-shedding only. After this he entered as our high priest into the holy place not made with hands, to appear in the presence of God for us. And as this was signified by the high priest's entering into the most holy place with the blood of the bullock and goat that were offered for a sin-offering, so it was necessary in itself to the application of the value and efficacy of his sacrifice to the church, according to the covenant between Father and Son before described.

What has been pleaded is sufficient to our present purpose, as to the declaration of the nature of the priesthood of Christ, his entrance upon it, and discharge of it. But there being another opinion concerning it, universally opposite in all particulars to the truth declared and vindicated, we must, for the security of the faith of the church, call it, with the ways, means, and artifices wherewith it is endeavoured to be supported, to an account; which shall be done in the ensuing exercitation.

9

THE NATURE OF THE PRIESTHOOD OF CHRIST

The opinion of the Socinians concerning the priesthood of Christ was expressed in general in our preceding discourse; but for the clearer apprehension and confutation of it, it is necessary that it be more particularly declared in the most important parts of it, as also that its contrariety to the faith of the church may be the more plainly demonstrated. And the sum of what they pretend to apprehend and believe herein may be reduced to the ensuing heads:

1. 'That the Lord Christ was not, nor is, a high priest properly so called, but only metaphorically, by reason of some allusion between what he does for the church and what was done by the high priests under the law for the Jews.' And here, if they please, they may rest, as having in design utterly overthrown or rejected this office of Christ. But further to manifest their intentions, they add—

2. 'That he was not at all, in any sense, a high priest whilst he was on the earth, or before his ascension into heaven.' And this because he did not any of those things on the earth on the account of which he is called a high priest; but he is called so in an allusion to the high priests under the law. Hence it follows that in his death he offered no sacrifice to God, nor

made any expiation of our sins thereby; which also that he did not they expressly contend.

3. 'That therefore he became a high priest when he entered into heaven, and presented himself alive to God.' Not that then he received any new office which he had not before, but only that then he had power to do those things from the doing whereof he is metaphorically denominated a priest. Wherefore they say—

4. 'That it is in heaven where he makes atonement and does expiate our sins, which is called his offering himself to God an expiatory oblation or sacrifice; which as it consisted not in his sufferings, death, and bloodshedding, so had it no virtue or efficacy from thence, but only as it was a condition pre-required thereunto.'

5. 'This expiation of our sins consists principally in two things— (a) Our deliverance from the punishment due to them, initially in this world by pardon, and completely at the last day, when we shall be saved from the wrath to come. (b) In our deliverance from the power of sin, by faith in the doctrine he taught and confortuity to his example, that we should not serve it in this world.' And—

6. 'Hence it follows that believers are the first proper objects of the discharge of the duties of this office, or of all the sacerdotal actings of Christ;' for they consist in the help, aid, relief, and deliverance from our spiritual enemies which we have by him, his gracious and merciful will of relieving us being that on the account of which he is called a high priest, and wherein that office does consist. Wherefore—

7. 'This priestly office of Christ is upon the matter the same with his kingly office;' or it is the exerting and exercise of his kingly power with love, care, and compassion; so called in the Epistle to the Hebrews, out of an allusion to what was done by the high priests of old.

8. 'Whereas his intercession does belong to this office of his, and is expressly assigned to him as a high priest, it is nothing but a note, evidence, or expression, to teach us that the power which the Lord Christ excercises and puts forth mercifully for

our relief, he received originally from God, as if he had prayed to him for it.'

SOCINIANS IN THEIR OWN WORDS

I have so included and expressed the apprehensions of these men concerning the priesthood of Christ in these positions, as that I am persuaded that there is no one who is ingenuous amongst them will except against any particular in the account. But that none may reflect in their thoughts about it, I shall repeat it in the words of one of their principal writers. To this purpose speaks Volkelius (*de Vera Relig*. lib. 3. cap. 37, 144):

> We will now explain the priestly office of Christ. In the first place we must notice that there is not much difference from his kingly office, if you put your mind to the matter. When the divine Spirit is brought forth by this figure and anology, by which manner Christ directs the performance of his reign, before our eyes he wished to establish him in the best way, and to reveal that he is not only able to procure our salvation, but also wishes to assist us, and furthermore to do it entirely and to be complete in it, that he might thoroughly atone for our sins. It is this: he saves us not only from sin itself but indeed chiefly from its guilt and penalty.

> Even if Christ was duly placed in this priestly office, it was not enough for him to be merciful to men, unless in addition his power was great enough by his most divine help to raise up oppressed men in their distress. And whenever this power was needed for any matter in the heaven and the earth it followed Christ before he ascended into heaven and achieved such great mastery of everything and was not yet finished as our high priest (146).

So he, and much more to the same purpose. In like manner (*Cat. Rac.* 'de Munere Christi Sacerdotali', Quaest. 1):

> The role of a priest in this is allowed because just as with the kingly office he is able to assist us in all our needs, so in the priestly office he is willing to and in fact does assist us. And this assistance of his or his method of bringing help is called his sacrifice.

Why is his method of bringing help called his sacrifice?
It is therefore called it by a figurative manner of speaking. etc.

What again is the atonement of sins?
It is liberation from the penalties with which sins both temporal and eternal are accompanied, and also from the sins themselves, so that we are not slaves to them.

Why is this sacrifice of Christ completed in the heavens?
Because such a great tabernacle was required. etc.

What? Can it be that he was priest before he ascended into the heavens and especially when he was hanging fixed to the cross?
He was not.

To the same purpose the reader may see Socin. *de Christo Servat.* p. 2, cap. 15; Ostorod. *Institut. Relig. Christian.* cap. 37; Smalcius *de Divinitate Jesu Christi*, cap. 23; Woolzogen. *Compend. Relig. Christian.* sect. 51, p. 11; Brenius in Hebrews 4:16, et cap. 8:4. 3.

VERSUS THE CHURCH'S FAITH

But the faith of the church of God stands up in direct opposition to all these imaginations; for it asserts—

1. That our Lord Jesus Christ was and is truly and properly the high priest of the church, and that of him all others vested with that office under the law were only types and representatives. And the description which the apostle gives of a high priest properly so called is accommodated and appropriated by himself to him (Heb. 5:1–3); as also all the acts, duties, or offices of the priesthood are accordingly ascribed to him (Heb. 7:26–7, 10:6–7, 9:24; 1 John 2:1–2).
2. That he was perfectly and completely a high priest whilst he was on the earth, although he did not perfectly and completely discharge all the duties of that office in this world, seeing he lives for ever to make intercession for us.
3. That he offered himself an expiatory sacrifice to God in his

death and bloodshedding, and was not made a priest upon his entrance into heaven, there to offer himself to God, where only the nature of his bloody sacrifice was represented.

4. That the expiation of our sins consists principally in the charging of the punishment due to them upon the Lord Christ, who took them on himself, and was made a sin-offering for them, that we may be freed from them and all the evil which follows them by the sentence of the law. And therefore—

5. God is the first proper object of all the sacerdotal actings of Christ; for to him he offered himself, and with him he made atonement for sin. And thereon—

6. This office of Christ is distinct from his kingly office, and not in any of its proper acts or adjuncts coincident therewithal.

All which assertions have been before declared and proved, and shall now be further vindicated.

No Empty Title

He who is supposed, and that not unjustly, to have amongst our adversaries handled these things with most diligence and subtilty is Crellius. I shall therefore examine what he on set purpose disputes on this subject, and that not by referring the substance of his discourses to the distinct heads before mentioned, but taking the whole of it as disposed in his own method and words; and that with a design to give a specimen of those artifices, diversions, ambiguous expressions, and equivocations, which he perpetually makes use of in this cause and controversy. And where he seems to be defective I shall call in Smalcius, and it may be some others of them, to his assistance. And I shall only transcribe his words in Latin, without adding any translation of them, as supposing that those who are competently able to judge of these things are not wholly ignorant of that language, and others may find enough for their satisfaction in our discourses so far as they are concerned.

In this controversy he expressly engages, in *Respon. ad Grotium*, cap. part. 56, p. 543:

(1.) We recognise the priestly office of Christ as distinct from (the offices of) prophet and king, though not distinct by position only. (2.) For, to put it briefly, it is in harmony with his kingly office and with his prophetic office. (3.) From these two offices, the king and of course the priest, in the sacred writings openly divided from one another, (4.) you see an embrace to a certain extent. For (5.) the author of Hebrews 3 from the beginning considers the dignity of Christ as a method of service committed to him by God. Wishing to place him before our eyes, and encouraging us to contemplate him, he mentions his two great offices, the prophetic office and the priestly one, one of which he carried out on the earth, and the other of which he continually conducts in the heavens. Then he says, 'Therefore, holy brothers, and participants in the heavenly calling, consider Christ Jesus, the apostle' (or 'ambassador') 'and priest of our confession.' He calls Christ the apostle or envoy or our confession, that is, of our religion and faith which we ought to declare, because he was once sent by God to proclaim it to us, and was among the prophets. However, he calls him a priest of that creed or religion. (6.) Since he constantly manages that protection and care, that is, he was established by God to direct everyything which they see and to lead us to the end; you speak as though he were the highest point of our religion and the guardian and administrator of the sacrifices, as below in chapter 12:2. He expresses these words while he calls him the leader and finisher of faith; because he went before us (to it) not only by word and example to us, but also he has now completed it since he likewise settled at the right hand of God, and guides us to the desired end.

That the Lord Christ is called a priest on some account or other, and is so, these men cannot deny, and therefore on all occasions they do in words expressly confess it. But their endeavour is, to persuade us that little or nothing is signified by that appellation as ascribed to him. At least, they will by no means allow that any such thing is intended in that expression as it signifies in all other authors, sacred and profane, when not applied to the Lord Christ. They will not have a distinct office to be intended in it.

Wherefore Crellius, although he acknowledges, in the entrance of this discourse, (1.) that the priestly dignity of Christ is distinct from his kingly and prophetical dignities, yet his whole ensuing endeavour is to prove that the priesthood is not a distinct office in him. And he sophistically makes use of the word 'dignity,' the 'priestly dignity,' to make an appearance of a distinct office from the kingly, which here he expresses by 'dignity' also. But he nowhere allows that he has a distinct sacerdotal office. And when he mentions *'officium pontificale'* as distinct from the *'officium propheticum,'* he expressly intends his kingly office. And they do constantly in their other writings call the one *'officium regium,'* the other *'munus sacerdotale,'* supposing the first word to denote an habitual power, and the latter only actual exercise, wherein yet they are mistaken. The priestly dignity, therefore, here intended, and by which word he would impose on the less wary reader, is nothing but the honour that is due to Christ for and in the discharge of his kingly office and power in a merciful, gracious manner, as the priests did of old.

Wherefore he adds, (2.) that notwithstanding this distinction, yet the sacerdotal dignity comes nearer or closer to the kingly dignity than the prophetical. But this assertion is not built on any general principle taken from the nature of these offices themselves, as though there were a greater agreement between the kingly and priestly offices than between the priestly and prophetical; for the prophetical and sacerdotal offices seem on many accounts to be of a nearer alliance than the sacerdotal and kingly, as we shall see afterwards. But this is only a step towards the main design of a total subverting of the sacerdotal office of Christ.

For on this assertion it is added immediately, (3.) that in the Scripture these two offices, the kingly and priestly, are never disjoined openly, or as contradistinct one to another. But yet his words are ambiguous. If he intend that they are not plainly, and so openly, distinguished in the Scripture one from the other, there is nothing more openly false. They are so in names and things, in the powers, acts, duties, and effects. If by *'A se invicem disjuncta et contradistincta,'* he intend such a divulsion and separation as that they should agree in nothing, not in their subject, not in their original, nor in their general ends and effects, so no offices of him are divided who in them all is the Mediator between God and men.

But they are nowhere so conjoined as that one of them should be contained and comprehended in the other (4.) 'quodammodo,' 'after a sort,' as he speaks; for this word also is of a large and ambiguous signification, used on purpose to obscure the matter treated of or the sense of the author about it. Is one so comprehended in the other as to be the same with it, to be a part of it, or to be only the exercise of the power of the other in an especial manner? If this be the mind of this author, it can be expressed by 'quodammodo' for no other end but because he dares not openly avow his sense and mind. But we deny that one is thus contained in the other, or any way so as to hinder it from being a distinct office of itself, accompanied with its distinct powers, rights, acts, and duties.

The argument from Hebrews 3:1–3, whereby he attempts to prove that one of these offices is contained in the other 'quodammodo,' whatever that be, (5.) is infirm and weak; yea, he himself knew well enough the weakness of it. It consists in this only, that the apostle in that place makes mention of the prophetical and priestly offices of Christ, and not of the kingly; for which Crellius himself gives this reason in his commentary on the place, namely, because, as he supposes, he had treated fully of the kingly office in the first chapter. In the third, the place here produced by him, as himself observes, he is entering on his comparing Christ with Moses, who was the prophet, apostle, ambassador, or legate of God to the people, and Aaron who was their priest; and with respect to this he calls the Hebrews to a due consideration of him, especially considering that they had a deep and fixed apprehension concerning the kingly power of the Messiah, but of his being the great prophet and high priest of the church they had heard little in their Judaism. It does not therefore follow hence that the kingly and priestly offices of Christ are comprehended one in another 'quodammodo,' but only that the apostle, having distinctly handled the kingly office of Christ before, as he had done both in the first and second chapters, now proceeding to the consideration of his priestly and prophetical offices, makes no mention thereof, nor indeed would it have been to his purpose so to have done; yea, it was expressly contrary to his design.

For what is nextly proposed, concerning the nature of these offices, it is agreed that the Lord Christ is called our 'apostle' as he was the prophet of the church, sent of God to reveal and declare his mind and love to us. But it is not so that he is called (6.) a 'high priest,'—that is, principally, firstly, and properly—because of the care he takes of our religion, and his administration of the affairs of it. Yea, there is nothing more opposite than their notion of the priesthood of Christ, not only to the general nature of that office, with the common sense of mankind concerning it, but also to the whole discourse of the apostle on this subject; for he not only asserts, but proves by sundry arguments, that the Lord Christ was made a priest to offer sacrifice to God, to make reconciliation for sin and intercession for sinners. It is his being constituted a high priest for ever, and having offered the one sacrifice of himself, whereby all that come to God are sanctified—he does as such a high priest preside over the spiritual worship of the house of God; so that in and by him alone we have access to the throne of grace, and do enter into the holy place through the blood of his sacrifice, wherein he consecrated for us a new and living way of access to God. Wherefore our author utterly fails in his first attempt for a proof of what he had asserted.

No New Testament Silence

His next endeavour towards the same purpose is from the silence of the other writers of the New Testament concerning this office of Christ. This he supposes would not have been, considering the excellency and usefulness of it, had it not been included in his kingly office, for so he expresses himself (p. 544):

> The rest of the New Testament scriptures (1.) more relate the kingly and prophetic offices, and none of them call Christ priest or high priest expressly. It would frequently be without doubt if it could not be understood and easily included in the other offices themselves and especially in that of king, when one has carefully considered the role surrounding that office in which Christ is like the priest of the law, and since it is on that office that our eternal salvation depends (Heb. 5:9–10, 7:24–5). Seeing that he thereupon sets out the remission and justiciation of our sins in which our blessing consists.

ANSWER. The intelligent reader may easily observe what is the judgment of this man concerning the priesthood of Christ, which is this, that in the exercise of his other offices he is so called, because of some similitude to the legal priests of old; which is plainly to deny and overthrow the office itself, and to leave no such thing in him, substituting a bare metaphorical, allusive denomination in the room of it. And it is but a noise of words which is added concerning the dependence of our salvation on the sacerdotal duty of Christ, because indeed it is denied that he is a priest at all; and all that is intended thereby is but the exercise of his other offices in some kind of likeness to the high priest under the law. To affirm on this supposition that forgiveness of sin, justification, salvation, blessedness, depend on this office—that is, on a name given from this allusion—is only to serve a present occasion, without respect to truth or sobriety. But in particular, I say (1.) there is more express mention of the distinct office of the priesthood of Christ, both as to its nature and its acts, than of his prophetical. Why (2.) they do not directly and expressly call him a priest, they are not bound to give an account to these men. It is enough for the faith of the church that they do really and expressly ascribe to him the acts and duties of that office, such as could be performed by none but a priest properly so called, and particularly such as in no sense belong either to the prophetical or kingly office—namely, to offer himself a sacrifice, to be a propitiation, to wash us in his blood, to make intercession for us, yea, to be made sin for us, and the like. But this epistle also belongs to the New Testament, nor is it as yet denied by the Socinians so to do; and herein this office of Christ is so plainly, fully, distinctly treated of and proposed, in its causes, nature, use, and effects, with its necessity and the benefits we receive thereby, as that no other office of his is in any part of the Scripture, nor in the whole of it, so graphically described.

The reason also why the full revelation of the nature of this office of Christ was, in the wisdom of the Holy Ghost, reserved for this Epistle to the Hebrews is so evident that our author need not think so strange of it. It was among them that God of old had instituted the solemn representation of it, in their typical priesthood. The nature of all those institutions they were now to be peculiarly instructed in, both that they might see the faithfulness of God in accomplishing what he designed by them, and the end that he put thereby to their administration. Now, though these things were of use to the whole church of God, that all might learn his truth, wisdom, and faithfulness, in the harmony of the Old Testament and the New, yet were the Hebrews peculiarly concerned herein, and therefore the Holy Ghost reserved the full communication of those things to his treating with them in an especial manner. But

(3.) all those acts of the sacerdotal office of Christ whereon the pardon of sin, justification, and salvation, do depend, are expressly mentioned by other writers of the New Testament; as 1 John 2:2; Ephesians 5:2; 2 Corinthians 5:21; Romans 8:3–4, 34; 1 John 1:7; Revelation 1:5; 1 Peter 1:19, with sundry other places.

Let it now be judged whether any thing of the least moment has as yet been offered in proof of the assertion laid down—namely, that the priestly office of Christ is contained in the kingly 'quodammodo.'

No Kingly Act

But he yet further enlarges on this consideration:

> When however the rest of the Holy Scriptures relate what more particularly concerns the priesthood of Christ, (1.) they do not in fact place this office or function in opposition to his kingly office or function. (2.) Paul once mentions the intercession of Christ for us in Romans 8:34, (3.) but mentions it secretly in a reference to his kingly power as it relates to our freedom from the penalty of sin, just as his special performance of intercession is afterwards included in it. For the work or kingly activity flows from Christ's power, and relates to our freedom from the penalty of sin and to the responsibility he undertakes on our behalf just as it is brought about and achieved. (4.) Indeed there the apostle mentions his kingly power in the words, 'who is also at the right hand of God,' and distinguishes his intercession from it; but he expressly does not mention the performance of his power, having striven to mention his intercession.

ANSWER. (1.) This condition is imposed on us without warrant, that we should produce testimonies out of the other writers of the New Testament where the priestly office of Christ is opposed to his kingly; nor do we pretend that any such thing is done in this epistle. Nor are the offices of Christ anywhere opposed one to another, nor ought they so to be; nor can any man show wherein there is an opposition made between his kingly and prophetical offices, which these men acknowledge to be distinct. And it suffices to our purpose that the kingly and priestly offices are, in their names, powers, acts, and duties, distinctly proposed and declared. And this author ought to have considered all the testimonies before mentioned, and not to have taken out only one or two of them, which he thought he could best wrest to his purpose; which is all that he has attempted, and yet has failed of his end.

It is here said (2.) that Paul in his other epistles does but once expressly mention the intercession of Christ in heaven. But he mentions his oblation on earth more frequently, as may be seen in the places quoted. And the mentioning of it in one place in words plain, and capable of no other sense, is as effectual as if it had been expressed in a hundred other places.

(3.) It is both false and frivolous, to say that in speaking of Christ's intercession he does tacitly include any act of his kingly power whereby he frees us from punishment. First, it is false, because as intercession is certainly no act of kingly power, nor formally has any respect to that—it denoting the impetration of something from another, whereas all the acts of kingly authority are the exerting of that power which one has in himself—so there is nothing in the text or context to give countenance to any such imagination. For what relates to the kingly power of Christ, namely, his sitting at the right hand of God, is expressed as a distinct act or adjunct of his mediatorial office, even as his dying and rising again are. And that his intercession is completely distinguished and separated from it is plain from the expression whereby it is introduced: Ὅς καὶ ἔστιν ἐν δεξιᾷ τοῦ Θεοῦ, ὅς καὶ ἐντυγχάνει ὑπὲρ ἡμῶν—'Who also is on the right hand of God, who also makes intercession for us.' If therefore his being at the right hand of God is distinguished from his dying and rising again, so as not to be included in them nor they in it, then are his intercession and sitting at the right hand of God so distinguished also. And the truth is, the apostle, for our consolation, here proposes distinctly all the offices of Christ in their most effectual acts, or the most eminent notations of them, and that in the proper order of their discharge and exercise. And whereas the acts of his sacerdotal office are so distinct as that between them the interposition of the actings of his other offices was necessary, he begins and ends with them, as the order of their exercise did require; for:

1. He died for us as a priest; then
2. He rose, giving testimony to the truth as the prophet of the church;

3. He possessed actually his kingly power, sitting at the right hand of God; and

4. There carries on the perpetual exercise of his priesthood by intercession.

Wherefore there is nothing in these words that should tacitly intimate an inclusion of any act of the kingly office, but it is expressed in a clear distinction from it, as an act quite of another nature. And it will, if I mistake not, be a very difficult task for these persons to manifest, in any tolerable, rational manner, how the intercession of Christ does include in it an act of his kingly, power. Secondly, it is frivolous, if by this 'tacitly comprehended' he intend that the intercession of Christ, which is an act of his priestly office, has its effects towards us by virtue of the interposition of some act or acts of his kingly office; for such a mutual respect there is between the acts of all the offices of Christ and their effects. The oblation of Christ, which is an act of the priestly office, is made effectual towards us by the interposition of the exercise of his prophetical office (2 Cor. 5:18–21, Eph. 2:14–17); and his teaching us as the prophet of the church is made effectual by those supplies of his Spirit and grace which are effects of his kingly power. Suppose, therefore, that the energy and operation of Christ's kingly power is put forth to make his intercession effectual towards us in the way mentioned by Crellius—which yet in his sense is false—this proves not in the least that his kingly power, or any act of it, is included in his intercession, which is so distinctly expressed.

Wherefore, (4.) that the apostle should here mention the kingly power of Christ, and name his intercession as the act thereof, seeing he names no other, is a fond imagination; for both does intercession in its proper nature long to another office, and also it is peculiarly ascribed to the Lord Christ by our apostle as a high priest, and not as a king (Heb. 7:25–7). The intercession of Christ as a priest is ordained of God as a means of making his sacrifice and oblation effectual, by the application of its virtue and efficacy to us; and the actual communication of the truth of it is committed to him as our Lord, Head, and King. For whereas all his offices are vested in the same person, belong all to the same general work of mediation, and have all the same general end, it is impossible but that the acts of them must have mutual respect and relation one to another; but yet the offices themselves are formally distinct.

1 John 2:2 Describes the Priestly Office

He yet proceeds on the same argument to another instance:

> John teaches that we have Christ as advocate before the Father, and likewise calls him the atonement for our sins. (1.) He mentions him in order to describe to us how the priestly office can be applied to him. (2.) However, he does not place the office of king in opposition to this. (3.) But since with regard to that consolation, which in this place John relates to sins, very many are concerned to know that Christ has complete power to bear the penalty of sins for us, (4.) it is secretly considered to be included in his words. 1 John 2:2.

ANSWER. Seeing he designed not to consider all the testimonies that are usually pleaded for the priestly office of Christ in the New Testament, I cannot but admire how he came to fix on this instance, which he can give no better countenance to his evasion from; for (1.) The apostle may not only be thought to describe the priestly office of Christ, but he does it so expressly as that the contrary cannot be insinuated with any respect to modesty. For the whole of the priestly office consists in oblation and intercession, both which are here distinctly ascribed to him; and to describe an office by proper power and its duties is more significant than to do it only by its name.

(2.) It is acknowledged that here is no mention made of Christ's kingly power; and it must also be acknowledged that the things here ascribed to Christ do no way belong to his kingly office. Hence it follows undeniably that the writers of the New Testament distinguish these offices, and do not include one of them in the other.

Yea, but says Crellius, (3.) 'The apostle is to be thought tacitly to include the kingly power of Christ;' that is, although he mentions it not, yet he ought to have done so, and therefore is to be thought to have intended what he did not express. That case is very desperate, indeed, which is only capable of such defense as this. But there is good reason to think why the apostle ought so to do—that is, to do what indeed he did not—Crellius being judge. For says he, (4.):

The full power that Christ has to deliver us from the punishment due to sin belongs to that consolation which the apostle intended to give to sinners.

ANSWER. (1.) I deny that the consideration of the power intended did at all belong to the consolation that the apostle designs for sinners, and that because neither directly nor indirectly is it mentioned by him. And he knew what belonged to the consolation which he intended better than Crellius did. This, therefore, is but a direction given the apostle (though coming too late) what he ought to have written, and not an interpretation of what he wrote.

(2.) Proposing the expiatory oblation and intercession of Christ as the ground of our consolation, because they are the reasons, causes, and means of the forgiveness of our sins, the apostle had no occasion to mention the certain consequents thereof, such as is our deliverance from the punishment due to sin.

(3.) The power of Christ to take away sins, or to deliver us from the punishment due to sin, fancied by Crellius, is indeed no principle of evangelical consolation, nor does belong to the kingly office of Christ, nor is consistent with the apostle's present discourse, which lays our consolation on the real propitiation and intercession of Christ, both which are excluded by this imaginary power of taking away the penalty due to sin absolutely, without respect to price, atonement, or satisfaction.

The Old Testament Calls Christ a Priest

And these are all the places which he thought meet to consider in pursuance of his assertion, 'That all the writers of the New Testament, excepting the author of this Epistle, did in a sort include the kingly and priestly offices of Christ the one in the other;' wherein how he has acquitted himself is left to the judgment of the indifferent reader. It was not, I confess, improvidently done of him, to confine himself to the New Testament, considering that in the Old he is expressly called a priest (Ps. 110:4), and that in conjunction with, and yet distinction from, his regal power (Zech. 6:12–13); he is also said to have his soul made a sin-offering, and that when, in and under his suffering, he bare our iniquities

(Isa. 53:10–11); whereby, when he was cut off, he made reconciliation for iniquity, and brought in everlasting righteousness (Dan. 9:24–5). Sundry testimonies also of the New Testament, before quoted, are utterly omitted by him, as those which will not by any means be compelled to the least appearance of a compliance with his design. But these artifices are wanted to the cause. Only I must add, that I cannot but admire with what confidence our adversaries talk of the priesthood of Christ, of his offering himself an expiatory sacrifice, of his intercession, when all these things, in the proper and only signification of the words, are expressly denied by them.

Christ's Priesthood Is not Subsumed in His Kingship

Our author proceeds, in the next place, to give a reason of that which neither is nor ever was, namely, why the holy writers do in some manner comprehend these offices one in the other; for they propose them to us distinctly, as their nature does require:

> It is not without reason that the Holy Scriptures include one office in the other (1.) to a certain extent. For whatever we hope for from Christ as priest, (2, 3) it is able to be said to proceed from him as king. (4.) It is the role of the priest to atone for and cleanse sins. (5.) This happens until the enemies of Christ and of us, sin itself of course, death and Satan who has the power of death, are destroyed. But Christ as King destroys and demolishes his and our enemies, according to 1 Corinthians 15:24–6, Philippians 3, and following. (6.) It is the role of the priest to supply ready help to those who approach the throne of grace, and to come promptly to the aid of the afflicted, according to Hebrews 2:17–18, 4:15–16. (7.) Can it also be the role of Christ the King to flee to his own throne to bring help to his people, and to carry their troubles?

ANSWER. (1.) We observed before the looseness and ambiguity of that expression, '*quodammodo*,' or 'after a sort;' for if it signify any thing in this case, it is the application of the distinct energies and operations of these distinct offices to the same end, wherein we own their agreement and concurrence. That which he should prove is, that they are one of them so contained in the other as that they are not two distinct offices.

(2.) If whatever we expect from Christ as a priest do really proceed from him as a king, as here it is affirmed, then is his priesthood οὐδὲν ἄλλο πλὴν ὄνομα—'a mere empty name' whereby nothing of any use is signified.

(3.) His arguments whereby he endeavours to prove that the holy writers did, not without cause, do that which indeed they did not at all, are sophistical, and in conclusion not proving what himself intends. For, what 'we do expect from a priest' is sophistical; for it respects our present expectation of what is future—our hope, faith, and desire of what he will do for us. But this is but one part of the office and duty of a priest, yea, that part which is expressly founded in what is done already; for Christ, our high priest, has already expiated and purged our sins, and we have no expectation that he should do it again. He did 'by himself'—that is, by the sacrifice of himself—'purge our sins,' and that before he sat down at the right hand of God (Heb. 1:3); and this he did once only, by his own sacrifice once offered, as we have proved.

Wherefore (4.) it is true that it belongs to a priest to expiate our sins and take them away. This we believe that Christ has done for us, as our high priest; but we do not expect that he should do it any more, any otherwise but by the application to us of the virtue and efficacy of what he has already done.

(5.) The description here given us of the expiation of sin—namely, that it 'consists in the actual subduing of Christ's enemies and ours, sin, death, and the devil'—is absurd, dissonant from the common sense of mankind in these things, destructive to the whole nature of the types of the old testament, and contrary to the plain doctrine of the Scripture. This is a blessed consequent and fruit, indeed, of the expiation of our sins, when he bare our sins in his own body on the tree, when his soul was made an offering for sin, when he offered himself a sacrifice, a propitiation, price, and ransom, to make atonement and reconciliation for sin; but expiation itself consists not therein. These, therefore, we acknowledge that Christ effects by various actings of his kingly power; but all on a supposition of the atonement made by him as a priest with respect to the guilt and demerit of sin. Hereby he obtained for us eternal redemption, and we have redemption in his blood, even the forgiveness of sins. The things intended are therefore so distinct that they prove the offices or powers from whence they proceed to be so also: for neither did Christ as a king expiate and purge our sins, which could be done only by a bloody sacrifice; nor does he as a priest subdue his enemies and ours, which is the work, and to which the power of a king is required. Nor has he any better success in the next instance, as to encouragements of coming to the throne of grace.

For (6, 7.) 'the throne of grace' mentioned in Hebrews 4:16, is not the throne of Christ as a king, 'his own throne,' as it is here rendered by Crellius, but the throne of God, where Christ as a high priest makes intercession for us. So that when he says that it is the office of a priest to 'succor them who come to the throne of grace,' and the part of Christ to relieve them who come for help to his throne, it is evident that he sophistically confounds the things that are to be distinguished. We go to the throne of God through the interposition of Christ as our high priest, our propitiation, and advocate; and we go to the throne of Christ as king of the church, on the account of the glorious power committed to him for our help and relief. Wherefore (2.) the encouragements we have to approach to the throne of grace, whereunto is our ultimate address, for help and relief, from the priestly office and actings of Christ, are different and distinct from them which we have from his kingly office, as the actings of Christ with respect to the one and the other of these offices are different and distinct. We go 'with boldness to the throne of grace,' on the account of Christ's being our high priest; as he who, by the oblation of himself, has procured admittance for us, and consecrated a new and living way for our access thereunto; as he who, by his intercession, procures us favorable audience and speeds our requests with God. See our exposition on the place. Our expectation of relief and aid from the Lord Christ as the king of grace and glory on his throne, arises from that all-power in heaven and earth which is given to him for that end. In brief, as a priest he interposes with God for us; as a king he acts from God towards us.

Psalm 2:7 Speaks of Relationship not Office

His last attempt to the same purpose is in the ensuing discourse:

> Likewise also from this the reverend author of the epistle to the Hebrews, in chapter 5:5–6, makes it apparent that (1.) this place in the psalm, 'You are my son, today I have begotten you' (4.) refers

clearly to (5.) the priesthood of Christ, and he teaches through this reasoning both the priesthood and the status granted to Christ by God. But they also speak openly concerning his reign. (2, 3.) For David, who was a type of Christ, unfolds in these words the decree of God, in which the king was appointed after long exile and placed on his royal throne, to the extent which the psalm we are considering will teach. From this Paul proved that Christ was risen from the dead, Acts 13:32–3. (7.) For then finally God, according to his promise, gave the king to his own people and established Jesus as Lord and Christ, or likewise the one who is the Son of God in power, according to Acts 2:36, Romans 1:4. And likewise the writer to the Hebrew argues this in chapter 1:5. (8.) In these words he shows the superiority which Christ has obtained beyond angels, since he has been placed at the right hand of the majesty on high. With respect to which, if the priesthood of Christ is entirely distinct from his kingly dignity, and Christ himself was priest when he suffered on the cross, no indeed, then particulary the office of priest was performed, inappropriate in heaven, how do these words, which they say concern the supreme reign and dignity of Christ, apply to the priesthood of Christ, which was then actually completed when Christ himself was most humbled, and appeared less than angels, according to Philippians 2:8, Hebrews 2:8?

ANSWER. If it were determinately certain what he intends to prove, we might the better judge of the validity of his proofs and arguments. But his limitation of 'to a certain extent', 'it seems' and 'in some part' leave it altogether uncertain what it is that he designeth to evince. It is enough to our cause and purpose if we manifest that nothing by him produced or insisted on does prove the kingly and priestly offices of Christ to be the same, or that one of them is so comprehended in the other as that they are not distinct in their powers, energies, and duties. And this is not done; for (1.) The words of the testimony out of the second psalm, which is so variously applied by the apostles, 'Thou art my Son, this day have I begotten thee,' do not formally express any one office of Christ, nor are used to that purpose. They only declare the relation and love of the Father to his person; which were the foundation and reason of committing all that authority to him which he exercises in all his offices; to which, therefore, they are applied. And therefore on several occasions does God express the same thing in words very little varied, 'This is my beloved Son, in whom I am well pleased' (Matt. 3:17, 17:5; 2 Pet. 1:17); for the declaration of Christ to be the eternal Son of God is all that is intended in these words.

(2.) That these words were firstly used of David and his exaltation to the throne of Israel after his banishment, is easily said, but not so easily proved. Let our reader consult our exposition on Hebrews 1:5.

(3.) The call of Christ to his offices of king, priest, and prophet, as it respects the authority and love of the Father, was but one and the same. He had not a distinct call to each office, but was at once called to them all, as he was the Son of God sent and anointed to be the Mediator between God and men. The offices themselves, the gifts and graces to be exercised in them, their powers, acts, and duties, were distinct, but his call to them all was the same.

(4.) The writer of this epistle does not accommodate these words to the priestly office of Christ, any otherwise but to evince that he was called of God to that office on the ground of his relation to God and his love of him; for he produces those words to declare who it was that called him, and why he did so, the call itself being expressed, as respecting the priesthood, in the other testimony, 'Thou art a priest for ever after the order of Melchizedek.' Wherefore there is not in these words any expression of the priesthood of Christ. See the exposition of the place.

(5.) These words are most eminently applied to the resurrection of Christ (Acts 13:32-3). Now, this principally belonged to his prophetical office, as that whereby the truth of the doctrine he had taught was invincibly confirmed. And you may by this means as well overthrow the distinction between his kingly and prophetical offices as between his kingly and sacerdotal. But the reason why it is accommodated to the Lord Christ with respect to either of his offices, is because his relation to God, therein expressed, was the ground of them all.

(6.) What if Crellius cannot prove that these words of the psalmist have any respect to the kingly office of Christ? I deny at present that he can do so, and refer the reader for his satisfaction herein to the exposition of them as quoted by the apostle (Heb. 1:5).

(7.) Those words whereby he enlarges herein, 'That then, when

Christ was raised from the dead, God gave to his people a king according to his promises, and appointed Jesus to be both Lord and Christ, or, which is the same, the Son of God in power,' for which Acts 2:36, Romans 1:4, are urged, are partly ambiguous and sophistical, and partly false. For—

1. The things mentioned in those places are not the same. In the one it is said that God made him 'both Lord and Christ;' in the other, that he was 'declared to be the Son of God with power.' And he does woefully prevaricate when he so repeats the words, as if it were said that he was made or appointed to be the Son of God with power by the resurrection, when he was only publicly determined or declared so to be.

2. He insinuates that Jesus was not made Lord and Christ, or the Son of God, until after his resurrection. But this is openly false: for (a) he was born both Lord and Christ (Luke 2:11); (b) when he came into the world the angels worshipped him as Lord and Christ (Heb. 1:6); (c) Peter confessed him before to be 'Christ, the Son of the living God' (Matt. 16:16); (d) he often affirmed before that all things were given into his hands (Matt. 11:27); (e) if it were so, the Jews only crucified Jesus, and not Christ the Lord, or only him that was so to be afterwards; which is false and blasphemous.

It is true, upon his ascension, not immediately on his resurrection, he was gloriously exalted to the illustrious exercise of his kingly power; but he was our Lord and King before his death. And therein also—

(8.) From what has been spoken, it is easy to know what is to be returned to the conclusion that he makes of this argument; for the words produced in testimony are not spoken immediately concerning any office of Christ whatever, as expressive of it, much less concerning his regal dignity in a peculiar manner. And God was no less the father of Christ, he was no less begotten of him, when he was humbled to death in the sacrifice of himself that he offered as a priest, than when he was exalted in glory at the right hand of the Majesty on high.

How the Kingly and Priestly Offices Differ

From this attempt to prove that the sacerdotal office of Christ is comprehended in the regal by the divine writers, Crellius proceeds to show what 'differences there are indeed between them;' and of this he gives sundry instances. But he might have spared that labour. This one would have sufficed, namely, that the Lord Christ is a 'king really and properly,'—he is a 'priest only metaphorically;' that is, he is not so indeed, but is called so improperly, because of some allusion between what he did and what was done by the priests of old, as believers are called kings and priests. A man would think this were difference enough, as amounting to no less but that Christ is a king indeed, but not a priest. There was therefore no need that he should take the pains to find out, indeed to coin, differences between two such offices, of which one is, and the other is not. And all the differences he fixes on, the first only excepted, to which some pretense may be given, are merely feigned, or drained out of some other false hypotheses of the same author. However, it may not be amiss, seeing we have designed the vindication of this office of Christ from the whole opposition that is made to it by this sort of men, to examine a little those differences he assigns between the real and supposed office of Christ, which he makes use of to no other end but to annihilate the latter of them.

According to Crellius

The distinction between the royal and priestly offices is primarily discerned in the way that the royal office, unlike the priestly office, presents itself concealed. This is why the priestly office is more frequently mentioned, for the task of a king is to punish, but the task of a priest is to expiate the sins of the people.

ANSWER. This may be granted as one difference in the exercise of the power of these offices; for the kingly power of Christ is extended to his enemies, the stubbornest of them and those who are finally so, but Christ is a priest offered and intended only for the elect. But he might also have instanced in sundry other acts the kingly power of Christ, as, namely, his law-giving, his universal protection of his people, his rule and government of the church by his Spirit and word, which belong not at all to his priestly office. But this was not to his purpose, nor does he design to evince any real difference between these two offices. For it is true that he opposes punishing and expiating sin the one to the other, assigning the former to the kingly, the latter to the sacerdotal office; but if to expiate sin be only to remove and take away the punishment of sin, or that which is contrary to punishing, then Crellius maintains that Christ does this by virtue of his kingly power and office. The sum, therefore, of this difference amounts to no more but this, that the Lord Christ as a king, and by virtue of his regal power, does both punish sin and take away the punishment of it; only he does the latter as a priest— that is, there is an allusion in what he does to what was done for the people by the priests of old. He adds another difference:

(1.) Then since we call Christ king, in himself unless we add someone else, (2.) we do not portray him as grasping this power from another person, and, whatever kindness proceeds from him as our king, (3.) we ascribe entirely to God who granted this power to him. (4.) For the office and name of king indicates no such responsibility unless God is also said to be the king (Matt. 5:35, 1 Tim. 6:15). But when we call Christ a priest (5.) we attribute to him the right to offer and intercede and we declare the remission of our sins by him as not being from him as the first cause, but set out by God. We declare that he does not have power to remit sins by himself (6.) and that he is not the supreme ruler of everything. For why else would he offer and intercede in the presence of another and be transformed into the role of priest to obtain our forgiveness? In what way, while he is marked by the name of priest by God Most High, (7.) to whom he is otherwise equal in power, is he openly distinguished, and publicly proclaimed as such before him by the prerogative and excellence of God? This easily increases such great excellence and glory which Christ in himself is lacking or able to conceal, and so he sought to take that glory from God by which he [ie. God] is exalted in Christ.

ANSWER. (1.) There is neither difference nor pretense of any difference between these offices of Christ assigned in these words, nor does this discourse seem to be introduced for any other end but only to make way for that sophistical objection against the deity of Christ wherewith it is closed. For whatever notion the first sound of these words, 'king' and 'priest,' may present to the minds of any prejudiced persons, in reality Christ does no less depend on God with respect to his kingly office than with respect to his priestly; which Crellius also does acknowledge.

(2.) When we call Christ Lord and King, we consider both who and what he is, and thereby do conceive and express his being appointed to that office by God the Father. And of all men the Socinians have least cause to fear that on the naming of Christ as king they should conceive him to be independent of God; for believing him to be a man, and no more, there cannot possibly an imagination thereof befall their minds.

(3.) It is not what we express when we call Christ a king, but what the Scripture declares concerning that office of his, which we are to consider; and therein it is constantly affirmed and expressed that God made him 'both Lord and Christ,' that all his power was given him of God, that he sets him his king on the holy hill of Zion, and gives him to be head over all to the church. Wherefore, to call and name Christ our king, and not at the same time to apprehend him as appointed of God so to be, is to renounce that only notion of his being so which is revealed to us, and is a folly which never any Christian fell into. Wherefore, when we call Christ king, we do acknowledge that he is made so of God, who consequently is the author and principal cause of all the good and blessed effects which we are made partakers of through the administration of the kingly office and power of Christ; nor did ever any sober person fall into an imagination to the contrary, seeing none can do so without an express renunciation of the Scripture.

(4.) When God, absolutely considered, is said to be king, the subject of the proposition limits and determines the sense; for the nature of him which is presented to us under that name, 'God,' will not allow that he should be so any otherwise but on the account of his infinite, essentially divine power; which the notion of Christ as mediator does not present to us.

(5.) The reasons taken from what is ascribed to the Lord Christ as a priest to prove that, in our notion and conception of that office, we look on him as delegated by God, and acting power for us on that account, are, although true in themselves, yet frivolous as to his purpose; because all the acts, duties, and powers of his kingly office, do affirm and prove the same. Christ has all his power, both as king and priest, equally from God the Father, and was equally called of God to act in both these offices;—in his name, majesty, and authority towards us, in one of them; and with or before him on our behalf, in the other.

(6.) Whereas he adds, and enlarges thereon, that by the oblation and intercession of Christ, which are ascribed to him as a priest, it is evident that he has not power of or from himself to pardon our sins, as also that he is not the supreme rector, but is distinguished from the most high God, to whom otherwise he is equal in authority, I ask—

1. Whether Christ as a king has power, of himself and from himself, to take away sin, as the supreme rector of all, and that power not delegated to him of God? I know he will not say so, nor any of his party, and therefore the difference between these two offices on that account is merely pretended.

2. To make the Lord Christ, whom they will have to be a man only, to be equal in power on any account with God, is a bold assertion. How shall any creature be equal, in any respect, to God? To whom shall we equal him? How can he who receives power from another for a certain end be equal in power to that other from whom he does receive it? How shall he who acts in the name of another be equal to him? But these great expressions are used concerning things which are false, only to cover the sacrilege of taking that from him wherein he was truly equal to God, and counted it no robbery so to be.

3. It is confessed that the Lord Christ, as the high priest of the church, was inferior to God, that his Father was greater than he, that he offered himself to God, and intercedes with him; but that he is not equal with God, of the same nature with him, under another consideration, this proves not.

And, (7.) on the other side, there is not the least danger that the prerogative of God, absolutely considered, with respect to Christ as mediator, should be obscured by the glory of the kingly office of Christ, among them who acknowledge that all the glory and power of it are freely given to him of God.

He yet proceeds:—

> (1.) He agrees that Christ is said to be priest and indeed presents himself as one, and that his death, without which he could not have offered himself, is included in that, and that mention of his reign completes any pact. (2.) And his exceedingly tender and concerned care which he carries for us, and by which he completed the atonement of our sins, is shown to be greater than the kingly office which has been mentioned. From this he agrees that there is not a little consolation for us in Christ's divine power (3.) is likewise able to drive away our worthlessness by his greatness and superiority, from which small matter we dare to do something so great as to flee to him with confidence of heart and to await help from him.

ANSWER. (1.) How, according to the judgment of these men, 'the death of Christ is more openly and plainly included in his being called a priest,' than in his being a king, I know not; for he was not, if we may believe them, 'a priest in his death,' nor did his death belong to his discharge of that office, only they say it was 'necessarily antecedent' thereunto. But so also was it to the discharge of his kingly office; for he 'ought first to suffer, and then to enter into his glory' (Luke 24:26). And his exaltation to his glorious rule was not only consequent to his humiliation and suffering, or to his death, but did also depend thereon (Rom. 14:9; Phil. 2:7-11). Wherefore, with respect to the antecedent necessity of the death of Christ, there is no difference between these offices, it being equal with regard to them both. Had he placed the difference between these two offices with respect to the death of Christ herein, that Christ as a priest died and offered himself therein to God, which no way belonged to his kingly office, he had spoken the truth, but that which was destructive to all his pretensions. For what is here asserted, it constitutes no difference at all between them.

(2.) It is acknowledged that the consideration of the priesthood of Christ bespeaks much care and tenderness towards the church, which is a matter of great consolation to us. But—

> 1. It is so when this care and tenderness are looked on as the effects and fruits of that love which he manifested and

exercised when in his death he offered himself a sacrifice for the expiation of our sins, and continues to intercede for us, thereby rendering his oblation effectual. Herein does the Scripture constantly place the love of Christ, and thence instructs us in his tender care and compassion thence arising (Eph. 5:25-7; Gal. 2:20; Rev. 1:5). Remove this consideration of the priesthood of Christ, which is done by these men, and you take away the foundation and spring of that care and tenderness in him towards us as a priest whereby we should be relieved and refreshed. Wherefore—

2. This consolation is nowhere proposed to us as that which arises absolutely from the office itself, but from what, out of his unspeakable love, he underwent and suffered in the discharge of that office; for being therein exercised with all sorts of temptations, and undergoing all sorts of sufferings, he is merciful and tender in the discharge of the remaining duties of this office. See Hebrews 2:17, 4:15-16, and 5:7-8, with our exposition on those places. I do not, therefore, see how they who deny that Christ suffered any thing in being our high priest, can, from the consideration of the priesthood, draw any other arguments for his care and tenderness than what may be taken from his other offices.

3. Christ as a king, absolutely considered, without respect to his sufferings, is no less tender to, no less careful of his church, than he is as he is a priest, his love and other qualifications for all his offices being the same; only his preparation for the exercise of his care and tenderness, by what he suffered as a priest, makes the difference in this matter; the consideration of which being removed, there remains none at all. To conceive of Christ as the king of his church, and not to conceive withal that every thing in him as such is suited to the consolation and encouragement of them that do believe, is highly to dishonour him. He is, as a king, the shepherd of his flock, his pastoral care belonging to his kingly office, as kings of old were called the shepherds of their people. But in his rule and feeding of the church as a shepherd, he is proposed as acting all manner of care and tenderness, as the nature of the office does require (Isa. 40:10-11).

(3.) It is a fond imagination, that believers should be frighted or deterred from going to Christ as a king because of their own vileness and his glorious dignity, seeing that glorious dignity was conferred on him on purpose to relieve us from our vileness. There is no office of Christ but contains its encouragements in it for believers to make use of it and improve it to their consolation; and that because the ground of all their hopes and comforts is in his person, and that love and care which he acts in them all. But that we should consider any one of them as a means of encouraging us with respect to another, the Scripture teaches us not, any otherwise than as the effects of his priestly office, in his oblation and intercession, are the fundamental reasons of the communication of the blessed effects of his kingly power to us. For all the benefits we are made partakers of by him flow from hence, that he loved us, and gave himself for us, washing us in his own blood. Even the glorious greatness of God himself—which, absolutely considered, is enough to deter us, as we are sinners, from approaching to him—as he is in Christ reconciling the world to himself, is a firm foundation of trust, confidence, and consolation; and therefore the glory of Christ in his kingly power must needs be so also.

He closes his discourse in these words:—

> Therefore this also was the reason why (1.) this name should be attributed to Christ; so that (2.) I could omit the many likenesses that there are between Christ and Melchizedek in their responsibility as a priest of the law: they both prays, just as each was in the same way a priest of the most high God; these facts provided the reason for this name; to these facts also should be added numerous similarities with regard to the sacrifices of the law.

ANSWER. Here (1.) the whole design is plainly expressed. There is the name of a priest, for some certain reasons, attributed to Christ, whereas truly and really he never had any such office from whence he might be so denominated. And this is that which, in this whole discourse, I principally designed to evince.

(2.) To say that Christ was 'called a priest from that likeness which was in sundry things' (not in the office of the priesthood and execution thereof) 'unto the legal high priest, and Melchizedek,' and the sacrifices of the law, is only to beg or suppose the thing in question. They were all instituted and made priests, and all their sacrifices were offered, principally to this end, that they might prefigure and represent him as the only true high priest of the church, with that sacrifice of himself which he offered for it; and without this consideration there would never have been any priest in the world of God's appointment. And this is the whole of what this man pleads, either directly or by sophistical diversions, to confound these two offices of Christ, and thereby utterly to evacuate his sacerdotal office. Wherefore, before I proceed to remove his remaining exceptions to the truth and reality of this office, I shall confirm the real difference that is between it and the kingly office, in a confounding it wherewithal the strength of their whole endeavour against it consists.

According to Scripture

The offices of king and priest may be considered either absolutely, or as they respect our Lord Jesus Christ. In the first way it will not be denied but that they are distinct. The one of them is founded in nature, the other in grace. The one belongs to men as creatures capable of political society, the other with respect to their supernatural end only. It is true that the same person was sometimes vested with both these offices, as was Melchizedek; and the same usage prevailed among the heathens, as we shall see afterwards more at large. 'King Anius, the same king of men and priest of Phoebus.'—AEn, 3:80.

But this hinders not but that the offices were then distinct in their powers and duties, as the regal and prophetical were when David was both king and prophet. But at present our inquiry is concerning these offices in Christ only, whether they were both proper and distinct, or one of them comprised in the other, being but a metaphorical expression of the manner of the exercise of its powers and duties. And concerning this we may consider—

Christ is Plainly Called a Priest

He is absolutely, and that frequently, called a priest or a high priest, in the Old Testament and the New. This was demonstrated in the entrance of these exercitations. Now, the notion or nature of a priest, and the office of the priesthood, or what is signified by them, are plainly declared in the Scripture, and that in compliance with the unanimous apprehension of mankind concerning them; for, that the office of the priesthood is that faculty or power whereby some persons do officiate with God in the name and on the behalf of others, by offering sacrifice, all men in general are agreed. And thereon it is consented also that it is, in its entire nature, distinct from the kingly power and office, whose first conception speaks a thing of another kind. Now, whereas the Scripture does absolutely and frequently declare to us that Christ is a priest, it does nowhere intimate that his priesthood was of another kind than what it had in general declared it to be in all others, and what all men generally apprehended of it. If any other thing were intended thereby, men must unavoidably be drawn into errors and mistakes. Nor does it serve to undeceive us, that some come now and tell us that the Scripture by that name intends no such distinct office, but only the especial qualifications of Christ for the discharge of his kingly power, and the manner of his acting or exercising thereof; for the Scripture itself says no such things, but, as we shall see immediately, gives plain testimony to the contrary.

Properly a King; Properly a Priest

His first solemn type was both a king and a priest, and he was so as to both of these offices properly. He was not a king properly, and a high priest only metaphorically, or so called because of his careful and merciful administration of the kingly power committed to him; but he had the office of the priesthood properly and distinctly vested in him, as both Moses and our apostle do declare (Gen. 14:18, Heb. 7:1). And he was more peculiarly a type of Christ as he was a priest than as he was a king; for he is said to be 'a priest,' and not a king, 'after the order of Melchizedek.' Therefore that consideration of him is reassumed by the psalmist and by our apostle, and not the other. And is it not uncouth, that God, designing to prefigure one that should be a priest metaphorically only, and properly a king, should do it in and by a person who was a priest no less properly than he was a king, and in his so being was peculiarly and principally designed to prefigure him? Who can learn any thing of the mind of God determinately if his declarations thereof may be thus interpreted?

The Law's Extensive Presentation of His Priestly Office

In the giving of the law God did renew and multiply the instructive types and representations of these offices of Christ. And herein, in the first place, he takes care to teach the church that he (whom all those things which he then did institute did signify) was to be a priest; for of any prefiguration of his kingly power there is very little spoken in the law. I shall at present take it for granted, as having sufficiently proved it elsewhere, and which is not only positively affirmed but proved with many arguments by our apostle, namely, that the principal end of Mosaic institutions was to prefigure, represent, and instruct the church, though darkly, in the nature of the offices, work, and duties, of the promised Messiah. This being so, if the Lord Christ were to be a priest only metaphorically and improperly, and a king properly, his priesthood being included in his kingly office, and signifying no more but the manner of his administration thereof, how comes it to pass that his being a priest should be taught and represented so fully and distinctly in so many ordinances, by so many types and figures, as it is, and his kingly power be scarce intimated at all? For there is no mention of any typical kings in the law, but only in the allowance which God gave the people to choose such a ruler in future times, wherein he made provision for what he purposed to do afterwards (Deut. 17:14–15). Moreover, when God would establish a more illustrious typical representation of his kingly office in the family of David, to manifest that these two offices should be absolutely distinct in him, he so ordained in the law that it should be ever afterwards impossible that the same person should be both king and priest, until He came who was typified by both; for the kingly office and power were confined, by divine institution, to the house and family of David, as that of the priesthood was to the family of Aaron. If these offices had been to be one and the same in Christ, these institutions had not instructed the church in what was to come.

Distinct Powers Proves Distinct Offices

A distinct office has a 'distinct power or faculty' for the performance of its acts in a due manner with respect to a certain end. And those things whereby it is constituted are distinct in the kingly and priestly offices of Christ; for—

1. Moral powers and acts are distinguished by their objects. But the object of all the actings of the sacerdotal power of Christ is God; of the regal, men. For every priest, as we have showed, acts in the name and on the behalf of men with God; but a king, in the name and on the behalf of God with and towards men, as to the ends of that rule which God has ordained. The priest represents men to God, pleading their cause; the king represents God to men, acting his power. Wherefore, these being distinct powers or faculties duties and acts, they prove the offices to which they do belong, or from which they proceed, to be distinct also, and this consideration demonstrates a greater difference between these two offices than between the kingly and prophetical, seeing by virtue of them both some men equally act in the name of God towards others. But that the priesthood of Christ is exercised towards God on the behalf of men, and that therein the formal nature of any priesthood does consist, whereby it is effectually distinguished from all other offices and powers that any men are capable of, we have the common consent of mankind to prove, the institution of God under the old testament, with express testimonies in the new confirming the same.

2. As the acts of these offices are distinguished by their objects, so also are they and their ἀποτελέσματα between themselves, or in their own nature. The acts of the sacerdotal office operate morally only, by way of procurement or acquisition; those of the regal office are physical, and really operative of their effects: for all the acts of the priestly office belong to oblation or intercession. And their effects consist either in, (1.) 'by the averting of evil or (2.) by the procurement of good' These they effect morally only, by procuring and obtaining of them. The acts of the kingly office are legislation, communication of the Spirit, helps, aids, assistances of grace, destruction of

enemies, and the like. But these are all physically operative of their effects. Wherefore the offices whence they proceed must be distinct in their natures, as also they are. And what has been spoken may suffice at present to evince the difference between these two offices of Christ, which those men are the first that ever called into doubt or controversy.

Deny Christ's Priesthood—Deny His Glory

I shall close this discourse with the consideration of an attempt of Crellius to vindicate his doctrine concerning the priesthood of Christ from an objection of Grotius against it, namely, that it 'diminishes the glory of Christ, in ascribing to him only a figurative priesthood.' For to this he answers, by way of concession, (1.) 'That indeed they allow Christ to be a priest metaphorically only, as believers are said to be kings and priests, and to offer sacrifices.' Now, this is plainly to deny any such real office, which sometimes they would not seem to do, and to substitute an external denomination in the room thereof. What are the consequents of this, and what a pernicious aspect this has upon the faith and consolation of all believers, is left to the judgment of all who concern themselves in these things.

He answers, (2.) 'That although they deny the Lord Christ to be a priest properly so called, yet the dignity which they ascribe to him under that name and title is not metaphorical, but real, and a greater dignity than their adversaries will allow.' For the latter clause, or who they are that ascribe most glory and honour to Jesus Christ, according as that duty is prescribed to us in the Scripture, both with respect to his person, his mediation, and all his offices, with the benefits redounding to the church thereby—they or we— is left to every impartial or unprejudiced judgment in the world. For the former, the question is not about what dignity they assign to Christ, nor about what names or titles they think meet to give him, but about the real honour of the priesthood. That this is an honour in itself, that it was so to Aaron, that it is so to Christ, our apostle expressly declares (Heb. 5:4–5). If Christ had it not, then had Aaron a real honour which he had not, and therein was preferred above him. But, says he, 'Although he is compared with Aaron, and his priesthood opposed to his, and preferred above it, yet it is not in things of the same kind, though expressed under the same name, whereby things more perfect and heavenly are compared with things earthly and imperfect.' But—

1. This leaves the objection in its full force; for whatever dignity Christ may have in other things above Aaron, yet in the honour of the priesthood Aaron was preferred before him; for it is a real priesthood which the apostle asserts to be so honourable. And although a person who has it not may have a dignity of another kind, which may be more honourable than that of the priesthood, yet if he have not that also, he therein comes behind him that has it.

2. It is true, where things fall under the same appellations, some properly, and some metaphorically only, those of the latter sort, though they have not so good a title as the other to the common name whereby they are called, yet may they in their own nature be more excellent than they; but this is only when the things properly so called have notable defects and imperfections accompanying of them. But this consideration has here no place; for the real office of the priesthood includes nothing in it that is weak or impotent, nor are the acts of it in any thing inferior to what may be fancied as metaphorical. And whereas the dignities of all the mediatory actings of Christ are to be taken from the efficacy of them, and their tendency to the glory of God and the salvation of the church, it is evident that those which are assigned to him as the acts of a real priesthood are far more worthy and honourable than what they ascribe to him under the metaphorical notion of that office.

3. If the priesthood of Christ is not opposed, as such, to the priesthood of Aaron, on what grounds or from what principles does our apostle argue to the abolishing of the priesthood of Aaron from the introduction of that of Christ, plainly asserting an inconsistency between them in the church at the same time? For there is no such opposition nor inconsistency, where the offices intended are not both of them properly so, but one of them is only metaphorically so called. So there is no inconsistency in the continuance of the kingly office of Christ, which is real, and all believers being made kings in a sense only metaphorically.

SMALCIUS' APOLOGY FOR THE HOLY SPIRIT

But Valentinus Smalcius will inform us of the original and occasion of all our mistakes about the priesthood of Christ: 'It was out of an excessive desire' (in the Holy Ghost or the apostles) 'to speak figuratively, that Christ is said to intercede for us, and consequently to be a priest' (*De Regn. Christ.* cap. 23). But he afterwards makes an apology for the Holy Spirit of God, why he spoke in so low and abject a manner concerning Christ; and this was, the care he took that none should believe him to be God. We have had some among ourselves who have traduced and reproached other men for the use of 'fulsome metaphors,' as they call them, in the expression of sacred things, though evidently taken out of the Scripture; but this man alone has discovered the true fountain of that miscarriage, which was the 'excessive desire of the holy writers to speak figuratively,' lest any one should believe Jesus Christ to be God from the things that really belong to him.

10

THE ACTS OF THE PRIESTHOOD OF CHRIST

Having declared and vindicated the nature of the sacerdotal office of our Lord Jesus Christ, it remains that we consider the acts of it distinctly, with some of the most important adjuncts of its exercise. And it is not so much the dogmatic declaration of these things that I design, which also has already been sufficiently discharged, as the vindication of them from the perverse senses put upon them by the Socinians.

GENERAL ACTS

The general acts of the Lord Christ as the high priest of the church are two—namely, oblation and intercession. These the nature of the office in general does require, and these are constantly assigned to him in the Scripture. But concerning these, their nature, efficacy, season, use or end, there is no agreement between us and the Socinians. And I know not that there is any thing of the like nature fallen out among those who profess themselves to be Christians, wherein persons fully agreeing in the same words and expressions, as they and we do in this matter, should yet really disagree, and that to the greatest extremity of difference, about every thing signified by them, as we do herein. And this sufficiently discovers the vanity of all attempts to reconcile the differing parties among Christians by a confession of faith, composed in such general words and terms as that each party may safely subscribe and declare its assent to. Neither is the insufficiency of this design relieved by the additional advice that this confession be composed wholly out of the Scriptures and of expressions therein used; for it is not an agreement in words and the outward sound of them, but the belief and profession of the same truths or things, that is alone to be valued, all that is beyond such an agreement being left at peace in the province of mutual forbearance. An agreement in words only parrots may learn; and it will be better amongst them than that which is only so amongst men, because they have no mind to act dissenting and contradicting principles. But for men to declare their assent to a certain form of words, and in the meantime in their minds and understandings expressly to judge and condemn the faith and apprehensions of one another about these very things, is a matter that no way tends to the union, peace, or edification of the church. For instance, suppose a form of words expressing in general that Christ was a high priest; that, the acts of the priesthood being oblation and intercession, Christ in like manner offered himself to God and makes intercession for us; that hereby he purges, expiates, and does away our sins, with many more expressions to the same purpose, should be drawn up and subscribed by the Socinians and their adversaries, as they can safely do on all hands; will this in the least further any agreement or unity between us, whilst we not only disagree about the sense of all these terms and expressions, but believe that things absolutely distinct and inconsistent with one another, yea, destructive of one another, are intended in them? For so really it is between us herein, as the further consideration of particulars will manifest.

Oblation

First, the oblation of Christ is that act or duty of his sacerdotal office whereby he offered himself, his soul and body, or his whole human nature, an expiatory sacrifice to God in his death and blood-shedding, to make atonement for the sins of mankind, and to purchase for them eternal redemption. So that—(1.) the nature of the oblation of Christ consisted in a bloody expiatory sacrifice, making atonement for sin, by bearing the punishment due to that. And, (2.) as to the efficacy of it, it has procured for us pardon of sin, freedom from the curse, and eternal redemption. (3.) The time and place when and wherein Christ, as our high priest, thus offered himself a sacrifice to God, was in the days of his flesh, whilst he was yet in this world, by his suffering in the garden, but especially on the cross.

For the application of the effects of this oblation of Christ to the church, and the completing of all that was foresignified as belonging to this, it was necessary that, as our high priest, he should enter into the holy place, or the presence of God in the heavens, there to represent himself as having done the will of God, and finished the work committed to him; whereon the actual efficacy of his oblation or the communication of the fruits of it to the church, according to the covenant between the Father and Son before described, does depend.

In all these things the Socinians wholly dissent from us. What they conceive about the nature of the office itself has been already called to an account. As for this act or duty of it, they apprehend— (1.) that the expiatory oblation or sacrifice ascribed to the Lord Christ, as a high priest, is nothing but his presenting of himself alive in the presence of God. (2.) This, therefore, they say he did after his resurrection, upon his ascension into heaven, when he had revealed the will of God, and testified to the truth of his ministry with his death, which was necessary to his ensuing oblation. (3.) That his expiation of our sins consists in the exercise of that power which he is intrusted withal, upon this offering of himself, to free us from the punishment due to them. (4.) That this presentation of himself in heaven might be called his offering of himself, or an expiatory sacrifice, it was necessary that, antecedently to this, he should die for the ends mentioned; for if he had not so done there would have been no allusion between his care and power in heaven which he excercises towards the church, and the actings of the high priests of old in their oblations and sacrifices, and so no ground or reason why what he did and does should be called the offering of himself. Wherefore this is the substance of what they affirm in this matter:—'The place of Christ's offering himself was in heaven, in the glorious presence of God; the time of it, after his ascension; the nature of it, a presenting himself in the presence of God, as one who, having declared his name and done his will, was gloriously exalted by him;—the whole efficacy of this being an effect of that power which Christ has received as exalted to deliver us from sin.'

In this imaginary oblation the death of Christ has no part nor interest. They say, indeed, it was previously necessary thereunto; but this seems but a mere pretense, seeing it is not intelligible, on their principles, how it should so be: for they affirm that Christ did not offer in heaven that very body wherein he suffered on the tree, but a new, spiritual body that was prepared for him to that end. And what necessity is there that one body should suffer and die that another might be presented in heaven? The principal issues to which these differences between them and us may be reduced shall be declared and insisted on.

INTERCESSION

The second duty of the priestly office is intercession. How frequently this also is ascribed to the Lord Christ as a high priest has been declared before. Now, intercession is of two sorts:

Formal and Oral

There is a formal, oral intercession, when any one, by words, arguments, supplications, with humble earnestness in their use, prevails with another for any good thing that is in his power to be bestowed on himself or others. Of this nature was the intercession of Christ whilst he was on the earth. He dealt with God, by prayers, and supplications, sometimes with cries and tears, with respect to himself in the work he had undertaken, but principally for the church of his elect (Heb. 5:7; John 17). This was his intercession as a priest whilst he was on the earth, namely, his interposition with God, by prayers and supplications, suited to the state wherein he was, for the application of the benefits of his mediation to the church, or the accomplishment of the promises made to him upon his undertaking the work of redemption.

Virtual and Real

Virtual or real intercession differs not in the substance or nature of it from that which is oral and formal, but only in the outward manner of its performance, with respect to the reasons of it as now accomplished. When Christ was upon the earth, his state and condition rendered it necessary that his intercession should be by way of formal supplications; and that, as to the argument of it, it should respect that which was for to come, his oblation—which is both the procuring cause of all good things interceded for and the argument to be pleaded for their actual communication—being not yet completed. But now, in heaven, the state and condition of Christ admitting of no oral or formal supplications, and the ground, reason, or argument of his intercession, being finished and past, his intercession, as the means of the actual impetration of grace and glory, consists in the real presentation of his offering and sacrifice for the procuring of the actual communication of the fruits thereof to them for whom he so offered himself. The whole matter of words, prayers, and supplications, yea, of internal conceptions of the mind formed into prayers, is but accidental to intercession, attending the state and condition of him that intercedes. The real entire nature of it consists in the presentation of such things as may prevail in the way of motive or procuring cause with respect to the things interceded for. And such do we affirm the intercession of Christ as our high priest in heaven to be.

It is no easy matter to apprehend aright what our adversaries judge concerning this duty of the priesthood of Christ. They all say the expression is figurative, and they will not allow any real intercession of Christ, although the Scriptures so expressly lay the weight of our consolation, preservation, and salvation thereon (Rom. 8:34; Heb. 7:25–7; 1 John 2:1). Neither are they agreed what is signified by it. That which mostly they agree on is, that it is a 'word used to declare that the power which Christ excercises in heaven was not originally his own, but was granted to him of God; and therefore the good that by virtue thereof he does to and for the church is so expressed as if he obtained it of God by intercession.' But it is, I confess, strange to me, that what the Holy Ghost left the weight of our consolation and salvation on should be no more but a word signifying that the power which Christ excercises in heaven for the good of his church was 'not originally his own,' but was conferred on him by God after his ascension into heaven.

From what has been discoursed it is evident how great and wide the difference is between us about these things, which yet are the things wherein the life of our faith is concerned. And so resolved are they in their own sentiments, that they will not admit such terms of reconciliation as may be tendered to them, if in any thing they intrench thereon; for whereas Grotius premised to his discourse on this subject, 'We are agreed with Socinus as to the name, that the death of Christ was an expiatory sacrifice, as is clearly testified in the Epistle to the Hebrews,'—Crellius renounces any such concession in Socinus, and tells Grotius how greatly he is mistaken in that supposition, seeing both he and they do perfectly deny that the death of Christ was the expiatory sacrifice mentioned in that epistle (cap. 10 part. 1, p. 472). Now, it is evident that these things cannot be handled to full satisfaction without a complete discussion of the true nature of the sacrifice of Christ. But this is not my present design, nor shall I engage into it in these exercitations. The proper seat of the doctrine thereof is in the 9th and 10th chapters of this epistle. If God will, and we live to arrive thereunto, all things concerning them shall be handled at large. Only, there are some things which belong peculiarly to the office itself under consideration. These we shall separate from what concerns the nature of the sacrifice, and vindicate from the exceptions of our adversaries. And they are referred to the ensuing heads: first, the time and place when and where the Lord Christ entered on and principally discharged the office of his priesthood. Secondly, the immediate proper object of all his sacerdotal actings, which having been stated before must now be vindicated and further confirmed. Thirdly, the especial nature of his sacerdotal intercession, which consists in the moral efficacy of his mediation in procuring mercy and grace, and not in a power of conferring them on us.

THE TIME AND PLACE OF CHRIST'S PRIESTHOOD

The first thing we are to inquire into is, the time and place of the exercise of the priesthood of Christ; and the state of the controversy about them needs only to be touched on in this place, as having been before laid down. Wherefore with reference to this we affirm —

1. That the Lord Christ was a high priest in the days of his flesh, whilst he was in this world, even as he was also the king and prophet of the church.
2. That he exercised or discharged this office, as to the principal acts and duties of it, especially as to the oblation of his great expiatory sacrifice, upon the earth, in his death, and the effusion of his blood thereon.
3. We say not that the priesthood of Christ was limited or confined to this world, or the time before his resurrection, but grant that it has a duration in heaven, and shall have so to the end of his mediation.

He abides, therefore, a priest for ever, as he does the king of his church. And the continuance of this office is a matter of singular use and consolation to believers, and as such is frequently mentioned. Wherefore, although he ascended not into heaven to be made a priest, but as a priest, yet his ascension, exaltation, and glorious immortality, or the 'power of an endless life,' were antecedently necessary to the actual discharge of some duties belonging to that office, as his intercession and the continual application of the fruits and benefits of his oblation.

The Socinians, as has been declared, comply with us in none of these assertions; for whereas they judge that Christ is then and therein only a priest, when and wherein he offers himself to God, this they say he did not until his entrance into heaven upon his ascension, and that there he continues still so to do. Whilst he was in this world, if we may believe them, he was no priest, nor were any of his duties or actings sacerdotal. But yet, to mollify the harshness of this conceit, they grant that, by the appointment of God, his temptations, sufferings, and death, were antecedently necessary to his heavenly oblation, and so belong to his priestly office metonymically. These being the things in difference, how they may be established or invalidated is our next consideration.

On the Earth

Our first argument for the time and place of the exercise of the priesthood of Christ shall be taken from the judgment and opinion of our adversaries themselves; for if the Lord Christ whilst he was upon the earth had power to perform, and did actually perform, all those things wherein they affirm that his sacerdotal office does consist, then was he a priest at that time and in that place; for the denomination of the office is taken from the power and its exercise. And themselves judge that the priesthood of Christ consists solely in a right, power, and readiness, to do the things which they ascribe to him. Neither can any difference be feigned from a distinct manner of the performance of the things so ascribed to him. In heaven, indeed, he does them conspicuously and illustriously; in the earth he did them under sundry concealments. But this alters not the nature of the things themselves. Sacerdotal actions will be so whatever various accidents may attend them in the manner of their performance. Now, that Christ did all things on the earth which they assign as acts of his sacerdotal office will appear in the ensuing instances.

He Presented Himself Ready to Do God's Will

On the earth he presented himself to God as one that was ready to do his will, and as one that had done it to the uttermost, in the last finishing of his work. This presentation they call his offering himself to God. And this he does, 'Lo, I come to do thy will, O God' (Heb. 10:7). That this was with respect to the obedience which he performed on the earth is manifest from the place of the psalmist whence the words are taken; for he so presents himself in them to God as one acting a principle of obedience to him in suffering and preaching the gospel: 'I come to do thy will; thy law is written in my heart' (Ps. 40:8–10). Again, he solemnly offered himself to God on the earth upon the consideration of the accomplishment of the whole work which was committed to him, when he was in the close and finishing of it. And herewith he made his request to God that those who believed on him, or should so do to the end of the world, might have all the benefits which God had decreed and purposed to bestow on them through his obedience to him—which is the full description of the oblation of Christ, according to these men (see John 17:1-6, etc.)

He Loved and Cared for the Church

He had and exercised on the earth a most tender love and care for his whole church, both his present disciples and all that should believe on him through their word. This they make to be the principal property of this office of Christ, or rather, from hence it is—namely, his tender care, love, and readiness to relieve, which we cannot apprehend in him under the notion of his kingly power alone—that he is called a high priest, and is so to be looked on. Now, whereas two things may be considered in the love and care of Christ towards his church; first, the evidencing fruits of it; and, secondly, its effects;—the former were more conspicuous in what he did in this life than in what he does in heaven, and the latter every way equal thereunto.

THE EVIDENCE. The great evidencing fruit of the love of Christ and his care of his church was in this, that he died for it. This both himself and all the divine writers express and testify to be the greatest fruit and evidence of love, expressly affirming that greater love there cannot be than what is so expressed (See John 10:14, 15:13; Rom. 5:6; Gal. 2:20; Eph. 5:25; 1 John 3:16; Rev. 1). If, therefore, Christ be denominated a high priest because of his love and care towards his church, as he had them in the highest degree, so he gave the greatest evidence of them possible, whilst he was in this world. This he did in dying for it, in giving his life for it; which, in what sense soever it be affirmed, is the highest fruit of love, and so the highest act of his sacerdotal office.

THE EFFECTS. The effects of this priestly love and care, they say, consists in the help and aid which he gives to those that believe on him, whereby they may be preserved from evil. But that he did this also on the earth, besides those other instances which may be given thereof, himself also expressly affirms, 'While I was with them in the world, I kept them in thy name; those that thou gavest me I have kept, and none of them is lost' (John 17:12).

He Exercised His Power According to His Love

There belongs nothing more to the priesthood of Christ, according to these men, but only a power to act what his love and care do incline and dispose him to. And this consists in the actual collation of grace, mercy, pardon of sin, and spiritual privileges, on believers. But all these things were effected by him whilst he was in this world. For—

1. He had power on the earth to forgive or take away the sins of men; which he put forth and acted accordingly (Matt. 9:2; Mark 2:5; Luke 5:20, 7:48). And the taking away of sin effectually is the great sacerdotal act which they ascribe to him.
2. He conferred spiritual privileges upon them who believed on him; for the greatest thing of this kind, and the fountain of all others, is adoption, and to 'as many as received him gave he power to become the sons of God' (John 1:11–12).
3. Whatever also Christ does for us of this kind may be referred either to his quickening of us with life spiritual, with the preservation of it, or the giving of us right and title to eternal life. But for these things he had power whilst he was on the earth, as he himself expressly declares (John 4:10, 5:21, 10:28, 11:25, 40, 14:6, 15:5, 17:22). And with respect to all these things does he require that we should believe in him and rely upon him.

Besides these three things, in general, with what belongs to them, I do not know what the Socinians ascribe more to the sacerdotal dignity or power of Christ or the exercise of it, nor what they require more, but that the name and title of the high priest of the church may be ascribed to him in their way—that is, metaphorically; for although they set these things off with the specious titles of expiating or purging our sins, of the offering of himself to God, of intercession, and the like names, as real sacerdotal acts, yet it is evident that no more is intended by them than we have expressed under these heads. And if they shall say otherwise, let them give an instance of any one thing which they ascribe to him as a priest, and if we prove not that it is reducible to one of these heads, we will forego this argument. Wherefore, upon their own principles, they cannot deny but that the Lord Christ was as really and truly a priest whilst he was on the earth as he is now in heaven.

WHENEVER AND WHEREVER HE MADE ATONEMENT

Secondly, let it be further remembered, that we plead only Christ to have been a priest and to have offered sacrifice on the earth *quoad* ἱλασμόν, as to propitiation, or the expiation of sin, granting on the other side that he is still so in heaven *quoad* ἐμφανισμόν, as to appearance and representation. Wherefore, whatever our adversaries do or can ascribe to the Lord Christ as a priest, which in any sense, or by virtue of any allusion, can be looked on as a sacerdotal act, is by us acknowledged and ascribed to him. That which is in controversy arises from their denial of what he did on the earth, or of his being a high priest before his ascension into heaven; which is now further to be confirmed.

When and where he made reconciliation and atonement for us, or for our sins, then and there he was a priest. I do not know that it is needful to confirm this proposition; for we intend no more by acting of the priest's office but the making atonement for sin by sacrifice. He that has power and right so to do is a priest by the call and appointment of God. And that herein principally consists the acting of the sacerdotal power, we have the consent of the common sense of mankind. Nor is this expressly denied by the Socinians themselves. For it was the principal if not the sole end why such an office was ordained in the world (Heb. 5:1). But this was done by the Lord Christ whilst he was on the earth; for he made atonement for us by his death. Among other testimonies to this purpose, that of our apostle is irrefragable, 'For if, when we were enemies, we were reconciled to God by the death of his Son, much more, being reconciled, we shall be saved by his life' (Rom. 5:10). He distributes the mediatory actings of Christ on our behalf into his death and his life. And the life which he intends is that which ensued after his death. So it is said, 'He died, and rose, and revived' (Rom. 14:9). He was dead and is alive (Rev. 1:18). For he leads in heaven a mediatory life, to make intercession for us, whereby we are saved (Heb. 7:25). Upon this distribution of the mediatorial actings of Christ, our reconciliation to God is peculiarly assigned to his death: 'When we were enemies we were reconciled to God by the death of his Son.' Reconciliation is sometimes the same with atonement (Heb. 2:17); sometimes it is put for the immediate effect of it. And in this place the apostle declares that our being reconciled and receiving the atonement are the same: Καταλλαγέντες...τὴν καταλλαγὴν ἐλάζομεν (Rom. 5:10–11). But to make atonement and reconciliation is the work of a priest. Unless this be acknowledged, the whole instructive part of the Old Testament must be rejected; for the end of the priest's office, as we observed, was to make atonement or reconciliation. And that this was done by the death of Christ, the apostle does here expressly affirm. He slew the enmity, made peace, reconciled Jews and Gentiles to God in one body, by the cross (Eph. 2:15–16).

Our adversaries would have the reconciliation intended to be only on our part, or the reconciling us to God; not on the part of God, or his reconciliation to us. But as this is false, so it is also, as to our present argument, impertinent; for we dispute not about the nature of reconciliation, but the cause and time of its making. Whatever be the especial nature of it, it is an effect of a sacerdotal act. Nor is this denied by our adversaries, who plead that our conversion to God depends on Christ's offering himself to God in heaven, as the effect on the cause. And this reconciliation, whatever its especial nature be, is directly ascribed to the death of Christ. Therein, therefore, was he a priest and offered sacrifice. Besides, the especial nature of the reconciliation made by the death of Christ is sufficiently declared; for we are so reconciled by Christ as that our sins are not imputed to us (2 Cor. 5:19, 21); and that because they were imputed to him when he was made a curse for us (Gal. 3:13)—when he hung on the tree, and bare our sins in his own body thereon (1 Pet. 2:24). And then he gave himself λύτρον, 'a ransom' (Matt. 20:28), and ἀντίλυτρον (1 Tim. 2:6), a price of redemption for us; and his soul was made a sin-offering (Isa. 53:10)—that is, '*sacrificium pro reatu nostro*,' 'a sacrifice for the expiation of our guilt,' and this he did as the sponsor or surety, or 'the mediator of the new covenant' (Heb. 9:15); and therefore he must do it either as the king, or as the prophet, or as the priest of the church, for within these offices and their actings is his mediation circumscribed. But it is manifest that these things belong to neither of the former; for in what sense can he be said to pay a price of redemption for us in the shedding his blood, or to make his soul an offering for sin, to make reconciliation by being made sin and a curse for us, as he was a king or a prophet? In like manner and to the same purpose we are said to have 'redemption in' (or 'by') 'his blood, even the forgiveness of sins' (Eph. 1:7); to be 'justified by his blood' (Rom. 5:9; Col. 1:14; 1 Pet. 1:18–19). Now, redemption, forgiveness and justification, consisting, according to our adversaries, in our delivery from the punishment due to sin, it is an effect, as they also acknowledge, of the sacerdotal actings of Christ. But they are all said to be by his blood, which was shed on the earth. Besides, it is in like manner acknowledged that the Lord Christ was both priest and sacrifice; for, as it is constantly affirmed, he 'offered himself' (Heb. 9:14, Eph. 5:2). And he was a sacrifice when and wherein he was a propitiation; for propitiation is the end and effect of a sacrifice. So the apostle distributes his sacerdotal acts into propitiation and intercession (1 John 5:1–2). His making oblation and being a propitiation are the same. And wherein God made him a propitiation, therein he was our propitiation. But this was in his death; for God set him forth 'To be a propitiation through faith in his blood' (Rom. 3:25). Our faith, therefore, respecting Christ as proposed of God to be a propitiation—that is, making atonement for us by sacrifice—considers him as shedding his blood to that end and purpose.

ON HIS ENTRANCE INTO HEAVEN

Thirdly, the Lord Christ entered into the holy place, that is, heaven itself, as a high priest, and that with respect to what as a high priest he had done before; for when the apostle teaches the entrance of Christ into heaven by the entrance of the high priest into the sanctuary, as that which was a prefiguration thereof, he instructs us in the manner of it. Now, the high priest was already in office, completely a high priest, before his entrance into the most holy place, and was not admitted into his office thereby, as they pretend the Lord Christ to have been by his entrance into heaven. Yea, had he not been a high priest before that entrance, he would have perished for it; for the law was, that none should so enter but the high priest. And not only so, but he was not, on pain of death, at any time to go into the sanctuary, but with immediate respect to the preceding solemn discharge of his office; for he was not to enter into it but only after he had, as a priest, slain and offered the expiatory sacrifice, some of the blood whereof he carried into the most holy place, to complete and perfect the atonement. Now, if the Lord Christ was not a priest before his entrance into heaven, if he did not enter thereinto with respect to, and on the account of, the sacrifice which he had offered before without the holy place, in his death and blood-shedding, all the analogy that is between the type and the antitype, all that is instructive in those old institutions, is utterly destroyed, and the apostle, illustrating these things one by another, does lead us unavoidably into misapprehension of them. For whosoever shall read that, as the high priest entered into the most holy place with the blood of bulls and goats, which he had sacrificed without, to appear in the presence of God, in like manner Jesus Christ, the high priest of the church, called of God to that office, by the one sacrifice of himself, or by his own blood, entered into the holy place in heaven, to appear in the presence of God for us, will understand that he was a high priest and offered his sacrifice before he so entered into the heavenly sanctuary, or he must offer violence to the plain, open sense of the instruction given to him.

Other Priests Were Types of Christ

Fourthly, other priests, who never entered into the sanctuary, were types of Christ in their office and the execution of it; which if he was not a priest on earth, nor thereon offered his sacrifice or executed his office, they could not be; for nothing they did represented the appearance of Christ in heaven. And this is evident in his principal type, Melchizedek; for he did so eminently represent him above Aaron and his successors as that he is peculiarly called a priest after his order. Now, Melchizedek discharged his office entirely, and an end was put to his priesthood, before there was any sanctuary erected, to be a resemblance of the holy place whereinto Christ, our high priest, was to enter. And whereas our adversaries say that he is called a high priest because of an allusion that was between what he does for the church and what was done by them, if his priesthood and sacrifice consisted in his entrance into heaven and presenting or offering himself there in glory to God, there was no allusion at all between it and what was done by him whom the Scripture expresses as his principal type, namely, this Melchizedek, who had no sanctuary to enter into, whereby there might be any allusion between what he did and what was done by Jesus Christ. Moreover, all the priests according to the law, in all their sacrifices, especially those that were solemn and stated for the whole people, were types of Christ; for whereas the original institution of all expiatory sacrifices, or sacrifices to make atonement for sin, was merely with respect to, and to prefigure, the sacrifice which Christ was to offer, without which they would have been of no use nor signification, nor had ever been instituted, as being a kind of worship no way suiting the divine nature without this relation; and whereas the Lord Christ, with respect to them, is called the 'Lamb of God that takes away the sin of the world,' and a 'Lamb slain from the foundation of the world,' as I have proved elsewhere; the priests that offered these sacrifices must of necessity be types of him in his.

Crellius replies to this (Chapter 10, To Grotius, part 21, page 413):

> Socinus wishes (1.) that the public and appointed sacrifices, and especially the annual one, be regarded as figures of the sacrifice of Christ. I deny that the rest are our spiritual sacrifices. (2.) For we offer such sacrifices by which our intervening sins are atoned for, or forgiveness of sins is obtained by the kindness of God: he thinks (3.) to answer that the high priest was also a type of Christ as High Priest, and that (4.) the rest of the ordinary priests are we who are now also priests; and thinks it is strange if anyone is doubtful about this matter.

(1.) It is acknowledged that other stated and solemn sacrifices besides the anniversary expiation were types of the sacrifice of Christ. But these were offered by the ordinary priests (Num. 28:15, 22, 30; 29:5, 11, 16, 19, 22), and were completed without the most holy place, no entrance into it ensuing thereon; for they consisted entirely in the death and blood-shedding of the sacrifices themselves, with their oblation on the altar. How, then, could they typify Christ and his sacrifice, if that consisted not at all in his death and blood-shedding, which they did represent, but in his entrance into heaven, and presenting himself there to God, which they did not represent at all? This concession, therefore, that the sacrifice of Christ was typified by any sacrifices whereof no part nor remembrance was carried into the sanctuary, destroys the whole hypothesis of our adversaries.

(2.) Nothing that we do is, in any sense, such a sacrifice as whereby sin is expiated. And although our faith is the means whereby we are interested in the one sacrifice of Christ by which our sins are expiated once and for ever, and we thereby, according to God's appointment, obtain the forgiveness of our sins, yet no duties of ours are anywhere called sacrifices, but such as are fruits of gratitude for the pardon of sin, received by virtue of that one sacrifice of Christ.

(3.) The high priest was a true, real type of Christ, but not his only type; Melchizedek was so also, and so were all the ordinary priests of the house of Aaron, who served at the altar.

(4.) He is greatly mistaken in his last assertion, of which he gives no other proof but only 'it is strange if anyone is doubtful about this matter;' and this is, that the priests under the law were types of all Christians, and their sacrifices of ours, and that 'this belongs to the economy of the new covenant.'

For I do not only doubt of it, but also expressly deny it, and that on such grounds as will leave none for admiration in any sober person; for—

1. All the priests of the house of Aaron were of the very same office with the high priest. Aaron and his sons were at the same time called to the same office, and set apart in the same manner (Exod. 28:1 and 29:9). If, therefore, the high priest was in his office the type of Christ, the other priests in their office could not be types of us, unless we have the same office with Christ himself, and are made mediators with him.

2. The sacrifices offered by the other priests were of the same nature with that or those which were offered by the high priest himself; for although the entrance once a year into the most holy place was peculiar to him, yet he had no sacrifice of any especial kind, as burnt-offering, sin-offering, or trespass-offering, peculiar to him, but the other priests offered the same. If, therefore, the sacrifice of the high priest was a type of the sacrifice of Christ, the sacrifices of the other priests could not be types of ours, unless they are of the same kind with that of Christ, which is not yet affirmed.

3. The truth is, the whole people under the law were types of believers under the gospel in the highest of their privileges, and therefore the priests were not so. We are now 'kings

and priests;' and the apostle Peter expressing this privilege (1 Pet. 2:5), does it in the words spoken of the body of the people or church of old (Exod. 19:6). Nothing, therefore, is more vain than this supposition.

Fifthly, The principal argument whereby we prove that Christ was a priest on the earth, is taken from the nature of the sacrifice which he offered as a priest. But whereas this cannot be duly managed without a full consideration and debate of all the properties, ends, and concernments of that sacrifice, which is not our present subject nor design, it must, as it was intimated before, be transmitted to its proper place.

DENIALS THAT CHRIST WAS A PRIEST ON EARTH

It remains that we consider the pretences and pleas of our adversaries in the defense of their opinion. It is that, I confess, which they have no concernment in for its own sake, being only a necessary consequent of their judgment concerning the office of the priesthood itself. Wherefore, for that the most part they content themselves with a bare denial that he was a priest on the earth, the proof of their negation they mix with the description of the office and its discharge. Wherefore, to show how little they are able to prove what they pretend to, I shall represent their plea in the words of one of the chief masters of that sect, that the reader may see what is the true state of the controversy between them and us in this matter, which they industriously endeavour to conceal, and then consider their proofs in particular.

Valentinus Smalcius

This is Valentinus Smalcius, in his book *De Regno Christ*. cap. 23, which is, De Christi Sacerdotio, whose words ensue:

> Then we must consider (1.) this whole matter, which is described by the term 'priesthood in Christ', to be figurative, which of course explains what once existed under the old covenant. Just as under the old covenant God wished there to be priests (2.) who acted before God on behalf of the people, so also Jesus Christ

is therefore considered to be a priest himself, because he acts before God in heaven on behalf of the people. And this work of his is called his priesthood. (3.) This can be completely evident if it is considered alone to a certain degree, since the Epistle to the Hebrews mentions Christ and his priesthood, because he is priest; however impossible it is that the other apostles make no mention of a matter so notable in their writings, and without which the dignity of Christ cannot exist.

ANSWER. (1.) It is not much that I shall observe on these words, and I shall therein principally respect the perpetual sophistry of these men. It is somewhat plain, indeed, that all things spoken about the priesthood of Christ are figurative, and nothing real or proper; and therefore he speaks of it as a thing utterly of another nature that is intended, only in Christ it is described 'by this word, the priesthood.' But the sober Christian reader will judge whether there be nothing but a mere occasional abuse of that word intended by the Holy Ghost in that full and large description which he has given us of this office of Christ, its duties, acts, adjuncts, and exercise, with the importance of these things to our faith and consolation.

(2.) Who would not think these expressions, first concerning the high priest, 'Who should deal with God on the behalf of the people,' and then concerning Christ, 'Who pleads the holy people's cause in heaven,' were so far equivalent, especially the one being produced in the illustration of the other, as that the things signified should, though they be not of the same kind, yet at least some way or other agree? But no such matter is intended; for in the first proposition God is expressly asserted as the immediate object of the sacerdotal actings of the high priest under the law, according to the Scripture; but in the latter, 'he pleads the cause of his people in heaven,' which is ascribed to Christ, nothing is intended but the exercise of his love and power in heaven towards his people for their relief—which is a thing quite of another nature. By these contrary senses of seeming equivalent expressions, all analogy between the old priesthood and that of Christ is utterly destroyed.

(3.) It is falsely pretended that this office of Christ is not formally mentioned by other divine writers besides the apostle in this Epistle to the Hebrews. He is expressly called a priest in the Old Testament by the way of prophecy, and all acts of this office are expressly mentioned and declared in sundry other places of the

New Testament, which have been before produced. And although it becomes not us to call the Spirit of God to an account, or to expect an express reason to be assigned why he teaches and reveals any truth more directly and expressly in one place of the Scripture than in another—it being an article of our faith that what he does he does wisely, and on the most rational motives—yet we are not altogether in the dark to the reason why the doctrine of the priesthood of Christ was more openly and plainly taught in this epistle than in any other place of Scripture. It was the prefiguration of it and preparation for it which the church of the Hebrews had received in their Mosaic institutions which was the occasion of this; and whereas the whole economy of their priesthood and sacrifices had no other end or use but to prefigure and represent those of the Lord Christ, upon his coming and the accomplishment of what was typified by them they were to cease and to be removed out of the church. But those Hebrews, by the long use of them, had contracted an inveterate persuasion that they had an excellency, use, and efficacy in the worship of God, upon their own account, and were therefore still to be continued and observed. On this occasion the declaration of the nature and use of the priesthood of Christ in the church was not only opportune and seasonable, but necessary and unavoidable. It was so, that those Hebrews who did sincerely believe the gospel, and yet supposed that the old legal institutions were in force and obligatory, might be delivered from so pernicious an error. And in like manner it was so with respect to them who, being satisfied in their cessation and removal, were to be instructed in what was the design of God in their institution, and what was their use; whereby they might at once discern that they were not a mere burden of chargeable and unuseful outward observances, and yet how great and excellent a glory was exhibited in their stead now under the gospel. Besides, whereas God was now giving up the whole Scripture to the use of the church, what better season or occasion could be taken to declare the harmony and relation that is between the old testament and the new, the analogy between the institutions of the one and the other, the preparations that were made in the shadows of the one for the introduction of the substance of the other, and so at once to present a scheme of divine wisdom and grace in both, than this of the instruction of the church of the Hebrews in their translation out of the one state into the other, which was peculiar to them, and wherein the Gentiles had no share? These things, I say (with holy submission to the sovereign will and wisdom of the Holy Ghost), rendered this time and place most convenient for the fixing and stating the doctrine of the priesthood of Christ in a peculiar manner. But our author adds:

> With respect to this therefore Christ himself, when he was still mortal, promised that 'he would be with his people always until the end of the age', that 'he would not leave them as orphans', but 'that he would give them a mouth and wisdom that no one could resist'. Likewise he said to John after he had been raised from the dead, 'Do not be afraid. Behold I am alive for ever.' And to St. Paul he said, 'Do not be afraid, but speak and do not keep silent, because I am with you.' Paul, when he was at last among the apostles, taught that Jesus Christ was the head of the church, and that the church was his body, that the church was cherished by him, and that Christ frees us from the wrath to come. This is, to the author of the Epistle to the Hebrews, what it means for Jesus Christ to be our priest. Add hereunto what he instructs us in a little afterwards: 'Christ himself was made both priest and offering. This is without figure of speech. When Christ ascended into heaven he was made immortal and by God's command began to live in that most holy place; he began to provide for our salvation and to conduct himself as excellently as he had promised before hand to do.'

ANSWER. This is in some measure plain dealing, and needful to the cause wherein these men are engaged; for although no great matter, at first view, seems to be contained herein, yet upon the truth of what he avers depends all the opposition they make to the real sacrifice and satisfaction of Christ. Hence, therefore, it is evident what is the true state of the controversy between these men and us about the priesthood of Christ. It is not, indeed, about the nature of that office, nor about the time and place of its exercise, though they needlessly compel us to treat about them also; but the sole question is, whether Christ have any such office or no. For if this be all they grant which this man asserts, as indeed it is—namely, 'That the Lord Christ, upon the account of some actings of his, which are no one of them properly or peculiarly sacerdotal, is only called a high priest figuratively by the author of the Epistle to the Hebrews'—then indeed he neither has nor ever had any such office at all. And this is the true state of our controversy with them, and with all by whom the satisfaction of Christ is denied, namely, whether he be the high priest of the church or no. And herein the Holy Ghost himself must answer for us and our profession.

This, then, is the substance of what they intend: the power, love, and care which the Lord Christ exercises in heaven towards his church makes him to be figuratively called our high priest; and in the same manner he is said to offer himself to God. But whence, then, comes it to pass, that whereas, according to the notion and understanding that is given us of the nature of these things (priest and sacrifice) in the Scripture—suited to the apprehension of all mankind about them, and which they answer or they are nothing— there is no similitude or likeness between them and what Christ was and did, they are expressed by these terms, which are apt to lead to thoughts of things quite of another kind than (as it seems) are intended? Why this, says Smalcius, was 'out of an excessive desire in the holy writers to speak figuratively;' an account which whether any wise man will, or good man ought to be satisfied withal, I do much question. And yet, according to Smalcius, they much fail in their design. For whereas no wise man does ever use figurative expressions unless he judge them necessary to set off the things he intends to express, and to greaten the apprehension of them, it is, if we may believe this author, unhappily fallen out otherwise with the writers of the New Testament in this matter; for instead of heightening or enlarging the things which they intended by all their figurative expressions, they do but lessen or diminish them. For so he informs us: 'We want to note this first here—not only because of other reasons but because of this one also—so that, by those same ways of speaking figuratively we can know that the highest pre-eminence anyone could perhaps consider possible can be bestowed on Christ in these matters; however less can be bestowed on him than is the case.' No men, certainly, could ever have steered a more unhappy course. For no doubt they designed to press the excellency of Christ and the usefulness of his mediation in these things to the church; but in the pursuit of it they wholly omit those plain and proper expressions whereby they might have fully declared it, to the comfort of the church and the establishment of our faith, and betake themselves absolutely to such figurative expressions as whereby the dignity of Christ is diminished, and less is ascribed to him than is due. Certainly men have used to make very bold with the Scriptures and their own consciences who can satisfy themselves with such imaginations.

But yet when all is done, all this, as has been manifested before will not serve the turn, nor disprove our assertion, that the Lord Christ was a priest whilst on the earth; for all the things which they thus ascribe to him were then discharged by him. Wherefore we shall further consider what direct opposition they make to this.

Woolzogenius

It is no matter at all whom we fix upon to call to an account herein. Their wits are barren in a peculiar manner on this subject, so that they all say the same things, one after another, without any considerable variation. The reader, if he please, may satisfy himself herein by consulting Socinus, Volkelius, Ostorodius, Smalcius, Moscorovius, Crellius, and Schlichtingius, in the places before cited. I shall therefore confine myself to him who has last appeared in the defense of this cause, and who seems to have put the newest gloss upon it. This is Ludwig Woolzogen., in his *Compend. Relig. Christianae*, sect. 51, whose words ensue:—

> In addition also this ought to be mentioned by we few because those who think that Christ finished and completed his atoning sacrifice for our sins on the cross do not properly understand the priestly office of Christ. For in the old covenant, (1) in which the sacrifices were a type of the sacrifice of Christ (2), the act of the atoning sacrifice was not in the slaughter of the victim or the animal, but the preparation of a certain victim for sacrifice was so great. For the sacrifice came about (3) (in this) when the high priest, with the responsibility of blood, entered into the Holy of Holies (4), and he offered it and sacrificed it to God. For sacrificing does not particularly consist of slaughtering (5), but of offering and setting apart for God.

ANSWER. (1.) It is acknowledged that the sacrifices under the old testament were types of the sacrifice of Christ; that is, all of them were so which were expiatory or appointed to make atonement. Although, therefore, these men are wary, yet they stand in such an unstable and slippery place as that they often reel and betray themselves; for if all expiatory sacrifices were types of the sacrifice of Christ, most of them being perfect and complete without carrying any of their blood into the sanctuary, that of Christ must be so before his entrance into heaven.

(2.) As for what he affirms of the expiatory sacrifice — that is, the anniversary sacrifice on the day of expiation — that it consisted not in the slaying of the sacrifice, which was only a certain preparation thereunto, it is either sophistical or false. It is sophistical, if by 'mactatio pecudis' he intend only the single act of slaying the sacrifice: for so it is granted that was not the entire sacrifice, but only a part of it; the oblation of it on the altar was also required to its perfection. But it is false, if he intend thereby all that was done in the offering of the beast, namely, its adduction to the altar, its mactation, the effusion of its blood, the sprinkling thereof, the laying of the offering on the altar, the consumption of it by fire — all which belonged to this. All these things, even all that preceded the entrance of the high priest into the most holy place, are distinguished from what was done afterwards, and are to be considered under that head which he calls the slaying of the victim. But then his assertion is false, for the sacrifice consisted therein, as we have proved.

(3.) That the expiatory sacrifice did not consist in the entrance and appearance of the high priest in the most holy place with the blood of the beast offered is manifest from hence, because he was commanded to offer the beast in sacrifice before his entrance into the sanctuary, which was a consequent of the sacrifice itself, and represented the effects of it.

(4.) That the high priest sacrificed the blood to God in the sanctuary, as he affirms, is an assertion that has no countenance given to it in the Scripture, nor has it so from any common notion concerning the nature of sacrifices; and the atonement that is said to be made for the most holy place by the sprinkling of the blood towards the mercy-seat was effected by the sacrifice as offered before, of which that ceremony was a sign and token.

(5.) That to sacrifice and to slay are the same in the original, so as that both these actions — that is, sacred and common slaying — are expressed ofttimes by the same word, I have before demonstrated. But withal I grant that to a complete sacrifice the ensuing oblation on the altar was also required. Hence was the sacrifice offered and consecrated to God.

But he endeavours to confirm his assertion with some testimonies of our apostle:

> And this is what the author of the Epistle to the Hebrews says: (1.) 'Into the second tent' (that is, into the Most Holy Place) 'only the High Priest entered once a year, not without blood, which he offered for himself and for the people in their ignornance'. These words in Hebrews 9:7 make it clear that the High Priest sacrificed only then, and presented an offering when he carried blood into the Most Holy Place, and with that responsibility appeared in the presence of God. (2.) It was in this service and offering in which atonement and redemption from sins consisted. So therefore even in Christ, who was destined to be both High Priest and also the victim, by the sacrifice of his body on the cross, there was no other preparation for the true sacrifice. But when he completed the sacrifice of himself, he entered into the heavenly sanctuary with his own blood, and there offered and presented himself to God as the victim. And indeed he intercedes for us before God as an eternal priest, and procures our atonement.

ANSWER. (1.) I understand not the force of the proof from this testimony to the purpose of our author. The high priest did enter into the most holy place with the blood of the sacrifice. What will thence ensue? Had it been common blood before, and now first consecrated to God, something might be collected thence in compliance with his design; but it was the blood of the sacrifice which was dedicated and offered to God before, the blood of the sacrifice that was slain, which was only carried into the most holy place and sprinkled there, as the representation of its virtue and efficacy. In like manner, Jesus Christ, the Lamb of God that was slain and sacrificed for us, after he had through the eternal Spirit offered himself to God, procuring thereby redemption for us in his blood, entered into heaven, there in the presence of God to represent the virtue of his oblation, and by his intercession (prefigured not by the offering, but by the sprinkling of blood) to make application thereof to us.

(2.) Redemption did in no sense follow the appearance of the high priest in the most holy place typically, nor the entrance of the Lord Christ into heaven really; but it is constantly assigned to his death and bloodshedding—which invincibly proves that therein alone his oblation of himself did consist (See 1 Pet. 1:18–19). Expiation may be considered either in respect of impetration or of application. In the first regard it did not follow, but precede the entrance of the high priest into the most holy place, for the sacrifice was offered without to make atonement for sin; and the same atonement was made in sundry sacrifices whose blood was never sprinkled in the most holy place. In the latter sense alone it may be said to follow it, which we contend not about.

His next testimony is from Hebrews 9:11–12, the words of which he only cites, without attempting any improvement or application of them: 'But Christ being come an high priest of good things to come, by a greater and more perfect tabernacle, not made with hands, that is to say, not of this building; neither by the blood of goats and calves, but by his own blood, he entered in once into the holy place, having obtained eternal redemption.'

Had he attempted any proof from these words, he would have found himself at a loss where to have fixed the argument. Wherefore, he contents himself with the bare sound of the words, supposing that may seem to favor his pretension. For it is plain from this text—

1. That Christ entered into heaven as our high priest, and not that he might become so; which is sufficient to scatter all his imaginations about this office of his.
2. That he entered into heaven 'by his own blood,' which was shed and poured out in his sacrifice before that entrance; for really he carried no blood with him, as the high priest did of old, but only was accompanied with the efficacy and virtue of that which was shed before.
3. He is said to have 'obtained eternal redemption' before his entrance into heaven, that being expressed as past upon his entrance; which invincibly proves that his sacrifice was antecedent to this.

His last testimony is Hebrews 8:4, which most of them make use of as their shield and buckler in this cause: 'For if he were on earth, he should not be a priest, seeing that there are priests that offer gifts according to the law.' But the plain design and intention of the apostle allows them no relief from these words. He had proved invincibly that the Lord Christ was to be 'an high priest,' and had showed in some instances the nature of that office of his. Here, to confirm what he had so declared, he lays it down, by the way of concession, that if there were no other priesthood but that which is earthly and carnal, or which belonged to the Judaical church, he could not have been a priest at all, which yet he had proved that it was necessary he should be. And the reason of this concession he adds, from the possession of that office by the priests of the house of Aaron, and the enclosure of its propriety to them (v. 5). Hence it unavoidably ensues that he must have a priesthood of another kind, or different from that of Aaron, which he expressly asserts as his conclusion (v. 6). A priest he must be; a priest after the order of them who offered gifts according to the law he could not be: and therefore he had another, and therefore a more excellent, priesthood.

More of Smalcius' Impieties

To these testimonies, which are commonly pleaded by them all to deprive the Lord Christ of this office, at least whilst he was on the earth, I shall add the consideration of one, with the argument from it, which I find not insisted on by any of them but only Smalcius alone (*De Reg. Chr.* cap. 23):

> When the author of the Epistle to the Hebrews wishes to refer to this offering of Christ, and to demonstrate clearly that it was only completed when Christ ascended into heaven, he says, 'For it was fitting for us to have such a high priest, holy, without fault, undefiled, separate from sinners, and made higher than the heavens.' And with Paul he says below, 'Christ offered himself spotless to God through the eternal Spirit.' He understood that by these epithets 'holy, without fault, undefiled, separate from sinners and innocent,' he did not consider the holiness of Christ in his behaviour, but the holiness which was in Christ's nature, for Christ was always perfectly described by these terms, even before he became our priest. With regard to this nature of Christ, as long as he was on the earth, he was made like his brothers in all their weakness and was even liable to mortality; now however he is free from this for all eternity.

ANSWER. (1.) These properties of 'holy, harmless, undefiled, separate from sinners,' which the apostle ascribes to our Lord Jesus as our high priest (Heb. 7:26), as also his offering himself 'without spot' (Heb. 9:14), this man ascribes to Christ as exalted in heaven, in contradistinction to what he was whilst on the earth; for thence he takes his argument that he was not a priest whilst he was on the earth, namely, because he was so holy, harmless, undefiled, and separate from sinners, in heaven. Now, if it do not hence follow that he was impure, defiled, guilty, like other sinners, whilst he was on the earth, yet it does undeniably—and that is the matter contended for—that he was not holy, harmless, and undefiled, in the sense here intended by the apostle. How this can be freed from open blasphemy I am not able to discern.

(2.) He is not secured by his ensuing distinction, that the Lord Christ was before, whilst on the earth, perfectly holy as to his manners, but that the epithets here used respect his nature: for, not to assign all these properties to the nature of Christ from the instant of his conception, or to deny them to belong thereunto, is no less contrary to the Scripture and really blasphemous than to deny him to have been holy with respect to his life and conversation; for he was the 'holy thing' that was born of the Virgin, and as he was born of her, by virtue of the miraculous creation and sanctification of his nature in the womb, whereof I have treated elsewhere at large.

(3.) Here is a supposition included, that all the difference between Christ and us, whilst he was in this world, consisted only in the use of his freedom to the perfect obedience wherein we fail and come short. That his nature was absolutely holy and impeccable, ours sinful and defiled, is cast out of consideration; and yet to deny this difference between him and us is no less blasphemous than what we before rejected.

(4.) Christ in this world was indeed obnoxious to sufferings and death itself, as having a nature, on that account, like to his brethren in all things. But to suppose that he was obnoxious to infirmity and mortality because he was not yet holy, harmless, undefiled, and separate from sinners, is injurious to his person, and derogatory from his love; for it was not from the necessity of his own condition in human nature that he was exposed to sufferings or to death, but he became so by voluntary condescension for our sakes (Phil. 2:5–8). We are obnoxious to these things on our own account, he only on ours.

(5.) In the death of Christ, when he shed his blood, he was ἀμνὸς ἄμωμος καὶ ἄσπιλος, 'a lamb without spot and without blemish' (1 Pet. 1:19); and he is said to offer himself ἄμωμον τῷ Θεῷ, 'without spot to God' (Heb. 9:14). He was therefore no less so before and in his death than after. And it is a surprisal, to be put, by one professing himself a Christian, to the work of proving the Lord Christ to have been, in his entire nature, in this world holy and harmless.

(6.) He does not in the least relieve himself from those impieties by his ensuing discourse on, 'That he might sanctify, and cleanse it with the washing of water by the word, that he might present it to himself a glorious church, not having spot, or wrinkle, or any such thing; but that it should be holy and without blemish' (Eph. 5:26–7). He contends that the making of the church 'holy and without blemish' in this place concerns its glorified state, because it is therewithal said to be a 'glorious church.' In the same sense, therefore, as he affirms, is Christ said to be 'holy' when he was 'glorified,' and not before. But he adds herein to the weight and number of his preceding enormities: for in what sense soever the church is said to be made holy or to be sanctified, whether it be in grace or as instated in glory, it is so by being washed and cleansed from the spots, stains, and filth which originally it had; but to ascribe such a sanctification or making holy to the Lord Christ is the highest blasphemy imaginable.

We may therefore firmly conclude, with the whole church of God, according to the Scripture and the nature of the thing itself, that the Lord Christ was a priest and executed his priestly office whilst he was on the earth, even then when he offered up himself to God with strong cries and supplications at his death on the cross.

THE OBJECT

Secondly, that which yet remains, as belonging to our present design, is the consideration of the direct and immediate object of the sacerdotal actings of Christ, or the exercising his mediatory power by virtue of his priestly office. This we have declared before and proved, namely, that it is God himself. Our meaning is, that the Lord Jesus Christ, as the high priest of the church, acts on its behalf with God, doing those things which are to be done with him, according to the covenant before explained. As a king and prophet he acts in the name of God towards us; as a priest he acts towards God on our behalf. This the whole economy of the Aaronic priesthood does confirm, and the very nature of the great duties of this office, oblation and intercession, do necessarily infer. Does Christ offer himself in sacrifice to God, or to us? Does he intercede with God, or with us? It is no small evidence of the desperate cause of our adversaries, that they are forced to put uncouth and horrid senses on these sacerdotal duties, to accommodate them to their sentiments. So after that Smalcius has told us that these things were thus expressed in Scripture 'out of an excessive desire to speak figuratively,' so traducing the wisdom and sobriety of the penmen thereof, he adds in the explication of that figurative expression, as he would have it, of Christ's intercession, 'Therefore, when it is said of Christ that he intercedes for us, nothing else is said about that power given to him to undertake and govern for us.' It is not easily conceivable how a greater violence can be offered to a sacred expression. By such interpretations it is possible to put an orthodox sense on all the writings of Smalcius. But in the vindication of his exposition of Christ's intercession he adds, 'That the power which Christ excercises in his care of the church, and all his actings towards it, he received of God, and therefore in the use of it he is said to make intercession for us'—that is, he does one thing, and is said to do another! What he does is not said—namely, that he acts his power towards the church; and what he does not, that he is said to do—namely, to make intercession with God for us. The arguments whereby we confirm the truth asserted have been before declared and confirmed. Wherefore, to put a close to this whole disputation, and to give the reader a specimen of the subtlety and perpetual tergiversation of our adversaries in this cause, wherein also occasion will be administered further to explain sundry things relating to this office of Christ, I shall examine strictly the whole discourse of Crellius on this subject, and therein give a peculiar instance of the sophistical ability of these men in evading the force of arguments and testimonies from the Scripture.

GOD

Grotius proves that the first actings of Christ as a priest were towards God, from Hebrews 5:1, and chap. 8:3, to which Crellius replies (cap. 10: part. 3, p. 474):

The following words were therefore compared, and they did not agree with Grotius, so that they would not disagree with the opinions of Socinus. For Socinus also admits and the author of Hebrews 2:17 teaches clearly enough that the action of Christ as priest, and in the same way his atoning sacrifice, were among a number of deeds which occurred on behalf of men in the presence of God. Another deduction is not useful here, when inquiring into matters concerning the sacrifice of Christ. An understanding of this is therefore sought, when the meaning of these words is agreed upon.

ANSWER. (1.) The agreement which he pretends between Grotius and himself in this matter, as to the words of the apostle, is enough, with sober men, to put an end to the whole controversy. The question is, whether Christ, as a high priest, did act principally towards God, or towards us? 'Towards God,' says the apostle, and Grotius from him. 'We are agreed,' says Crellius, 'about these words; all the question is about their sense.' As how? 'Namely, whether they signify that Christ excercises this office towards God, or towards us;' for this is that which, after a long tergiversation, he comes to: 'The apostle intimates plainly, that such is the (sacerdotal) acting of Christ in this matter that it is first exercised towards us, and not towards God' (p. 477). Whatever, therefore, is otherwise pretended, the question between him and us is about the words themselves and their truth, and not about their sense and meaning. For if it be true that the Lord Christ καθίσταται ὑπὲρ ἀνθρώπων τὰ πρός τὸν Θεόν, 'is appointed as a priest for men,' (or on their behalf) 'in the things belonging to God,' or to be done with God (Heb. 5:1), and that in an especial manner, εἰς τὸ προσφέρειν δῶρά τε καὶ θυσίας (Heb. 8:3), 'to offer gifts and sacrifices to God,' the whole sense is granted which we plead for. If he is not so appointed, if he does not do so—that is, if he was not ordained to act with God in the behalf of men, if he did not offer sacrifice for them or the expiation of their sins—then are not these words true, and it is in vain to contend about the sense of them.

(2.) I shall only further observe the sophistry of that expression, 'That action of Christ whereby he is a priest;' for he intends that Christ is only denominated a priest from some action he does perform, whereas in truth he performs those actions by virtue of his priesthood, and could not perform them were he not a priest in office.

Having laid this foundation, Crellius enters upon a large discourse, wherein he does nothing but perpetually divert from the argument in hand, and by a multitude of words strive to hide himself from the sense of it. Take him when he supposes himself out of its reach and he speaks plainly. So he does, *Lib. de Caus. Mort. Christi*, page. 7: 'When Christ is considered as a priest, although he bears the likeness of one that does something with God on the behalf of men, yet, if you look more narrowly into the matter itself, you will find that he is such a priest who acts towards us in the name of God.' If we may but hold him to this plain declaration of his mind (which, indeed, he must keep to or lose his cause), the vanity and tergiversation that are in all his other evasions and pretences will be evident.

Crellius' Errors Concerning Expiation and Sacrifice

But because we have resolved on a particular examination of all that can be pretended in this matter on the behalf of our adversaries, we may consider his plea at large in his own words:

(1.) Grotius therefore without doubt understands these words and whether God was said to be moved by sacrifices to bless men and wished, indeed by atonement, to grant forgiveness of their sins. (2.) This is accepted, by the opinion in which Grotius is otherwise accustomed to take up words in our discussion, (3.) to show that God is angry and desiring punishment, and while he does not turn from anger by laying it aside, is appeased by sacrifices, and caused to forgive. (4.) It is not with regard to all atoning sacrifices, yet particularly those said to grant - no indeed concering those which are particularly so called – (5.) if not quite repentence, humility of mind and contrition of heart and spirit, which one may know concerning other prayers made by men. (6.) For the sacrifices under the law did not always move God from the covenant especially laid down by him himself: but since God had already decreed beforehand that he wished to forgive transgressions and wrongdoings on the basis of those intervening sacrfices. By those offerings, (7.) by the strength of that decree what was carried out before God achieved this: even if he was not actually angry, indeed the sacrifices were therefore offered in advance, they acted so that he would not become angry if they were by chance neglected, rather than him being appeased when already angry. If, moved by my voice, you accept this manner of interpretation, and the rest of the metaphors, which we have also explained elsewhere, you will see that they show they are carried out by the agreement supplied before God. In his decree he blessed what is done by men, and erases the charge or sin and withdraws its penalty, whether through himself, as under the law, or through another, as in the time of the New Covenant. It is as Grotius says, done then through the legal sacrifices and now also through the death of Christ. (8.) That is the true sacrifice and we confess that it is indeed atoning although it is not yet complete through him in this generation.

ANSWER. (1.) There was no need at all of this large and ambiguous repetition of the whole state of the controversy about the nature and use of sacrifices in this place, where the argument concerned only the proper object of Christ's sacerdotal actings. And he knew well enough the mind of Grotius, as to the sense of what he asserted; only it was necessary to retreat into this long diversion, to avoid the force of the testimonies produced against him.

(2.) The sense which we plead for, as to the expiation of our sins by Jesus Christ, is plain and evident. God was the author and giver of the law and the sanction thereof; the supreme, righteous, holy rector, governor, judge of all persons and actions relating to this; the dispenser of the rewards and punishments, according to the sense and sentence of it. Man transgressed this law by sin, and did what lay in him thereby to cast off the government of God. This rendered him obnoxious to the sentence, curse, death, and punishment, threatened in the sanction of the law; which God, as the righteous, holy, supreme governor of all, was, on the account of his righteousness, authority, and veracity, obliged to execute. This respect of God towards the transgressors of his law the Scripture represents under the notion and expression of his anger against sin and sinners; which is nothing but the engagement of his justice to punish offenders. On this account God would not, and without the violation of his justice and veracity could not, forgive sin, or dismiss sinners unpunished, without an atonement made by an expiatory sacrifice; wherein his justice also was to be satisfied and his law to be fulfilled. And this was done by the sacrifice of Christ, according to the tenor and compact between God and him before described.

(3.) The advantage that Crellius seeks from the words of Grotius, in the entrance of his discourse, of God's being 'angry with sinners, yet not so as to depose all thoughts of reconciliation,' will stand him in no stead; for he intended no more by them, but that although God was provoked, as the righteous governor of his creatures, yet he determined not absolutely to destroy them, when he had found a ransom: that is, provided his justice were satisfied, his honour repaired, his law fulfilled—all which his own holiness and faithfulness required—he would pardon sin, and take away the punishment from sinners. That whereby this was done was the sacrifice of Christ; whose object, therefore, must be God himself, and consequently he is so of all his sacerdotal actings.

(4.) All expiatory sacrifices did, in their way and kind, procure the remission of sins by the way of atonement, and not otherwise. Nor can Crellius give any one instance to the contrary. Their first and principal design was to atone and pacify anger, or to turn away wrath and punishment as due from the displeasure of God; and, therefore their first effect was towards God himself.

(5.) The means on our part for the obtaining of the actual remission of sin, and a sense thereof in our consciences, as prayer, repentance, humiliation, contrition of heart and spirit, are not means of making atonement, wherein there is always the nature of compensation and satisfaction. If we apply ourselves to God by them to any such purpose, or rest upon them to that end, we render them useless, yea, an abomination. Yea, they are all enjoined to us on supposition of atonement made for sin in and by the blood of Christ; and so they were from the foundation of the world. From the giving of the first promise, wherein the Lord Christ was a 'lamb slain,' as to the efficacy of his future oblation, God forgave sins for his sake, and not otherwise. And the duties enjoined us in order to actual remission, or a sense of it in our consciences, are all to be founded in the faith of that atonement, which is supposed, and is to be pleaded in them all; for in Christ alone it is that we have 'redemption through his blood, even the forgiveness of sins.' But all this is a diversion from the present argument and inquiry, which concerns only the proper object of the sacerdotal actings of

Christ, and not the nature of his sacrifice, which shall be spoken to elsewhere. And those very duties whereby we make application for actual remission or pardon, upon the atonement made, have God for their object also; and so must every thing which has an influence of any kind into the pardon of sin.

(6.) The account he gives concerning the influence of expiatory sacrifices in procuring the pardon of sin is false and sophistical. That God, not being angry with sin, should decree that upon the offering of sacrifices he would pardon it, and would have such sacrifices offered, not because he was angry, but that he might not be so, is a vain imagination; for all sacrifices were offered for sins that were past, and all application we can make to God by the sacrifice of Christ for the pardon of sin respects it as past. And therefore were sacrifices instituted to make atonement; that is, to avert and turn away wrath already deserved and due to the offender. To say this was done, not because God was angry at sin, but that he might not be so, when it was already committed, is inconsistent with truth and reason: for God is angry with sin because it is committed; and if he be not so, he is never angry with it. That which we intend hereby is, that he forbids every sin, and has annexed a threatening of punishment to that prohibition. This is his anger.

(7.) That expression, '*vi decreti*,' that God pardons sin by virtue of his decree, contains sundry secrets of these men's doctrine. For it is intimated that all that belongs to the expiation of sin by sacrifices was a mere free constitution; nothing in them, nothing which they had any respect to, or in the atonement made by them, was any way necessary on the account of the righteousness or holiness of God. For this decree of God is nothing but a voluntary constitution of this order of things, that sacrifices should go before remission, and not contribute any thing to this. There is therefore nothing in that discourse, '*Conditione praestita spud Deum efficere ut vi decreti sui*,' etc., but that sacrifices, by God's appointment, were an act of worship antecedent to the remission of sins. It is true, there is nothing done, in the whole matter of the expiation of sin, but it depends on God's decree and appointment; but the things disposed of by virtue of that decree have this relation one to another, that the sacrifice of Christ shall be, and is, the procuring cause of the pardon of sin. God may therefore be said to pardon sin '*in decreto suo*,' as

the original disposing cause; but he does it not without respect
to the sacrifice of Christ, as the meritorious procuring cause. It is
not, therefore, merely an antecedent condition, making way for
the accomplishment of a voluntary decree; but it is a moral cause,
appointed of God in his decree for the effecting of pardon.

(8.) I wonder with what confidence he here affirms that the death
of Christ was an expiatory sacrifice, when he knew himself that he
did not believe it so to be. That Christ offered but one sacrifice
both they and we agree. But that this was not in his death, that it
was in heaven, when he presented himself to God—that indeed it
consists in the power which he has, as glorified and exalted, to free
us from the punishment due to sin—is the sum of what he pleads
for in this part of his book. Both here and elsewhere he endeavours
to prove that Christ was not a priest whilst he was on the earth, that
his death was only a prerequisite condition (and so was his life also)
to the offering of himself. But from all these open contradictions
he shelters himself by saying that it was not as yet perfect in this
kind. But why does he say that it was not a perfect sacrifice, while
he believes that it was none at all? Or if it be not a perfect sacrifice,
was it a part of the perfect sacrifice that was afterwards completed
in heaven? If it was so, then was Christ a priest whilst he was on
the earth—then did he offer himself to God in his death—then
was God the object of that sacerdotal act, as we contend and plead
for. If these things belong not to it, then it was neither a perfect
sacrifice nor imperfect, neither complete nor incomplete, neither
part of a sacrifice nor the whole; which we shall find him granting
in his next words.

What Takes Away Our Sin?

But if you speak (1.) of the sacrifice or offering which Christ
completed for atonement, which he completed in the heavens,
and which the author to the Hebrews explains, and which
Grotius, who names it in addressing it, acknowledges;
concerning this much must be said. (2.) For he did not intervene
to forgive sins, as if by some bare agreement, or of just a matter
of business with another. He supplies salvation itself, which is
to certain extent compared with intercession. But chiefly, just as

he carries it out by his strength, he supplies the forgiveness of our sins by God's decree, and by the execution of his power by which we are condemned and liable to be handed over to divine punishment, he extinguishes and blots our our sins.

ANSWER. As the former discourse was a mere diversion from the present question and argument, so this is partly a begging of the question in general, and partly a concession of what he labors to avoid the inconvenience of. For (1.) it is a plain begging of the main question, to say and suppose that the perfect expiatory sacrifice of Christ consisted only in what he performed in heaven; the contrary whereunto we have sufficiently proved before, and which they shall never evince whilst the Scripture is owned to be the word of God.

(2.) The latter part of his discourse plainly grants what he would seem to deny, but proves it not. He denies that the sacrifice of Christ respects God so much as a condition pre-required to the forgiveness of sin. But he will have it to be the efficient cause of pardon; that is, the Lord Christ, being intrusted with power from God to that end and purpose after his ascension into heaven, does take away our sin, or free and deliver us from the punishment due to it. Now, though this be true, yet this is not the oblation or sacrifice of himself. Nor can any man reconcile the notion of a sacrifice with this actual efficiency in delivering us from the punishment of sin, so as that they should be the same. Concerning this it is granted that we, and not God, are the first and immediate object; but that the oblation or sacrifice of Christ consists herein is wholly denied, nor does he here attempt to prove it so to do.

(3.) What account, on this supposition, can be given of the intercession of Christ, which is his second great sacerdotal duty? Does this also consist in a powerful efficiency in us of what God has decreed concerning his pardoning, blotting out, and extinguishing of sin? Is this the nature of it, that whereas God had decreed freely to pardon sin, and to take away the punishment due to it, this intercession is his powerful taking away of that punishment, and his actual delivery of us from sin? Is it possible that an act and duty of this nature should be expressed by a word of a more opposite signification and importance? For my part, I value not that use of right reason, that these men so much boast of, which is exercised in giving a wrong signification to words expressive of so weighty truths and duties. Who but they can possibly understand any thing, by Christ's intercession in heaven at the right hand of God, but his procuring from him grace, mercy, and pardon for us, by virtue of his antecedent oblation? And God is the object of his actings herein.

Christ's Death Was an Expiatory Sacrifice

But he proceeds to give countenance to what he has asserted:

(1.) Therefore to a certain extent the expression 'offering', as clearly set out below, was transferred to this action of Christ (2.) on account of its likeness to the sacrifices of the law, (3.) because that anger and utterance which was destroyed or came about, before God on behalf of men. (4.) It is in this likeness that (5.) to a certain extent the sacrifices of the law were therefore offered to God and (6.) were accomplished before his face, as the men by whom they were offered carried them out (7.) by the strength of his decree, and received from him the forgiveness of sins. (8.) Therefore by the intercessory offering of Christ, whether by appearing before the face of God (9.) through the act of his shed blood, and united by the highest desire for our completed salvation, (10.) men receive freedom from punishment from God by the strength of his decree and by his merit, which he grants them in the end through Christ. (11.) The Holy Spirit wished to show by these words that the forgiveness of sins, which Christ supplies for us as he waits in the heavens before the Father, proceeds in the first place from God and his kindness. Whatever was accomplished by it for us, it is only by his merit and authority, by Christ, since he gained it, and so he himself is able to free us from the penalty of sin, since he poured out his blood, and entered heaven with the longing to give it [ie. forgiveness] completely. (12.) Therefore, it portrays not only the entrance of Christ into the heavens and his approach to God, who caused him to sit down at his own right hand; and, satisfied, he obtained the power to forgive our sins, and also a perpetual dwelling before him, and thus considered what relates to the oversight of our salvation. It portrays whether or not God was moved by any other reason to forgive our sins and to pardon us by the strength of his decree, (13.) and so between this and that act of God himself, he presents himself as favourably disposed towards us, and he intervenes to free us from punishment. When Christ himself however reaches out to free us from punishment, he does it by the power, once and now, ordained to him by God, and by the entrance into heaven which has been granted to him. He does it all by his name.

ANSWER. (1.) The name of oblation and sacrifice is not applied at all to that action of Christ which this man intends, namely, his appearance in heaven; which, as to its efficacy on our behalf, belongs to his intercession (Rom. 8:34; 1 John 2:1). There is more also in the sacrifice of Christ than the transferring the name of oblation to any action of his which is not so indeed. These little artifices and insinuations, which when discovered are a mere begging of the thing in question, make up the principal parts of Crellius' defense.

Wherefore—(2.) The name of oblation is not transferred to that action of Christ wherein his sacrifice did truly and really consist, namely, his death and blood-shedding, merely by an allusion taken from the legal sacrifices; but it is so called by the Holy Ghost because it is so indeed, as having the true, proper nature of a sacrifice, so as that it was the pattern or idea in the mind of God of all the other sacrifices which he appointed, and which, therefore, were ordained to no other end but to prefigure the nature and exhibit the efficacy thereof.

(3.) That expression, of doing things '*apud Deum*,' or doing for men the things that appertain to God, cannot, on the hypothesis of these men, be ascribed to Christ out of a similitude to what was done by the priests of old: for whatever they did, as priests, they did it to God; but the Lord Christ, according to these men, did nothing as a priest to God. And how can that which he does towards us be called by the name of what the priests did of old towards God, because of its likeness to this, seeing there is no likeness between these things? For what similitude is there between the offering of a bloody sacrifice to God, thereby to make atonement for the guilt of sin, and the actual powerful deliverance of us from the punishment due to sin? What such similitude, I say, is there between these things, as to warrant their being called by the same name, which answers to one of them properly, and to the other not at all?

That, therefore, which is here pretended amounts to no more than this, namely, that whereas he does nothing in his offering with God, but with men, he is said to offer himself by reason of a similitude in what he did to what the priests did in their oblations, who did nothing with men therein, but with God! As, therefore, we know that the sacerdotal acting of Christ was not called an oblation, offering, or sacrifice, merely out of the similitude that was between it and the sacrifices of old—although we grant that indeed there was more than a mere similitude between them, even a typical relation, the one being designed to represent the nature and exhibit the virtue of the other, whence they are both properly called by the same name—so, according to the opinion of our adversaries, we deny that there is any such likeness or similitude between what Christ does in taking away of sin and what was done by the priests of old, as that any denomination could or ought thence to be taken, or any name assigned to it. As for the death of Christ, Crellius peremptorily denies it to have been Christ's perfect expiatory sacrifice; and for his offering himself in heaven, he affirms, that whatever other appearance may be of it, yet indeed it is wholly conversant about us, and not about God. It is therefore in vain to inquire after reasons and grounds on which Christ may be said to do those things in his sacrifice 'those things that must be done that appertain to God,' when it cannot be truly spoken at all, and is directly denied by them.

(4.) Let it therefore be observed, that the similitude that was between the sacrifices of the law and that of Christ was not a bare natural or moral similitude, whence the one of them might be called by the name of the other, that name belonging to the one properly, to the other metaphorically; but whereas there is a generical identity between them, both of them agreeing in the same general nature of being proper sacrifices in their own special kind, the one of them, namely, those of the priests under the law, were instituted and ordained to represent the other, or the sacrifice of Christ, whence arose a similitude between them, as there was a real difference on many other accounts. And the relation that was between them, which these men would have to be a similitude only, arose from these three respects:

1. That the sacrifice of Christ was the pattern in heavenly things according to the idea whereof all legal sacrifices were appointed to make a representation; that is, God having designed his Son Jesus Christ to be the high priest of his church, and to expiate their sins by the sacrifice of himself, did appoint the

legal priesthood and sacrifices, obscurely to delineate that design before its actual accomplishment, and indeed here lies the true difference between us and the Socinians in this matter; for they suppose that God having, for certain ends, instituted the office of priests and duty of sacrificing in the church of old, some things that were done afterwards, and are yet done by Christ, because of their allusion to, and some kind of likeness with, what was done in and by those institutions, are called by their names. We judge, on the other hand, that God originally designing the priesthood and sacrifice of Christ, that he might represent his purpose therein, to be accomplished in the fullness of time, and grant an outward means or pledge to the church of an interest in the nature, efficacy, and benefit thereof, and for no other end, appointed the typical priesthood and sacrifice of the old testament, as has been proved at large before.

2. Seeing they were types appointed of God to set out, teach, and prefigure, the sacrifice of Christ, whatever was in them that did not arise from the natural and indispensable imperfections of them by whom they were offered and the nature of the offerings themselves, but was directly of divine institution, was in the mind and will of God instructive beforehand of the nature and use of the sacrifice of Christ. If, therefore, those priests offered sacrifice to God, so did Christ; if they made atonement by blood, so did Christ; if those sacrifices consisted in the slaying, and oblation on the altar, of the victim, so did Christ's in his death and blood-shedding; if God was the principal immediate object of their sacerdotal actings, so he was of Christ's.

3. They were, by God's ordinance, figuratively communicative of the real virtue of the sacrifice of Christ; that is, God appointed them to this end, that the church making use of them in the faith of the promise concerning the future sacrifice of Christ, should through them be made partakers of the benefits thereof, they being means of communicating spiritually what they did carnally represent. Crellius thinks that all sacrifices were only conditions required antecedently to the free pardon of sin, which he calls the 'pardoning of sin by virtue of God's decree,' but that they had no influence to the procuring of the

remission of sin; which is, in effect, that they did no way make atonement for sin. But then no man living can give an account of their special nature, or why God did institute a condition of that kind, when any duties or acts of obedience of any other sort would have served to the same end. It is plain that all expiatory sacrifices did at least make a representation of commutation, satisfaction, pacification of wroth, turning away of evil, the procurement of mercy, reconciliation, and atonement; and if they did nothing of this nature, it is hard to find any reason for their institution. Wherefore the similitude invented by Crellius is of no consideration in this matter, but is only found out on purpose to destroy the true analogy that is between the legal sacrifices and that of Christ.

(5.) There is indeed, according to the opinion of these men, no similitude between them; for the legal sacrifices did not consist in the representation of the beast sacrificed, much less in any exaltation and power that it had afterwards, but in the slaying and offering of sin on the altar, to which there is not the least resemblance in that which they call the perfect expiatory sacrifice of Christ.

(6.) The offering of sacrifices 'before the face of God,' is true, but not in his sense; for he confines it to the presence of God in the sanctuary only, whereas that which was done at the altar was also said to be done before God, and nowhere else were any sacrifices offered.

(7.) The use of legal sacrifices here granted by him is indeed none at all; for the decree of God—that is, the free pleasure of God—is made the only cause of the remission of sin, without respect to any procuring cause or means whatever. And if propitiatory or expiatory sacrifices had no influence into the remission of sin, if they made not atonement for it, they were of no use at all. Nor is there any thing found in the application of these things to Christ and his sacrifice; for—(8.) the oblation or sacrifice of Christ was not the same with, nor did consist in, his appearance in the presence of God in heaven, but was antecedent to this. He 'offered himself,' and afterwards 'appears in the presence of God for us,' as is plainly expressed.

(9.) This oblation of Christ is said to be 'by the shedding of his blood;' but how or in what sense? The words are used to keep to some seeming compliance with the Scripture, wherein our redemption, forgiveness, freedom from wrath—all the effects of the sacrifice of Christ—are frequently and signally ascribed to his bloodshedding. But is there any intention to intimate that the effusion of his blood had any interest or concern in his oblation? We know it had not, according to these men, but only as an antecedent condition to his exaltation, as was his whole life and humiliation.

(10.) The manner of the expiation of sin by the sacrifice of Christ, here at large described by Crellius, is absurd, dissonant from reason, and contradictory to the Scripture in itself, and in the manner of its declaration sophistical. The words are to this purpose, 'That Christ, as a priest, offered himself to God through the effusion of his blood, to obtain for us mercy, pardon of sin, and deliverance from punishment.' But the meaning or sense intended is, that being exalted to heaven, after his death, by the power that he has received from God he pardons our sins, and delivers us from the punishment due to them. But this is such a way of teaching things as becomes neither the holy penmen of the Scripture, nor any man of common sobriety. And to increase the fondness of the story, Christ is said to do these things with God, or towards God, when men are the express objects of what he does; and this in his ensuing discourse he directly asserts and contends for.

(11.) This is that, it seems, which the Holy Ghost would intimate by these expressions, of Christ's being a priest, of his offering himself to God an expiatory sacrifice, of our redemption thereon by his blood in the forgiveness of our sins, namely, 'That whatever Christ does in heaven towards the pardon of sin, or the pardon of sin which he affords us, proceeds in the first place from the kindness and benignity of God, because he has given power to him for that end and purpose.' But if no more be indeed intended in this expression, if the sacrifice of Christ did in no sense procure our redemption, or pardon of sin, or deliverance from the punishment due to it, to what end the Holy Ghost should use these expressions, why he should largely and particularly insist upon them and their explanation for our instruction, seeing the only thing intended by them—namely, that the pardon of our sins proceeds originally from divine benignity and grace, and that the Lord Christ, as mediator, has received all his power from God the Father—is taught and expressed a thousand times more plainly and clearly in other places and words, and whereas these things and expressions signify no such things as those intended, no man living can divine. Let him that can, assign a tolerable reason why the exercise of the power of Christ in heaven, because it is given him of God, should be called his feting, sacrifice, or oblation of himself, as the high priest of the church. All men freely acknowledge, that whatever power Christ has, as mediator, to forgive us our sins, actually to free us from the punishment deserved by them, he received it of God, who gave all things into his hands, because he laid down his life for his sheep; but that his priesthood consists in the exercise of this power, and that the exercise thereof with love and care is his oblation and sacrifice of himself, being indeed only a consequent thereof, and the means of the administration of its virtue and efficacy, is a fond imagination.

(12.) In the mention of those things whereby God should at least seem to be moved to grant to us the pardon and remission of sin, Crellius utterly omits the death of Christ, reckoning up only his entrance into heaven, his great desire of our salvation, his access to God, and sitting at his right hand; wherein he seems not much to aim at a compliance with the Scripture, which everywhere ascribes all these effects directly and immediately to the death and blood-shedding of Christ.

(13.) The sum of what remains of his discourse amounts to this, 'That although in what Christ did for us there is an appearance as though God, upon the consideration of what was done by him, was moved to pardon sin and free us from punishment' (which yet exclusively to his death is not true), 'yet indeed there is no such thing intended; but only this is so, that Christ does all this by virtue of the power he received from God, and in his name.' The sum of the whole is, that there is an appearance of Christ's being a high priest, an appearance of his offering himself a sacrifice to God for us, an appearance of his acting with God on our behalf, an appearance of his procuring redemption and pardon of sins for us; but in truth and really there is nothing intended but that he has received power from God, after his humiliation, to pardon our sins and deliver us from punishment, which he excercises with love and tenderness.

But yet all this while he has not directly denied that Christ, in his offering himself as a priest, had first respect to God—which was the only thing in question—and that because he had not long before granted that the Scripture in express terms affirms it; but he would make a show of reasons why though the thing be not so indeed, yet it is mentioned as though it were; which is first to assign a falsehood to the holy writers, and then to excuse it. His ensuing discourse in this place, wherein he designs to prove that God is said to do something for Christ, which yet he does himself (as the subduing of his enemies, and the like) by virtue of the power he has received of God, is so exceedingly impertinent to the present occasion, as being designed only for a diversion from the cause in hand, as that I shall pass it by, and come to that part of his disputation wherein he begins to speak his mind with more openness and freedom than before.

Hebrews Does not Neglect Allusions to the Levitical Priesthood

Sometimes, however, the writer to the Hebrews with regard to the priesthood and sacrifice of Christ, because he wishes to lay the matter bare before our eyes, eloquently neglects other allusions and comparisons with legal ceremonies. He clearly points out such action on the part of Christ which concerns us firstly, but certainly not which concerns God (p. 477).

ANSWER. (1.) This is plain dealing, and to the purpose. To what end have we been led about by all the long discourse which we have examined? Grotius affirmed and proved that the actings of Christ as a priest did in the first place respect God, and not us. This Crellius durst not grant, lest he should prejudice his cause; nor at first deny, until he had endeavoured to cast a mist before the eyes of the reader. But now, supposing him sufficiently entangled or engaged, he expressly denies what Grotius affirmed. Be it so, then, that we, and not God, are the immediate objects of Christ's sacerdotal actings: then did he offer himself to us, and not to God; and makes intercession with us, and not with God—for these are the only general sacerdotal actings of Christ, and if God be not the object of them, he did neither offer himself to God nor intercede with him.

But (2.) he supposes that all which seems to be asserted to that purpose proceeds from the neat fitting of these things by way of allusion to the legal sacrifices; which when the apostle neglects, he declares his intention to be quite otherwise. Let us consider the testimonies he produces in the confirmation of this bold assertion:

He teaches this, as we saw above in the place itself at the end
of chapter two and chiefly the last verse, where he unfolds the
manner in which Christ, as a priest among those who are in the
presence of God, atones for people's sins. The method from
ancient times is this: 'For because he himself suffered when he
was tempted, he is able to help those who are being tempted.'
'He is able', he says. This means that he is leaning forward to do
it, or that he is accustomed to doing it freely. Also the words of
the chapter, similarly at the end, teach what sustains this position.

ANSWER. (1.) He is mistaken in supposing that the apostle, in
the places alleged, does omit or neglect the consideration of the
analogy between the ancient priesthood and sacrifice and those
of Christ. For, in the first place, these words, Πιστὸς ἀρχιερεὺς τὰ
πρὸς τὸν Θεὸν, εἰς τὸ ἱλάσκεσθαι τὰς ἁμαρτίας τοῦ λαοῦ—'A faithful
high priest in things pertaining to God, to make reconciliation for
the sins of the people' (Heb. 2:17), does respect both the office and
whole work of the priests of old, in making atonement for sin by
expiatory sacrifices. And in Hebrews 4:14, the entrance of Christ
into heaven asserted in opposition to the entrance of the legal high
priest into the carnal sanctuary.

(2.) The help which the Lord Christ to us, expressed Heb. 2:18,
is founded on and proceeds from the reconciliation or atonement
which he is affirmed to have in the first place (v. 17).

(3.) The question under consideration is, whether the oblation
of Christ does in the first place respect God or us; and to prove
that it respects us, and not God, he cites this testimony of verse 18,
wherein there is no mention of his oblation at all, and omits the
preceding words, where his oblation is so described by its effects
as to prove unavoidably that it respected God in the first place.

(4.) The succor which Christ affords to them that are tempted is
no act of his priestly office; but it is the act of him who is our priest,
and who was, as enabled thereunto by virtue of the reconciliation he
had made by his oblation as a priest, so the discharge of that office
he underwent and suffered those things whereby he is disposed
and inclined to put forth his power in our behalf.

(5.) In Hebrews 4:15–16, the apostle treats not of the oblation of
Christ, but of his personal qualification fitting him for his office.
And that which he has a principal eye to is his intercession, and
the fruits of it; and we shall conclude that this is with God, at least

until our adversaries can affix some other tolerable sense to that expression, or make intelligible their new kind of intercession with God for us, by acting his own power and love towards us. But he yet undertakes to prove that what is here mentioned is the whole of what Christ does as a priest for us, his discourse whereof, because it comprises the substance of all that he has to plead this cause, I shall at large transcribe and examine.

An Argument the Causal Particle Cannot Support

I deny that these are included to strengthen and enlighten what is added by the author at the begnning of chapter 5, as he indicates with the word 'for', which is at the beginning of the chapter and which connects it to the preceding chapter. How from this is he able to cut what the author himself wishes from these words, since they ought to be applied to Christ, which Grotius urges here, and which we reckon the whole passage is about? It is however in this way: 'We do not have a priest who is unable to sympathise with our weaknesses; but was tempted in everything like us yet without sin. Therefore let us approach the throne of grace with confidence, that we may find mercy and grace for the help we need. For every priest accepted from among men is established on behalf of men in matters relating 'to [or 'before'] God, to offer gifts and sacrificial victims for sins: he is able to guide and emphathise with the ignorant and those going astray, since he himself is also surrounded by weakness etc.' When you see these words in chapter 5, 'the priest is established in matters relating to God,' to 'offer gifts and sacrificial victims for sins' there is nothing to answer on account of that in what has gone before, because we will through Christ receive 'mercy and grace for the help we need.' He brings this about, because he suffers with us, and helps us exceedingly in our trembling, so that we will not give in to temptation when pressed down with the weight of evil, and we are freed from the penalty of our sins. Then, when the wicked pay the penalty for their sins, he upholds us and we will not be enveloped along with them in destruction, for he intercedes for us by his divine power. Likewise, as we see, it is indicated in these words in chapter 2, in which is explained the manner of the atonement, which Christ completed before God. But this action firstly concerns us, not really God, unless we speak inappropriately.

ANSWER. (I.) I have at large transcribed this whole passage, that we may see what is the only foundation which he builds upon, or argument he has to prove that the sacerdotal acts of Christ respect us in the first place, and not God. The whole of what he pleads issues from this single supposition, that the apostle in the beginning of the fifth chapter intends nothing but the confirmation of what he had delivered in the end of the fourth; and therefore, that the offering of 'gifts and sacrifices for sins' to God is only his giving help and succor to us in our temptations—which is the most uncouth expression and explication of one thing by another that ever was in the world. Now, this supposition is evidently false, and the connection of the discourse, which he feigns at pleasure, every way insufficient to enforce us to such a fond and brainless exposition of the words. That which alone he pleads in justification of his assertion, is the introduction of this near discourse by the causal particle γάρ, 'for;' as though it intimated that the apostle designed no more but to give a reason of what he had before laid down concerning the help and succor which we have in all our temptations and sufferings from our high priest. This, indeed, he does also, in the description he gives us of the nature and duties of this office; wherein he does not merely explain what he had before delivered, but adds other considerations also of the nature and acts of that office confirming our faith and expectation therein. But his principal regard is to the whole subject-matter treated of, as being now to give his reasons why he does so industriously instruct them in the doctrine of the priesthood of Christ. And this use of the same particle in his transitions from one thing to another—wherein it respects not so much what immediately went before in particular, as the relation of what ensues to his whole design, and is also sometimes redundant—we have manifested by sundry instances in our exposition. Wherefore, the apostle having occasionally digressed from the priesthood of Christ, which he had proposed to consideration in the end of the second chapter, through the third and to the 14th verse of the fourth, he there returns again to his first design. And this he does by declaring in general the glory of Christ as a priest, his eminency above those of the order of Aaron, and the spiritual advantage which we receive, not from his being a priest, but from his being such a person, so qualified for the discharge of his office, as he is there by him described. Having expressed this in the last verses of the fourth chapter, and thereby stirred up the Hebrews to a diligent attention to what he had to instruct them in with respect to this, in the beginning of the fifth he lays the foundation of all his subsequent discourses about the priesthood and sacrifice of Christ, in a general description of that office and the duties thereof, with what belongs essentially thereunto in all that are partakers thereof, adding some particular instances of the imperfections that attended it in the priests under the law, making application of the former to Jesus Christ, and discarding the consideration of the latter. As, therefore, in the end of the fourth chapter, he prepares his way to his intended declaration of the nature and duties of the sacerdotal office of Christ, by declaring in general the advantage we have by his susception of that office who was the Son of God incarnate; so here, in the beginning of the fifth, he adds a description of the power, acts, and duties of that office, whence our benefits by it do originally arise. There is therefore no such coherence between these passages as should warrant us to look on Christ's helping and assisting of them that are tempted to be the same with his offering gifts and sacrifices to God. Yea, suppose that the apostle in these words does only give the reason of what he had before asserted—which is all that is pleaded by Crellius to impose this nonsensical sense upon us—yet thereby also his pretension would be everted; for the reason of any thing differs from the thing itself. And if he proves only that we may have help and succor from Christ, as our high priest, on this ground, that every priest does offer gifts and sacrifices for sin, it does not follow that his helping of us and his offering of sacrifice are the same, yea, it does that they are distinct and different, the latter being given in as a reason and cause of the former.

(2.) What is here further discoursed concerning our deliverance by the power and care of Christ from sin and destruction, even then when wicked and impenitent persons shall be utterly destroyed, is true; but yet it is not his offering of sacrifice to God for sin, but it is a consequent thereof. The consideration of it is indeed a matter of great consolation and encouragement to believers, but it is not to be asserted to the exclusion of that which is the fountain of all the benefits which we receive by his mediation. And now it may be considered whether any thing be here offered by this author, either to prove that we are the first object of all the sacerdotal actings of Christ, or in answer to the testimonies alleged that God alone is so. But he has yet somewhat more to add, and therefore proceeds:

> It is to be noticed, however, in each place, but more clearly in the next, because of (1.) the allusion to the priesthood of the law and a certain similitude which there might be between Christ and the Aaronic high priests, (2.) infirmity was accommodated to Christ—infirmity which existed in those very high priests and by which they ought to have been driven to expiate the infirmities of others all the more promptly; when nevertheless (3.) something of a kind other than those infirmities which were nothing other than from the fall and from ignorance or were misdeeds arising from weakness – when these are set in comparison to Christ, to his temptations and afflictions which everybody knows, and mindful of which he is accustomed to succour us all the more promptly when we have been tempted and afflicted.

ANSWER. (1.) This man seems to aim at nothing but how he may evade the force of truth, and therefore lays hold of every appearing advantage, though indeed contradicting himself therein; for in the entrance of his production of these testimonies, he tells us, 'That they are such places as wherein the apostle, neglecting the allusion to the priesthood of old, does plainly and openly declare the nature of that of Christ.' But here, in the pressing of those testimonies, he pleads the express mention of that allusion as the principal reason of his exposition.

(2.) It is not true that those infirmities of the priests of old which consisted in their sins and ignorances are any way accommodated to Christ. The things here spoken of the nature of the priest's office, and the discharge of it by them with whom it was intrusted, are distributed to the subjects intended, according to their capacity. In the priests of old there were such infirmities as that they had need to offer for their own sins also; in Christ there was no such thing, nor any thing that answered thereunto. But in all priests there were infirmities, such as inseparably attend our human nature in this mortal life; and these our high priest, Christ Jesus, was subject to, whence he was liable to be tempted and to suffer. These the apostle does not accommodate to Christ, but really ascribes to him (see v. 7–8, with our exposition).

(3.) This one concession of Crellius, that Christ our high priest, that is, as our high priest, was subject to temptations and sufferings—which he must be, or there is no similitude between him and the high priests of old in this matter of infirmities—utterly overthrows his whole cause; for he was no way subject to them but as and whilst he was in this world. His glorified nature in heaven is liable neither to temptations nor sufferings. If therefore any of these infirmities were found in him as our high priest, which the apostle expressly affirms, and Crellius acknowledges, he was our high priest whilst he was on the earth. But he adds:

> From this is it clear that the Aaronic priests, to respond to our temptations and sufferings in these places, needed to atone for their own sins also, on the strength of which they are said to atone for our sins. They had these sins to our ruin, but the wings are raised and from these sins we are snatched by the help of Christ. Therefore it is not remarkable to apply the rest of what is said about the Aaronic priests to Christ in another sense, and to accept something particularly concerning them to be inappropriate concerning Christ, although in an excellent sense.

ANSWER. (1.) Where there is any mention made of the offering of Christ for us, it is constantly with respect to our sins, and not to our temptations and sufferings, at least not in the first place. What he is affirmed to do with respect to them, as to the aid, relief, and deliverance which he gives us, is all consequential to his once offering of himself to take away sin.

(2.) The foundation of the inference which is here made we have already taken away, namely, that the sinful infirmities of the priests of old were accommodated to Christ with respect to natural infirmities, or obnoxiousness to temptations and sufferings; which we have showed to be false. Yet hence he would infer that the sins of the people of old, for which the priests offered sacrifice, do correspond in this matter with our temptations and sufferings; that as they offered sacrifices for real sins, so Christ's sacrifice is our relief from temptations and sufferings. The force of the reason pretended lies in this, that because the priests of the order of Aaron had sins themselves, therefore they offered sacrifices for the sins of the people, those which were truly and really so; but whereas the Lord Christ had no sins of his own, but only temptations and sufferings, therefore the sins offered for were temptations and sufferings. Nothing can be more absurdly imagined; for both those qualifications, that he 'had no sin,' and that he 'was tempted,' were necessary to his offering for us and for our sins. Being 'made sin for us, and sent in the likeness of sinful flesh, yet without sin, he condemned sin in the flesh, bearing our sins in his own body on the tree.' Is this all, therefore, that the great discourses of Crellius concerning 'the expiatory sacrifice of Christ, his being a propitiation for our sins, his offering himself to God for us,' with the like magnificent expressions of sacerdotal actings, do amount to—namely, that he frees us by his power from temptations and afflictions, with all the efficacy they have to destroy us? Is this, I say, to offer himself to God a true, perfect, complete expiatory sacrifice? Were it not much better wholly to deny that Christ was a high priest, or that he ever offered himself to God, than to put such strained and futilous senses on these expressions.

(3.) And because these men will have it so, all things must be spoken properly of the Aaronic priests, though they were umbratile, typical, figurative, temporary, and liable to such infirmities as exceedingly eclipsed the glory of the office itself; but all things spoken of the Lord Christ to the same purpose must be improper and metaphorical, and denote things of another nature, only called by the names of priesthood and sacrifice in allusion to them and those things, who and which were appointed and ordained of God for no other end or purpose but that they might prefigure him in the discharge of his office. And then, to salve the matter, the things so improperly assigned to Christ must be said to be more excellent than the things that are properly ascribed to the Aaronic priests, when indeed they are not, nor to be compared to them; and if they were, yet would not that prove but that Aaron, though not absolutely, yet as to the office of the priesthood, was more excellent than Christ, as being properly a priest, whereas the Lord Christ was so only metaphorically, which is a diminution as to that particular.

He closes his discourse:

Before we move away from this we would like to note that Paul, in Romans 15:17, although he speaks about his apostolic office, the strength of which dwells with men primarily, and which, if we are to speak with Grotius, was on behalf of God or Christ before men, yet he alludes to the sacrifices and priesthood by saying that he has boasting or that he glories in Christ Jesus in the matters which are before God, τὰ πρὸς Θεόν.

ANSWER. This observation does no way impeach the force of the testimony produced by Grotius. He intended no more by that expression, Τὰ πρὸς τὸν Θεόν, but to declare in the words of the apostle that God was the object of what was so performed; which certainly, unless some great reason be produced to the contrary, must be acknowledged to be the sense of the words. But Grotius proves his intention from the matter treated of, which is sacrifices; and if they are not offered to God, and that for men, they are not at all what they are called. And in compliance with this sense the apostle respects the discharge of his conscience towards God in the work of his ministry, wherein he had immediately to do with him; for although men were the object of his ministry, yet he received it from God, and to him he was to give an account thereof.

Wherefore he only declares how he had acquitted himself sincerely in that whole work, which was in an especial manner committed to him of God, and whereof he was to give to him a peculiar account.

Tergiversations, Equivocations, and Plausible Diversions

I had sundry reasons why I chose to insist on a particular examination of these discourses of Crellius; for it is confessed that none among our adversaries have handled those things with more diligence and subtilty than he has made use of. It was necessary, therefore, to give a specimen, as of his strength, so of his way and method, whereby he seeks to defend his opinions. And every impartial reader may see, in the discussion of what he alleges or pleads, that the whole of his defense is made up of tergiversations, equivocations, and plausible diversions from the cause under debate. Besides, I have had sundry opportunities hereby to declare many things belonging to the nature and discharge of the priesthood of Christ which could not conveniently be reduced to other heads. And I was willing, also, to cast these things into this place by themselves, to avoid all controversies as much as possible in the exposition itself, though I constantly detect the falsehood of this man's interpretations, as those of others who either follow him or comply with him. And hereby also, perhaps, some who are less exercised in the sophistry of these men may learn somewhat how they are to be dealt with.

11

PREFIGURATIONS OF THE
PRIESTHOOD AND SACRIFICE OF CHRIST

Sundry things concerning the priesthood of Christ, and those the most material that relate thereunto, we have now passed through. But we know withal that although the foundations of this were laid in the eternal counsels of God, and a revelation was made of them in the first promise, immediately upon the entrance of sin, yet the Son of God was not actually 'manifested in the flesh,' for the execution of those counsels and discharge of this office, until 'the fullness of time' came, after the expiration of a multitude of ages In the meantime, there were certain prefigurations of it instituted of God in the church, to keep up and direct the faith of mankind to what was to come, in sacrifices and a certain typical priesthood, with emanations from them into the practice of the nations of the world. Now, what is worth our inquiry into, with reference to these prefigurations of the priesthood of Christ, may be referred to these four heads:

1. The state of things in general, with respect to priesthood and sacrifices in the church, before the giving of the law.

2. The peculiar priesthood of Melchizedek, which fell within that period of time.
3. The institution of the Aaronic priesthood at Mount Sinai, with the nature and duration of that office, the garments, sacrifices, laws, and succession, of the high priests in particular.
4. The rise, occasion, and usage, of a priesthood among the nations of the world.

From all these we may learn both what God thought meet previously to instruct the church in concerning the future glories of the priesthood of Christ, and what presumptions there were in the light of nature concerning the substance of that work which he was to accomplish.

Before the Law

Our first inquiry will be as to what monuments remain of either sacrifices or the order of priesthood, from and after the first promise and the institution of expiatory oblations, to the solemn giving of the law in the wilderness, when all things were reduced into a methodical, instructive order.

The first institution of sacrifices, and revelation of an acceptable worship of God in and by them, I have declared before, and elsewhere discussed and proved at large. Hereupon, as is evident from many particular instances recorded in the Scripture, sacrifices were offered before the law. It is highly probable that Adam himself, after he had received the promise, which gave life and efficacy to that kind of sacred service, did offer sacrifices to God. And this some do suppose, and that not unwarrantably, that he did with the beasts with whose skins he was clothed, and that by the immediate direction of God himself. Hereby the whole of those creatures were returned to God, and their carcasses not left to putrefy on the earth. And so the whole was an illustrious exemplification of the promise newly given, or a type and representation of Christ and his righteousness; for as he was to be our real sacrifice of atonement to expiate our sins, so are we said to put him on, or to be clothed with his righteousness. So typically was our first father, after his receiving the promise, clothed with the skins of the beasts which were offered in sacrifice to make atonement; and therein was Christ a 'lamb slain from the foundation of the world.' And those beasts seem rather to have been sheep or goats than the greater cattle of the herd, their skins being more meet for clothing.

The Jews suppose that Adam sacrificed an ox or a bullock. So in the Targum on Psalm 69:32—

קרנוי למלפוהו ותשפר צלותי קדם יי מן תור פטים
ובחיר דקריב אדם קדמי דקדימו

> My prayer shall please God more than the fat and choice bullock, which Adam, the first man, offered, whose horns went before the dividing of the hoofs.

To the same purpose Rashi comments on the place:

משור פר הוא שור שהקריב אדם הראשו שנברא בקומתו (.etc)

> This is the ox which Adam, the first man, offered, which was created in his full stature; and they called him שׁוּר, an ox or bullock, in the day wherein he was brought; and he was like a bullock of three years old. And his horns went before his hoofs; for his head came first out of the earth when he was made, and his horns were seen before his hoofs.

It may be there is no more intended in this fable but an account of the order of these words, מַקְרִן מַפְרִיס, wherein the order of nature, the bringing forth of horns being placed before dividing of the hoofs, seems to be inverted, though nothing indeed be intended but the description of a bullock fit for sacrifice. But the authors of the fable may yet have had a further reach. The psalmist in that place prefers the moral and spiritual duties of obedience before sacrificing. This they will not allow to be spoken with reference to the sacrifices of the law, and therefore put it off to that of Adam, which they make their conjectures about. After this example Cain and Abel offered sacrifices (Gen. 4:3–4); and Noah (Gen. 8:20); and Melchizedek, as we have showed (Gen. 14:20) and Abraham (Gen. 15:9–10, 22:13); and Isaac (Gen. 26:25); and Jacob (Gen. 28:18, 35:3, 7; Job 1:5, 42:8). Express mention of more before the giving of the law I do not remember. Not that I think these were all the sacrifices which were offered according to the mind of God in that space of time.

I doubt not but all the persons mentioned and multitudes besides did in those days offer sacrifices to God, thereby testifying their faith in the promise and expectation of the great expiatory sacrifice that was to come. Oblations were not yet, indeed, fixed to times and seasons, as the most of them, especially the most solemn, were afterwards under the law; and therefore I suppose their offering was occasional. Upon some appearance of God to them, on great mercies received, in times of great dangers, troubles, or perils, to themselves or families, when they were in doubts and perplexities about their affairs, and would inquire of God for direction, they betook themselves to this solemn service, as the instances on record do manifest. And the only solemn sacrifices we read of among the heathen, traduced by imitation from the patriarchs, were for a long season such as were offered in the times of approaching wars, after victories, and upon the solemn covenanting of nations or rulers; who yet in process of time also made use of stated solemn sacrifices, and of those that were confined to the interests of private families.

INDIVIDUAL SACRIFICE

It does not appear that there was as yet any peculiar office of priesthood erected or instituted. But the persons who enjoyed the revelation of the promise and the institution of sacrifices may be considered two ways: (1.) Personally; (2.) As members of some society, natural or political. Families are natural societies, greater voluntary combinations, for the preservation of human conversation to all the ends of it, we may call political societies. Consider men in the first way, and every one was his own priest, or offered his own sacrifices to God. Not that every one was instated in that office: for, to, make an office common to all is to destroy it; as it includes an especial privilege, faculty, power, and duty, which being made common, their being ceases. But every one was to perform that duty for himself, which upon the erection of the priesthood was confined and limited to this. It does not, therefore, follow that because every one was to offer sacrifice, therefore every one was a priest in office. God giving out the prefigurations of the priesthood and sacrifice of Christ πολυμερῶς, by distinct parts and degrees, he ordained the duty of sacrificing before he erected an office for the peculiar discharge of it. Thus Cain and Abel, as we have before observed, offered their own sacrifices, but could not both of them be priests; nor indeed was either of them so: nor was Adam, nor was it possible he should be so, before the increase and multiplication of his family; for a priest is not of one, but must act in the name of others. Wherefore, sacrifice being a worship prescribed to believing sinners, every one in his own person was to attend to it, and did so at stated times or on solemn occasions, according as they apprehended the mind of God required it of them.

CORPORATE SACRIFICE

Secondly, as persons were united into any community, natural or political, this worship was required of them in that community; for this is a prescription of the law of nature, that every society, wherein men do coalesce according to the mind of God, should own their dependence on him with some worship common to them, and to be performed in the name of the society. Especially is it so with respect to that which is the foundation of all others, in a household or family. So God gives to Abraham the testimony of sincerity, that he would order and take care of his worship in his family (Gen. 18:19). Hence there were sacrifices peculiar to families before the law, wherein it cannot be doubted but the father of the family was the sacred administrator. So Job offered burnt offerings for himself and his family (Job. 1:5); and Jacob for his (Gen. 35:3, 7). Yet are they not hereon to be esteemed priests by office, seeing they had their warrant for what they did from the light and law of nature, but the office of the priesthood depends on institution. And such family sacrifices were famous among the heathens. An eminent instance of this the Roman historian gives us in C. Fabius, who, when Rome was sacked by the Gauls, and the Capitol besieged, upon the stated time of the solemn worship and sacrifices of the family of the Fabii, passed through the enemy's camp to the Quirinal Hill, and discharged the accustomed 'sacra,' returning to the Capitol without disturbance or affront from the enemy (Liv. lib. 5). And the family ceremonies, in the sacrifice of an ox to Hercules, by the Potitii and Pinarii, were adopted by Romulus and Numa into the use of the whole people, the posterity of those families being made as it were their public priests thereby. And after they had confirmed the administration of their 'sacra' in public

solemnities for the whole community, yet they left it free to single
persons and families to sacrifice for themselves as they saw good;
for as they took up the former course probably from the form and
example of Mosaic institutions, so they retained the latter from the
original practice and tradition of the world. Even the meanest of
the people continued their family libations. 'Sacrima' they called
the wine which their countrymen offered to Bacchus, as Festus
testifies; and 'carpur' the vessel out of which they drew the wine
whereof they made a libation to Jupiter. 'Struferta' and 'suovetaurilia'
were the sacrifices of poor families. And something in resemblance
of this original practice continued among the people of God after
the giving of the law. So the family of Jesse had an yearly sacrifice,
which was a free-will offering, and a feast thereon (1 Sam. 20:6).
But it may be by the הַיָּמִים זֶבַח, there was intended only a feast
at which there was a slaughter of beasts. If a sacrifice be intended,
the time and place were irregular. Or if the whole was pretended
by David, yet is it hence evident that such things were in common
use at that time, or no pretense could have been made of it. And if
it was a sacrifice, it was offered by a legal priest, or the whole of it
was an abomination. Philo (lib. in. de Vita Mosis), admits all the
people afresh to this duty at the passover: Νόμου προστάξει σύμπαν
τὸ ἔθνος ἱερᾶται, τοῦ κατὰ μέρος ἑκάστου τὰς ὑπὲρ αὐτοῦ θυσίας
ἀναγόντος τότε καὶ ἱερουργοῦντος·—'By the appointment of the
law the whole nation sacrifices' (or 'is employed in sacred duties'),
'whilst every one brings his own sacrifice and slays it.' But this saying
of his is not without its difficulties, and deserves further inquiry.

Pre-Levitical Priests

Persons united into greater societies for the ends of human
conversation had, as we observed, the use of sacrifices among them
as such, and which they were by the light of nature directed to.
So was it among the Israelites when the twelve original families,
being multiplied into so many numerous tribes, were, by common
consent, united into one people or nation, without any polity,
rule, or order peculiarly accommodated to the whole community.
This was the condition of that people before the giving of the
law, the bonds of this union being consanguinity, agreement in
design, outward state in the world with respect to other nations,

all under the conduct of divine Providence to a certain designed end. In this state there were some that offered sacrifice for the whole people: 'Moses builded an altar under the hill, and twelve pillars, according to the twelve tribes of Israel. And he sent young men of the children of Israel, which offered burnt-offerings, and sacrificed peace-offerings of oxen to the LORD' (Exod. 24:4–5). It is probable these young men were the same with those who are called 'the priests' (Exod. 19:22, 24), when as yet the office of the priesthood was not erected.

WHO WERE THOSE PRIESTS?

There has been great inquiry who those priests were, or who they were who thus offered sacrifices for families or greater associations, and by what means they were invested with that privilege. By most it is concluded that they were the first-born of the families and tribes, and that the right of the priesthood before the giving of the law was a branch of the primogeniture. But whatever similitude there may be in what the light of nature directed to and what was after sacredly appointed, yet this opinion will not easily be admitted by them who judge it necessary to resolve the original of the priesthood into a voluntary institution, as that which was to be typical and representative of the priesthood of Christ, which must be an immediate effect and emanation of divine wisdom and grace. Yet some suppose this opinion may be confirmed by the example of Melchizedek, who was the first called a priest of God in the world, being [according to them] Shem, the eldest son of Noah. But the whole of this argument is composed of most uncertain conjectures. It is uncertain whether Shem was the eldest son of Noah, and most probable that he was not so; more uncertain whether Melchizedek was Shem or no; yea, it is at the next door to the highest certainty that he was not so. And it is absolutely certain that he was not a priest on any account common to him with others, but by the immediate call or appointment of God; for had it been otherwise, when the Lord Christ was made a priest according to the order of Melchizedek, he must have been so according to that common order whereof his priesthood was, which is contrary to his singular call to that office. And if an extraordinary instance may contribute any thing to satisfaction in this inquiry, that of Moses is express to the contrary. He was a priest to God: 'Moses and Aaron among his priests' (Ps. 119:6). And there is not any thing peculiar to a priest but he discharged it in his own person. Yet was not he the eldest son of Amram his father, but younger than Aaron by three years, who was alive all the while he executed his priesthood. But from these extraordinary instances nothing certain in this case can be concluded. Micah afterwards, when he fell off from the law of institution in setting up teraphim and graven images, consecrated אֶחָד מִבָּנָיו, one of his sons from amongst them, which he thought meet, without regarding the primogeniture (Jdg. 7:5). I have formerly thought that the הַכֹּהֲנִים הַנִּגָּשִׁים אֶל־יְהוָֹה (Exod. 19:22–4), 'The priests which drew nigh to the LORD,' which, as was now said, I still suppose and judge to be the same with the young men employed by Moses in the first solemn sacrifice in the wilderness (Exod. 24:5)—were the first-born of the families: but I now rather judge that they were persons delegated by common consent, or immediate divine designation, which in that extraordinary dispensation supplied the room thereof, to act representatively in the name of the people; for the other opinion is attended with many difficulties, and exposed to sundry exceptions not to be evaded.

The Right of Primogeniture

The rise of this opinion concerning the office of the priesthood, or peculiar right of sacrificing for themselves and others, being annexed to the primogeniture, is usually taken from the words and fact of Jacob with respect to Reuben his eldest son: 'Reuben, thou art my first-born, my might, and the beginning of my strength, the excellency of dignity, and the excellency of power: unstable as water, thou shalt not excel' (Gen. 49:3). The Targums make jointly this interpretation of the words, 'Thou hast a threefold right above thy brethren—בכראותא; the primogeniture, the priesthood, and the rule. But seeing thou hast sinned, the primogeniture shall be given to Joseph, the priesthood to Levi, and the rule or dominion to Judah.' But their authority, without further evidence, is not sufficient to determine this case. The privileges of the first-born were certainly great from the beginning. There was מִשְׁפַּט בְּכוֹרָה, a right of primogeniture, founded in the law of nature, determined in the judicial law to Israel, and generally owned in some degree or other among all nations in the world. The foundation of it is expressed in these words of Jacob, כֹּחִי וְרֵאשִׁית אוֹנִי —'My might, and the beginning of my strength;' that is, the spring to all power and excellency that was to arise out of his posterity. In him it began, and in him was the foundation of it laid. And the same reason is repeated in the establishment of the law: הוּא רֵאשִׁית אֹנוֹ לוֹ מִשְׁפַּט הַבְּכֹרָה;—'He is the beginning of his strength; his is the right of primogeniture' (Deut. 21:17). Hence this right was confined to the firstborn of the father only, and not to the first-born of the mother, if her husband had had a son by another wife before. And if a man had more wives at the same time, he that was the first-born of any of them was to have the privilege of the birthright, against all disadvantages on the mother's part, as if she were hated in comparison of the others; which manifests that it was a law of nature not to be transgressed, nor the right to be forfeited but by personal sin and disobedience, as it was with Esau and Reuben (Deut. 21:15-17). There was, indeed, a privilege that belonged to the first-born of every mother, by virtue of the especial law about פֶּטֶר רֶחֶם, him that opened the womb; for every such an one was to be 'sanctified' or separated to the Lord (Exod. 13:2); which among men was restrained to the male: 'The first-born of thy sons shalt thou give to me' (Exod. 22:29). And therefore we have added, in way of exposition of this law, in our translation, 'All that opens the matrix is mine' (Exod. 34:19, that is, the males). And it was instead of the first-born males only that the Levites were taken in exchange (Num. 3:40-42). But this was a peculiar ceremonial law and privilege. There were two things that eminently belonged to the πρωτοτοκεία, or right of primogeniture, before the law, the one whereof was confirmed also under it; and this was the privilege in '*familia herciscunda*,' or distribution of the estate and inheritance of the family. For whereas every son was to have שְׁכֶם אַחַד (Gen. 48:22), 'one part' or 'shoulder,' to bear the charge of his own especial family, so the first-born was to have פִּי שְׁנַיִם (Deut. 21:17), that is, διπλᾶ, or μέρος διπλοῦν, 'a double portion' of the inheritance. And this evidently Jacob took from Reuben and gave to Joseph, when he adopted his two sons, and gave each of them the inheritance of a tribe (Gen. 48). And there also belonged to this civil pre-eminence and right to rule. The first-born had a principal honour among his brethren, and when rule and dominion was erected, without especial cause and alteration made by God himself, it belonged to him. So do the words of God to Cain plainly signify: 'Unto thee shall be his desire, and thou shalt rule over him' (Gen. 4:7). And when God transferred in prophecy the birthright from Esau to Jacob, he did it in these words, 'The elder shall serve the younger' (Gen. 25:23); which Isaac also in the confirmation of it so expresses, 'Be lord over thy brethren, and let thy mother's sons bow down to thee' (Gen. 27:29). And so he tells Esau afterwards, 'Behold, I have made him thy lord, and all his brethren have I given to him for servants' (v. 37). And this was by Jacob taken from Reuben and given to Judah. Both these are expressly mentioned, 'Reuben was the first-born; but, forasmuch as he defiled his father's bed, his birthright was given to the sons of Joseph: and the genealogy is not to be reckoned after the birthright. For Judah prevailed above his brethren, and of him came the chief ruler; but the birthright was Joseph's' (1 Chron. 5:1–2). I confess the birthright here seems to be confined to the double portion only, and is therefore proposed as totally transferred to Joseph, and to have comprised all that was lost by Reuben. The matter of rule is introduced so as that when God would erect it, he gave it to Judah without depriving any other of a right to it. I will not therefore be positive that, by the law of nature, or any previous constitution of God, right to rule belonged to the primogeniture, but suppose it might be disposed to the most worthy, as the Roman epitomator affirms it was at the beginning of all governments. However, here is no mention of the priesthood, which we inquire after.

A Shadow of the Christ in His Offices

The Mishnical Jews, in *Masseceth Becaroth Peresh*. 8, divide the rights of the primogeniture in נחלה and כהנה, 'the inheritance' and 'the priesthood,' and thereon make many distinctions concerning them, who may be the first-born, or have the right of primogeniture, as to the one, but not to the other. But by 'the priesthood' they intend only the dedication of the first-born to God upon the law of opening the womb. Now, this had no relation to the priesthood properly so called. As far as it had its foundation in the law of nature, it was an offering to God of the first-fruits of the family, all *primitiae* being due to him; and hereby was the whole family made sacred and dedicated to God: for 'If the first fruit be holy, the lump is also holy' (Rom. 11:16). The place, therefore, mentioned in *Becaroth* intends not the priesthood. But in *Bereshith Rabba* (fol. 71), some of them do plainly ascribe the priesthood to the primogeniture; and so does Jerome from them (on Gen. 17:27, *Epist. ad Evagr.*, and elsewhere), as do others also of the ancients. But in the whole law and order of the primogeniture, it is plain that God designed to shadow out the Lord Christ in his offices, when, by his incarnation, he became the first-born of the creation, as to rule (Col. 1:15, 18, Rev. 1:5, Heb. 1:6); as to inheritance (Heb. 1:3–4, Eph. 1:20); and as to sanctifying the whole family (Heb. 2:11).

Fathers of Families

Yet all that has been spoken, or that may further be pleaded to the same purpose, does not necessarily conclude that the right to sacrificing by way of office was enclosed to the first-born before the giving of the law; and afterwards we know how it was disposed of by divine institution. There was, therefore, in that state of the church, no office of priesthood, but every one performed this duty and worship of sacrifice, '*ex communi jure*,' with respect to himself. As all were obliged to attend to this worship of God, and express their faith in the promise thereby, so every one who was '*sui juris*,' or had the free disposal of himself in all his moral actions, did in his own person attend to his own duty herein. As persons were united into families, and made up one body naturally-political by God's appointment, the '*pater familias*' had the duty of sacrificing for the whole committed to him. Herein it is probable he had the especial assistance of the first-born of the family, whereby he might be initiated into his future duty. Yet was it not afterwards confined to him; for Abel, who was the youngest son of his father, offered sacrifices for himself in his own person, his father and elder brother being yet alive. I no way doubt but that all the persons on the patriarchal line before the flood offered sacrifices to God; yet is it most uncertain whether they were all of them the first born of their respective parents. Abraham after the flood offered sacrifice whilst the eldest son of Noah was yet alive, neither was he himself the first-born of his immediate parents. Afterwards it is probable that the order and solemnity of public sacrificing went along in a peculiar manner with the birthright; not that it was a privilege thereof, but that the privilege of the birthright made what they did more extensive and illustrious. But this was continued only whilst a family continued by consent. When it divided, all things returned to their primitive right and practice. So was it when the younger sons of Noah were separated from the elder; they lost not the right of solemnizing the worship of God thereby. And in case the firstborn was incapable, through sin, idolatry, or apostasy from God, the right of the remainder was not prejudiced thereby, but every one might personally attend to the discharge of his duty herein; which after the giving of the law was not provided for. But this respected men only. Women were afterwards, among the heathen, admitted into the office of the priesthood, especially in the idolatries of Juno. But there was no induction towards any such practice in the light of nature or original tradition; for 'the head of the woman is the man.' And the whole sex generally being supposed under the power of their parents or husbands, nothing remains on record of their solemnizing sacred worship in their own persons, though some conjectures have been made about Rebekah's inquiry of God upon her conception of twins.

Throughout the World

When greater political societies, being the products of the light, of nature acting by choice, and on necessity, were established, it was judged needful, or at least useful, not only that every one should offer sacrifice for himself that would, nor only that the head of each family should discharge that duty in the name of the whole family—which expresses the first two directions of the law of nature—but also that some one or more should offer sacrifice for the whole community, which had the solemn representation of a sacerdotal office. How these persons came originally in the world to be designed to this work and office is a matter left much in the dark and obscure. The ways whereby God erected this office, and constituted any in the possession and enjoyment of it, are plain and evident: for he did it either by an immediate call from himself, as it was with Melchizedek in one manner, and Aaron in another, or by the constitution of a legal succession of priests, as it was with all the posterity of Aaron; concerning both which we shall treat afterwards distinctly.

How Priests Were Appointed

Our present inquiry is, how this order of things came to pass in the world, or when—that some certain persons, under the name of priests, should have the administration of things sacred in the behalf of political communities committed to them. And these are the ways that may be pleaded with good probability to this purpose.

Elected

The first is, that the people or communities judging the duty of public sacrificing and religious administrations to be their duty, and necessary for them as a community, did choose out from among themselves, either by lot or suffrage—the two original ways of all elections—such as they judged meet for that purpose. So Virgil would have Laocoon designed to be a priest to Neptune by lot: 'Laocoon, priest led by Neptune's oracle' (AEn. 2:201). And in Statius it was by the choice of the people that Theodamas was made the priest of Apollo in the room of Amphiaraus. So he speaks to them, 'You do not call them from our breast: He sings to the one who will serve me and compels him to take up your band of faith and not be at variance' (*Thebaid.* lib. 10:189). And when, among the Romans, the care of sacred things had been devolved on their kings, upon their removal the people created priests by suffrage among themselves, and one under the name of '*rex sacrorum*,' that by the continuance of the name therein the office might not in any thing be missed, the civil power being fully transferred to the consuls (see *Dion. Halicarnass*, lib. 5). So Livy: 'Then he gave his attention to religious matters; and since certain public religious duties had been done by the kings themselves, he created a "king sacrificing priest", so that there would never be a desire for a king' (lib. 2. cap. 2). And the king of the '*sacra*' at Athens had the same original, as is manifest in Demosthenes. The Dacians so far improved this power as that, having at first made priests to their gods, they at length made one of their priests to be their god. And this I take to be one of the principal ways whereby, in the first coalescences of human society, the order of priesthood came to be erected among them. Possibly in their elections they might suppose themselves to have received guidance by some supernatural indication, of which afterwards; but it was consent and choice that gave them their authority and office.

Rulers Took Priestly Duties Upon Themselves

Secondly, those who had by any means obtained the rule of the community, knowing that with their power over it they had an obligation on them to seek its good, did take upon themselves the care of sacrificing for it, and performed it in their own persons. And there seems to be a natural traduction of the power and right of this kind of priesthood from the fathers of families to the heads of political societies, which have a resemblance to them. And thence the heathen writers do generally grant that the care of the administration of sacred things accompanied the supreme power, so that the kingdom and the priesthood amongst them for a season went together. So Aristotle informs us of the kings in the heroic times—that is, such as they had tradition but no history of: Κύριοι ἦσαν τῆς δὲ κατὰ πόλεμον ἡγεμονίας, καὶ τῶν θυσιῶν ὅσαι μὴ ἱεροτικαί· —'They were rulers of things belonging to the conduct of war, and had the ordering of sacrifices that were not in an especial manner reserved to the priesthood;' of the reason of which exception I shall afterwards give an account. And again: Στρατηγὸς ἦν καὶ δικαστὴς ὁ βασιλεὺς καὶ πρὸς τοὺς τεοὺς κύριος (Aristot. Polit. lib. 3)—'The king was general, judge, and lord of things sacred.' And Cicero: 'In the presence of the ancients, who grasped matters and held the same auguries; so that they might understand, and so prophesy and lead by the royal one' (*De Divin.* lib. 1. cap. 40). The truth is, the use of sacrificing among the Gentiles, by the time we meet with any probable records of things among them, was much restrained, and principally attended to in and with respect to war, or an apprehension of the approach of public calamities. Hence it came to pass that they who had the chief command in war had power of sacrificing also. But if it was so that not only a right of sacrificing for the community occasionally, in the times of danger, belonged to him who presided therein, but that the supreme power and priesthood went together in any greater societies, as traduced from the practice of families, it is evident that they were very quickly separated again, and vested in diverse persons, yet so as still to reserve to kings and generals the privilege of sacrificing expiatory oblations in war; which they did sometimes by the death of beasts, sometimes of persons, and sometimes of themselves: for the first mention we have of priests in the world is distinct from kings in the same place. This was in Egypt, where we find the '*cohanim*,' or priests, an order of men by themselves, under the power and care of their kings, how they came by that office originally, if we shall suppose that the right of sacrificing for the community went along with regal power and rule, I know not. It may be said that kings grew weary of that employment, as their greatness, wealth, and empire increased, and so suffered others to be chosen to it, or designed them thereunto by their own power; or, that ambition and luxury rendering them unfit for the discharge of that office and negligent in it, the people provided for themselves as they could. Or it may be thought that some such things fell out in those early days of the world as did in later ages among the caliphs of the Saracens; for the world in all its varieties varies not from itself. These caliphs, being originally the successors of Mohammed, had all power civil and sacred in their hands; but through the sloth of some of them, military men, who had the power and charge of armies in their hands and disposal, took the civil power from them, and, making themselves emperors, left only the pontificate to the caliphs, the principal dignity remaining to them being an allowance to wear those garments and colours which they did as successors to Mohammed, when they had all the power (See *Elmacin. Histor. Saracen.* lib. 3. cap. 2). It might have so fallen out with those priests of Egypt. Being originally both princes and priests, they were confined to the sacerdotal function by some of more heroic spirits, who deprived them of rule and government; which alteration might constitute one of those changes in their dynasties which are so much spoken of. And thence, it may be (which Athenaeus observes), the priests of Egypt did always wear kingly garments. But these things are only conjectures, and that about matters wrapped up in the greatest obscurity. I rather judge that there was never an ordinary concurrence of both these offices in the same persons, though it sometimes so fell out on extraordinary occasions; as 'King Anius, the same king of men and priest of Phoebus.' And the most ancient reports among the heathen, both in the Eastern and Grecian traditions, mention these offices as distinctly exorcised by diverse persons. Homer has his priests as well as his kings, though that which then was peculiar to them was divination, and not sacrificing.

Claims to Special Divine Calling

Thirdly, priests among the heathen might have their original from some extraordinary afflatus, real or pretended. It was with respect to their gods that men had thoughts of sacrificing, or of the way of it. And the world was generally now become utterly at a loss both as to the nature and manner of religious worship, though the light of nature kept them up to a persuasion that the Deity was to be worshipped, and some small remainders of original tradition that sacrificing was an acceptable mode of religious worship still continued with them. But how to exert these notions in practice, or how to express their impressions from tradition, they knew not. But yet they still had an apprehension that the knowledge of this dwelt with the gods themselves, and that from them they were to expect and receive direction. In this posture of the minds of men and their consciences, it is no wonder if some quickly pretended themselves to be divinely inspired, and were as easily believed; for men who are utterly destitute of all means of divine and supernatural direction are given up to as great an excess in facile credulity, as they are to an obstinate unbelief of the most evident truths by whom such light and direction has been rejected. And as this latter frame at this day discourages men wise and sober in the proposal of sacred truths, upon the highest and most evident warranty, to the sceptical atheism of rebels against the light; so the former encouraged crafty impostors to impose their pretended inspirations on the credulous multitude, as that they easily gave up to them the entire conduct of their religious affairs. And Satan himself was sure not to be wanting to so great an occasion of promoting his interest in the world; and therefore, as he had diverted the minds of men before from the true and only object of all religious worship,

Men who are utterly destitute of all means of divine and supernatural direction are given up to as great an excess in facile credulity, as they are to an obstinate unbelief of the most evident truths by whom such light and direction has been rejected.

entangling them in an endless maze of abominable idolatries, so, to secure them to himself in those tormenting, disquieting uncertainties whereinto he had cast them, he did actually intermix himself and all his power in the minds and imaginations of some persons, whom he had designed for the guides of others in their superstitions. And an appearance of his power and presence with them was that which instated and fixed them in a peculiar office of managing things esteemed sacred and religious. This was the certain and undoubted original of the stated solemn priesthood among the heathen, as will yet further appear.

ANCIENT EGYPT

To return, therefore, whence we have digressed, next to him who was the first priest in office in the world, and that by virtue of divine appointment—of whom I must treat afterwards distinctly and by himself—those first mentioned under that name are the priests of Egypt (Gen. 41:45, 47:22, 26). Concerning them, therefore, in the first place, our inquiry shall be.

It is very probable that the Egyptians began to have their stated 'sacra' very early in the world; for they were the posterity of him who unquestionably made the first defection from true religion after the flood, and therefore most likely they first improved that superstition which they embraced in the room thereof. And hence it came to pass that having chosen both their deities and the manner of their veneration in the times of barbarity and darkness, before mankind had leisure to improve the remaining light of nature by contemplation, arts, and sciences, they fixed on, and tenaciously adhered to, such observances in their superstition as were ridiculous and contemptible to all the world besides. In process of time they received many customs and usages in sacred things from Abraham and his posterity whilst they dwelt amongst them; much, it may be, particularly under the rule of Joseph, and more upon the fame and renown of their glorious law and divine order in religious worship. These customs and usages being observed among them by some Grecian writers long afterwards, divers of late are inclined to believe that the Israelites took them from the Egyptians, and not on the contrary. I mean not any of those superstitious and idolatrous customs which that people learned from the Egyptians, as weeping for Tammuz, even as they borrowed idolatries and superstitions from all their neighbors round about them, as I have elsewhere declared, but those institutions themselves which Moses gave them in the wilderness, and some that God had peculiarly given to Abraham. Whether a due reverence to divine revelations and institutions has been observed herein, I shall elsewhere, God willing, make inquiry. In brief, the plainest state of the difference is this: God gives a law of divine worship to his people in the wilderness, declares all the parts and observances of it to be of his own immediate appointment And in the declaration of his mind he allowed not Moses the interposition of any one word or conception of his own, but made him a mere internuncius, to make known his express commands and will to the people; nor did he allow him to do any thing but what he expressly and immediately ordained. In the meantime, making known to the people that all they were enjoined was from himself, he straitly forbids them to do any thing in his service after the manner whereby other nations served their idol gods. Yet notwithstanding it appears afterwards that sundry of the things which were so instituted and observed amongst them were observed also by the Egyptians. Hereupon it is inquired whether the Egyptians learned those things and took up the practice of them from the Israelites, or whether Moses (who, indeed, had no more to do with the intruding or appointing of those sacred institutions than has the present reader, whoever he be) did not learn them in Egypt and prescribe them in the wilderness to the people. But whereas the inquiry ought to be, not what Moses might learn of and receive from the Egyptians, but what God himself did so (for if we believe the Scripture at all, they were all of his own immediate appointment, without the interposition of the wit, invention, or memory of Moses), so I shall say, that if any learned man can produce any one evident testimony, or but such an one as whose pretence to a probability of truth I cannot make manifest to be vain, of the observation of any one sacred institution belonging peculiarly to the system of Mosaic ordinances among the Egyptians before the giving of the law, I will pass on among the captives in their triumph for so great an achievement. But certain it is that men are exceedingly apt to take up with learned conjectures out of heathen writers, though pressing hard on the reputation of sacred truth.

Hyksos—A Fable or a Hebrew Story

An instance of this, if I mistake not, may be taken from that space of time, and what sets out therein what we have now under consideration. Josephus in his *Discourses Against Apion* (lib. 1) reports somewhat of the history of the Egyptians out of Manetho, a priest of Heliopolis, who wrote his story in the days of Ptolemy Philadelphus, about sixteen hundred years after Abraham's being in Egypt. Out of this man's writing, and in his own words, he gives an account of a nation that was called Hyksos, which in the Egyptian language signifies 'kingly shepherds.' This nation, as he says, entered Egypt and subdued it, holding it for about five hundred years, erecting an especial dynasty therein. By these shepherds and their king, with Josephus, Manetho intended the Israelites and their abode in Egypt, although he mixed the story of it with many fabulous traditions; for under that name and character were they known to the Egyptians, and on the account of that profession of life whence they were so denominated lived separately from them. This story, with allowances for the fabulous tradition and invention of the reporter, is for the substance of it fairly reconcilable to our sacred writings; yea, no other interpretation of it is consistent with them, as we shall manifest. But our late learned chronologers are generally of another mind. They will have a nation called by the Egyptians Hyksos, leaving no memorial of any name of their own, nor ground of any tolerable conjecture from whence they came, nor what became of them in the issue, nor why the Egyptians gave them that name, being a composition of what they most adored and most abhorred, to have entered Egypt presently after the death of Joseph, and conquering the whole kingdom, or at least all the lower and principal parts of it, to have erected a kingdom of their own therein. These, they say, were they who oppressed the Israelites, as is related in Exodus; and under their rule was the people delivered, as in the same story, in the reign of Apophis, leaving them to rule in Egypt two or three hundred years after. Concerning this people, the principal things observed out of Manetho are:

1. That they invaded the country in the reign of one Timaus, God being angry with the nation; and that they had no king of their own at their first entrance.

2. That after their entrance they made one from among themselves a king, whom they called Salatis.
3. That this Salatis took care about corn and its measures, with the stipends of soldiers.
4. That he and his successors endeavoured to root out all the Egyptians.
5. That they kept Abatis (that is, Pelusium) with a garrison of 240,000 soldiers building of some other cities.

Now, leaving to others the liberty of their judgment, I cannot but declare that to me either this whole story is a mere coined fable, or it is the Hebrews alone that are intended in it, or that credit is not to be given to our sacred story, as I shall evidently demonstrate. For—(1.) If the Hebrews and their abode in Egypt be not intended in this story, what credit is to be given to the writings of this Manetho, and the skill he pretended in the antiquities of his country, or the sacred records from whence he boasts to have transcribed his commentaries? For if the state of the Israelites be not here expressed, it is apparent that he had not any notice of it; for Josephus, searching of him no doubt with diligence, to find what he could discover concerning the antiquity and affairs of his own nation, could find nothing in his book concerning their coming into and departure from Egypt but this passage only. For what he mentions afterwards about the lepers and mixed people has no consistency with the story of the Hebrews, but was a mere figment of the Egyptians, designing their reproach. And if this Manetho was utterly ignorant, and had no tradition of what befell his country in that terrible desolation and ruin, the like of which never befell any nation under heaven, what reason have we to give the least credit to any of his reports? A man may soberly judge, on such a supposition, that all his dynasties and kings, and what fell out under them in ancient times, were mere figments of his own brain, like the story of Geoffrey of Monmouth concerning the succession of kings in this island from the coming of Brutus, which in like manner is pretended to be taken from sacred monastical archives.

(2.) The Israelites were at that time known by the name of shepherds, professing themselves to follow that course of life whence they were so denominated; and as such they were 'an abomination to the Egyptians.' These things concurring with the ruin that befell Egypt at their departure, issued in such a fame and tradition as might easily be fabled upon by Manetho, an idolatrous priest, so long after. But that there should be two sorts of persons, two nations, at the same time in Egypt, both strangers, both called shepherds, the one oppressing the other, the Egyptians as it were unconcerned in both, seems rather to be a dream than to have any thing of real tradition or story in it. Besides, who the one sort of shepherds at that time were is known to all; but as to the other sort, none can imagine whence they came, nor what was the end they were brought to.

(3.) They are said by this Manetho to come into Egypt without a king, but afterwards made one of themselves so, who 'in time of harvest ordered the measures of corn, and paid men their allowances' (ἐνθά τε κατὰ ζέρειαν ἤρχετο τὰ μὲν σιτομετρῶν καὶ μισθοφορίαν παρεχόμενος); which things have so plain a respect to Joseph as that he must shut his eyes who sees him not therein, especially since the times agree well enough.

(4.) Joseph had the exercise of all regal power committed to him, who was one of the shepherds, and made laws and statutes, yea, changed the whole political interest of Egypt and the tenure of their lands, making the king the sole proprietor of the whole soil, leaving the people to hold it of him in a way of tenancy at a certain rate, by the way of acknowledgment and rent. This might well raise a fame of his being a king amongst them. And there is that herein which overthrows the whole fabulous supposition of the invasion and conquest of Egypt at that time by another nation. For Moses affirms that those laws of Joseph were in force and observed in Egypt to the day of his writing that story (Gen. 47:20–26). Now, this story supposes that immediately after the death of Joseph came in a new nation, who utterly dispossessed the Egyptians of their country and whole interest therein, taking it into their own power, possession, and use. And can any man think it probable that the laws made by Joseph about the rights of the king and the people should be in force and be observed by this new nation, who had conquered the whole, and at first, no man knows for how long, had no king at all? For they were these Hyksos, and not the Egyptians, who, according to Manetho, as interpreted by our chronologers, ruled in Egypt in the days of Moses. This, in my judgment, so long as men will acknowledge the divine authority of the writings of

Moses, is sufficient to discard the whole story; for it is most certain that things could not be at the same time as Moses and Manetho report, if the Hebrews be not intended by him. And setting aside such considerations, certainly he who was a person renowned for wisdom and righteousness in the world, the ruler and conductor of a mighty nation, the first and most famous lawgiver on the earth, writing of things done in his own days and under his own eyes, is to be believed before an obscure, fabulous priest, who lived at least sixteen hundred years after the things fell out which he undertakes to relate.

(5.) The nation or people to whom Abraham went down was to afflict him and his posterity four hundred years, and afterwards to be judged of God for their oppression (Gen. 15:13–14). Now, this cannot be affirmed, if they first went down to one nation, and then were afflicted by another, as this story imports.

(6.) The people with whom the Israelites had to do from first to last, in a way of kindness and oppression, are called Mizraimites or Egyptians constantly; and although these Hyksos should have been in Mizraim, or Egypt, yet if they were not of the posterity of Mizraim, it could not be said in what they did that it was done by the Mizraimites. They were Egyptians who first received them and kindly entertained them; Egyptians they were who oppressed them and were their taskmasters; an Egyptian it was that Moses slew for his cruelty; Egyptians they were whom the people spoiled at their departure; and so in all other instances: whereas, if this story be rightly applied to another nation, they received nothing but kindness from the Egyptians, and were oppressed wholly by another people.

(7.) The places which Manetho reports these Hyksos to have held peculiarly in garrison were most probably those built by the Israelites whilst oppressed by the Egyptians. It is generally agreed that Pithom, which was built by them (Exod. 1:11), was the same with Pelusium, and this the same with Abaris, which the Hyksos are said to maintain with 240,000 men; which great number are said afterwards to have been driven out of Egypt, and to have entered into Syria. He that shall reflect on the truth of the story in Moses, and withal consider the nature of the reports concerning the Hebrews leaving Egypt, in Trogus, Tacitus, and others, will not easily think that any but they are intended.

(8.) It is evident that whoever ruled Egypt at the departure of the Israelites, both himself, his whole host, and all the strength of the kingdom, were utterly destroyed. If it be supposed that those were the Hyksos, and not the Egyptians, and withal as it is said that the Egyptians in Thebais always waged war with these Hyksos, and expected an opportunity to recover their liberty, can it be imagined that they would have let go the advantage now put into their hands, when there was no strength left to oppose them? But this, according to the story, they did no way make use of; but after their destruction and desolation, the Hyksos continued to rule in Egypt two or three hundred years. Wherefore, this story, as it is framed by Manetho, and applied by some late learned chronologers, is inconsistent with the writings of Moses; and therefore, with those by whom their sacred authority is acknowledged, it can be no otherwise esteemed but as a fabulous declaration of that obscure tradition which the Egyptians had so long after of the Hebrews being in their country, and of the desolation which befell it thereby. 'Evil dwells in the giving up of the estate.' Had there not been somewhat of real truth in the business, there had been no occasion for this fabulous superstructure. The like account I shall give in its proper place of that other bold, and to speak plainly, false hypothesis, that many of the Mosaic religious institutions were taken from the usages and customs of the Egyptians in their sacred rites.

The Priests Were Princes

But to return. The כֹּהֲנִים, or 'priests,' mentioned among the Egyptians, were probably princes of the people at the first. And translators are yet dubious whether they should render the word in its places 'priests' or 'princes.' At first they were designed by common consent to take care of the 'sacra' which belonged to the community, which grew into an hereditary office; nor can I give any other probable conjecture concerning them. Appointed they seem to have been to comply with the catholic tradition of sacrificing, or doing something in lieu of it, for the good of the community. And their function continued in principal reputation in after ages, increasing in popular veneration and esteem as superstition increased among them, which was fast enough, until it had even tired itself with its own extravagancies and excess.

Jugglers, Impostors, and Conjurers

Besides these 'cohanim,' there were in Egypt at the same time other sorts of men, whom we call 'magicians and sorcerers,' whose arts or delusions were afterwards generally followed by the priests of other nations; or, it may be, upon some neglect of the service of their gods, these men, pretending to a familiarity and acquaintance with them, took the office upon themselves, promising supernatural effects in the execution of it. There seem to be three sorts of them expressed (Exod. 7:11). There are the חֲכָמִים, 'chacamim', and מְכַשְּׁפִים 'mecashshephim', and חַרְטֻמִּים, 'chartummim.' The 'chacamim,' which we render 'wise men,' are here distinguished from the 'mecashshephim,' or 'sorcerers;' but the 'chartummim,' or 'magicians,' seem to comprise both the other sorts, the 'chacamim' and 'mecashshephim'. 'Then Pharaoh called the wise men and the sorcerers: now the magicians of Egypt, they also did in like manner with their enchantments.' But Genesis 41:8, the 'chacamim,' or 'wise men,' are distinguished from the 'chartummim,' or 'magicians,' as they are here from the 'mecashshephim,' or 'sorcerers;' and therefore we shall consider them distinctly.

The חֲכָמִים are constantly rendered by the LXX σοφοί, and all other translations are compliant, the word being of a known obvious signification, and commonly taken in a good sense, 'wise men;' for they were they who afterwards, when the contemplation of things secret and hidden first found acceptance and then applause in Greece, were called σοφοί and then φιλόσοφοι. But the original of their studies seem to have been in things magical, curious, and diabolical; in which arts philosophy made its last attempt in the world under Apollonius and some other Pythagoreans—so, like an *'ignis fatuus,'* expiring as it began. Wherefore these 'chacamim,' now of such reputation in Egypt, were such as had separated themselves to the study of curious arts and the speculation of hidden things; into whose contemplations Satan variously insinuated himself, giving them an esteem and honour among the common people on the account of their skill in things to them unknown; they gratifying him, on the other hand, in promoting his design for superstition and idolatry. This gave them the title of 'wise men;' which yet possibly, in the judgment of those who really were so, was confined to their trade and profession, for we hear not of their use on any other occasion. Exodus 7:11, the LXX render חֲכָמִים by σοφισταί, 'Men subtle to deceive.' Hence, probably, in the expression of what was done by their counsel, Luke uses κατασοφισάμενος, 'dealt subtly' (Acts 7:19).

Those joined in one place with these wise men are the מְכַשְּׁפִים. The name is originally Hebrew, from כָּשַׁף, '*praestigias exercuit*.' The LXX render it by φαρμακοί, 'venefici;' and the Targum by חרש, '*praestigiator*,' 'jugglers, impostors,' and also 'conjurers.' They seem to have pretended to the revelation or discovery of things secret and hidden; whence the Arabic כשף signifies 'to cover,' 'to reveal,' 'to make known.' Such a sort of impostors the world was always pestered with, which were of old in great reputation, though now the scorn of the multitude. Probably they had an access to the administration of things sacred, whence the word in the Syriac denotes 'to pray,' 'to administer in things holy,' and 'to sacrifice.' The 'chartummim' are those to whom all magical effects are peculiarly assigned. It does not appear whether they were a peculiar sect distinct from the other two, or some of them more eminently skilled in magical operations than the rest. The name is foreign to the sacred language, probably Egyptian, though in use also among the Chaldeans, to whom this diabolical skill and practice were traduced from Egypt. The LXX render them ἐξηγηταί (Gen. 41:8), 'interpreters,' according to the matter in hand, it being the interpretation of the dreams of Pharaoh which was inquired after, wherein also they boasted their skill. Exodus 7:11, they render it ἐπαοιδοί, '*incantatores*, enchanters.' The Vulgar Latin omits the name, and to supply that omission renders בְּלַהֲטֵיהֶם, 'per incantationes Egyptiacus,' 'by their Egyptian enchantments.' Some render it by '*genethliaci*,' which Aben Ezra gives countenance to on Daniel 2:2, calling them תכמי התלדות, 'men skilled in casting nativities;' others by '*malefici, arioli, magi, necromantici*,' 'witches, conjurers, magicians;' Targum, הרשים; in the common translation, Genesis 41:8, '*magistri*,' without any reason. It is plain and evident that they were a sort of persons who pretended to a power of miraculous operation, and made use of their skill and reputation in opposition to Moses. Their chiefs at that time were Jannes and Jambres, mentioned by our apostle (2 Tim. 3:8), as they are likewise spoken of in the Talmud, and are joined with Moses by Pliny, as persons famous in arts magical. It is not unlikely but that this sort of men might have been cast under some disgrace by failing in the interpretation of the dreams of Pharaoh, the knowledge of which was of so great importance to the whole nation. This being done by Joseph, whose eminent exaltation ensued thereon, it is not improbable but that they bore a peculiar malice towards all the Israelites, being, moreover, instigated and provoked by the knowledge and worship of the true God that was among them. This made them vigorously engage in an opposition to Moses, not only in compliance with the king, but, as our apostle speaks, ἀντέστησαν —'they set themselves against him;' which includes more than a mere production of magical effects upon the command of Pharaoh, whereby they attempted to obscure the lustre of his miracles—even a sedulous, active, industrious opposition to his whole design. And besides, whereas they knew that Moses was skilled in all the learning of the Egyptians, and not perceiving at first any peculiar presence of divine power with him, they thought themselves sufficient for the contest, until they were forced, by the evidence of his miraculous operations, to acknowledge the energy of a divine power above what they could imitate or counterfeit. The name, as was said, is Egyptian, as was the art they professed. And it is not unlikely but that those which Moses calls כֹּהֲנִים, 'cohanim,' were in the Egyptian language called הַשְׁמַנִּים, 'chashmannim,' who are mentioned in Psalm 68:32, which we render 'princes,' who are said to come out of Egypt in the profession of subjection to the kingdom of Christ; for the word is Egyptian, and nowhere else used.

More Devil-excited Artists

To these Egyptian artists two other sorts were added among the Babylonians, Daniel 2:2. Besides the 'chartummim' and 'mecashshephim,' which managed these arts in Egypt, whence their skill and names were traduced to the Chaldeans, there were among their wise men אַשָּׁפִים, 'ashshaphim,' and כַּשְׂדִּים, 'casdim' also. How these two sorts were distinguished between themselves, or from the others named with them, is altogether unknown. Strabo tells us that the astrologers, magicians, and philosophers, among the Chaldeans, were called by various names: Καί γὰρ Ὀρξηνοί τινες προσαγορεύονται, καί Βορσιππηνοὶ, καὶ ἄλλοι πλείους (lib. 16, cap. 1)—'Some were called Orcheni, and some Borsippeni; as also there were other sorts of them.' 'Ashshaphim' are rendered 'philosophers, astronomers, astrologers, physicians,' merely on conjecture, and not from any signification of the name, which is unknown. The 'casdim,' or Chaldeans, seem to have been a sort of people that claimed their pedigree in an especial manner from the first inhabitants of those parts, being the posterity of Chesed, the son of Nahor. These, probably, being overpowered by a confluence of other sects of men, betook themselves to those curious arts which afterwards were famous, or [rather] infamous, throughout the world under their name; for the prognostication of future events, which they pretended to, is a thing that the world always despised and yet inquired after. So Strabo describes them: Ἀφώριστο δ' ἐν τῇ Βαζυλωνίᾳ κατοικία τοῖς ἐπιχωρίοις φιλοσόφοίς, τοῖς Χωλδαίοις προσαγορευομένοις, [*ubi supra*;]—'There is in Babylonia a peculiar place of habitation assigned to philosophers born in or deriving their race from the country, called Chaldeans.'

We may take a brief view of them all in their order, expressed in Daniel 2:2. The first are the 'chartummim.' They were they to whom all the magical operations in Egypt are ascribed; and the name itself is Egyptian, though some would have it of a Hebrew extract. R. Saadias would derive it from הוּר, 'a hole;' and אָטוּם, 'shut,' or 'closed;' supposing they gave their answers from a hole in the earth, as the oracle at Dodona out of an oak. Some deduce it from חָרַט, as Avenarius and Manasseh Ben Israel, judging them a sort of persons who used a style or graving tool to cut characters and pictures to work their enchantments by (see *Fuller. Miscellan.*, lib. 5: cap. 11). Hottinger, with most probability, conjectures the name to be taken from חרד, which in the Persian language still signifies 'to know,' ד being changed into ט, as is usual. For all such impostors do always represent themselves as persons endued with excellent skill and knowledge; and as such are they by the common people esteemed. A sort of people they were pretending to supernatural operations by virtue of a hidden power present with them—that is, diabolical. The next mentioned are the 'ashshaphim,' distinguished from the 'chartummim,' as another sort and sect, by vau copulative. Aben Ezra renders them by הרופאים, 'physicians.' Some would have the name the same with the Greek σοφοί, and so a general name for all professors of secret knowledge, and of the causes of things natural. In the Concordance of Rabbi

Nathan, אשף is חוזה, 'a seer, a prophet, a prognosticator.' The third sort are the 'mecashshephim,' from כָּשַׁף, 'to divine' (see 2 Chron. 33:6; Deut. 18:10; Exod. 22:17). Maimonides, and many that follow him among the Jews, suppose these to have been such as, framing images and pictures of things above, included such powers in them by incantation as could intercept the influences of the heavenly bodies, and thereby produce rare and wonderful effects, but always hurtful and noxious. Of the 'casdim' we have spoken before. (He that would further satisfy himself in the nature of the arts they professed may consult Maimonides in More Nebuchim, lib. 3 cap. 37; Polydor. Virgil de Rerum Incantor. p. 85; Rhodigni. Var. Lec., lib. 9:cap. 23; Sixtus Senensis, Biblioth. Tit. Curio Sacrarum Artium libri; Danaeus de Praestigiatoribus; Kircher. OEd. tom. 2, part. 2, fol. 456; Bantus Coelum Orientale; Pictures of Witchcraft; Delrio, Disqusit. Rerum Magicarum, lib. 1, cap. 2, lib. 2; Pelan. in Daniel 2:2; Geierus Daniel; Agrippa de Occults Philosophia, etc.) Strabo informs us that in his time they had lost all their skill and arts, and that the remainders of them were only a kind of priest that attended to sacrificing, lib. 17; and he says that one Chaeremon, who went along with AElius Gallus, the governor of Egypt, undertaking still to practice their arts, was ridiculous to all for his ignorance and arrogance.

I have diverted to the consideration of these sorts of men, as finding some of them in this space of time, before the giving of the law, looked on as those who had more acquaintance and intimacy with the deities in common veneration than ordinary, and were thereon esteemed as priests and sacred. But it is plain that they were such as the devil excited, acted, and after a sort inspired, to draw off the minds of men from the knowledge and fear of the only true God and his worship. Wherefore, notwithstanding their pretense of interposing between men and a divine power, which Satan made use of, to discover things hidden, and to effect marvellous operations, as also that at length they became public sacrificers, yet are they to be utterly excluded from all consideration in those prelibations and prefigurations of the priesthood of Christ which derived themselves from divine institution through the catholic tradition of mankind.

Having made this entrance into what I had designed concerning the prefigurations of the priesthood of Christ in the church and in the world, I find the full discussion of all things thereunto belonging will require larger discourses than either my present indisposition as to health will allow me to engage into, or the printer's haste admit of a stay for. Wherefore, having despatched the whole doctrinal part of the sacerdotal office of Christ, which was my principal design in these exercitations, I do crave the reader's pardon to transmit the remainder of our historical observations to the publication of another part of our exposition of the epistle, if God shall be pleased to afford that occasion and opportunity.

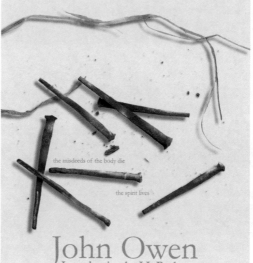

THE
MORTIFICATION
OF SIN

A Puritan's View of how to Deal with Sin in your Life

John Owen

John Owen insisted on the importance of the Christian dealing effectively with their sinful tendencies and attitudes. He believed that God, through his Word and Spirit, had provided the guidelines and the power for this to be achieved.

In this book, John Owen effectively dismisses various excuses for not engaging in self-scrutiny and yet avoids the current trend of self-absorption. In so doing he provides principles to help believers live lives of holiness.

'I owe more to John Owen than to any other theologian, ancient or modern, and I owe more to this little book than to anything else he wrote.'

J.I. Packer,
Regent College, Vancouver

ISBN 978-1-85792-107-6

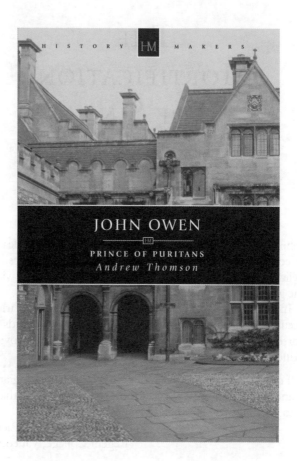

JOHN OWEN

PRINCE OF PURITANS
Andrew Thomson

JOHN OWEN

Prince of Puritans

Andrew Thomson

John Owen (1616-1683) was one of the defining theologians in the Christian era. His books have been continually in print and are still influential today. Educated at Queen's College, Oxford, he was a moderate Presbyterian who became a Congregationalist after reading a book by John Cotton. He later helped draw up the Savoy Declaration, the Congregational Basis of Faith.

During the English Civil War Owen was wholly on the side of the Parliamentarians, accompanying Cromwell on expeditions to Scotland and Ireland as Chaplain. Owen was influential in national life and was made Vice-Chancellor of Christ Church Oxford. After the Restoration of the Monarchy he was ejected from this position and devoted his energies to developing 'godly and learned men', in writing commentaries and devotional books, and in defending nonconformists from state persecution.

Andrew Thomson uses various sources for this biography including Owen's adversaries 'who could not be silent on so great a name or withhold reluctant praise.'

Andrew Thomson (1814-1901) was minister of Broughton Place United Presbyterian Kirk, Edinburgh.

ISBN 978-1-85792-267-7

CHRISTIAN
HERITAGE
Useful Books of Lasting Value

THE HOLY SPIRIT
HIS GIFTS AND POWER
JOHN OWEN

'Whenever I return to read Owen I find myself
at least in part wondering why I spend
time reading lesser things.'
Sinclair B. Ferguson

The Holy Spirit

His Gifts and Power

John Owen

John Newton spoke of Owen's work on the Holy Spirit as, 'An epitome, if not the masterpiece of his writings.' No one who cares about the church in the 21st century can afford to ignore this exhaustive guide.

This is the orginal text with a new layout and is fully subtitled which makes it more accessible to a new generation of readers!

'Whenever I return to read Owen I find myself at least in part wondering why I spend time reading lesser things.

Part of the contemporary value of Owen's work lies in the way it gives us biblical teaching and principles that can be applied to what we observe in the life of the churches today. He provides the tools we need to be discerning Christians in an undiscerning world. In the pages that follow you will find yourself quarrying theological treasures, and spiritual and pastoral riches, from the Owen Goldmine.'

Sinclair B. Ferguson, Senior Minister,
First Presbyterian Church, Columbia, South Carolina

'I assert unhesitatingly that the man who wants to study experimental theology will find no books equal to those of Owen for complete scriptural and exhaustive treatment of the subjects they handle. If you wish to study thoroughly the doctrine of sanctification I make no apology for strongly recommending Owen on the Holy Spirit.'

J.C. Ryle, First Bishop of Liverpool (1816 - 1900)

ISBN 978-1-85792-475-6

THE GLORY OF CHRIST

HIS OFFICE AND GRACE

JOHN OWEN

'A great and beautiful book...his final testimony
to the grace of God in the gospel'
Sinclair B. Ferguson

THE GLORY OF CHRIST

His Gifts and Power

John Owen

'Take time to read this book. Savour each page. Appreciate the depths of what Owen says. Allow yourself to be analysed, searched, exposed, deconstructed, edified, enlightened, engraced, and refocused on the glory of Jesus Christ.'

Sinclair B. Ferguson, Senior Minister,
First Presbyterian Church, Columbia, South Carolina

'I'm here today, absolutely certain that the subject we ought to think about together is the glory of Christ. And the reason that I was absorbed with it at the time is that I was reading a book and I want to commend that book to you; I think it is one of these sell-your-shirt books that you really need to buy and read. It is of course called the Glory of Christ, and this is a new edition of it. It was written in the seventeenth century by John Owen, probably the greatest of the Puritans. And John Owen's book on the Glory of Christ is the classic writing on that subject. This edition was published five years ago by Christian Focus and we're greatly in the debt of Philip Ross, who is known to some of you, who has edited the book for modern readers. And it is really made infinitely easier to read. I do commend it to you. It has one other notable feature and that is an introduction by Sinclair Ferguson explaining who Owen was and how to read his book...I commend that book to you very warmly and anything that I've learned of the Glory of Christ you will find elaborated considerably there. '

Eric Alexander,
formerly minister St George's Tron, Glasgow

ISBN 978-1-85792-474-9

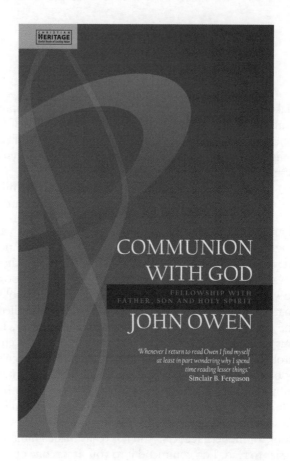

COMMUNION
WITH GOD

FELLOWSHIP WITH
FATHER, SON AND HOLY SPIRIT

JOHN OWEN

'Whenever I return to read Owen I find myself
at least in part wondering why I spend
time reading lesser things.'
Sinclair B. Ferguson

COMMUNION WITH GOD

Fellowship with the Father, Son and Holy Spirit

John Owen

In 1657, John Owen produced one of his finest devotional treatises: probably originating from the substance of a series of sermons. He examines the Christian's communion with God as it relates to all three members of the trinity. He assures that every Christian does have communion with God, no-one is excluded and that this communion takes place distinctly with Father, Son and Holy Spirit.

Our relationship with...

- God the Father is primarily through love and faith.
- God the Son is through fellowship & grace.
- God the Holy Spirit is primarily through comfort and sanctification.

This was a controversial work in ecclesiastical circles of the 17th century. Twenty years after its publication, the rational ecclesiastical elite were scoffing at it's contents. Owen strongly defended the ideas within this book, and history has shown him to be right! It is a classic of Christian devotional thought that still influences the church today.

'I owe an incalculable debt to these pages. For forty years now this has been a favourite volume to which I continue to return for more "angel food"'

Sinclair B. Ferguson, Senior Minister,
First Presbyterian Church, Columbia, South Carolina

'Owen was by common consent the weightiest Puritan theologian, and many would bracket him with Jonathan Edwards as one of the greatest Reformed theologians of all time.'

J.I. Packer,
Regent College, Vancouver

ISBN 978-1-84550-209-6

Christian Focus Publications

publishes books for all ages. Our mission statement –

STAYING FAITHFUL
In dependence upon God we seek to impact the world through literature faithful to His infallible Word, the Bible. Our aim is to ensure that the Lord Jesus Christ is presented as the only hope to obtain forgiveness of sin, live a useful life and look forward to heaven with Him.

REACHING OUT
Christ's last command requires us to reach out to our world with His gospel. We seek to help fulfill that by publishing books that point people towards Jesus and help them develop a Christ-like maturity. We aim to equip all levels of readers for life, work, ministry and mission.

Books in our adult range are published in three imprints.

Christian Focus contains popular works including biographies, commentaries, basic doctrine and Christian living. Our children's books are also published in this imprint.
Mentor focuses on books written at a level suitable for Bible College and seminary students, pastors, and other serious readers. The imprint includes commentaries, doctrinal studies, examination of current issues and church history.
Christian Heritage contains classic writings from the past.

Christian Focus Publications, Ltd
Geanies House, Fearn,
Ross-shire, IV20 1TW, Scotland, United Kingdom
info@christianfocus.com
www.christianfocus.com